UNITED STATES
in 1808

WITHDRAWN

CANADA

Quebec

ST. LAWRENCE R.

DISTRICT OF MAINE

Montreal

L. SUPERIOR

MISSISSIPPI R.
PIKE 1805-6

L. MICHIGAN

L. HURON

MICHIGAN TERRITORY

INDIANA TERRITORY

Detroit

L. ERIE

Erie

L. ONTARIO

Oswego

Albany

NEW YORK

VT.

Portland

N.H.

MASS.

Boston

CONN.

R.I.

New Haven

New York

N.J.

PENNSYLVANIA

Pittsburgh

Philadelphia

Baltimore

OHIO

MD. DEL.

Washington

VIRGINIA

OHIO R.

KENTUCKY

Richmond

St. Louis

Raleigh

TENNESSEE

NORTH CAROLINA

MISSISSIPPI R.

TENNESSEE R.

Wilmington

SOUTH CAROLINA

GEORGIA

Charleston

MISSISSIPPI TERRITORY

Savannah

TERR. OF ORLEANS

SPANISH WEST FLORIDA

Pensacola

St. Augustine

New Orleans

SPANISH EAST FLORIDA

ATLANTIC

OCEAN

GULF OF MEXICO

N

BAHAMAS

Havana

CUBA

Mainstream of America Series ★

EDITED BY LEWIS GANNETT

THE SHACKLES OF POWER

Books by John Dos Passos

Historical Narratives

THE GROUND WE STAND ON

THE HEAD AND HEART OF THOMAS JEFFERSON

THE MEN WHO MADE THE NATION

MR. WILSON'S WAR

THE SHACKLES OF POWER

Contemporary Chronicles

CHOSEN COUNTRY

THREE SOLDIERS

MANHATTAN TRANSFER

THE 42ND PARALLEL

NINETEEN NINETEEN

THE BIG MONEY

THE MOST LIKELY TO SUCCEED

ADVENTURES OF A YOUNG MAN

NUMBER ONE

THE GRAND DESIGN

THE GREAT DAYS

MIDCENTURY

Rapportage

JOURNEYS BETWEEN WARS

STATE OF THE NATION

TOUR OF DUTY

BRAZIL ON THE MOVE

THE SHACKLES OF POWER

POWER

Three Jeffersonian Decades

JOHN DOS PASSOS

1966   DOUBLEDAY & COMPANY, INC.   Garden City, New York

LIBRARY OF CONGRESS CATALOG CARD NUMBER 66–12237

COPYRIGHT © 1966 BY JOHN DOS PASSOS

PRINTED IN THE UNITED STATES OF AMERICA

FIRST EDITION

Contents

Acknowledgments

First I want to thank the staff of the Peabody Library in Baltimore for their kindness and consideration over so many years. I'm particularly grateful to Mr. Percy W. Filby for introducing me to the bound set of Niles's *Register*. Everybody in the Manuscript Division of the Library of Congress was as helpful as ever. The quotations from the letters of Jefferson, Madison, Monroe, from the Samuel Harrison Smith papers, the Nicholas N. Trist papers, the John Henry papers, the Burr Folder, Plumer's memorandum and autobiography and other letters of the period are from these collections.

I want to thank the New-York Historical Society for allowing me to go through the Gallatin papers and their recently acquired collection of material relating to Aaron Burr's later life. It was most useful to be allowed to compare the manuscript copies of the Burr and Wilkinson letters in the collections of the Newberry Library in Chicago with the published versions. Power's letter about Wilkinson's performances in New Orleans is printed with their permission.

The office of the curator of manuscripts at the Alderman Library was most helpful in making available photo copies of William C. Cabell's notes on the grand jury proceedings which preceded the Burr trial. Parts of two letters in the Cobell papers are quoted by the kind permission of Mrs. Hartwell Cobell of Warminster, Virginia.

On the Dusky Sall story I am very much obliged to Mr. James A. Rodabaugh of Kent State University in Ohio for bringing the Madison Hemings narrative to my attention, to Mr. Douglass Adair of Claremont, California, for letting me read an advance copy of his carefully reasoned article on the subject, and to Mr. Julian Boyd for taking the time to write me a letter full of useful suggestions. Randall's letter to Parton is quoted by courtesy of the Harvard University Library. The quotations from the Tocqueville and Beaumont letters are by permission of the Yale University Library, and of Mr. George Wilson Pierson.

CHAPTER I

A Reception at the President's House

1. Morning Thoughts of a Virginian

Thomas Jefferson was an early riser. On the morning of the first of January 1807 he woke as was his wont before day in his curtained bed in an upstairs room in the unfinished mansion which John Adams was accused of having called the palace but which Jefferson referred to as the President's house. While his body servant stirred up the coals in the grate and lit the candles with a sliver of lightwood the President bundled himself in a warm dressing gown against the cold and prepared to resume the neverending drudgery of his official paper work.

He was going on sixtyfour but, except for the sick headaches that had plagued him all his life and an occasional twinge of rheumatism in his broken wrist, his health was good. His reddish sandy hair was fading to gray, but his long freckled countenance still had an outdoor look. Visitors reported that he looked more like a farmer than a statesman. His tall spare frame was still unbowed. When he rode out in the afternoon, often to visit the local nurserymen and market gardeners whom he furnished with seeds and slips of unusual plants, and whose plantings he watched with breathless interest, his seat in the saddle was firm as ever. When he stepped forward to greet a friend or a stranger it was with the long stride of a man accustomed to walking in the hills.

His headaches had grown more frequent as problems and perplexities multiplied. In spite of the petitions from all over the Union begging him to run for a third term he was determined to follow George Washington's precedent and to retire on March 4, 1809. Meanwhile there was much to be done if his second administration were to end as triumphantly as his first.

War must be avoided, but somehow the two Floridas must be acquired, as Louisiana had been acquired, for the United States. An agreement must be reached with Great Britain to free American shipping from harassment by the Royal Navy. Some means short of war must be found by which the government of the United States could impose its will on an aggressor.

One stumbling block at home was the intrigue of certain Federalists for the secession of the New England states which only encouraged the highhanded behavior of the British government. Another was the madcap scheme of Aaron Burr. The discredited retired Vice President, having been foiled by the voters of New York in his ambition to head an independent New England confederacy, was trying to foment a similar scheme among the settlers on the Ohio. Problems. Perplexities.

Jefferson took a certain pleasure in close application to a mass of papers. When he adjusted his spectacles to read and write he forgot everything but the question in hand. He had given up the oldfashioned quill pens that needed continual trimming and was using one of the new steel nibs put out by a Baltimore stationer. He had a habit of humming as he worked.

Jefferson was a sanguine man. He had the knack of throwing off anxieties when he rose from his writing desk. He was looking forward to greeting his wellwishers in a happy frame of mind on this New Year's Day that was dawning so clear.

For one thing, Meriwether Lewis had ridden into Washington just three days before to give him an eyewitness report of the extent and potential wealth and diversity of the territory acquired by the Louisiana Purchase. The Louisiana Purchase had very nearly doubled the land area of the United States. Even Jefferson's political enemies were beginning to admit that it was the great achievement of his first administration.

Captain Lewis, the son of an Albemarle County neighbor, was one of the young men in whose education Jefferson took a warm interest. An explorer and naturalist, he was living one of the lives Jefferson himself might have liked to live if his destiny had proved different. Early in his administration as President he called young Lewis to Washington to act as his private secretary.

Together they planned every detail of the expedition. The exploration of the West had been one of Jefferson's dreams ever since he had listened as a boy to the heady talk of his father's friends in the Loyal Land Company about finding a river route to the Western Ocean.

Lewis chose George Rogers Clark's brother William to be his associate on the venture. William was the youngest of the redheaded Clarks of another Albemarle County family whose careers as frontiersmen Jefferson had followed with sympathy for many years. The

President put such a lilt of enthusiasm into the instructions he wrote out for Lewis and Clark that they are bloodheating to read.

For many weeks, until expresses telling of their safe return reached Washington from St. Louis in the fall of 1806, Lewis and Clark were given up for dead. Now Lewis was back and Clark was on his way. They had followed Jefferson's instructions to the letter. In thirty months they had led their Corps of Discovery up the Missouri almost to its headwaters, across the Continental Divide and down the green Columbia to the Pacific Ocean; and back to St. Louis with the loss of only a single man who died of what was described as a colic early in the journey.

Though Meriwether Lewis' first words dispelled any lingering hope of a water route to the Pacific, the news he brought of the new territory Jefferson had acquired for the young republic was exciting to the last degree. Along with him in his pack train Lewis brought crates of dried specimens of the flora and fauna of the Rocky Mountains and the great river valleys beyond, a huge mass of geographical data in notebooks and diaries, a family of palefaced Mandans from the upper reaches of the Missouri, and two grizzly bear cubs.

The success of the Corps of Discovery was Jefferson's most immediate cause for jubilation but there were other reasons for satisfaction as he looked back on his first six years in the presidency.

In his message to Congress at the beginning of December he had reported another successful expedition. Lieutenant Zebulon Pike had explored the Mississippi River virtually to its source; Pike's journal and map were almost ready to be presented to the lawmakers. The dispute with Spain about the boundaries of Louisiana was far from settled, but at least hostilities had been averted and General Wilkinson was negotiating with the Spanish authorities for agreement on a provisional boundary between the United States and Spanish Texas. Though the President didn't mention Aaron Burr by name, he reported that measures had been taken to forestall any unauthorized attack upon the Spanish dominions, or any insurrection west of the Appalachians. He expressed his wholehearted satisfaction that only one year remained before Congress could constitutionally abolish the slave trade.

He was proudest of the state of the national finances. Jefferson had early proclaimed his intention of making the bookkeeping of the federal government so simple that any farmer could understand it. Now he was able triumphantly to report the results of his friend Gallatin's thrifty measures in the Treasury. By the close of the current year, even allowing for the expenses of the naval war against the Barbary pirates, and of Louisiana and for the two million dollars laid aside as a secret fund for the acquisition of Florida, the administration would have paid off twentythree million dollars of the national debt.

In his message he recommended that the duty on salt be eliminated but that the Mediterranean Fund, levied from imposts on luxuries, be continued for a short time in view of the disturbed state of Europe. It had given him real satisfaction to point out that the Treasury would soon have more revenue than would be needed to service the remaining national debt. He suggested that the surplus be spent on rivers, canals, and roads to open new channels of communication between the states; and on education.

George Washington had made a bequest for a national university in his will. It was Jefferson's dearest hope that in the two years left to him in the presidency he might see this national university established in Washington City. He wanted it so much he spoke of it most guardedly—knowing that many a congressman didn't care a fig about book learning or natural science—as a "national institution" to supply "those sciences, which though rarely called for, are yet necessary to complete the circle, all parts of which contribute to the improvement of the country and some of them to its preservation."

He suggested that a constitutional amendment would be needed to specify exactly what internal improvements the federal government should take in hand.

Jefferson still hoped for one further success. By the destruction of the Prussian army during the past summer Bonaparte—now the Emperor Napoleon—had extended his empire over most of continental Europe. At the same time Great Britain, by a series of naval victories of which Trafalgar was the most impressive, had become undisputed mistress of the seas. There seemed no end in sight to the war between the two greatest powers in the world. Jefferson's foreign policy was based on the theory that there were advantages to be gained for the United States from this war. The Louisiana Purchase had proved him right.

Now he hoped that wartime necessities would force the British to ease their harassment of American shipping, and that Napoleon, always in need of hard cash, would somehow force Spain to sell the Floridas to the United States, as he himself had sold Louisiana when he was First Consul. This dual negotiation, which engaged Jefferson's envoys in London and Paris and Madrid and which could not from the nature of things be made public, accounted for the President's request to Congress that the act prohibiting importation of certain British goods be suspended, and for the gingerly manner, so maddening to Anglophile Federalists, in which his administration tried to avoid hurting the French Emperor's feelings.

Any newspaper reader could judge the delicacy of the Napoleonic sensibilities by following the dispatches which described the trial and execution of two unfortunate Germans accused of printing a pamphlet thought to libel His Imperial Majesty's troops. The British gazettes were making heroes of Schroderer and Palm.

Jefferson's latest negotiations in Europe had not been successful, but they had not entirely failed. He could still cling to the hope of repeating the miracle of Louisiana and of rounding out his presidency by adding Florida to the United States. At least, in spite of provocations from both sides, he had managed to keep the country out of war with either of the warring powers.

At home the prospects were good. Having devoted the best years of his life to its development, Jefferson tended to see national prosperity in terms of the continued growth of his own Democratic Republican party. Even in New England rightminded men were beginning to outvote the Federalists. Since the disruption of the secessionist plans of Pickering and his friends the only threat to domestic tranquillity was Burr's mysterious scheme in the West.

The President's desk was piled with reports, some signed, some anonymous, of a complicated but still mysterious intrigue of the ex-Vice President's. Jefferson had been moving with caution. He had sent John Graham, a friend of the Clintons in New York, presumably well versed in Burr's style of operations, to the Ohio for a personal report. Burr's most successful argument in enlisting young men for his expedition seemed to be his claim that his plans—whatever they were —had the sub rosa approval of the administration. To counter that falsehood the President had published a proclamation on November 27 warning good citizens against joining any unauthorized expedition against the Spanish dominions. The response was excellent. The President felt all he needed now to dispose of Mr. Burr was to give him enough rope to hang himself. Events were justifying his confidence in the devotion to the Union of the Western settlers.

Though Jefferson disliked large entertainments and preferred small dinners of not more than twelve he kept open house on New Year's Day and the Fourth of July. Anybody could come in to shake his hand. Usually the company was enlivened by the playing of the Marine Band in their scarlet uniforms, stationed on one of the platforms which were to be the bases of the porticoes the President was planning for the north and south entrances. The large east room was still unfinished and contained a collection of curiosities, notably the reconstructed skeleton of a mammoth, Indian paintings on buffalo hide, Indian weapons and examples of pottery, basketmaking, and sculpture which Jefferson showed his guests to prove his contention that the culture of the Indian tribes was on a high enough level; so that, if they could only be induced to take up agriculture instead of hunting as their means of subsistence, the red aborigines would eventually be admitted to citizenship on an equality with the whites.

Here also reposed the remnants of the gigantic cheese sent by the

President's New England admirers. Its maggoty condition afforded great sport to the Federalists.

Though much of the mansion remained unfurnished, some of the upstairs and the dining room and what was known as the cabinet room had been made habitable. The drawing room was equipped with the chairs and sofas upholstered in crimson damask which George Washington had bought in Philadelphia nearly twenty years before. Even the wife of the editor of the fervently Jeffersonian *National Intelligencer* found the additional furniture Jefferson brought in "plain and simple to excess."

Mrs. Smith, the niece of Congressman James A. Bayard of Delaware, was brought up a Federalist. It was with misgivings that she followed the inclinations of her heart and married a Philadelphia Republican. When Samuel Harrison Smith, who had been secretary of the American Philosophical Society, moved, at Jefferson's urging, to Washington City to set up the capital's first Republican newspaper, she looked forward with pious horror to the prospect of having to meet the infidel President.

Her diary and her letters to her sisters record her change of heart. Admitting that Mr. Jefferson was an eccentric, she was soon describing her meetings with him with a warmth of affection which was almost daughterly.

Except when his own daughter Martha Randolph and her children were visiting him Mrs. Smith found President Jefferson to be a lonely man. Particularly since the death of his younger daughter Polly, who was so sweet and pretty and was said to favor his dead wife, there had been a solitude about him. There was a bleakness about his widower's life in the great unfinished mansion. According to Mrs. Smith, the cabinet room was his refuge. There he sat at the desk where his vast correspondence was carefully filled. In one drawer he kept a set of carpenter's tools and in another his gardening trowels and shears "from the use of which he derived much amusement." Round the walls were maps, charts, and bookcases stuffed with books. On the bookcases stood globes and surveyors' instruments.

"In the window recesses were stands for flowers and plants which it was his delight to attend, and among his roses and geraniums was suspended the cage of his favorite mockingbird—which he cherished not only for its melodious powers but for its uncommon intelligence and affectionate disposition, of which qualities he gave surprising instances. It was the constant companion of his solitary and studious hours. Whenever he was alone he opened the cage and let the bird fly about the room. After flitting for a while from one object to another it would alight on his table and regale him with its sweetest notes or perch on his shoulders and take its food from his lips. Often when he retired to his chamber it would hop up the stairs after him

& while he took his siesta would sit on his couch & pour forth its melodious strains. How he loved the Bird! How he loved his flowers! He could not live without something to love & in the absence of his darling grandchildren his bird and his flowers became the objects of his tender care."

While Mrs. Smith came to love the President like a father she admitted his oddities. "He was called even by his friends a notional man, full of odd fancies in little things, and it must be confessed that his domestic arrangements were full of contrivances, conveniences as he called them, peculiarly his own." She described the revolving shelves in the diningroom wall and what she called a "dumbwaiter" set at each place, when he had something important to discuss with the members of his cabinet at dinner, so that no waiters need come into the room. "Often the practical was sacrificed to the fanciful," according to Mrs. Smith.

She agreed with the general report that the food furnished by his French cook, Monsieur Julien, was magnificent. "Republican simplicity united to epicurean delicacy." The wines were of the finest. What service there was was excellent, because the President paid the best wages in Washington. She reported that his servants loved him because he watched over them in a paternal way and never kept them up late at night.

2. *Morning Thoughts of a New Englander*

At the other end of Pennsylvania Avenue, Washington City's only thoroughfare, which Jefferson had managed to get planted with a double row of Lombardy poplars on either side, at Frost and Quinn's new boardinghouse on Capitol Hill, another early riser sat at his desk writing.

William Plumer of New Hampshire had set himself to chronicle events in the national capital as seen from the Senate chamber. As he wrote he occasionally looked with satisfaction round the wellappointed room for which he paid eleven dollars a week with board. He had described it to his daughter in a chatty letter a few days before, assuring her with a down to earth literalness which was very close to humor, that he kept it very neat: no hose or shoes under the bed, nothing tucked in behind the mirror. Though an abstemious man and careful of his pennies he noted that he had a demijohn of madeira in his closet to regale an occasional friend with.

During the earlier years of his term he had boarded at Coyle's, which was patronized only by Federalists. Now he was beginning to have doubts about his New England associates. For this session, which would be his last, since he had failed of reelection, he had decided to live in a place where he could associate with Republicans too. He hadn't dared invite a Republican to his old lodgings for fear he might be insulted by one of his Federalist friends.

Five years in Washington had broadened Plumer's outlook. He was beginning to plan a career for himself as a historian rather than as a politician.

At fortyseven Senator Plumer was a spare sallow sharpfaced man with wavy black hair that grew close to his head. Though he belonged to a good old New England family he had been raised to the plow on a farm which his father bought with his savings as a cordwainer in Newburyport. Plumer had to scratch for his education. As a youth he'd been possessed with the New Light promulgated by Jonathan Edwards and George Whitefield, but, being a pragmatic sort of fellow, by the time he was twentytwo he became a convinced Deist who tried to base his religion on reason.

He entered New Hampshire politics as an advocate of religious toleration. For a while he toyed with the idea of medicine, but decided, after some reading, that too little was known to justify an honest man's taking up doctoring as a profession. Already elected justice of the peace by his fellow townsmen, he went into a country attorney's office to study law. He applied the same hard common sense to the law that he did to religion. He was successful as a lawyer, and in state politics, and became a man of some means, raising a family of five children in his plain white weatherboarded farmhouse. In 1802 the New Hampshire legislature elected him to the United States Senate.

He arrived in Washington a straitlaced Federalist, who regarded all Republicans with abhorrence as lowlives and Jacobins. As late as the fall of 1804 he was writing a friend: "The high office of President is filled by an infidel, and that of Vice-President by a murderer"; and adding that, "to increase the gloom," the House of Representatives had just elected a Massachusetts Republican as their chaplain. He shared the Federalist dismay over the Louisiana Purchase and went so far as to join Roger Griswold, Uriah Tracy, and Timothy Pickering in their plot to dissolve the Union and to set up a separate New England confederacy; but gradually, as he carefully kept note of the proceedings in Congress, his common sense began to get the better of his partisanship. Particularly after Aaron Burr's failure to win the governorship of New York and the Republican victories that accompanied Thomas Jefferson's reelection in 1804, Plumer began to deplore the obstinacy of such highflying Federalists as his friend Timothy Pickering.

Pickering's political ideas had developed in the radically opposite direction. Like Plumer, Timothy Pickering was a rockribbed denizen of a rockribbed coast. He came of a family of hardbitten seafaring people long established in Salem.

He liked to tell his children the story of his uncle William in Queen
Anne's War. Uncle William was master of a small fishing vessel which
was attacked by a boatload of about thirty Frenchmen while drifting
helpless in a calm off Cape Breton. Since they only mustered seven
the Salem men wanted their skipper to surrender. Not so Uncle
William. Each man had a musket. He told them all they needed to do
was load. He'd attend to the Frenchmen. He started firing from the
cabin windows. When the Frenchmen swarmed over the stern he and
his crew ran forward to the forecastle where there were loopholes
for ventilation. Firing his seven muskets in turn through the loopholes,
he made it so hot for the Frenchmen that, carrying off their dead and
wounded, they piled back into their boat and rowed off in a hurry.
For this exploit Uncle William was placed in command of the *Boston
Galley*, specially built and outfitted to defend the fishing fleet.

Pickering noted with some pride in his memorandum book another
anecdote of this same uncle.

"Being afflicted with a corn on one of his toes, he went to a
joiner's shop, put his foot on a block, and taking up a mallet and
chisel struck off the offending toe."

After graduating from Harvard College, Pickering served as a clerk
with John Higginson, the Register of Deeds for Essex County. His
hobbies were music and closeorder drill. He owned a spinet and gave
lessons in sacred music. The year he came of age in 1766 he was
commissioned lieutenant in the Essex County militia. Though he
studied law his chief concern was for county politics.

In the dispute with the mother country he was one of the few
collegebred Salem men who took the Whig side. He developed a
pungent pen. He filled the columns of the *Essex Gazette* with controversy on all sorts of topics from foreign affairs to inoculation for
smallpox. As a result of a theological dispute with the Presbyterian
minister of his church he announced himself a Unitarian. He served
five terms as selectman of Salem, was a member of the Committee of
Correspondence and of the Committee of Safety. In 1774 he drafted
the address of the people of Salem protesting the shutting up of the
port of Boston.

He devoted a great deal of his time to training the local levies and
that same year published "An Easy Plan of Discipline for the Militia."
The Essex County militiamen elected Timothy Pickering their colonel.

In spite of Colonel Pickering's enthusiasm for martial exercises the
Salem contingent failed to reach Lexington in time for the fighting
there. There were charges of cowardice. When Pickering was involved in an affair, controversy and recrimination tended to follow in
its wake.

In 1776, almost immediately after marrying a Boston girl whose
father was an officer in the Royal Navy, Pickering left home with his

militiamen to join Washington's Continentals. His first child was born while he was in Westchester, chafing under the military inefficiency he saw all around him during the disastrous campaign which resulted in the loss of New York. "I speak my mind freely," he wrote his wife. "You know I am apt to do it."

Colonel Pickering spoke his mind with such good effect that he was appointed by General Washington to the important administrative post of Adjutant General. Recommending him to Congress, the Commander in Chief described him as "a Gentleman of liberal education, distinguished Zeal and great Method and activity in Business."

Though Pickering never for a moment doubted the correctness of his own opinions, he was subject to fits of doubt of his abilities. He wrote General Washington a selfdeprecating letter explaining that he feared the position was beyond his capacity. Furthermore he was extremely nearsighted. His spectacles clouded up so in rain or sleet he couldn't tell one body of troops from another. That letter was hardly in the hands of the postrider before he changed his mind. He dashed off a second letter to the Commander in Chief. After all he could see pretty well through his spectacles. If the post were still open he would accept.

"I am very happy in the General's family," he confided to his dear Becky. "His secretaries and aides de camp are gentlemen of education, and of the most polite engaging manners."

He served as Adjutant General with such distinction that during the dark winter of Valley Forge he was appointed to the Board of War which Congress set up in a desperate attempt to coordinate the military effort. He told Becky he had reached a low opinion of the citizens of the confederated states outside of New England. Especially he railed against the Pennsylvanians as lukewarm and selfseeking. "Not that I have a great opinion of the *morality* of the Americans in general," he complained, "but there are none that have more *public* virtue than the Pennsylvanians. However should the contest depend on the goodness, the *moral virtue* of my countrymen I should despair of success. But for the *justice of our cause* and the sake of the *righteous* in the land, I hope and I doubt not, God will in the end grant us victory."

For Timothy Pickering "the righteous in the land" abode mostly in Essex County, Massachusetts.

He was Quartermaster General on Washington's staff during the triumphal encirclement of Yorktown. With the coming of peace he set up as a merchant in Philadelphia but, though diligent in the public business, he had no knack for moneymaking. Caught up in the wave of speculation in Western lands, he enthusiastically bought up military grants in northern Pennsylvania. When the conflict between the settlers in the Wyoming Valley who had come from Connecticut and the settlers who relied on their Pennsylvania patents threatened to reach the proportions of a civil war, Pickering got himself commissioned by the authorities in Philadelphia to set up a county government in the Wyoming region. He laid claim to many acres in those forests. His peremptory behavior set everybody by the ears. He proved as stubborn as his uncle William. His selfrighteous manner may well have saved his life when he was kidnapped by a group of insurgents with blackened faces who planned to kill him. Instead of showing fear he lectured them like schoolboys until they lost their nerve.

He developed a knack with the Indians and often spoke up for them. The Indians were impressed by his tall stooped frame and the long dour countenance under the stringy black hair. Pickering was an unsmiling frozenfaced man; the Indians liked that. Just as he hated slavery and dueling he objected to the way the Indians were being despoiled. One of the few points on which he agreed with Thomas Jefferson was on the practicality of setting the Indians to farming.

Like Jefferson, he felt that farming was the proper life for a man. Though he'd worked at a desk from his youth up he insisted on speaking of himself as a farmer.

George Washington retained a high regard for Colonel Pickering. As soon as he was elected President he sent Pickering out to Painted Post to counteract British influence among the Senecas, and further commissioned him to draw up a treaty with the entire Six Nations. Soon after he made him Postmaster General; and, when Knox resigned in 1795, Secretary of War.

When the governing groups of the new nation split into political parties Pickering became a vehement Federalist. He denounced the agitation against the Jay treaty. "Such proceedings," he wrote, "are flagrant violation of the fundamental principles of our republican governments which are not simple democracies, but governments by *representation*." When the Federalist faction in Washington's administration forced Edmund Randolph out of the cabinet, Pickering took his place as Secretary of State. He continued to serve under John Adams.

In the controversy over the French war Pickering sided with Oliver Wolcott, who was taking all his cues from Hamilton. When President Adams discovered that Hamilton was trying to use his influence on Wolcott and Pickering to direct the affairs of his administration right under his own nose, he threw his wig on the floor in a rage and demanded first Wolcott's and then Pickering's resignation.

Pickering refused to resign. The President sent him a note discharging him forthwith. For the rest of his life Pickering was to conduct a bitter public feud with the Adamses.

In 1800 he found himself on the street without a penny to bless himself with. The victory at the polls of Jefferson's Democratic

Republicans had cut him off from any hope of public employment. His salary of thirtyfive hundred dollars as Secretary of State, though raised to five thousand in the last year, had proved barely sufficient to support his numerous family; he had nothing saved. He still had boys to educate. His land speculations had left him some ten thousand dollars in debt.

At the age of fiftyfive he decided to settle on one of his own tracts in the Great Bend of the Susquehanna River. He borrowed a thousand dollars, induced his eldest son to give up a good business opening in Philadelphia to join him, and set out in a cart with a couple of hired laborers. They cleared fields, planted a crop of wheat, built log houses. Though his hands got terribly blistered Pickering insisted on felling trees himself, lopping off branches, grubbing roots. He wrote home that his health had never been better but that he had been almost incapacitated by the loss of his spectacles.

Pickering's Massachusetts friends were appalled. They feared their spokesman for uncompromising Federalism would kill himself trying, at his age, to take up the life of the frontier. The Lowells and Cabots and Higginsons, who were getting every day richer and more powerful in the countinghouses of Boston, had like Pickering their home and family ties rooted in Essex County. They echoed each other's opinions so heartily that their opponents got to calling them the Essex Junto. Knowing how set in his ways the man was, they clubbed together to perpetrate a friendly hoax.

Making him believe that they were interested in his holdings as a business venture, they collected a group of subscribers who raised twentyfive thousand dollars to buy out his land grants. After paying his debts Pickering would be left with a sum which, properly invested, would assure him a comfortable income. To lure him home they rented him a farm at Danvers near Salem.

Timothy Pickering went home to Essex County more convinced than ever that the New Englanders—excepting perhaps the Adams family and the Jacobins of Marblehead—were "the righteous of the land." Though he boasted of being a plain farmer he couldn't keep away from the hustings. The Republicans defeated him for the House but his Essex friends had enough influence at the General Court to send him to the Senate. His companion senator was John Quincy Adams, John Adams' waspish son, who was to become Pickering's prime opponent in a quarter of a century of invective in the public press.

Plumer of New Hampshire had been hand in glove with Pickering of Massachusetts during his first years in the Senate. They lived in the same boardinghouse, they ate and drank and walked and rode together. Confident that righteousness was the perquisite of New

Englanders and New Englanders alone, they lashed up each other's scorn for the President and his democratic mob.

The Federalists were struggling for a foothold against a rising tide. With the Louisiana Purchase and settlers flocking out to the lands beyond the Ohio they saw that New England would be increasingly outnumbered and outvoted by Jacobins and slaveholders. "I do not believe," Pickering wrote in desperation to George Cabot in 1804, "in the practicality of a long continued union. . . . But when and how is a separation to be effected? . . . We suppose the British Provinces in Canada and Nova Scotia, with the consent of Great Britain may become members of the Northern League."

When Pickering began to discuss these plans with Mr. Anthony Merry, the British minister, Plumer felt he was going too far. "At this session," he wrote in his autobiography for the year 1806, "I found that the federalists were impudent and disposed to evil. Pickering and Talmadge said, at our lodgings, that they were in favor of such a measure 'because it would embarrass the president.' . . . Such unprincipled declarations disgusted me with them and the party."

From the beginning Plumer had refused to join in the boycott of the President's social gatherings pursued with so much relish by the New Englanders. Native curiosity if nothing else took him to the President's as often as he was asked.

The entries in his "memorandum" and the descriptions in his letters of doings at Mr. Jefferson's recorded a gradual change in attitude. The first time Plumer went he told of Jefferson's coming into the room with so little ceremony that he claimed to have taken him for one of the servants. He described the President as "a tall highboned man," "drest, or rather undrest, with an old brown coat, red waistcoat, old corduroy small clothes much soiled, woolen hose and slippers without heels." Even then he admitted that Jefferson was "easy of access & conversed with great ease & freedom."

Plumer was disgusted by the rail fence that protected the grassy enclosure round the mansion. "The house . . . is a palace but the fence is not fit for a barn yard; but perhaps it is in as much unison with the house as its theoretical tenant is with the dignified office he holds."

Long before he came to approve the policies of his administration he began admitting the charm of Mr. Jefferson's conversation. The President began to seem better dressed. Invited to dinner not long after the President's reelection for a second term, he wrote admiringly that Mr. Jefferson appeared "in a new black suit, wearing silk hose and shoes and with his hair highly powdered." His linen was clean. Plumer remarked that the dinner was "elegant and rich, his wine very good. There were eight different kinds . . . rich Hungary & richer Tokay . . ." at a guinea a bottle. The only thing he found to criticize was the cheese, part of the mammoth cheese contributed by the cheesemaking Republicans of Massachusetts, which he found "very far from being good."

Each time he was invited to the President's house he noted the quality of the wine. In spite of his Federalism Plumer enjoyed himself there. He didn't even mind the rule of *pêle-mêle*.

Mr. Jefferson was always the last one into the dining room but Plumer made a point of trying to sit near him at dinner. "My usual course, when invited to dine with him, is to converse very little with him, except on the weather & such common topics untill I come to the dining table, nor then untill the more substantial dishes are disposed of—& we have drank a glass or two. I do not mean that the President is under the influence of wine, for he is very temperate. But as I am generally placed next to him—& at that time the company is generally engaged in little parties eagerly talking—& thereby gives him & me More freedom in conversation—& even two glasses of wine oftimes renders a temperate man communicative."

Plumer had begun to soften towards Thomas Jefferson as a man. "The more critically I examined the character & conduct of Mr. Jefferson the more favorably I tho't of him," he wrote in retrospect when he copied his notes into a definitive autobiography. "A city appears very different when viewed from different positions; so it is with man. . . . The result of my enquiries as to Mr. Jefferson was that he possessed more honesty & integrity than most men in the higher ranks of society usually have. That he was a man of science & literature; that as to what is called *revealed religion* he was an infidel, but on all other subjects too credulous. Tho' he had made the tour of Europe, been minister at the court of Versailles, & enjoyed various means of being acquainted with the world, he had not acquired a thorough knowledge of it. That he had more knowledge of books & *natural philosophy* than of the human mind; that he was more a closet politician than a practical statesman, had more of *fine sense* than *common sense* so essential to business & which in fact governs the world. Man is a bundle of contradictions. Mr. Jefferson had too much cunning to be considered a model of wisdom & goodness; yet the errors of his public life proceeded more from the head than from the heart & particularly more of the errors of judgement & credulity than of depravity. . . . Yet with all his defects he was a great man possessed of a vast fund of knowledge, loved his country & was useful to it. We have no reason to expect we shall always have so good & safe a man for President."

Plumer was a cogitative man. New Year's Day for most people is a time for introspection and reminiscence. His term as senator would end with the close of this last session of the Ninth Congress. Already his letters to his friends were taking on a valedictory tone. He was leaving public life "without regret or disgust." A neat but not a flashy dresser, he was preening himself that morning with unusual care because he planned to attend the President's midday reception. The knowledge that it would be for the last time made the prospect poignant.

As he dressed he thought back over his career as a senator. "I have done my duty—I have acted according to the convictions of my own heart." What he most regretted, he noted in his journal, was the prospect of parting with men whose friendship he had come to prize, most of whom he feared he would never see again.

In those five years in Washington Plumer had learned to think of himself as an American rather than as a New Hampshireman. The change in his political notions was fairly typical of a process going on in the minds of many other moderate Federalists. While the Essex Junto was hardening in its opposition to democracy, practical New Englanders, in spite of the clamor of pulpit and press, were ceasing to believe that Thomas Jefferson was an imp of the devil.

"At twelve o'clock, the usual hour, I attended the President's levee," wrote Plumer. "The day being pleasant, there was a great concourse of people. The Vice President, many senators, representatives, heads of departments, foreign ministers, ladies, gentlemen, strangers, gentlemen of the vicinity—& several Indian Chiefs with their wives and children attended." Plumer's erstwhile friends, the irreconcilable Federalists, were noticeable by their absence. "There was a great plenty of ice creams, apple pies, cakes & a variety of wines. I tarried till two o'clock in the afternoon—at which time few visitors remained."

3. *President Jefferson's Heads of Departments*

There was no trace of a guard at the President's house. Samuel Harrison Smith wrote jokingly in a letter that he arrived one afternoon to introduce a friend to Mr. Jefferson and found nobody home at all. They wandered over the mansion, admired the Indian curiosities, and finally thought it a great lark to carry off one of the mammoth's smaller bones as a souvenir.

Even on open house days there was no ceremony. The President stood in the center of the drawing room and shook hands with all comers. He made no distinction of rank. On New Year's Day 1806 the secretary of the British Legation had noted ruefully in his journal that Mr. Jefferson merely bowed to the diplomatic corps and spent all his time talking through an interpreter with a group of Indians and their squaws.

This year the British diplomats may have expected special consideration because of the replacement of Anthony Merry by David Montague Erskine. This was the son of Thomas Erskine, Lord Chancellor in the "Ministry of All the Talents" which took office after Pitt's death. Thomas Erskine, who defended Tom Paine, was considered the most successful advocate of civil liberties at the British bar. Charles James Fox, the longterm friend of America, appointed the younger Erskine to Washington before his term at the Foreign Office was cut short by his last fatal illness. Alas, President Jefferson paid Erskine little heed. His interest was centered on a Mandan chief, known as the Wolf, whom Meriwether Lewis brought along, and on the grizzly bears on show behind the new stone wall which had recently been built to keep cattle from straying into the presidential grounds. The Federalists started spreading the word that Jefferson was turning the President's house into a bear garden.

Often on these occasions the ruffled feelings of the diplomats were soothed by the cordial ways of Mrs. James Madison, who acted as hostess when Mrs. Randolph was absent. A brunette with flashing dark eyes, Dolley Madison was as vivacious as her husband, the Secretary of State, was reserved.

Madison was eight years younger than Jefferson. They had been friends ever since they served together in the first Virginia Assembly in 1776, where Madison, with the look of a rosycheeked boy much too young to be elected a delegate, represented Orange County. Fresh from the study of Hebrew and ethics under John Witherspoon at Princeton, he espoused the cause of the nonconformist preachers harassed by the established church. Immediately he joined forces with Jefferson in his campaigns for religious toleration and public education. A taste for the classics, an aptitude for hard reading, and a profound belief in man's perfectibility drew them together.

When Jefferson was minister to France they corresponded constantly. At the Constitutional Convention in Philadelphia Madison performed the extraordinary feat of taking a leading part in the debates at the same time as he kept a meticulous journal of the proceedings. His papers, in collaboration with Hamilton, in *The Federalist* played a major part in explaining the theoretical groundwork of the Constitution to the American people. In Congress during the Federalist period, along with Gallatin, he was the chief organizer of the Republican party. He collaborated with Jefferson in the Virginia and Kentucky Resolutions, which were the basis of the states' rights theory. As Secretary of State he became the architect of the American doctrine of freedom of the seas.

In a pamphlet published in 1806 he ransacked the literature of international law for arguments against the British revival of the Rule of 1756 by which virtually any neutral goods could be declared contraband. Although John Randolph jeered at his work as "a shilling pamphlet hurled against eight hundred ships of war," Madison's scholarship and close reasoning managed to keep the legal basis of neutral rights alive in the public mind during the free for all of the Napoleonic wars.

As Secretary of State Madison appeared a small quiet man. He always dressed in black. Some said he looked like a Methodist minister. He wore his thinning hair powdered and pulled back into a little black silk bag behind.

The Federalists claimed his face was expressionless as a withered crabapple, but his friends found his deadpan remarks often witty and always to the point. Many a foreign diplomat discovered to his chagrin that it was a mistake to underrate Mr. Madison.

Madison made the State Department the cornerstone of Jefferson's administration. Mrs. Smith wrote warmly of his "plainness" and of the mild benevolence of his manner. After dinner, when the cloth and the ladies had been removed, Mr. Madison would sometimes astonish the company by coming out with a smutty story which, according to his contemporaries, was invariably funny.

The third member of the triumvirate that made up the executive arm of Jefferson's government was a striking looking man who spoke English with a foreign accent. Albert Gallatin was born in Switzerland of an influential Geneva family. He came to America at the age of eighteen with a friend of his own age in search of the wild free life of the frontier. They landed in the fall of 1780 at Gloucester on Cape Ann with a shipment of tea which they hoped would set them up in trade. Neither of the young Genevese developed a knack for business. Their first winter was spent at Machias in downeast Maine, where Gallatin chopped wood and marched with the militia and had his first experience with the Indians, whose languages and customs were to be his private study throughout his long career. The going was rough, but Gallatin never lost his zest for the wilderness settlements he saw building themselves into a nation.

He learned English at Machias, taught French at Harvard College, qualified as a surveyor in Virginia. During his early twenties he explored the Ohio and its tributaries in search of lands for the settlement of Swiss immigrants. Winters he spent among the hospitable Richmonders. There he became friends with John Marshall, and with the aging Patrick Henry. He so impressed George Washington during a short meeting at George's Creek on the Monongahela that the general asked him to become one of his land agents. He married the daughter of a French Huguenot and settled, with some associates from his native Geneva, a picturesque tract of Pennsylvania land he named Friendship Hill, which he later described, with a lack of illusion which was wholly characteristic, as "a troublesome and unproductive property which has plagued me all my life."

When his first wife died he threw himself into local politics. Being an industrious clearheaded young man with an excellent command of two languages, he found himself cast in the role of secretary in every political group he joined. He became a specialist at drafting bills and resolutions. After several terms in the Pennsylvania legislature he was elected at thirtytwo to the United States Senate. He asked far too many questions there to suit Alexander Hamilton; Hamilton's friends voted him out under the pretext that he was a foreigner, though he had long been naturalized in both Virginia and Pennsylvania. He showed great courage during the Whisky Rebellion in opposing the sedition and, at the same time, defending the just grievances of his constituents; and was reelected to the House of Representatives where he became the floor leader of the growing Republican party. Meanwhile he had tightened his links with the Republicans by marrying Hannah Nicholson, the sprightly daughter of James Nicholson, of a seagoing family of Nicholsons from the Eastern Shore of Maryland. Commodore Nicholson, after a couple of particularly bloody sea battles with His Majesty's ships during the Revolutionary War, had retired to New York where he played the old sea dog in politics in vigorous opposition to Alexander Hamilton.

Gallatin's personal friendship with Jefferson dated from his early days in the Senate. He brought to the Treasury a rare combination of the best European education of the time with a thorough knowledge of the needs and feelings of the Western settlers. Perhaps ten years Madison's junior, he was a swarthy stocky man with piercing black eyes. He had a jutting nose and a sharp chin. His dark hair, dressed back into a small tail, accentuated the pale height of his forehead. Gallatin looked like an able man and he was.

Through crowds of congressmen and Maryland countrymen and Georgetown and Alexandria merchants and their wives moved the rather mum Secretary of War, Henry Dearborn, who had served with brilliance as a young officer under Washington and never shown a trace of talent since; aggressive Senator Samuel Smith of Baltimore and his brother Robert, who the Federalists claimed was proving a nonentity as Secretary of the Navy; and Postmaster General Gideon Granger of Connecticut, the recipient of many a handshake as chief dispenser of patronage. With them on this occasion appeared Vice President George Clinton of New York, a dour old Irishman with a face gnarled as a shillelagh under beetling gray brows.

Powdered heads, and even an occasional wig worn by an oldtimer, mingled with the curled lovelocks and cropped bangs of the younger men who copied the fashions of the Napoleonic court.

Ladies were still rare enough in Washington for their presence in any number to be reported in the newspapers. The more daring dressed in the clinging lowcut "Grecian" style fashionable in London and Paris, but few went so far in that direction as did Napoleon's sisterinlaw, Madame Jerome Bonaparte, nee Patterson, a connection of the wealthy Baltimore Smiths, who had caused a great hubbub in the society of the capital city a couple of years before by the revealing flimsiness of her costume. "She has made a great noise here," wrote the wife of the editor of the *National Intelligencer*, "and crowds of boys have crowded around her gilded equipage to see what I hope will not often be seen in this country, an almost naked woman."

It had been Jefferson's hope to make Washington a center of science and literature. The President's good friend Joel Barlow, coming home from France with a comfortable fortune invested in French government funds, had recently bought himself, at Jefferson's suggestion, an estate on the hills to the northwest which he named Kalorama. As author of the *Columbiad* Barlow was by way of being the administration's poet laureate.

Visiting him during this winter was his best friend, Robert Fulton, painter and engineer, in Washington at the moment to try to interest the Navy Department in a submarine boat and an underwater torpedo he had invented. Recently arrived from France, he was taking advantage of a short period of leisure, while the hull of his *Clermont* was being prepared for the installation of the steam engine he had imported from Boulton and Watt in Birmingham, to visit his beloved Joel and Ruth Barlow, and to elicit Mr. Jefferson's assistance in getting his inventions considered by the proper authorities.

Both Barlow and Fulton were enthusiasts for a national university. Though a lazy man, under Jefferson's prodding Barlow had set to work on a prospectus. Jefferson had not yet given up the hope of inducing Joel Barlow to write a history of the early years of the Republic which would contradict the falsehoods he found in John Marshall's *George Washington*.

4. A Report from the Western Waters

Sometime during that first of January, possibly after the guests at the noonday reception had thinned out—leaving the tables along the walls, which had been heaped with such an abundance of cakes and wines, thoroughly gutted—a man in a flat black hat strode in and presented himself to the President. It was Jefferson's Quaker friend Isaac Briggs. His clothes were travelstained, his boots were covered with mud. He had ridden twelve hundred miles over wintry trails from Natchez to bring a personal message from General Wilkinson. He must see Mr. Jefferson alone.

Isaac Briggs was a man after Jefferson's own heart. A member of the Sandy Spring Meeting, he had helped found an agricultural society in Maryland and was tireless in promoting the use of manure and other good farming practices. With his brother he had invented a steam engine. By trade a surveyor, when Jefferson first knew him he was teaching school in Washington. When the President organized a government for the newly acquired regions along the Mississippi River he appointed Isaac Briggs surveyor general for the Mississippi and Orleans Territories with the special mission of laying out a mail road, if possible with the cooperation of the Spanish, who still held Baton Rouge, from New Orleans up the east bank of the river. Briggs's arrival was no surprise because Jefferson had received a few days before a letter from him, enclosed with dispatches brought by an express rider from Benjamin Hawkins, the U.S. agent with the Creek nation, explaining that Briggs was on his way to Washington but that, since he could find only this single half sheet of paper among the Creeks, he begged Mr. Jefferson to let his wife know that he was well.

The President immediately led Briggs into an empty room and closed the door behind them. As soon as he had glanced at General Wilkinson's wordy epistle, he turned to Briggs and, looking him in the eye, asked—as Briggs remembered when he described the scene to a congressional committee a few days later—with earnestness: "Is Wilkinson sound in this business?"

"I replied very promptly," Briggs quoted himself as saying, "there is not the smallest doubt of it."

Jefferson had a high regard for Isaac Briggs personally and he had a high regard for the truthfulness of Quakers.

He listened carefully while Briggs told of his interview with General Wilkinson. Somewhere between the eleventh and the seventeenth of the Eleventh Month, as Briggs put it, Quaker fashion, the general had asked him to come out to Major Minor's plantation near Natchez. Major Minor was an American who had long been in the Spanish service. His rank was in the Spanish army. At Minor's house the general had received Briggs in a state of great agitation. This could partly be accounted for by the fact that Mrs. Wilkinson lay desperately ill upstairs. "His manner was solemn and impressive."

Wilkinson told Briggs that Aaron Burr, Jonathan Dayton, and Commodore Truxton were about to attack New Orleans with a force of twelve thousand men. They would take over the banks and the artillery the French had left there. Their plan was to set up a separate government and to use what shipping they could seize in port to make a descent on Vera Cruz with the help of the British fleet. This would be the first stage of their conquest of Mexico.

"How does thee know these things?" asked Briggs.

"I have certain information," said Wilkinson.

"May not all this be a deception?" insisted Briggs.

Wilkinson then produced a letter of introduction, presented by young Sam Swartwout of New York, and an epistle in a mysterious cypher which he claimed to be from the retired Vice President himself. Wilkinson told Briggs that he and Burr had agreed on this cypher eight or ten years before. Then he read off what he claimed to be the decoding.

Briggs recited the phrases he remembered. He might not have retained the exact wording but he was sure of the general sense.

"I have crossed the mountains, never to return. . . . I am surrounded by a band of worthies, men of tried courage and talents, the best blood in our country. . . . Our force will move down the rivers in detached parties to rendezvous at Natchez . . . there to meet you"—Wilkinson—"when we shall determine whether Baton Rouge shall be taken or passed.

"You shall be second in command and shall dictate the rank of our officers . . . you may draw on me for any sum not exceeding a hundred thousand dollars.

"Truxton has gone to Jamaica to arrange with the admiral for naval assistance."

Jefferson immediately pronounced this to be a lie. Commodore Truxton had refused to have anything to do with the plot and had informed the President of every detail of it that he knew. Far from being in Jamaica he was at that moment residing quietly at his home in Perth Amboy.

Next Wilkinson read Briggs a letter from Jonathan Dayton, informing the general that he would surely be replaced as Commander in Chief at the next session of Congress. This was obviously an argument to induce Wilkinson to cooperate. As Briggs remembered it, Dayton's letter was even more lurid than Burr's. "The gods are with us. . . . Heaven smiles on our plan. . . . Success is certain. . . . Louisiana and Mexico . . . Glory, honor and wealth."

Briggs went on to quote Wilkinson's comments on these extraordinary epistles.

" 'I fear that Col. Burr has many associates and that he will be able to collect a very powerful force, for he is a man of consummate address and both he and General Dayton are capable of the *ruse de guerre* in a high degree; and I fear that my force is much too small to give an effectual check to the torrent that is about to descend upon me unless the government of the United States take some immediate step I am apprehensive all is lost. I shall, however, as in my judgment it will be the best defense I can make, concentrate all the force of which I can avail myself at New Orleans, fortify myself and consider myself as at the Straits of Thermopylae, where it appears very probable I shall lay down my life for my country, either by the assassin's dagger or the traitor's sword.'"

"Is Wilkinson sound?" the President asked again. Briggs replied that he had had his doubts. Wilkinson knew it.

When Briggs and Wilkinson first met during the taking over of New Orleans by the United States, Briggs asked the general outright in plain Quaker fashion if it were true that he had received ten thousand dollars, in freshminted Mexican coins packed in campeche bags, from the Spaniards. Wilkinson answered with every show of frankness that indeed it was true. It was the balance due him on "former mercantile contracts." During their conversation at Major Minor's plantation Wilkinson had admitted to Briggs that it was a suspicious circumstance, his staying in the house of a Spanish officer, but explained that he was willing to remain under a cloud if he could thereby help trap the conspirators. He added that his wife was so ill he could not move her. Briggs agreed with him that the major might be useful in his crisis because no man knew better than he who was dependable and who was not.

General Wilkinson expressed alarm because the mail hadn't come through for the last three weeks. He feared that the Burrites were already intercepting the postriders. He asked Briggs to undertake the mission of riding directly to Washington to carry his report to the President. Briggs replied that he would do it and here he was.

The President thanked Briggs heartily, said he would get his travel expenses refunded, and sent him off to see his wife at Sandy Spring.

Two days later, in a tone calculated to quiet the heroics of that *miles gloriosus*, Jefferson wrote General Wilkinson that he was confident that Burr's attempt had already failed: "I do not believe that the number of persons engaged with Burr ever amounted to five hundred . . . the greater part were engaged under the express assurance that the projected enterprise was against Mexico and secretly authorized by this government. many were expressly enlisted in the name of the United States. the proclamation which reached Pittsburgh, December 2nd, and other parts of the river, successively, undeceived both these classes. . . . I believe therefore that the enterprise may be considered as crushed, but we are not to relax our attentions until we know what passed at Louisville. . . . Be assured that Tennessee and particularly General Jackson are faithful . . . we had considered Fort Adams as the place to make a stand because it covered the mouth of the Red River. you have preferred New Orleans on the apprehension of a fleet from the West Indies. be assured there is not any foundation for such an expectation, but the lying exaggerations of those traitors to impose on others and swell their pretended means. the very man whom they represented to you as gone to Jamaica, and to bring the fleet, has never been from home, and has regularly communicated to me everything which has passed between Burr and him. no such proposition was ever hazarded to him . . . still I repeat that these grounds for security must not stop our proceedings or preparations until they are further confirmed. go on therefore with your works for the defence of New Orleans, because they will always be useful, only looking to what should be permanent rather than means merely temporary."

The President added that Wilkinson's confidential messenger had arrived. The cypher letters and all other evidence must be dispatched to Washington. "It is necessary that all important testimony should be brought to one center, in order that the guilty may be convicted, and the innocent left untroubled."

A few days later he summed up the plot that fizzled in a letter to his old friend the Reverend Charles Clay, a clergyman in backcountry Virginia:

"Burr's enterprise is the most extraordinary since the days of Don Quixot. it is so extravagant that those who know his understanding would not believe it if the proofs admitted doubt. he has meant to place himself on the throne of Montezuma, and extend his empire to the Allegheny, seizing on N. Orleans as the instrument of compulsion for our Western States. I think his undertaking effectually crippled by the activity of Ohio. whether Kentucky will give him the coup de grace is doubtful; but if he is able to descend the river with any means we are sufficiently prepared at New Orleans. I hope however Kentucky will do its duty & finish the matter for the honor of popular govmt and the discouragement of standing armies."

CHAPTER II

The Arch Traitor Burr

1. *A Hero at Twenty*

Aaron Burr was born to eminence if ever a man was. The ministry formed the aristocracy of colonial New England. Both Burr's father and mother were descended from long lines of distinguished divines. In spite of a stain of madness which had appeared in both families, the Burrs and the Edwardses had for generations taken it for granted that they were better than other men were. His father, the Reverend Aaron Burr, was the second president of the College of New Jersey. His mother was a daughter of Jonathan Edwards, the expounder of the New Light who painted the doctrine of predestined damnation in such terrifying colors that even his own congregation at Northampton rebelled and drove him out.

Aaron Burr the younger was born in 1756 at his father's rectory in Newark, New Jersey, while his father was riding about the country raising money for the building of Nassau Hall and the transfer of his college to Princeton. The Reverend Mr. Burr's labors proved too much for him. Little Aaron's grandfather, Jonathan Edwards, called to take his soninlaw's place, hardly reached Princeton before he, too, died, of a fever that followed inoculation for smallpox. Six months later Aaron's mother died and his grandmother Edwards soon after. The Burr children were left orphans.

The boy proved a persistent runaway. After he had been passed from household to household, his uncle Timothy Edwards, who thought himself somewhat of a pedagogue, was induced by the family to take charge. Aaron used to tell his friends that his uncle "licked him like a sack," but the uncle's report was different. He claimed that, though he believed in the rule of "spare the rod and spoil the

child," in Aaron's case he'd had to resort to "maple sugar government."

Running away to sea was the first thing rebellious boys thought of
in those days. When he was ten Aaron sneaked off to New York and
shipped as a cabin boy on a vessel being rigged for an ocean voyage.
The story told in the family was that when he saw his uncle coming
down the wharf to fetch him home he ran up the shrouds like a
monkey and refused to come down from the topgallant masthead
until his uncle had made a formal promise not to punish him. In later
years Timothy Edwards ruefully referred to his nephew "as one
whom I brought up, or suffered to grow up, without the rod."

Aaron developed into a small graceful lad with a rather large head
and dark luminous eyes. He was stronger than he looked. There was
another boy of about the same age being brought up under his
uncle Timothy's supervision, Matthias Ogden, his uncle's wife's
younger brother. The two formed a lifetime attachment. Aaron was
early developing a gift for attracting friends. The river was nearby.
Whenever they could sneak away from their books the two boys
spent their days rowing and sailing and fishing and crabbing together
on the broad tidal estuaries of the Jersey shore.

Education was the family creed. The family and friends couldn't
imagine any other career for Aaron than to follow his forebears into
the pulpit. He was a boy of quick intelligence and winning ways.
When he wanted to he could apply himself mightily. He learned so
fast when his uncle brought an agreeable young Princeton man
named Tapping Reeve into the family as a tutor that, by the time
he was eleven, he thought himself ready to apply for admission to
the college. He already had supreme confidence in his own abilities.

The College of New Jersey was now under the management of a
liberal Scot who had been brought over from North Britain to assume
the presidency. Dr. John Witherspoon was a good Presbyterian, but
of the commonsense school that believed in works rather than grace.
To the boy's great mortification he was turned down as insufficiently
prepared, even if his name was Aaron Burr.

It wasn't until two years later that Dr. Witherspoon admitted him,
grudgingly, to the sophomore class. At Princeton Burr cultivated
the Chesterfieldian approach of the coffeehouse wits of Queen Anne's
London. Already his dark eyes and charming manners fluttered the
hearts of the village girls. When he graduated *magna cum laude* in
1772 with first place in English declamation, at Commencement, while
his classmates were making the rafters ring with arguments for and
against the nonimportation agreements, Burr contributed an Addisonian essay on building castles in the air.

Graduated from Princeton at sixteen, Burr delighted his family
connection by taking up a course of study with his cousin Joseph

Bellamy at Bethlehem, Connecticut. Dr. Bellamy, who had a famous library on philosophical and theological topics, was the foremost disciple of the late Jonathan Edwards. He took young men into his household to study for the ministry.

After a winter of close reading, and some heated argument with the learned divine, Burr took French leave, riding off on one of the best horses in the doctor's stable, which his uncle Timothy eventually had to pay for. The doctrine of predestined damnation left Burr cold. He told his friends that his theological reading had convinced him that God was a great deal better than most people supposed and that the road to heaven was open to all and sundry. Thereafter his attitude towards the Christian religion and Christian ethics was one of amused condescension. Let others await the joys of heaven; little Aaron would seek his pleasures on earth.

He decided to study law and settled at his sister Sally's house in Litchfield. Sally was the only relative Aaron really loved. She had married their erstwhile tutor Tapping Reeve, who was already so well thought of as a lawyer that students were coming to him for instruction. Aaron found Litchfield a congenial town. The Connecticut blue laws were somewhat relaxed there. The neighborhood was full of revolutionary fervor and charming young women. Burr, well-born, goodlooking, and reputed to be rich, was the focus of all the girls' eyes. Indeed the young lady who was about to marry John Hancock, the great Boston merchant, wrote home that Burr was "a remarkably handsome young man with a pretty fortune." The Litchfield girls took up a great deal more of Burr's time than did Coke's Littleton.

He had just turned nineteen when war flared in earnest between the colonists and what they still called the ministerial troops. News of Lexington and Concord and of the pitched battle on Bunker's Hill caused young Burr to drop his lawbooks and to take to reading Caesar and Frederick the Great instead. The Prussian drillmaster became one of his lifelong admirations.

When Congress appointed George Washington generalissimo of the Continental forces, volunteers started flocking to his headquarters. Armed with a letter from John Hancock, who was an old family friend of the Burrs, Aaron and his pal Matt set out for Cambridge.

Matthias Ogden, only a year older than his companion, immediately found himself commissioned a major, but Burr was passed over. Perhaps the shrewd gray eye of the Commander in Chief glimpsed something arrogant and supercilious under the courtly manner and the almost girlish good looks, or perhaps it was just that Burr looked too frail and diminutive to impose his will on other men. The slight stung him to the bone. He hung around Cambridge and Watertown, reading Frederick's memoirs and planning campaigns in makebelieve until he came down with one of the fevers so prevalent in the camp. He was still in bed when he heard that Benedict Arnold was organizing an expedition to take Quebec.

Colonel Arnold was the hero of the hour. The New Haven apothecary had been with Ethan Allen's Green Mountain Boys at Ticonderoga. His bringing back the British cannon which the Commander in Chief had so sighed for was being hailed as the first successful feat of Continental arms. Now Arnold proposed a pincers movement. He would lead twelve hundred men north through the wilderness of the province of Maine to surprise Quebec, while another army was to move from Crown Point down the St. Lawrence Valley against Montreal. He assured the Commander in Chief that the British in Canada lacked sufficient troops to defend both cities at once. This was a plan to heat the blood of any young student of military strategy.

Right away Burr dragged himself out of bed and proved that he had a flair for leadership by getting together a group of volunteers who would pay their own way. Matt had already gone off with the officers in a train of carriages. Burr and his lads shouldered their muskets, strapped on their knapsacks, and trudged the thirtytwo miles to Newburyport on foot.

Eleven schooners were to transport Arnold's expedition to Point Angry near Fort Western on the Kennebec, where bateaux were being built to take them upriver. While the flotilla waited for a favorable wind messages from doting friends poured into Newburyport begging Aaron not to go.

Crowded into the rank holds of smacks and cargo schooners, Arnold's troops were thoroughly seasick, but they reached the quiet waters of the Kennebec without mishap. At Fort Western they made up for lost meals with barbecued bear meat and smoked venison washed down with stout New England rum.

It was mid-September. The trip up the Kennebec turned out to be a race with the season. Rowing and poling the clumsy boats against the current was heavy work. Burr's training as a boatman served him in good stead. His mates were astonished by the little fellow's hardihood. He never seemed hungry. He never seemed tired.

Little Aaron proved himself a man. Though chary of words he had a quiet way of dramatizing himself. Stories about his exploits went from boat to boat. He had seduced a halfbreed Indian girl who tagged along with the expedition helping him track game and catch fish. She became legendary as Aaron Burr's first paramour under the name of Jacataqua.

He was reputed to be a capable steersman but when one of Dan Morgan's boats plunged over a fall in the Chaudière River and split on a rock, young Burr was at the steering oar. The supplies were all lost; one man was drowned, but Burr scrambled ashore, wet but imperturbable.

By that time they were eating their dogs and trying to boil up old moccasins and leather straps for soup. Some chewed roots and bark. Arnold, who was not much on sharing privations with his men, had gone ahead with a group of Indians in canoes to buy provisions from the habitants who were supposed to favor the Continental cause.

When the weary troop straggled into Point Levis across the St. Lawrence from Quebec, Colonel Arnold could barely muster five hundred men fit to shoulder a musket.

Burr had attached himself as informal aide to the staff officers. Matt Ogden was working to get him a commission. At the end of the month Arnold sent Burr on a liaison mission to General Montgomery, who was still a day's march from Quebec, with a note describing him as a volunteer, "son to the former President of New Jersey College . . . a young gentleman of much life and activity and has acted with great spirit and resolution on our fatiguing march." Perhaps Arnold had no commissions to give or perhaps he felt the young gentleman was a little too smart for his own good. He intended Montgomery to keep him. "His conduct," he added, "will be a sufficient recommendation to your favor."

Burr thereafter spoke disparagingly of Arnold as a moneygrubbing tradesman more interested in collecting loot to send home than in the fine points of strategy and tactics, but big laughing Montgomery he considered a gentleman. Montgomery had studied at Trinity and, as a friend of Burke and Charles James Fox and of the group of fashionable Whigs in Parliament who had worked for conciliation with America, he had moved in the best society in England. He threw up his commission in the British army before the troubles began and bought himself an estate at King's Bridge on the Hudson. There he married a daughter of Robert R. Livingston and so became a member of the powerful Livingston clan. On Montgomery's staff Burr could feel at home. Young Aaron induced the cheerful Irishman to commission him a captain forthwith.

Montgomery's part in the Canadian expedition had so far been highly successful, but he had suffered one mischance which was to prove fatal. When Montreal surrendered, the Americans let Sir Guy Carleton, the British governor, slip through their fingers.

Carleton was one of the ablest men in His Majesty's service. He was experienced in the Canadian North. He had a knack for conciliating the French and the Indians. He was a subtle and determined fighter. While the Americans were digging in to besiege Quebec, he smuggled himself through their lines, disguised as an Indian as some said, and went to work to make the fortress city impregnable. He kept himself posted on every move the Americans made. Many of the French habitants Arnold thought so friendly were spying for Carleton.

Winter had closed down. On the last day of 1775 Arnold and Montgomery tried to storm the lower town. Their troops started moving before day in a raging blizzard. Montgomery insisted on leading the vanguard in person. Captain Burr walked by his side. Carleton was ready for them. The advanced detachment fell into a trap and was cut down by a burst of grapeshot from a hidden battery. Of the twelve men in the first rank every man fell except Burr. The ranks behind broke and bolted. As they ran they saw little Burr tugging desperately at Montgomery's great body as he tried to drag it back through the snow. Bullets spattered all about him. A Colonel Campbell who took command ordered him to retire with the rest. The day ended in failure and disgrace. About all the Americans had to brag about was Montgomery's rash courage and Captain Burr's brave effort to retrieve his general's body. Not quite turned twenty, Aaron Burr found himself a national hero.

2. Colonel Burr of the Malcolms

With the failure of the assault Captain Burr lost interest in the Quebec campaign. He foresaw that the American attempt to besiege that fortress city would end in disaster. Prospects for glory and advancement beckoned him from the southward. The redcoats had evacuated Boston but they were mounting an attack on New York. Matt Ogden, who had been wounded on the fatal morning and was home convalescing, wrote that prospects were good for his friend Aaron on Washington's staff. Family and friends were beating the drum for him in New Jersey and Connecticut.

Burr miserably dragged out the winter in camp on the Plains of Abraham. Four feet of snow. Temperatures of forty below zero. The army suffered more from cold and smallpox and dysentery than from the harassments of the enemy. He was "dirty, ragged, moneyless and friendless," he wrote his sister Sally.

When Congress, as soon as the ice broke in the spring, withdrew Arnold and his raddled troops and substituted fresh levies under General Wooster, Burr wrote home that Arnold was "not to be trusted anywhere except under the eye of a superior." British reinforcements were arriving. The Canadian expedition was falling to pieces. Burr had had enough. In spite of repeated refusals of a leave of absence, he took off from Arnold's camp at Sorel one fine morning with a boatload of militiamen whose enlistments were up. Many a man in the Continental Army was shot for less.

Burr found General Washington making his headquarters at Richmond Hill outside of Greenwich Village on Manhattan Island. Friends had set the stage for the young hero of Quebec. He was well received by the Commander in Chief and invited to join his "military family." Part of Burr's work as a staff officer was to copy the general's letters and orderbooks.

Burr appreciated the elegance of the Richmond Hill mansion and the beauty of the great trees in the park that surrounded it, but he did not appreciate his Commander in Chief. He professed to be sickened by the air of adulation that surrounded him. He told his friends that the Virginian was devoid of military talent. Oblivious of the superb rhetoric in which George Washington couched his phrases, Burr made sport of his errors in spelling. The general had not had the advantage of an education at Nassau Hall. When Major Burr tried to enlighten his commander with certain ideas of his own about the defense of New York he received a rebuff. Washington was no man to take unsolicited advice from young whippersnappers. If Burr didn't appreciate the general, it became obvious that neither did the general appreciate Burr.

Before a month was out Burr was writing John Hancock, who took a paternal interest in his career, that he wanted to resign from the army. Instead the president of Congress arranged a transfer to the staff of General Israel Putnam. Putnam was a hearty old soul who had been an innkeeper in private life. His spelling was far worse than General Washington's, but as a Connecticut man he would presumably appreciate the deference due Burr for his lineage.

Putnam's headquarters were on the Broad Way, near the Battery. The general had kindly taken a young girl named Margaret Moncrieffe into his family. She was the daughter of a British army officer, whom the rapid movements of the armies had somehow left stranded in Jersey. She was reputed to be an irresistible beauty. She made a dead set for young Major Burr. When she began to talk about marriage Burr seems to have taken evasive action. He induced the general to discourage her and privately expressed suspicions that she might be a British spy. In the end he managed to have her sent back to her father, who was with the British fleet anchored in the outer bay, in a congressional barge under a flag of truce.

The lovely Margaret became one of London's most fashionable courtesans, and years later, having fallen on evil days, listed the names of her more prominent lovers in a publication called *The Confessions of Mrs. Coghan*. Though she didn't name Burr she referred to him as an American officer who might have saved her from a life of shame, had their marriage been permitted. She remembered him in the most romantic terms, as the one pure love of her life, but Burr's biographer insisted, unabashed, that young Aaron was the gay deceiver who started her on the primrose path.

The British investment of New York cut all romances short. Burr expected the worst. He wrote his friends bitterly criticizing Washington's plans for defense. During the desperate days of the retreat after the Battle of Long Island he acquitted himself well, so well that in the following summer he received from Washington, who was then making his headquarters at Peekskill up the Hudson, his formal appointment as lieutenant colonel in the Continental Army. His orders were to join Colonel Malcolm's New York regiment.

Burr was not satisfied. In his letter of thanks he observed tartly "that the late date of my appointment subjects me to the command of many who were younger in the service. . . . I would beg to know whether it was any misconduct in me, or any extraordinary merit or services in them, which entitled the gentlemen lately put over me to that preference?"

There is no answer on record. A lieutenant colonel Burr remained so long as he served in the Continental Army. His friends felt his courage and ability deserved more recognition but George Washington, no matter what exploits were imputed to Burr, never developed confidence in the little colonel.

Already a man with a grievance, at Valley Forge Burr joined the grumblers around Conway and Charles Lee who were trying to induce Congress to remove Washington from his command. His hero was Horatio Gates, whose forehead still shone with the glory of Burgoyne's surrender. He tried to get transferred to Gates's staff but the Commander in Chief wouldn't permit it.

At Monmouth Court House came the opportunity for military glory he'd so long waited for. Though still a lieutenant colonel he was given the duties of a brigade commander. He led three regiments in General Stirling's division. Washington's plan was to attack Clinton's redcoats, pausing for breath in their retreat from Philadelphia, when their cumbersome wagon trains should start moving at the dawn of day. Willfully or not, General Lee misunderstood Washington's orders and pulled his men back at the first British opposition. This maneuver almost threw the whole Continental Army into a rout. There followed the legendary interview, where Washington "cursed till the leaves shook on the trees." By rapid improvisations of a sort his critics hadn't believed him capable of, Washington saved the day.

Colonel Burr, meanwhile, had been ordered to hold a strong position on the flank overlooking one of the many swamps that made the terrain so difficult, while the center advanced to attack. There Hamilton and Lafayette, contemporaries whose advancement Burr had complained of, were winning reputations under fire. After the American artillery mangled a British battalion that tried to bridge the swamp,

Burr, tired of standing idly by, ordered his men to cut off the stragglers. An aide arrived on a lathered horse to forbid the move. Burr disobeyed orders. Crossing the little bridge, Burr's regiments were enfiladed by a British masked battery on the edge of the swamp and took such punishment that they lost two thirds of their men, dead or wounded. A cannon ball cut Burr's horse from under him and spilled him in the mud.

The British made good their retreat but the Continentals were left in command of the field. Burr was not courtmartialed, as General Lee was after the battle for his fumbling of the orders, but he never after was trusted with an important command. The disparagement of Washington became one of his obsessions.

The Battle of Monmouth was fought in scorchingly hot weather. Both armies suffered as much from thirst and sunstroke as from the bullets of the enemy. When night brought the engagement to an end Burr threw himself down under some trees in an agony of fatigue and frustration. When he awoke he found he could barely walk.

Whether the disease was rheumatic fever or some sort of shell shock Colonel Burr was almost a cripple for many months. He suffered from chronic diarrhea. His resignation from the army was accepted.

3. The Fair Widow of Paramus

In letters to his friends he complained of hypochondria. "It is an object of importance to me to be not only secure from alarms, but remote from the noise of war," he wrote William Paterson, the New Jersey jurist whom he was consulting about continuing his studies for the bar. He found consolation in the arms of a lady ten years his senior.

Theodosia Prevost was one of the great hostesses of the day. Her letters reveal a charming sensible woman, well read almost to the point of becoming a bluestocking. Her father Theodosius Bartow had been a lawyer at Shrewsbury, New Jersey. After his death her mother married an officer in the British regular army and she herself at an early age married another, a Colonel Prevost by whom she had five children. The two older boys were already serving as ensigns in the British army when the American war broke out. Added to her social graces there was a good deal of finesse in Mrs. Prevost's makeup. She had friends on both sides. She entertained the officers of whichever army was occupying the Ramapo Valley. General Washington held her in high esteem. In spite of being related to no less than five British officers she managed to keep her fine stone house, The Hermitage, near Paramus, and its farms and dependencies, out of the hands of the Whig committees greedy to expropriate Tory possessions.

It seems likely that Aaron Burr was first introduced to her as far back as 1777. He spent a night at Paramus at the time of his only really successful military exploit, when he managed to capture the bulk of a British raiding party sent out by the redoubtable Tryon to ravage the Ramapo farmsteads. Burr's friends took it for granted that his continued visits to the Hermitage meant that he was courting Mrs. Prevost's younger and unencumbered half sister Catherine de Visme, but the older lady was the real attraction. Their intimacy from the beginning was warmer than friendship.

When news came of Colonel Prevost's death in the West Indies their liaison became so open that talk began to spread. Burr begged her to marry him. Mrs. Prevost held him off. When Burr threatened to throw up his law studies and go to the dogs she gave him a good scolding. She had been trying to argue him out of his adolescent cynicism with motherly advice. She pointed out that she was a middleaged woman. Her face was marred by a scar. Her figure showed the effects of having borne five children. Burr had an irrepressibly boyish air. She didn't want to make herself ridiculous by marrying a man who looked young enough to be one of her sons.

In the end Aaron Burr prevailed. Aside from the pleasures of her bed Mrs. Prevost was a wellconnected lady. Marrying the hostess of the Hermitage was a step up in the career of an ambitious young man. Burr had abandoned the study of law with his friend Paterson. Paterson was a legal scholar who wanted him to put in three years for a thorough grounding. Burr had run through his inheritance, paying the expenses of his regiment, so he always claimed. He had to make money fast. He found an Albany lawyer with whom he crammed night and day to meet the questions that would be put by the judges who conducted examinations for the New York bar.

"The Law is anything that is boldly asserted and plausibly maintained," was to be the motto of Burr's law practice throughout his life. With Theodosia holding his hand, and her connections joining his own to pull all strings, he got himself licensed a counselor at law at Albany in the spring of 1782.

It was in the nick of time: he hadn't a penny. When, later in the same summer, he and Mrs. Prevost were married, they made it a double wedding with Catherine de Visme and Dr. James Browne to save money. Theodosia, already on terms of warm friendship with her new sisterinlaw, described the ceremony in a jocular letter to Sally Reeve: "You asked . . . the particulars of our wedding," she wrote. ". . . It was attended with two singular circumstances. The first was that it cost us nothing. Browne and Catty provided abundantly and we improved the opportunity. The fates led Burr on in his old coat. It was proper my gown should be of suitable gauze. Ribbons, gloves etc. were favors from Catty. . . . The parson's fee took the only half Joe Burr was master of. We partook of the good things as long as they lasted and then set out for Albany where the want of money is our only grievance."

4. The Napoleon of Richmond Hill

The want of money was to be Burr's grievance all his life. He had the tastes of a Hudson River magnate but no income to support them. With an attractive wife to calm his nerves he could devote every energy to the law. He accepted his family responsibilities with zest. There was Theo's brood to launch in life. A passion for education, traditional in the Burr and Edwards families, had caused him, even before his marriage, to take over the schooling of the Prevost children and to direct his intended's reading through a series of somewhat pedantic letters.

It was a time of opportunity for a smart lawyer. Since the legislature had disbarred every lawyer who practiced under the British occupation the Whig attorneys who flocked into New York on the coattails of Washington's Continentals found rich pickings.

New York was still a wealthy city. The Revolution had left land titles and commercial contracts in a tangle which proved a lawyer's paradise. Added to that were bluesky speculations in upstate lands from which the lawyer who drew up the papers could expect a cut in the profits. Young attorneys like Alexander Hamilton and Aaron Burr, who could point to a patriotic war record, would virtually have the courts to themselves.

As soon as the redcoats evacuated New York Burr moved his growing family into the Verplanck house on Maiden Lane. Before leaving Albany his wife had produced a daughter whom he named after her—Theodosia. Then came two stillborn boys and a little Sally who died in infancy. When the two older Prevost boys resigned from the British army after the peace, they joined the family in New York. Burr took them into his office as apprentices and saw to it that they were admitted to citizenship.

With success at the bar came easy credit. Though personally an abstemious eater, Burr liked to give fine dinners. His cook was a German supposed to be the best chef in town. He was collecting a library second to none. He patronized rising young painters. He became a connoisseur of furniture. He collected a stable of fine horses. When he took his wife and little Theodosia, whose development into girlhood he followed with allconsuming affection, out driving, he sported a coach and six with outriders in livery.

The downtown house soon became too cramped for his style of living. He first rented and then bought Richmond Hill, the elegant mansion near the Hudson which he'd known as Washington's headquarters, and which Vice President Adams so enjoyed during the two years when New York was the national capital. Burr spent a fortune redecorating the house. He acquired another place called The Shrubberies on Pelham Bay. He speculated in real estate along the projected course of the Boston Post Road. He dabbled in upstate lands. None of his biographers was ever able quite to disentangle Burr's finances. A millionaire in prospect, he was always pressed for cash to pay his bills.

Burr hadn't been in the city six months before he became involved in politics. When he was first elected to the legislature, New York politics was the private preserve of three great families, the Livingstons, the Clintons, and the Schuylers. The saying was that the Livingstons had the money, the Clintons had the votes, and the Schuylers had Alexander Hamilton.

Burr and Hamilton were friendly rivals at the bar. When occasionally they appeared for the same client, it was Hamilton who read the law and Burr who improvised the courtroom strategy. It was as a moderate Federalist, a supporter of Alexander Hamilton's, that Burr first appeared at the hustings. Then when George Clinton almost missed reelection for a fourth term as governor and felt he had to draw support from the opposition, he offered the job of attorney general to Aaron Burr. Burr accepted and his political coat began to take on Republican hues.

He conducted himself so much to the satisfaction of the Clinton men in the legislature that when General Schuyler's term expired Burr was elected United States senator in his stead. He left the attorney general's office under a cloud, however. As attorney general he had sat as one of the commissioners of the Land Office entrusted with the sale of public lands. An enormous sale at a suspiciously low price to a speculator named Alexander McComb, who happened to be a legal client of Colonel Burr's, raised such a storm that the commissioners barely escaped indictment. Burr cleared his own skirts by coolly announcing that, having been absent from the meeting of the commissioners the day the sale was recorded, he had no responsibility in the matter. Even before he became acquainted with Talleyrand, when that serpentine statesman passed through New York, fleeing the Paris terror and eager to make a fortune in Ohio lands, Burr was putting the Frenchman's favorite motto into practice. *"Les grands âmes se soucient peu des petits moraux."*

At thirtyfive Aaron Burr appeared in Philadelphia as junior senator from New York. In the courts he had established himself as a master of stratagem, a dangerous opponent with whom few dared to match wits. At political meetings he behaved with the saturnine air of a man who had plans lesser spirits would not dare conceive of. His speeches were short and uncommunicative. He cultivated an atmosphere of mystery. Ever since as a boy he wrote in cypher to his sister Sally, he had reveled in cryptograms. His military bearing, his fierce black eyes, his freethinking quips, his look of truculence just restrained by aristocratic punctilio, made him irresistible to romantic young men at the point of kicking over the traces.

With women he was the dedicated charmer, never too busy to linger over the flirtatious conversations, full of theatrics and literary allusions, that constituted the romance of the day. So long as his wife lived all this play acting was kept within bounds by her watchful common sense. Having raised a family of boys, she treated him as much like a son as a husband. But his dear wife was ailing. A certain impatience with her continued illness made itself shown in his letters from Philadelphia.

Young Theodosia would take her place. Little Prissy, as she was known in the household, was developing her mother's charm and her mother's brains. She had her father's good looks besides. In the army Burr had the reputation of a martinet. He kept a tight rein on his daughter. All his obsession with education went into planning her schooling. Not the slightest detail escaped him. She must study Latin and Greek and learn French and dancing and singing and to play the harp. She must not be afraid of the dark. She must be a graceful and courageous rider. Aaron Burr's daughter must be supremely beautiful, fearless, learned, irresistible.

When the child was eleven her mother died, after a horrible illness, of cancer of the stomach. Young as Theodosia was, she had to take over as the hostess of Richmond Hill.

After the elder Theodosia's death Burr took up with a succession of mistresses. He seemed to glory in having his name linked with every loose woman in New York. Gossip had it that he and Hamilton vied for the favors of a Rhode Island girl named Elizabeth Bowen who was Manhattan's most successful prostitute. There was a lady who signed herself Leonora who dedicated a book to him about the revolution in Haiti. He cultivated the reputation of providing well for his bastards.

Senator Burr was frankly bored by the sessions of Congress. Except where his own interests were directly affected it was hard for him to keep his mind on the public business. An early riser, his mornings hung heavy on his hands. To while away the hours before the Senate convened he took to studying documents at the State Department. He hinted to his friends that he might write a history of the Revolutionary War.

Thomas Jefferson, who was still Secretary of State, was no man to stand in the way of such a project, particularly in the hands of a Republican. He let Burr have a key to the small brick building which housed foreign affairs, the patent office, and a couple of other agencies besides. Every morning Burr would send his servant over to light the fire and a little later would arrive with a copyist to dictate notes as he thumbed through the files of the public correspondence. His breakfast would be sent over from the excellent establishment managed by a respectable Quaker widow named Mrs. Payne, where he boarded. Over coffee and cold meat and hot muffins he would sit planning his history, gloating over the reputations that would go by the board. "These documents," he told a lawyer friend some years later, "detailed things which would falsify many matters now supposed to be gratifying national facts."

As soon as President Washington got wind of Burr's project he informed his Secretary of State that he must keep his records locked up. He wasn't going to leave his place in history to the mercy of Aaron Burr. The little colonel dropped the project as lightly as he might have some land speculation that had gone awry, or a young woman who had shut her bedroom door in his face.

Though Burr took little interest in the party strife between Jeffersonians and Hamiltonians that bedeviled the last years of Washington's administration, his newer friends were mostly among Jefferson's adherents. Congressman Madison, after Jefferson the chief architect of the Republican party, was still a bachelor. At Madison's request Burr introduced him to Mrs. Payne's lovely young daughter Dolley Todd, whom he promptly married. Burr had become so much the familiar of the Payne household that Dolley had appointed him after her first husband's death guardian of her infant son in her will. When Madison's and Jefferson's mutual friend James Monroe came close to a duel with Alexander Hamilton, in a contest of veracity over the Reynolds scandal just before Hamilton's retirement from the Treasury, it was Colonel Burr who appeared as Colonel Monroe's second. Indeed when Burr failed of reelection to the Senate, Madison and Monroe went together to the President to suggest that he appoint Burr minister to France. George Washington squared his jaw. Either of them, he said, he would appoint with pleasure, but not Aaron Burr.

In the Federalist reaction during the period of the near war with France during John Adams' administration, Burr was thrown back into local politics. Though President Adams recommended him for a commission in the national army, which George Washington and Alexander Hamilton were building up in case actual hostilities should break out, Washington turned him down.

Burr was elected again to the New York legislature. To offset his frustration on the national scene he speculated wildly in Genesee Valley lands and threw his sleepless energy into building himself a political machine in New York City.

Richmond Hill, where great fires blazed in every fireplace and where fourteenyearold Theodosia presided so prettily at the festive table, graced by the daringest wit and the best conversation and the finest dining on Manhattan, became the center of a group of young men about town. Bonaparte's romantic career in Europe stirred their imaginations. They were bored with the stodgy idealism of the past generation. They had the will; they would find a way. Theo called them her father's Tenth Legion. They were a wild and various crew but they had one thing in common: love for Theodosia and devotion to their leader.

New York was full of Irish immigrants and English radicals who had fled Pitt's repressive regime. French refugees talked Liberty, Equality, Fraternity. Up to now Hamilton's friends, merchants and manufacturers who made no bones about telling their employees they would lose their jobs if they voted Republican, had controlled the city wards. Now Burr's young men went around telling the voters all the things Colonel Burr would do for them if they voted the Rights of Man. A man had to own property to vote. The Burrites added new names to the voting rolls by helping artisans and mechanics and day laborers to club together to buy enough of a freehold in common to qualify.

Some years back an upholsterer named Mooney had organized a New York branch of the Sons of St. Tammany. The popular patriotic society had lost membership since President Washington's denunciation of Jacobin clubs. Burr's young men revived the Wigwam and turned it into a political organization. Though Colonel Burr himself never set foot in Martling's Long Room where the Tammany braves drank their beer, they cheered his coach when it drove past. "Aaron's rod shall blossom in New York" became the workingman's toast.

All this cost money. Burr was a great borrower. The only banks in the city, the Bank of the United States and the Bank of New York, were controlled by Hamilton and his friends. Burr decided the city needed a bank which would extend credit to Republicans. Characteristically he went roundabout. He put a charter through the legislature for a Manhattan Company which was to furnish New York with pure water. The project worked. A steam engine was set up to pump water through wooden pipes to the householders. The water system was a real boon, but not even the sharpesteyed Federalist had noticed a provision that Representative Burr wrote into his charter to the effect that surplus capital might be used in any way not incompatible with the laws. When Burr and his directors took advantage of the fine print to open a Bank of Manhattan, Hamilton's Federalists stormed but there was nothing they could do.

Though Colonel Burr and General Hamilton were outwardly on civil terms Hamilton was already warning his friends against Burr in private: "He is determined, as I conceive, to make his way to the head of the popular party and to climb *per fas aut nefas* to the highest honors of the State. . . . In a word if we have an embryo Caesar in the United States, 'tis Burr."

The Bank of Manhattan proved a setback to the Burrites politically. The popular element Burr's Little Band most appealed to considered banks inventions of the devil.

Furthermore there was damaging talk in the coffeehouses about Burr's connection with a Swiss gentleman named Cazenove who was spending money freely among New York politicians in behalf of the Holland Land Company, which dealt in enormous tracts of virgin lands in upstate New York and western Pennsylvania. The epidemic of bankruptcies that followed the failure of Robert Morris, the great financier of the Revolution, left many speculators holding worthless paper.

John B. Church, who as husband of another of General Schuyler's attractive daughters was Alexander Hamilton's brotherinlaw, was heard to criticize the manner in which Colonel Burr was allowed to wriggle out of a twenty thousand dollar claim this company had against him. Although Burr wrote a friend it was "the first time in my life that I have condescended to refute a calumny," the little colonel took such umbrage that he invited Mr. Church to meet him on the Jersey shore.

Burr was becoming a professional veteran, a pillar of the Society of the Cincinnati, a great stickler for the delicacy of his military honor. Mr. Church, besides holding Holland Land Company stock, was a director not only of the Bank of New York but of the Manhattan Company. There was no real antagonism between him and Burr. Their duel passed off as a joke. Burr had a new set of pistols that his second didn't load properly. The gentlemen let fly at each other. As neither was hit in the first encounter Mr. Church was induced to admit that he might have been mistaken about Colonel Burr's dealings with Monsieur Cazenove, and both parties were rowed home across the Hudson in high good humor to breakfast.

An old colored man named Harry who had been a slave of Burr's told the story years later that from that time on Colonel Burr took seriously to target practice. He made Miss Theo practice too. Sometimes after dinner at Richmond Hill he would hand out pistols to his guests. The servant would go out in the garden and throw an apple in the air. The other gentlemen often missed but Colonel Burr never did.

The news of the little colonel's marksmanship possibly had a quieting effect on idle tongues because, although he was known to be dangerously in debt, and besieged by his creditors, the May election of 1800 was a personal triumph. His whole slate was carried into the legislature. Nationally the Federalists were split among Hamiltonians,

New England secessionists, and adherents of John Adams. The coming presidential election was in the grasp of the Republicans, and Burr's adherents, dominating the New York legislature, would hold the balance of power. Burr demanded firm assurances from Jefferson's party in Virginia that he would have their votes for Vice President.

When the returns came in late in 1800 it was found that, because of a flaw in the Constitution, Burr and Jefferson were tied with seventy-three votes each for the presidency. Burr hastened to assure Jefferson that he had never aspired to anything more than second place. Jefferson wrote Burr that intriguers must not be allowed to come between them. It would be up to the House of Representatives to choose a President.

The Federalists saw their chance to impose an administration nearer to their liking. They would vote for Burr as the lesser evil. The result was a stalemate that lasted dangerously long. The Federalist plan was thwarted by Alexander Hamilton, who sat up nights in his law office on Broadway writing tirelessly to friends and supporters that though he disapproved of Jefferson's policies, Aaron Burr's "whole spring of action is inordinate ambition . . . without probity . . . a voluptuary by system—with habits of expense that can be satisfied by no fair expedients." He considered him "the Catiline of America."

Burr continued to sit with the legislature in Albany. He blew hot and cold. He wrote Jefferson reassuring letters. At the same time he hinted to certain Federalists that they would never regret it if they brought about his election. Though at home he would dramatically toast Bonaparte at the dinner table with a significant flash of his black eyes, when the test came on the national stage he failed to make the bid for power that Hamilton so dreaded. Instead he buried himself in mystery. The Federalists lost interest.

It was a time of rumors and denials, of plots and counterplots. Virginia and Pennsylvania were calling out their militia to resist a coup d'état in Washington in case the tie should not be broken. Burr declared he would throw all his weight against a new Federalist plan to appoint a temporary President. While suspicions and intrigues hummed about his name he busied himself, with his usual air of sang-froid, with the marriage of his adored Theodosia to a young plantation owner who belonged to a rich and powerful South Carolina family.

Some of Theodosia's friends were scandalized. Maria Nicholson, Albert Gallatin's sisterinlaw, whose father was a fervent Republican and a warm supporter of Burr's in New York, wrote Mrs. Gallatin in Washington, where Gallatin was directing Republican strategy in the House of Representatives: "I know you are interested in Theodosia Burr, I must tell you that Mr. Alston has returned from Carolina it is said to be married to her this month. . . . Report does not speak well of him; it says that he is rich, but he is a great dasher, dissipated, ill-tempered, vain and silly. I know that he is ugly and of unprepossessing manners. Can it be that the father has sacrificed a daughter so lovely to affluence and influential connections? They say it was Mr. A. who gained him the eight votes in Carolina at the present election, and that he is not yet relieved from pecuniary embarrassments. . . . He loves his child. Is he so devoted to the customs of the world as to encourage such a match?"

Perhaps Burr thought better of his soninlaw.

Though the salary was only five thousand a year, Burr's connection with the wealthy Alstons combined with his high federal office to hold off his creditors. He started negotiations for the sale of the farmlands of Richmond Hill which were eventually purchased by an energetic German immigrant named John Jacob Astor. He presided over the Senate with punctilious decorum.

Meanwhile he importuned the administration for jobs for his Little Band and intimated that there might be broader fields for his own talents than presiding over the Senate. Mr. Jefferson wrote back that he recognized Mr. Burr's great services to the Republican cause, that he had planned to offer him one of the departments, but that of course he couldn't expect him to resign the vice presidency. When Burr intimated that he would quite gladly resign the vice presidency Mr. Jefferson became very deaf.

Tales of Burr's maneuverings in Albany during the period of the presidential election had dampened Jefferson's enthusiasm for that gentleman's political collaboration. On his part Burr began to show signs, always in private, of dissatisfaction with Jefferson's administration. On Washington's Birthday, 1802, he appeared at a strictly Federalist dinner and toasted "The Union of All Honest Men." The inference was that the honest men were all Federalists.

Though Jefferson continued to invite him to his little dinners, Burr was left outside of the intimate circle of the administration. Whenever he went back to New York he found the city seething with bloodheating schemes. New York State was crucial in the plan of the New England Federalists to form a new confederacy free from the domination of the Virginia Republicans. The man who could deliver New York to the Essex Junto could write his own ticket for the new government. The stumbling block was Alexander Hamilton.

While Hamilton deplored republicanism and democracy he believed passionately in the federal Union. He did not find Jefferson's policies as wrongheaded as he'd expected them to be. Though the Republican victories had wrecked his political machine his personal influence was still great. All through Jefferson's first term New York City was torn by bitter personal warfare between Burrites and Hamiltonians. The printshops were busy with vituperative pamphlets. Columns of abuse filled the newspapers. Dr. Peter Irving, whose main claim to fame was to be as Washington Irving's elder brother, published the Federalist *Morning Chronicle*, friendly to Burr. Hamilton had William Coleman's ably written editorials in the *Evening Post*.

The code duello became an obsession. Hamilton's twentyyearold son Philip, whom Hamilton loved more than anything in the world, overheard a man named Eaker making disparaging remarks about his father at the theatre, called him out, and was shot dead.

The Swartwout brothers were of the inner ring of Burr's Little Band. John Swartwout called out George Clinton's brilliant son De Witt and was duly peppered by him through both legs. The story circulated that as young Clinton strode back to his boat he muttered that he wished he'd had the master to shoot at instead of the man. Swartwout recovered.

Burr's old friend Jonathan Dayton, another land speculator whom defalcations at home forced to move from New Jersey to greener pastures in Ohio, called out De Witt Clinton, but a duel was somehow averted. Richard Riker, who'd been Clinton's second, accepted the challenge of John Swartwout's younger brother Sam and was severely wounded. Then the Republican harbormaster, Thompson, offended by something Hamilton's favorite editor wrote in his paper, called out William Coleman and was killed by him in an obscure back alley in New York.

The Clintonians, now marshaled by young De Witt, united with the Livingston clan to shut Burr's machine out of state politics. When it became certain that the Republicans would not renominate him for the vice presidency, Burr ran for governor as an independent. His Little Band carried the city for him, but he was swamped upstate.

He had lost hopes of preferment from the Republicans. His only chance now was with the Federalists. There Alexander Hamilton stood in his way. Behind each frustration he could see Hamilton's pale face bent over his writing desk: "a dangerous man who ought not to be intrusted with the reins of government."

Burr's creditors were pressing. During the last few years he'd seen many a powerful speculator end his career, like Robert Morris, in debtor's prison. Alexander Hamilton's son John Church Hamilton told an odd tale of Colonel Burr's ringing their doorbell at the Grange before the family was up one morning, and begging his father for a loan of ten thousand dollars. Hamilton, a softhearted man, who always claimed he felt no personal ill will towards Burr and that his opposition was all political, told Burr he would try to raise the money but that it would take a few days. Before Hamilton had completed his arrangements a note came from Burr saying that he wouldn't need the loan; he had decided to put an end to himself.

During the same spring Burr was writing Theodosia facetious letters about his courtship of "La G." He was making his young daughter the confidant of his amours. He would solve all his problems by marrying a wealthy widow.

Aaron Burr was on the verge of madness. His ambition's every path was blocked. Always it was Hamilton who stood in the way. He knew he was a dead shot. The report went around New York that one afternoon he collected his Little Band in front of a roaring fire at Richmond Hill—he wrote Theodosia that he was always cold these days in spite of the summer weather—and told Matthew Davis and the Swartwouts and the Van Ness boys and the rest to vote which of his enemies he should kill first. Hamilton was elected. Immediately Billy Van Ness was sent off with a letter couched in the pedantic delicacies of the code inviting General Hamilton to disavow certain statements attributed to him in an Albany newspaper.

The bullet that killed Alexander Hamilton that early July morning on the Weehawken shore put an end to Aaron Burr's political career. By a further ricochet, as Hamilton had expected, his death ruined the plans of the New England secessionists. Republicans and Federalists united to mourn the great man dead. Burr was denounced as a murderer. Proceedings were instituted to indict him for murder in New York and New Jersey. In spite of his high office he became a fugitive from justice.

Years later an old colored man known as Professor Jim, who was at that time owned by a Colonel Robart in Yonkers, told about a rider arriving with a note for his master during the afternoon of the day after General Hamilton's death "as we were putting up a new yard fence." Colonel Robart shouted to his slaves to get a room ready "for that little devil is coming."

"Pretty soon he came up himself in his four horse coach. His head was bowed down and he didn't say a word but then his head was always bowed down. He caught right hold of my master's hand and they went into the house and I didn't see him again till the next evening. The day Hamilton was buried was a bad day for him, and he didn't eat any dinner, nor go out for his walk along the river, but he walked to and fro along the corridor upstairs, with his hands behind him. We could hear the funeral guns sounding up from New York. Burr kept his servant in the room with him night and day and he had a case of pistols and a sword in his room with him. He stayed with my master for some time and practiced a good deal at target shooting down by the river bank and I myself have seen a white birch tree where he had shot twelve balls into a space no larger than my hand."

From Yonkers, doing everything he could to keep his identity secret, Burr hurried to his friend Charles Biddle's house in Philadelphia. August 2 he wrote his daughter from there that he planned a secret trip to Spanish Florida. He yearned to see her but he didn't dare risk crossing the flat lands of South Carolina during the sickly season. He kept her posted on his affairs of the heart. "If any male friend of yours should be dying of ennui, recommend to him to engage in a duel and a courtship at the same time—prob. est." Another day he wrote her to pay no attention to "all manner of nonsense and lies" that filled the newspapers, particularly to stories of attempts to assassinate him. . . . "Those who wish me dead prefer to keep at a very respectable distance. . . . I am very well and not without occupation and amusement."

5. Burr's Castle in the Air

The occupation he found so amusing in Philadelphia was plotting with Jonathan Dayton a breathtaking project to recoup both their fortunes.

The news of Bonaparte's crowning himself Emperor had a profound effect on Aaron Burr. Bonaparte's successes tantalized every ambitious schemer of the age. When Burr's creditors forced the sale of Richmond Hill he wrote Theodosia that he was saving for her and his grandson, along with portraits of himself by Stuart and Vanderlyn and the rest of his excellent collection of paintings, his "beautiful" bust of Napoleon. Though thirteen years younger than Burr, Bonaparte, by sheer gall, had with the help of intriguers like Talleyrand and, of course, of the efficient army developed under the First Republic, made himself master of Europe. It all seemed very close because Burr himself was acquainted with Napoleon's young brother Jerome, who had run off to America and married the lovely, the audacious, the wealthy Miss Patterson of Baltimore, whose costumes in the Grecian mode had so shocked the Washington ladies.

With Burr in the role of the little corporal, and Dayton in the role of Talleyrand, the two near bankrupts made plans to carve themselves out a Napoleonic empire on the Mississippi. Disgraced at home Jonathan Dayton was working up a new career beyond the Ohio. He came of a distinguished Revolutionary family, had served as the youngest delegate to the Constitutional Convention, and as Speaker of the House of Representatives, but speculation in land had been his ruin. Now he had acquired new claims in Ohio. The legislature of the new state was sending him back to the United States Senate. Dayton and Burr were masking the early stages of their mad enterprise behind a perfectly reasonable project to build a canal round the falls of the Ohio opposite Louisville.

Since anyone who summered in Washington City was thought to be risking his life from malaria most of the diplomatic corps spent the hot months in Philadelphia. Waiting on the British minister, Mr. Anthony Merry, the gentleman who had been so disgruntled by Jefferson's reversal of protocol at the President's house, was a Colonel Charles Williamson, with whom Burr had been associated in land deals in upstate New York. Though Williamson had assumed American citizenship in order better to take title to real estate, he was a retired British army officer and an agent of the Foreign Office. Williamson had for years been urging on His Majesty's Government a scheme to curb the growing power of the United States by spreading British influence down the Mississippi. The Louisiana Purchase had ruined these plans. At Burr's suggestion that he might induce the settlers west of the Appalachians to secede from the Union Williamson caught fire.

Mr. Merry, who had nothing but scorn for President Jefferson and his leveling theories, could hardly conceal his pleasurable astonishment when Burr declared to him outright that, given a naval force and financial backing, he would "effect the separation of the Western States." Though he had had to forgo his hopes for the secession of New England, Aaron Burr was still Vice President. If he could split the Union, Merry's reputation would be made at the Foreign Office.

On August 6, 1804, Merry urged consideration of Burr's plan in a dispatch to the Foreign Office. He added that Colonel Williamson, soon to set sail for England, would explain the details. Though Merry admitted "the profligacy of Mr. Burr's character" and that he was "cast off as much by the democratic as by the Federal Party," he insisted that Burr "still preserves connection with some people of influence, added to his great ambition and a spirit of revenge against the present administration"; and that these factors "may possibly induce him to exert the talents and activity which he possesses with fidelity to his Employers."

Burr had to keep out of the way of the sheriff until Congress opened in the fall. At the same time he wanted to get a look at the Spanish settlements in Florida. He wangled an invitation from Major Pierce Butler, one of the Georgia senators, to visit his plantation on St. Simon's Island. With young Sam Swartwout in attendance he set out in high spirits on a coastal vessel from Newcastle.

Aaron Burr was a naturalborn traveler. While the ship beat her way down the coast against light summer breezes he had plenty of time to indulge himself with castles in the air. When Burr dreamed an enterprise it became true. That was why he was so convincing to others.

He was desperate for cash. His interview with the British minister had opened up the possibility of getting his hands on a large sum of money. Williamson, a congenial spirit, would carry his proposition to William Pitt, the imperial Prime Minister, who had already shown his interest in weakening the grip of the Spanish Bourbons on their American colonies by encouraging an expedition on the river Plate as well as Miranda's scheme for a revolt in Caracas. With British help Burr would launch a twopronged expedition against Mexico. An army would march overland and a naval expedition would land at Vera Cruz. The Mexicans would flock to his standard. He was already counting on all the fresh silver dollars that would flow from the Mexican mint.

No more republican nonsense. Mexico would proclaim him Aaron I. He would govern with the aid of a council of worthies made up of the best brains in the land.

Twenty days after sailing out of the Delaware he wrote Theodosia happily from St. Simon's: "I am now quite settled. My establishment consists of a housekeeper, cook, and chambermaid, seamstress and two footmen. There are besides two fishermen and two bargemen always at command. The department of laundress is done abroad. The plantation affords plenty of milk, cream, and butter; turkeys, fowls, pigs, kids, geese and mutton, fish, of course in abundance. Of figs, peaches and mellons there are yet a few. Oranges and pomegranates just begin to be eatable. The house affords Madeira wine, brandy and porter. . . . A neighbor," he added, "had sent over an assortment of claret sauturne and champagne, all excellent."

He amused himself cruising among the islands, frightening the alligators, shooting ricebirds, catching sea trout, looking for wild honey. "You perceive," he wrote Theodosia, "that I am constantly discovering new luxuries for my table. Not having been able to kill a crocodile, (alligator) I have offered a reward for one which I mean to eat, dressed in soup, fricassees and steaks. Oh how you long to partake of this repast!"

His spirits were hardly dampened when his preparations to travel to Florida by canoe were interrupted by a September hurricane that caught him on a neighboring island. Part of the piazza was carried away from the house where he was staying, "two or three of the windows bursted in. The house was inundated with water and presently one of the chimneys fell."

Next day he managed to get himself paddled back to the Butler plantation and found that nineteen of the major's Negroes had been drowned. A tide seven feet above normal high water had destroyed two hundred and fifty acres of rice.

While he was noting down this information for Theodosia's benefit "a smoking sheepshead" appeared on the table to call him to dinner. "*Madame j'ai bien diner,*" he continued in his own private French, "*and j'ai fait mettre mon writing desk sur le table a diner.* What a scandalous thing to sit here all alone drinking Champagne—and yet— (*Madame je bois a votre santé et a celle de monsieur votre fils*)."

Two days later he was off for Florida. The weather turned bad again and kept him from reaching St. Augustine. About all the news he brought back for Theodosia from the mouth of the St. Johns River was "It is a fact that Spanish ladies smoke segars."

He was determined to visit the Alstons on his way north. "Pray let A.B.A. [his grandson] know that *gamp* is a black man . . . not brown but a true quadroon yellow: whether from the effects of climate, or travelling four hundred miles in a canoe is no matter."

By early December he was back in Washington presiding with his usual punctilious gravity over the Senate. Plumer found him changed. "He appears to have lost those easy graceful manners that beguiled the hours away last session—He is now uneasy, discontented & hurried.—So true it is 'great guilt ne'er knew great joy at heart.'"

Plumer set to wondering what Burr's future would be. "He can never I think rise again. But surely he is a very extraordinary man & is an exception to all rules. . . . And considering of what materials the mass of men are formed—how easily they are gulled—& considering how little restraint laws human or divine have on his mind, it is impossible to say what he will attempt—or what he may obtain."

Burr's saturnine charm was irresistible. He was a man it was hard to stay angry with for long. The Republicans were now taking the attitude that Burr had killed Hamilton in a fair fight. Plumer professed to be shocked by the cordiality of the administration towards him. "I never had any doubts of their joy for the death of Hamilton; my only doubts were whether they would manifest that joy by caressing his murderer. These doubts are now dispelled—Mr. Jefferson has shown more attention and invited Mr. Burr more often to his house within three weeks than he ever did before. Mr. Gallatin . . . has waited upon him at his [Burr's] lodging. . . . Mr. Madison, formerly the intimate friend of Hamilton, has taken his murderer into his carriage."

The chief business of that winter session of Congress was the impeachment of Judge Chase before the Senate. Burr was in a position to be useful to the administration.

The Vice President presided with stern dignity in accordance with what he had read of the pomp and circumstance of the impeachment of Warren Hastings before Parliament, but he made no move to help the Republicans. The administration's failure to make a case caused rejoicing among the Federalists. Burr seems to have relished every moment. Plumer noted with some asperity: "Mr. Burr has for the last few weeks assumed the airs of a pedagogue."

Burr ruled from the chair that senators should cease wearing over-coats or eating cake or apples at their desks. In a letter to his daughter he quoted with pleasure the phrase of a journalist who wrote that the Vice President behaved "with the impartiality of an angel, but with the rigor of a devil."

His last appearance before Congress wound up all business on March 2 was impressive; he pronounced the most effective address of his career. "This house is a sanctuary," he declaimed, "a citadel of law, of order, and of liberty; it is here, if anywhere, it is here in this exalted refuge, here will resistance be made to the storms of political phrenzy and the silent acts of corruption; and if the constitution be destined ever to perish by the sacrilegious hands of the demagogue or the usurper, which God avert, its expiring agonies will be witnessed on this floor."

When he walked out of the hushed chamber many senators were in tears.

Two weeks later he was back in Philadelphia telling Anthony Merry that the French inhabitants of Louisiana were ripe for revolt against the United States and ready to ask for the protection of Great Britain. He suggested that the Foreign Office send as consul to New Orleans a confidential agent who spoke French and arrange for a flotilla of two or three frigates and some smaller vessels to be ready to blockade the mouth of the Mississippi when the time came for Burr to establish his government there. For himself he requested an immediate loan of a hundred thousand pounds.

The same day that Merry transmitted this request for the consider-ation of his government Burr wrote Theodosia that he was off for the West. "As the objects of the tour, not mere curiosity or *pour passer le tems,* may lead me to Orleans and perhaps further, I contemplate the tour with gaity and cheerfulness."

6. *A Serpent in Eden*

Burr found the trip a tonic to his spirits. By the end of April he was writing Theodosia from Pittsburgh describing delightedly the ark that was going to float him down to the Mississippi as "properly speak-ing a floating house, sixty feet by fourteen, containing dining room, kitchen with fireplace with two bedrooms; steps to go up and walk on the top the whole length; glass windows etc. This edifice costs a hundred and thirty three dollars, and how it can be made for that sum is beyond my comprehension."

Below Marietta he stopped at an island that was one of the show-places of the region. A wealthy Irishman named Harman Blennerhasset had built himself a mansion there with gardens and parklands in the English style and almost ruined himself in the process. Blennerhasset was a graduate of Trinity College, a big gangling man with some learning but not a trace of common sense. He was so desperately near-sighted he couldn't recognize a man at three paces away. He was known, half in affection, half in derision, as Blanny to the settlers up and down the Ohio.

Blanny was away during Burr's first visit but Burr was entertained by Mrs. Blennerhasset, described as an accomplished and welleducated woman, who was pining for talk of music and books on that far frontier. Colonel Burr had at his tongue's tip all the fashionable conversation of the age. Humphrey Marshall, a cousin and brotherinlaw of Chief Justice John Marshall and of the same Federalist and Unionist stripe, made great sport in his *History of Kentucky* of the little colonel's playing Ulysses to Mrs. Blennerhasset's Calypso. Be that as it may, from that moment on the Blennerhassets man and wife were as fascinated by Aaron Burr as a pair of cuckoos by a snake.

By mid-May Burr was in Cincinnati, being entertained by Jonathan Dayton's colleague in the Senate, a busy jack of all trades named John Smith, who was storekeeper, land speculator, Baptist preacher, politician, and commissary to General Wilkinson's forces. The plan burgeoned.

They felt that Kentucky, where the secessionists had almost carried the day nine years before, was sure. Burr's old friend James Wilkinson, the very man who had almost put a separation through at one of the territorial conventions, was now commanding general of the Army of the United States and governor of Louisiana. Though he had had little to do with it Burr could take credit for the latter appointment. One of the few appointments Burr really had managed through the Jefferson administration was that of his brotherinlaw Dr. Browne, who financed the double wedding of the Visme sisters at Paramus, as Governor Wilkinson's territorial secretary. Burr considered him a devoted adherent. Dayton and Smith admitted that Ohio was a little doubtful, but Andrew Jackson, who commanded the Tennessee militia, would be enthusiastic for any expedition against the dons.

Leaving his ark to follow the curve of the river, Burr rode briskly across country, stopping off to visit a Kentucky secessionist, also named Brown, into Tennessee. The early summer weather was fine. He enjoyed the riding. No word in public of secession, only of a coming war with Spain. His progress became a personal triumph.

Without quite saying so he managed to give the impression that his good friend Dearborn, the Secretary of War, was only waiting for a declaration of war to put him in command of an expedition against the Spanish possessions. In Nashville he was tendered a public dinner. Andrew Jackson grasped him warmly by the hand and took him home to The Hermitage.

An enthusiastic duelist himself, Jackson considered the hue and cry against Burr damnable persecution. Any expedition against the dons had his hearty approval.

General Jackson furnished Colonel Burr a boat to take him down the Cumberland River to Fort Massac on the lower Ohio where he was to meet his ark again. At Fort Massac Burr at last caught up with the man he'd determined on as his second in command, Brigadier General James Wilkinson.

Burr had known Wilkinson as a youth on the Quebec expedition. Both of them as young officers had joined in the cabal against Washington at Valley Forge. They had corresponded for years in a private cypher. Even more than Burr, Wilkinson was the conspirator incarnate. Double dealing was as natural to him as breathing. He too looked with hungry eyes on the silver of Mexico. Like Burr the general was a lavish entertainer. Though continually raking in money by various skulduggeries, he too was always short of cash. Wilkinson had particular reason to feel warmly towards Burr at this point because it was the elimination of Hamilton that had left him the ranking general in the United States Army.

7. *Agent Number Thirteen*

James Wilkinson at the time of this meeting with Burr was a man near fifty, short, redfaced and corpulent from high living; grown gray before his time, so he liked to put it, in the service of the United States. He was the son of a planter on the Patuxent River who came of a family of Maryland Episcopalians. When he was seventeen he was sent off to study medicine at the College of Pennsylvania. The outbreak of the Revolutionary War found him practicing as a physician up on Monocacy Creek in the mountain country of the upper Potomac Valley. He volunteered for a Pennsylvania rifle company and, being a plausible young man, wound up as aide to General Nathanael Greene. He remained a headquarters officer. Like Burr he served under Arnold in the botched Canadian expedition but unlike Burr he found promotion quick and easy.

Arnold seems to have been too much of a frontline general to suit Wilkinson. He managed to transfer himself to General Gates, whose headquarters were usually out of the sound of musket shot. He was promoted to brigade major. Luck always seemed to be with young

Wilkinson. By a series of fortunate chances he caught Washington's eye in a fortunate moment at Trenton. Back with Gates, who found him pliable and sympathetic, a young officer adept at scrounging up a meal or a drink or a wench, he was promoted to deputy adjutant general. In his memoirs he took credit for choosing Gates's fine position on Bemis Heights and thereby bringing about Burgoyne's surrender.

Horatio Gates entrusted to Wilkinson the dispatches to Congress which described his victory at Saratoga; but the young man lingered so long on the way that when he did appear before the continental delegates in session at York, Pennsylvania, John Witherspoon jocosely suggested in his broad Scots that, instead of the sword or the medal Congress was distributing to the victorious officers, maybe this laddie should have a horsewhip and a pair of spurs.

Wilkinson explained in his memoirs that illness, bad weather, and the courting of a young lady combined to make him tardy. He further confessed that, at dinner with Lord Stirling at Reading on the way, he babbled, over a flagon of wine, some details of the intrigue to unseat George Washington as Commander in Chief which was developing out of the swelled heads of Gates and his staff.

Although the results of these indiscretions were eventually to bring about a farcical near duel with General Gates, and to put an end for a number of years to his army career, Wilkinson was successful in his immediate designs. He returned to the Northern Department, not only with the brevet rank of brigadier general which Gates had requested for him, but with the plighted troth of Ann Biddle, the attractive daughter of the Quaker host of the Indian Queen in Philadelphia.

The Biddles were a rising family of seafaring men, merchants and financiers. One of them was later to be the friend on whom Aaron Burr most relied. Both Burr and Wilkinson remained friends of the Biddles for many years. Wilkinson was still barely twenty. Already this pocketsized Falstaff had gone far toward making his way in the world.

James Wilkinson had turned twentyone when he and Ann Biddle were married at Christ Church in Philadelphia. On account of his connection with the discredited Gates-Conway Cabal, he thought it prudent to resign from active service. Not long after he somehow managed to get himself appointed clothier general. Though anxious for money, he found he had a poor head for business. There were complaints that he took more interest in his position as master of the Philadelphia dancing assembly, where he called the numbers and arranged the country dances, than in seeing that the troops had proper clothing. General Washington insisted that he resign the office. Somehow in the process he secured possession of a confiscated Tory estate.

Washington never took the dislike to Wilkinson that he did to

Aaron Burr. Plump, popeyed, and convivial, the young man had a way of ingratiating himself. He slipped in and out of scrapes and scandals without leaving hard feelings behind. Becoming friendly with Washington's old aide, Joseph Reed, who was now president of Pennsylvania, he dipped into politics and was made brigadier general of the militia. He served two terms in the legislature. Finding a living hard to come by on his Bucks County farm, he sold it, piled his wife and two children into a carriage and his household goods into a Conestoga wagon, and set out for Kentucky. As agent for the Philadelphia firm of Barclay, Moylan and Co., he opened a general store in Lexington.

In Kentucky he was in his element. Storekeepers were making fortunes. Speculation in military land grants held out prospects of wealth to every settler. Politics was a hive of intrigue. Not many months passed before young Wilkinson had outrun George Rogers Clark as the spokesman for the gripes and grievances of the frontiersmen along the Ohio. Virginia, so they claimed, was neglecting to protect them from Indian raids. The natural flow of the trade that resulted from their bountiful crops was down the Ohio and the Mississippi to Spanish-held New Orleans. Wilkinson was among the moving spirits of the various Kentucky assemblies that petitioned Richmond for assistance and set the stage for secession from Virginia.

Nobody was more surprised than Wilkinson at his success as a public speaker. "I pleased myself, & what was more consequential, everybody else except my dead opponents," he boasted to a friend, "—these I with great facility turned into an object of ridicule and derision." Even the sarcastic Humphrey Marshall, who certainly was one of his "dead opponents," described him in his *History of Kentucky* as "a figure . . . not quite tall enough to be perfectly elegant, compensated by symmetry and appearance of health and strength: a countenance open, mild, capatious, and beaming with intelligence: a gait, firm, manly and facile: manners bland, accommodating and popular. . . . By these fair terms he conciliated: by these he captivated."

Wilkinson was a useful man in a frontier settlement. He could turn his hand to all sorts of things. He was enough of a soldier to drill a squad of militia, enough of a physician to purge or plaster a patient, enough of a surveyor to help lay out the new town of Frankfort. He had a book on gardening and imported seeds of garden vegetables and melons. He never cared how much he spent on eating and drinking. His charming wife won many hearts.

Wilkinson, wrote Humphrey Marshall, knew "that the way to men's hearts was *down their throats*. He lived freely and entertained liberally. If he paid for his fare it was well for those who furnished it; if he did not it was still well for himself and those who feasted on it.

He surrounded himself with idle young men, of both town and country, who loved him dearly, because they loved his beef, his pudding,
and his wine. They served to propagate his opinions, to blazon his
fame, to promote his popularity, and to serve him in elections."

When the Spanish closed the Mississippi to American commerce it
meant ruin to the Kentucky traders. Their prosperity depended on
shipping tobacco, flour, and hams to New Orleans; there selling them
for piasters or Mexican dollars, and then sailing north with their bags
of specie to Philadelphia to buy merchandise which would be shipped
out by wagon train to Pittsburgh and thence by flatboat down the
Ohio. Wilkinson dealt in land. He invested in cargoes for export. Along
with Judge Harry Innes and Benjamin Sebastian, he joined a faction
convinced that the future of Kentucky depended on accommodation
with the Spaniards.

Wilkinson believed in the personal touch. He started a correspondence with a gentleman named Cruzat who commanded the Spanish
fort at St. Louis. He helped a Spanish merchant obtain satisfaction for
goods seized at Vincennes by freebooters under George Rogers Clark.
He warned Señor Cruzat of a possible American attack. In the spring
of 1787 he made his way downriver with a bargeload of tobacco. The
gift of a pair of blooded horses assured him welcome by the Spanish
authorities at Natchez. With their help he drifted downriver past
drowsy Spanish sentries to the French and Creole capital.

Though it never seems to have occurred to Wilkinson to learn Spanish he developed a real flair for dealing with the dons. He had the
grand air, the ceremonious manner, the gaudy uniform, and a seeming frank cynicism in his way of putting things, exactly suited to the
taste of representatives of the court of Carlos IV and María Luisa
and the Prince of Peace.

The governor Don Esteban Rodríguez Miró was a man of some
experience in America. He had taken part in the expedition that occupied the two Floridas during the Revolutionary War. His mission
was to conciliate. He had to deal with a mixed and unruly population:
local Creoles, Irish adventurers, American squatters armed with bowie
knives and squirrel rifles, Cajuns and Indians, and Canadian French
fur traders spread over a vast unmapped region reaching to the domain
of the Viceroy of Mexico. He was subordinate to the captain general
at Havana and was subject to a stream of regulations emitted by the
Madrid bureaucracy which had no possible bearing on the situation
in Louisiana. Personally he needed money to supplement his four
thousand dollar salary and he needed intelligence reports to keep his
name lustrous among officials back home.

During the two summer months Wilkinson spent in New Orleans
he became thick as thieves with Don Esteban. He charmed the Spanish governor as a man of the world who could talk of books and natural

philosophy and tell tall stories about the Indian aborigines. Though the general's conversation, as translated by Don Esteban's Irish secretary, continually sought high ground, he did manage to let it be known that a monoply of the tobacco trade down the Mississippi would be profitable both to him and to His Excellency. Tobacco which you could buy for two dollars a hundredweight in Kentucky sold for nine and a half at the royal warehouse in New Orleans.

Don Esteban was no mean horse trader. In return for joining Wilkinson in a monopoly, which would demand a somewhat hazardous interpretation of the royal regulations of the Mississippi trade, he demanded a quid pro quo.

The illustrious brigadier intimated that there might be services he could perform for His Most Catholic Majesty. Always an eager penman, Wilkinson set to work to indite a *Memorial* setting forth for the Spanish officials the benefits that would accrue to them from a separation of the Western settlements from the Atlantic states.

Don Esteban developed an appetite for news of dissatisfaction in Kentucky. In the course of their negotiations he pointed out furthermore that it would be a graceful gesture, as a mere formality between men of the world, if the general would sign an oath of allegiance to Don Carlos. That grateful monarch furnished pensions to his retainers. Wilkinson's name was duly entered in the secret ledgers of the Ministry for the Colonies as Agent Number Thirteen.

By mid-September General Wilkinson was ready, his baggage well weighted with dollars and pieces of eight, to tear himself away from his Spanish friends. He left his commercial arrangements in New Orleans in the hands of the prosperous Irish merchant, Daniel Clark, whose nephew was entrenched in the government as one of Don Esteban's secretaries. After a seasick journey the general reached Richmond in time to be present at that fall's convention and to inject some glib arguments into the proceedings against ratification of the Constitution. Though he spoke loftily of politics as his "old hobby," his present interest in Richmond was to acquire warrants for Kentucky lands.

Winter had settled down, so he could not make it to Mount Vernon, but he did his best to keep his memory fragrant with General Washington by sending Mrs. Washington some Indian fabrics as a souvenir. An aide of the general's rode along with him on his wintry journey to Pittsburgh.

After the hardships and hazards of a winter trip down the Ohio, which he described in lurid terms to sundry correspondents, he was back in mid-February in Lexington with his wife and three boys in the unfinished mansion which he now would have funds to complete. He set to work at once to interest Harry Innes and other friends in a vast trading combine on the Mississippi. Any shipment with General Wilkinson's name on it would slip through the Spanish customhouses without interference.

In spite of Governor Miró's cooperation the course of the enterprise failed to run smooth. Shipments were lost. Cargoes of tobacco were ruined on leaky flatboats. A galley planned for the upriver trade proved a failure; and, worst of all, the wave of national enthusiasm that accompanied the ratification of the Constitution boded ill for the separatists. Most Kentuckians were now intent on joining the Union as the fourteenth state.

While admission to statehood hung fire the dissatisfaction of the settlers along the Ohio tempted another crafty fisherman to wet his line in those waters. Sir Guy Carleton, now Lord Dorchester, King George's governor general of Canada, sent a certain Colonel Connolly down to Lexington and Frankfort to offer "rank and emoluments" to leading Kentuckians if they would steer their territory out of the Union into the arms of His Majesty's Government. The colonel found General Wilkinson most attentive. Wilkinson had already rewritten the *Memorial* he compiled for the Spaniards in the form of a report to one of the Kentucky Assemblies. Now he revamped it again, seasoned this time to the British taste, and entrusted it to Colonel Connolly for the private inspection of Lord Dorchester. At the same time he scared the British emissary half to death with a lot of melodrama about an attempt on his life, and earned his gratitude by furnishing him a safe escort north to the border posts which the British still held around the lakes.

By every southbound express Wilkinson was sending off to Governor Miró long redundant tales in cypher of the plots and machinations of the British against the Spanish possessions. By mule and bateau Miró continued faithfully shipping a couple of sacks of silver coins a year to his assiduous agent.

Wilkinson's trading ventures failed to thrive. His monopoly of the Mississippi traffic lasted barely eighteen months. It had been hard to enforce at best, and soon orders came from Spain to reopen the port of New Orleans. The general came a cropper in a speculation in the Yazoo lands. Planters he had neglected to pay for the produce they had furnished for his trading ventures began to clamor for their money. Merchants protested bills. Whenever a fresh note was presented Wilkinson complained of his poor head for figures. He was engaged in so many speculations he couldn't tell one from the other. One of his partners went bankrupt. The man who kept his books committed suicide.

By the spring of 1791 Wilkinson turned over his affairs to Judge Innes. He had pioneered the navigation of the Mississippi, let others reap the profit in the years to come. He would leave it to the judge to take care of his creditors.

His lands were disposed of, and the fine new mansion he was building on Wilkinson Street in Frankfort. Horses, oxen, mules were sold. Even the old family phaeton went on the auction block. Nothing to it but to go back into the service. He wrote his ruined partner he would return to the army in search of "Bread and Fame."

As soon as George Washington was elected President, Wilkinson paid a ceremonious call on his old Commander in Chief at Mount Vernon. Back in Kentucky, he volunteered with the militia for a campaign against the Indians. When the small Army of the United States was set up he got himself commissioned a lieutenant colonel. Among recommendations from prominent Kentuckians the most unexpected came from Humphrey Marshall, the bitter opponent of his separatist plans. "I considered Wilkinson well qualified for a commission," Marshall explained, "I considered him dangerous to the quiet of Kentucky, perhaps to her safety. If the commission does not secure his fidelity, it will at least place him under control."

As a garrison commander Wilkinson earned the approbation of the War Department. He was adept at military housekeeping. Placed in command of the 2nd Regiment, he led a detachment to bury the dead after General St. Clair's disgraceful defeat by the Indians on the Wabash, and built Fort Recovery on the scene of that tragedy. President Washington spoke favorably of Wilkinson's "zeal and ability" in a letter to Secretary Knox. They raised him to the permanent rank of brigadier general.

Stationed at Fort Washington to protect the thriving settlement of Cincinnati, he made himself popular by his lavish table. Somehow he always managed to produce the best madeira. His larder abounded in wild turkey and buffalo meat and vension hams. He found gardeners to grow salads and root vegetables. He had a way with the Indians. He stuffed the visiting chiefs so with food and drink that a couple of them died of their excesses. The chief flaw in his career as a military man was that he couldn't abide a superior officer.

When Anthony Wayne was sent out with a new army grouping called the Legion to punish the Indians of the Illinois country, all Wilkinson, now second in command, could think of was how to make General Wayne's life miserable. He bombarded Secretary Knox with malicious epistles. All he could see in Wayne's victory at Fallen Timbers was a series of infractions of military regulations.

Wayne was a loyal, gallant, and simplehearted man. Trying to disentangle the web of Wilkinson's treasons embittered the last years of his life. Worry over Wilkinson's undercutting him at the War Department may well have helped bring him to his untimely death at Presque Isle in the early winter of 1796.

Wilkinson hated Wayne particularly because he knew that Wayne was on the trail of his relations with the Spaniards. In spite of his increased pay as brigadier and as commissioner for the Indians his high living and rash speculations kept him continually in debt. His only source of ready cash was the governor's palace in New Orleans. As one governor succeeded another he astonished each new incumbent with tales of the prodigies he was accomplishing in the Spanish cause. Besides foiling the British, he had, at the cost of exactly eightysix hundred and forty dollars, aborted George Rogers Clark's expedition, inspired by the revolutionary French, against Natchez.

He acquired several personal agents among frontiersmen eking a hazardous living out of the smuggling and skulduggery of the border region. There was Philip Nolan, who bought him mules in the Texas country, and an engaging scoundrel named Thomas Power, who was listed as an officer in the Spanish army. Power brought the general's Mexican dollars upriver hidden in barrels of flour.

These comings and going did not pass unnoticed. Conversations in taverns were overheard. Rumors got bruited about. The general himself was notoriously indiscreet. Wherever he went he was pointed out as a pensioner of Spain.

In the fall of 1796 he decided that the best way to silence malicious tongues was to appear in person at the seat of government so that President-elect Adams could see for himself what a fine fellow he was. With his wife and a party of friends he journeyed upriver to Pittsburgh and over the mountains to Philadelphia. There, saddened as he was by the death of his son John, the news that reached him of Major General Wayne's demise was a source of a certain compensating satisfaction. He was now General in Chief of the United States Army. In that capacity, wearing enormous epaulets and spurs described as of pure gold, he attended President Adams' inauguration.

Each in his own way, President Adams and Vice President Jefferson managed to give literary and scientific flavor to society in the national capital. Wilkinson had always been assiduous in sending bags of pecans or boxes of oranges or other exotic products of the Mississippi Valley to persons in authority. Now he interested himself in prehistoric bones and Indian relics and geographic data. He joined a Masonic lodge. Returning to the frontier to superintend the taking over of Detroit and Michilimackinac, he kept a meteorological journal for the benefit of the American Philosophical Society.

That learned body, of which Jefferson was president, and of which his friend Owen Biddle was a member, elected him to membership in 1798.

The general had generally been rated a Federalist in politics, but when Jefferson led the Democratic Republicans to victory at the turn of the century, Wilkinson signalized his adherence to the new regime by ordering his officers and men to cut off their queues. Hereafter, like the victorious legions of the French Republic, the American soldier must wear his hair cropped.

In 1803 General Wilkinson and W. C. C. Claiborne were appointed by the President to raise the Stars and Stripes at New Orleans. Jefferson, inspired by the success of peaceful methods of national aggrandizement such as the Louisiana Purchase, didn't too much disapprove of Wilkinson's cordial relation with the Spaniards. He was delighted by the general's interest in exploration and discovery.

While Jefferson was still Vice President, Wilkinson had sent his man Nolan to him to regale him with eyewitness accounts of the Texas plains. Now whenever he could he forwarded fossils and Indian artifacts to the President's house. He used their common membership in the Philosophical Society to the hilt. Even his reputation for cowardice redounded to his credit with the administration. Jefferson, who distrusted military men and military methods, was quite content to have a general on the frontier whom he could trust not to start a war.

In February of 1804 Wilkinson found himself in New Orleans lodging in the same house with his good friend Governor Vincente Folch of Spanish Florida. Folch was a congenial fellow, a Catalan who spoke excellent English. Amid successive dinings and winings the American General in Chief pointed out to Folch that he was somewhat low in funds. The Marqués de Casa Calvo, retired governor of the territory who was now active as boundary commissioner, must surely need his advice. Folch consulted the governor. The governor was agreeable. The General in Chief dashed off twenty pages of *Reflections* which Folch translated sheet by sheet.

Jefferson would hardly have been pleased by Wilkinson's recommendations to the Spaniards, which were that they must on no account dispose of the Floridas and should promptly arrest Lewis and Clark, who were carrying out the President's favorite plan of exploring the upper Missouri. Casa Calvo bought the *Reflections* for twelve hundred dollars which Wilkinson invested in a cargo of sugar to ship to New York.

The General in Chief had such a high opinion of the value of his literary efforts that, sailing north, whenever he found surcease from the seasickness that made a living death of his ocean trips, he reworked his *Reflections* into a report to Thomas Jefferson on the geography and commerce of the regions which the President had acquired for the United States.

Wilkinson stayed in New York long enough to dispose of his sugar and to engage in a long evening conference with Aaron Burr at Richmond Hill. In the desperation of political and financial reverses, Vice President Burr was letting his head swell with Napoleonic dreams.

Wilkinson had firsthand knowledge of the disintegration of the Spanish dominions. If the Spanish court had let Louisiana go without a struggle why shouldn't Mexico be next?

Leaving Burr aglow with castles in the air, he drove through Princeton to see his two surviving sons and arrived in early June at the President's house, bringing as a gift a handsome portfolio of Spanish and French maps of the Mississippi Valley.

Jefferson had been entertaining Baron von Humboldt, who was on his way home from a geographical and ethnographic tour of Mexico. Wilkinson bubbled with chitchat about exotic fruits, native customs, and mines of salt and silver and gold. Undoubtedly Jefferson found the General in Chief good company. Jefferson and Humboldt were the two great geographers of the age. From their conversation Wilkinson's eager mind stored away many hints which would be useful later in planning explorations in the West.

General Wilkinson didn't leave Washington until he had the President's commission as governor of the upper Louisiana Territory in his pocket. That meant two thousand dollars more than his salary as brigadier. Mexico beckoned from beyond the plains that spread out from St. Louis. "The country is a healthy one," he wrote one of the Biddles from there, "and I shall be on the highroad to Mexico."

8. *The Throne of Montezuma*

Burr and Wilkinson spent congenial days together in St. Louis tracing out the Mexican trails on their maps. To Burr his project now seemed certain of success. Louisiana, Tennessee, Kentucky, Ohio, the War Department; they were all in the palm of his hand. Now he must sound out the Creoles in New Orleans. The general may have had his doubts, but if Burr did manage his coup he wanted to be in on the loot. He offered the little colonel every accommodation.

"The general and his officers," Burr wrote Theodosia, "fitted me out with an elegant barge, sails, colors and ten oars, with a sergeant and ten able faithful hands."

Burr arrived at New Orleans in style. Wilkinson had given him a letter to the younger Daniel Clark, who had recently become an American citizen and inherited his uncle's trading firm. To keep a business going through these years of changing sovereignties a New Orleans merchant had to have a finger in every pie. Daniel Clark made himself useful to the Jefferson administration. At the same time he managed to remain on friendly terms with the Spanish and French.

On the side he dabbled in the activities of a group known as the Mexican Association made up of buccaneering characters on fire to make their fortunes by promoting a revolution in Mexico.

In New Orleans Burr stayed with Edward Livingston, who had ducked out of New York to escape his creditors and was trying to recoup his fortunes by real estate deals in the newly acquired territories. Edward Livingston, Chancellor Robert R. Livingston's much younger brother, was one of the most dashing of the Livingston clan. He had been a fellow student of Burr's in a law office in Albany. A tall man with a quizzical expression on his wide mouth, he was a great dresser, nicknamed in his youth Beau Ned. He was an inveterate punster and as much a ladies' man as Burr.

An early supporter of Jefferson's, after showing brilliance at the New York bar, Livingston was elected to Congress and with Albert Gallatin led the Republican minority in the House during the Republican campaign for the presidency. In Philadelphia he was said to "live like a nabob and talk like a Jacobin." Finding himself to a certain extent the intermediary between Jefferson and Burr during the contested election, he managed to retain the friendship of both. Jefferson appointed him federal district attorney for New York. He was appointed mayor at the same time.

He held both offices with éclat, until during the yellow fever epidemic of 1803, having gallantly remained at his post to do what he could for the sick and dying, he caught the fever himself. When he recovered he found that a French clerk had absconded with customhouse bonds amounting to some fortythree thousand dollars.

He resigned both offices and turned his whole estate over to a trustee to be sold to satisfy his debt to the Treasury. His wife had died some time before. Leaving his children with relatives, he took ship for New Orleans where he started a fresh career as a courtroom lawyer. Burr looked on Livingston as a source of ready cash, as Livingston still owed him a considerable sum of money from transactions connected with land speculations in New York.

Colonel Burr was the toast of the Vieux Carré. He was dined by the very Jeffersonian Governor Claiborne and set up to grand turnouts by Daniel Clark and members of the Mexican Association. He fluttered the hearts of the Creole beauties. He became fluent in bad French. He was attentive to the Catholic bishop who, like much of the Spanish clergy, was disgusted with the subjection of his homeland to the infidel French, and eager for the independence of Mexico.

As Burr told the story, the bishop sent off three Jesuit priests to prepare the Mexicans for the arrival of his expedition. Burr was so much the nine days' wonder that the bishop took him to visit, at the prioress' request, a fashionable convent of Ursuline nuns. The nuns offered the fascinating colonel a light collation of wine, fruit, and cake and promised "with great promptness and courtesy" to pray for him.

New Orleans seemed so ripe for Burr's plans that he felt he had to have fresh interviews with Jackson and Wilkinson. Clark furnished him a schooner across Lake Pontchartrain, and horses and a guide to take him to Natchez. Burr was a tireless rider. After laying up a few days in Natchez—"and saw some tears of regret as I left it"—he kept boasting of his conquests in his letters to his daughter—he rode north across the Natchez Trace—"drinking the nasty puddle-water, covered with green scum, and full of animalculae—bah!"—into the clear air of the Tennessee Mountains.

From Nashville he wrote Theodosia: "For a week I have been lounging at the house of General Jackson, once a lawyer, after a judge, now a planter; a man of intelligence, and one of those prompt, frank, ardent souls I love to meet." To Andrew Jackson he said not a word about secession or funds from the British, but talked long of Santa Fé and his contacts with the Mexican patriots. He declared that the wealthy Daniel Clark and his Mexican Association in New Orleans were behind him to a man.

A new castle in the air rising on his horizon as a coverup for his secret aims. An enormous grant of fertile land on the Ouachita River made by the Spaniards to a Baron de Bastrop was supposedly on the market. Burr would find funds to acquire it. President Jefferson himself had spoken of the urgent need for settlements west of the Mississippi. Land and harrying the Spaniards were two topics dear to Andrew Jackson's heart. They parted the best of friends.

Burr's energy was inexhaustible. From Nashville he rode four hundred and fifty miles to St. Louis for a second strategic conference with Wilkinson. The two men had always enjoyed each other's company. Wilkinson was a great trencherman and amusing over his wine. Now Burr could report to him amid considerable merrymaking that their ally Daniel Clark was on his way to Vera Cruz, under cover of a trading voyage, to spy out the political situation in Mexico. General Jackson would march at the drop of a hat. The Bastrop lands, which by this time Burr felt he already owned, would make them all rich, if everything else failed. They reached the point of drawing up lists of suitable officers for their army.

After four days of conference Burr rode posthaste to Vincennes carrying a letter from Wilkinson to William Henry Harrison, the governor of Indiana Territory, suggesting that it would be a good idea "for the sake of the Union" to have Colonel Burr elected territorial delegate to Congress. In Vincennes Burr met his first rebuff. General Harrison entertained him civilly but showed no interest in his plans.

Burr turned eastward again. His prospects were bloodheating but there was no cash in the till. He must hurry back to Washington where the British Minister would surely have funds for him. Writing his daughter to meet him with little A.B.A. and her husband, whom he referred to as Mari, in late October at Bedford Springs in Pennsylvania, he set off through Chillicothe and Marietta to Pittsburgh.

By mid-November Burr was back in Washington City waiting on Anthony Merry. Merry had disappointing news. His first dispatches had been lost at sea when a British packet was captured by the French. Duplicates had so far elicited no response from the Foreign Office. Jonathan Dayton, who Burr had hoped would be on hand during the summer to fan Merry's enthusiasm for the scheme, was delayed by illness and had just arrived.

Burr, so Merry wrote the Foreign Office on November 25, showed every sign of distress at the bad news. It didn't take him long to rally his spirits. He now demanded a hundred and ten thousand pounds and three ships of the line as well as the frigates and smaller vessels to cruise off the mouth of the Mississippi. He said he had encouraging letters from Colonel Williamson. He set March of the following year for the beginning of operations. The revolution in New Orleans would follow in April or May. He had found a deposit there of ten thousand stand of arms and fiftysix pieces of artillery abandoned by the French. "Pecuniary aid" must be in his hands by February.

He gave the names of Daniel Clark in New Orleans and John Barclay in Philadelphia as his financial agents. He held out a glittering prospect to the Foreign Office. As a result of the coup d'état "The Eastern States will separate themselves immediately from the Southern;—and that thus the immense power which has risen up with such rapidity in the Western Hemisphere will, by such a division, be rendered at once informidable."

A few days later Colonel Burr dined with President Jefferson. It didn't take much conversation to discover another check to his plans. Jefferson believed his envoys in Paris were about to accomplish a deal through Talleyrand to purchase the Floridas. He had dropped any plan for war with Spain.

News of all these goings and comings could hardly be kept out of the newspapers. For all his successful intriguing, Wilkinson was famous for his indiscretions when he'd had too much to drink, and that was almost every time the wine was uncorked after dinner. Burr himself, usually enigmatic in his utterances, had been so intoxicated by the prospects of grandeur that he had allowed himself to be overheard making jeering remarks about the need for a change from the "imbecility" of the administration in Washington. Rumors circulated and multiplied. Hostile conjectures about Colonel Burr's plans echoed from newspaper to newspaper from Philadelphia to New Orleans.

The premature publicity alarmed Daniel Clark. Before setting sail for Vera Cruz in early September on the ship *Caroline* which he had purchased for this voyage for trade and intelligence, he wrote Wilkinson a facetious letter obviously intended as a warning:

"Many absurd and wild reports are circulated here, and have reached the ears of the officers of the late Spanish government, respecting our ex-Vice President. You are spoken of as his right hand man, and even I am not supposed to be of enough consequence to combine with Generals and Vice-Presidents. . . . The tale is a horrid one if well told. Kentucky, Tennessee, the state of Ohio, with part of Georgia and Carolina, are to be bribed with the plunder of the Spanish countries west of us, to separate from the Union. . . . But how the devil I have been lugged into the conspiracy, or what assistance I can be of to it, is to me incomprehensible. . . . Vous qui savez tout can best explain this riddle. Amuse Mr. Burr with an account of it, but do not let these great and important objects, these almost imperial doings, prevent you from attending to my land business. Recollect that you then—, if you intend to become Kings and Emperors, must have a little more consideration for vassals; and if we have nothing to clothe ourselves with . . . or if the Congress take the lands for want of formalities, we shall then have no produce, we shall make a very shabby figure at your courts. Think of this and practice the formalities that are necessary that I may have from my Illinois lands wherewith to buy a decent court dress, when presented at your levee."

Clark was teasing Wilkinson about Burr's inflated projects and at the same time dropping just the faint hint of blackmail necessary to cause the governor of Louisiana to do the right thing by his old partner's nephew by securing him title to a tract of public land.

The month before a query published in the *United States Gazette* in Philadelphia had been widely reprinted: "How long will it be before we shall hear of Col. Burr being at the head of a revolution party on the western waters?"

On December 1 Thomas Jefferson received an anonymous letter warning him against Burr's conspiracy.

"You admit him to your table, and you held a long and private conversation with him a few days ago after dinner at the very moment that he is meditating the overthrow of your administration. . . . Yes Sir his abberations through the Western states had no other object. . . . Watch his connections with Mr. M——y and you will find him a British pensioner and agent."

Burr's grievance at that moment was that he hadn't succeeded in becoming a British pensioner. It was only by drawing bills on the Alstons that he paid his traveling expenses. Senator Dayton too was flat broke. When the conspirators journeyed to Philadelphia in search of funds they found there a fresh impediment to their schemes in the shape of a rival revolutionist.

Francisco de Miranda was on his way to Washington to seek the administration's countenance for his perennial scheme to throw the Spaniards out of Caracas. His backers in New York were among the same speculators on whom Burr was relying for funds. Though officially the two adventurers met on courtly terms of mutual admiration, to his intimates Burr expressed a low opinion of General Miranda's abilities.

The sight of Miranda and Burr in Dr. Benjamin Rush's drawing room set all tongues wagging. Another anonymous correspondent hastened to inform President Jefferson that Miranda's instructions came from the same source as Burr's. "Although ostensibly directed against a foreign power, your ruin and the material injury of the Atlantic states are their true object."

These rumors were mistaken. Even before the President received this piece of unsolicited advice, which he discounted as he did all anonymous communications, Jonathan Dayton, having given up hope of getting money from the British, was trying to shake down the Spanish minister with a set of proposals so fantastic as to verge on lunacy.

The Marqués de Casa Yrujo, a sprightly redheaded gentleman who was married to Governor McKean's daughter and dabbled in Pennsylvania politics, was so on the outs with the Jefferson administration that he spent his time in Philadelphia. He viewed the meeting between Miranda and Burr with professional curiosity. Though he had indulged in a guarded intimacy with Burr, when Burr was Vice President, in the interest of the perennial intrigue of the Spanish envoys to attract the Mississippi settlers into the Spanish orbit, he had recently been warning his government against Burr's ambitions and had politely refused to furnish that enthusiastic traveler with a passport to Mexico. When Senator Dayton paid him a visit, the marqués, regarding him rightly as an emissary of Burr's, was all ears.

Dayton started by declaring that the information he was about to give should certainly be worth thirty or forty thousand dollars to the Spanish government. Only two other men besides himself were privy to the plot. He went on to describe in detail Burr's proposal to Anthony Merry as if the Foreign Office had actually accepted it. Yrujo, who was no fool, concluded that if the British really were backing the scheme the conspirators would not come telling tales to him in the hope of raising a few thousand duros. He explained to Dayton that he couldn't dispose of such a large sum without consulting his government but encouraged him to go on talking. At the same time he made Dayton tell him everything he knew about the expedition Miranda was outfitting in New York.

A number of interviews followed in which, as Burr and Dayton became more desperate for cash, Dayton's disclosures became more and more sensational. In the coming spring, while the British fleet was blockading the coast, Burr's troops would seize West Florida and New Orleans. An expedition to take Mexico would land in the mouth of the Río Pánuco.

Yrujo kept inciting Dayton to further revelations by hints that authorization to pay for his information might come any day. At length Dayton blurted out Colonel Burr's newest plot. That was to introduce five hundred wellarmed men into Washington City, who would arrest the President, the Vice President, and the presiding officer of the Senate and proclaim a new government. If that failed they would plunder the banks and seize the ships at the navy yard and sail down the coast to revolutionize New Orleans.

Yrujo half believed him. . . . "For one who does not know the country," he wrote home to his government, "this plan would appear almost insane but I confess, for my part . . . it seems to me easy to execute . . . there exists in this country an infinite number of adventurers, without property, full of ambition, and ready to unite at once under the standard of a revolution which promises to better their lot. . . . Burr and his friends, without discovering their true object, have succeeded in getting the good will of these men."

Though the Spanish government refused to encourage any dealings with Burr, Dayton did manage to shake down the Spanish minister for twentyfive hundred dollars as a reward for informing on Miranda. From that moment Dayton's and Burr's great conspiracy, which started out at best as a doubtful speculation, degenerated into a common swindle. Each new dupe was goldbricked for what money could be had out of him.

While Dayton was raising petty cash from the Spaniards, Burr did his best to recruit the adventurers without property about whom Yrujo wrote his government. He sought out men with grievances. To each man he told as much as he figured the man wanted to hear.

Commodore Truxton of Perth Amboy had got into a tiff with the administration and lost his command. An old acquaintance of Burr's, he was intimate with Burr's best friend in Philadelphia, Charles Biddle, who had been a seafaring man in his youth. Burr knew Truxton was pining to go to sea again. He tried to entice him into the enterprise by painting the glories of a descent on Vera Cruz. When Truxton discovered that the government had authorized no such expedition the old sea dog refused. The elder Stephen Decatur was approached and also turned a cold shoulder.

William Eaton, who was American consul in North Africa during the hostilities against the Barbary pirates and who was loudly complaining, in the lobbies of Congress and in every Washington tavern, of the administration's neglecting to reward him for his impromptu capture of Derna which helped force peace on the Bey of Tripoli, was a man with a grievance and a loud one.

He was a noisy brawling kind of fellow who called himself General Eaton, and stamped around wearing a great silk sash and a martial uniform, boasting of his exploits in Tripoli. When Burr offered him the command of a division which Burr claimed he was enlisting (with the administration's approval) for service against the dons, Eaton was delighted; but when Burr presumed on their sudden intimacy by telling him that if he could win over the Marine Corps he would "turn Congress neck and heels out of doors," declare himself Protector, like Cromwell, of an energetic government and throw the President into the Potomac, Eaton, so Eaton reported later, looked Burr straight in the eye and told him he would get his throat cut if he tried it.

From that moment their friendship cooled. Eaton told the story to his friends in Congress and in a guarded way to the President himself. When he suggested that Jefferson get Colonel Burr out of the country by offering him a foreign mission, Jefferson showed every sign of impatience.

In fact, at about the same time, Colonel Burr himself visited the President to make the same request. Burr's attitude, as Jefferson described it in his *Anas*, was half threatening, half cajoling. He complained that though the President had always treated him politely he had never given him the position of trust Burr felt was due him as one of the architects of Republican victory. He hinted that he could do Jefferson "much harm" but said he would rather collaborate with his administration. Jefferson answered Burr bluntly that the public had no confidence in him and cited as proof the fact that Burr hadn't got a single vote for Vice President in the last election. They parted on their usual terms of chill civility.

9. *The Road to Failure*

Burr fails to enlist any man of consequence in the East. Though he may have raised a few thousand dollars from one of the New York Ogdens, Joseph Alston, whom Theodosia, who views her father's every word as gospel, keeps completely bemused, is still his chief source of funds. Meanwhile Burr casts his spell on Blennerhasset from afar.

Blanny proves even more credulous than Alston. He writes Colonel Burr that his island estate is up for sale and that he is looking for a profitable way to invest his capital. He tenders his services as a lawyer. Burr answers that he can offer Mr. Blennerhasset not only fortune but fame. He congratulates him for giving up "a vegetable existence" for a life of activity. He cannot explain the details of his magnificent enterprise until they meet face to face. This very autumn Colonel Burr is planning a fresh tour of the Western Waters. Blanny is left panting to give his all.

Though Burr must by this time know in his heart that his conspiracy has no real chance of success he has gone too far to turn back. He must act the part to the end. He recruits a German secretary and the services of a down at the heels French officer named Julien de Pestre to act as chief of staff. He sends Comfort Tyler, a ruined contractor with whom he had served in the New York legislature, to recruit hands in upstate New York. Burr and Dayton have dropped the fiction of the Ohio canal. The young men enlisted for service on the Mississippi are now being told that, in accordance with the secret policy of the administration, they are to establish an armed settlement on Colonel Burr's lands up the Ouachita River. Each man is to have a hundred acres of his own.

Though they are old friends Burr fails to stir Benjamin Latrobe, Jefferson's architect of the public buildings in Washington, with offers of a commission to lay out a city; but Latrobe's associate Dr. Bollmann swallows the scheme hook, line, and sinker.

Dr. Erick Bollmann is the German physician who helped Madame de Staël and her friends escape from the Terror in 1792 and who then was subsidized by John Barker Church and a group of Americans in London in an unsuccessful effort to free Lafayette from prison at Olmütz. Arriving in America, he was acclaimed as a hero and married the daughter of a wealthy Philadelphia banker who promptly cut her off without a cent. When the poor lady died Bollmann scandalized Philadelphia by recognizing as his a baby borne by his children's nurse. He founded an import-export business which after a spectacular success ended in an equally spectacular bankruptcy. When Burr invites him to join in his plans he holds out to Bollmann the prospect of acting as his diplomatic representative in Europe.

Somehow Burr scrapes up funds to ship Bollmann and a pair of associates to New Orleans by sea while Sam Swartwout of the Little Band and Dayton's nephew Peter V. Ogden start off crosscountry to seek out General Wilkinson. Both carry copies of the cypher letter which Wilkinson is soon to be quoting to Jefferson's Quaker friend Isaac Briggs. With the dispatch of this letter Burr burns every bridge behind him:

". . . I have at length obtained funds and have actually commenced; the eastern detachments, from different points and under different pretenses, will rendezvous on Ohio on 1st November . . . naval protection of England is secured. Truxton is going to Jamaica, to arrange with the admiral there, and will meet us at Mississippi—England—a navy of the United States ready to join, and final orders are given to my friends and followers. It will be a host of choice spirits. Wilkinson shall be second to Burr only. . . . Burr will proceed westward 1st of August never to return. With him go his daughter and grandson. The husband will follow in October, with a corps of worthies. . . . Our project my dear friend is brought to the point so long desired. I guarantee the result with my life and honor, with the lives, the honor and fortunes of hundreds, the best blood of our country. Burr's plan of operation is to move rapidly down from the Falls on the 15th November, with the first 500 of 1000 men in light boats now constructing for that purpose, to be at Natchez between the 5th and 15th of December: there to meet you; there to determine whether it will be expedient in the first instance to seize or pass by Baton Rouge. . . . The gods invite us to glory and fortune."

In early October Sam Swartwout delivers this message to the general whom, after many hundred miles of weary riding, he finds in camp at Natchitoches on the Red River. Ogden hands Wilkinson the even more extravagant epistle from Jonathan Dayton that so startled Isaac Briggs. "Are you ready? Are your numerous associates ready? Wealth and glory. Louisiana and Mexico."

In the solitude of his tent, with the help of a pocket dictionary that furnishes the key, the general sits up half the night decyphering the hieroglyphics. Food for thought indeed. General Wilkinson is a gentleman with the profoundest regard for the safety of his own skin. It strikes him at once that the enterprise in its present form is crackbrained. Besides Burr is lying to him. Wilkinson knows that the administration has decided against hostilities with the Spaniards. His orders are to patch up a truce with the Spanish force which has advanced across Texas to meet the rumored American invasion, and to agree to the Sabine River as a provisional boundary.

Furthermore even to this distant outpost news has come of Pitt's death and that Charles James Fox, the most pro-American of British statesmen, is now Foreign Minister. Wilkinson has no way of knowing that one of Fox's first acts in office was to recall the eager Mr. Merry, thereby putting a quietus on any hope of British help for Burr, but it is obvious that Fox is no man to back an insurrection against the United States. Wilkinson knows too that the Western settlers are "bigotted to Jefferson," as he put it a few months later, and that the conspiracy has no backing among the people.

After some cogitation the general decides that the safest thing for him to do is to inform on Dayton and Burr. Once that decision is made he lashes himself up into a storm of righteous indignation. He writes the President in heroic vein. He will defend the Union with his life. He writes Governor Claiborne of New Orleans to be on his guard: "You are surrounded by dangers of which you dream not and the destruction of the American Union is seriously menaced. The Storm will probably burst at New Orleans, when I shall meet it & triumph or perish in the attempt."

Not a word to Swartwout and Ogden, who must continue to believe that he is one of them, but among his officers, in the privacy of the wine after dinner, he swells like a bullfrog. How better can he squelch the libelous rumors of his being on the Spanish payroll than by saving New Orleans for the Union? He is the man who will stamp out this foul conspiracy, so help him God. He and his little force will stand like the Spartans at Thermopylae.

Aaron Burr meanwhile is building the most fabulous of his castles in the air for the ears of Theodosia, and her husband, and little Gampillo amid the crisp mountain breezes of Bedford Springs. In imagination he has them already living in the splendor of Montezuma's court. They will put the Emperor Napoleon to shame. Theodosia shall be the Empress of Mexico, and little Gampillo—Burr and his grandson each call the other Gamp—heir to the throne. He hasn't yet found a title for Joseph Alston. Alston announces that he will earn one by his deeds "in council and in the field."

Leaving the Alstons to follow by slow stages, Burr, attended by his secretary and chief of staff, rides off to Pittsburgh. There he sets up his headquarters at O'Hara's Tavern and starts recruiting young men of mettle. He contracts for twenty thousand barrels of flour and five thousand barrels of salt pork. He pays for everything with his own bills of exchange, when need be guaranteed by the infatuated Alston.

Burr talks so big in Pittsburgh that a number of military gentlemen become alarmed and send warnings to Washington. Burr has already gone downriver. On Blennerhasset's island he conquers all hearts. Blanny is transfigured by the prospect of glory. He sets energetically to work collecting fowling pieces and muskets, and whiskey by the barrel. His hands build a kiln for drying Indian meal. They roll out tubs of salt pork and corned beef. Mrs. Blennerhasset packs her trunks. She thinks Theodosia the loveliest woman she ever met, but she admits in a letter she can't stand Alston.

Blanny hypothecates what's left of his fortune to raise funds. Alston has told him he'll guarantee every dollar. They sign a contract for fifteen boats with the Woodbridges at Belpré across from the island. Blanny puts his name on every bill of exchange Burr places under his nose. He retires to his study to write four articles for the *Ohio Gazette* advocating the secession of the settlements west of the mountains.

Poor Blanny is even less discreet than Burr. He whispers to his gardener that settling the Bastrop grant is merely a pretext for the conquest of Mexico. If any recruit refuses to go along "I'll stab him." When John Graham, the man Jefferson sent out to make him a private report on Burr's doings, stops off at the island, Blanny, acting on Burr's hints that Graham is a confederate, confides the whole plan to him.

Burr moves on in a fever of activity. He can't stay in one place long enough to complete his arrangements. Leaving Blennerhasset and Alston to recruit riflemen, and to follow with the provisions when the boats are ready, he hurries to Cincinnati. A mob denouncing disunion and treason surrounds a house where Burr has put up for the night. Fife and drum play "The Rogue's March." Colonel Burr declares coolly that there is nothing he enjoys more than martial music. The outcry can't refer to him because his plans are all for the honor and glory of the United States. His disclaimer is so plausible that he's tendered an apology and the mob goes home.

Mobs or senators, Burr pulls the wool over all eyes. General John Adair, an old Indian fighter associated with Wilkinson in his wars against the Miamis, who, in spite of a recent humiliating defeat at the hands of Chief Little Turtle, is now senator-elect from Kentucky, joins Burr and lends a willing ear to his Mexican project. They ride through Kentucky in company.

Back in Nashville Burr finds the Republican part of the population in a fever to march on the Spaniards. General Jackson has alerted his militia, but he has doubts. When he confronts Burr with rumors of secessionist talk drifting downriver from Ohio, Burr shows him a blank commission signed by President Jefferson. Furthermore Burr produces thirtyfive hundred dollars in Kentucky bank notes to pay for the boats Jackson's partner John Coffee is building at Clover Bottom. Some time before he has paid five thousand (in his own paper) to a Colonel Lynch for the colonel's equity in the foggy claims a group of speculators, including Edward Livingston of New Orleans, have on the Bastrop lands. He draws sight drafts on all and sundry. According to the newspapers, he is spending two hundred thousand dollars on boats and provisions. Blanny's money flows freely. Thoroughly reassured, Andrew Jackson puts on his best uniform to introduce Colonel Burr to the citizens of Nashville at a public ball.

To the Marshall connection in Kentucky this is all a red flag to a bull. The Spanish conspiracies all over again. Humphrey Marshall has set up a newspaper named the *Western World* to expose the old Spanish intrigue to separate Kentucky from the Union in which he charges that two Republican judges are implicated. Joseph Daveiss, United States district attorney, another brotherinlaw of Chief Justice Marshall's, has been writing President Jefferson all summer warning him that Wilkinson and Burr are engaged in plots dangerous to the Union. November 8 he presents an affidavit in federal court, charging Aaron Burr and John Adair with illegally promoting an expedition against Mexico. The presiding judge is none other than Harry Innes, under attack in the *Western World* as a pensioner of Spain. Motion dismissed.

Aaron Burr, ever eager to assume the role of injured innocence, rides back to Lexington and demands an inquiry. A few days before he has written Senator Smith of Ohio, denying any intention of subverting the Union by force. Smith has warned him that rumors of secession continue to cause an uproar in Ohio. At about the same time Burr sends de Pestre east to reassure Yrujo in Philadelphia that he plans no harm to the Spanish possessions.

Popular sentiment in Kentucky is still with Burr. He has induced a rising young lawyer named Henry Clay to act as his counsel. When a grand jury is empaneled to hear Daveiss' charges, Daveiss is unable to present them because his witnesses have taken to the woods. Daveiss has to ask for a postponement. Burr makes an address to the court and walks out in triumph.

He is heard by a bystander to remark that Daveiss must think him a great fool if, supposing he did have an unlawful enterprise in view, he should conduct it in such a manner as to leave any loophole by which it might be proved on him.

When this news of Daveiss' charges reaches Andrew Jackson he is assailed by doubts again. November 12 he writes his old friend Governor Claiborne of New Orleans one of his tempestuous epistles: ". . . I fear treachery is become the order of the day . . . put your Town in a State of Defence organize your Militia, and defend your City as well against internal enemies as external. . . . Keep a watchful eye on your General—and beware of an attack, as well from your own Country as Spain . . . your government I fear is in danger, I fear there are plans on foot inimical to the Union . . . —beware the month of December—I love my country and government, I hate the Dons—I would delight to see Mexico reduced, but I will die in the last ditch before I would yield a part to the Dons or see the Union disunited. This I write for your own eye and your own safety, profit by it and the Ides of March remember. . . ."

It is not until November 25 that President Jefferson in Washington City receives Wilkinson's first warning of the conspiracy, which the general dispatched from Natchitoches some twelve days after the inconsistencies in Burr's cypher epistle decided him to turn state's evidence. On that same day, in Frankfort this time, the district attorney renews his motion for Burr's indictment. When Henry Clay demands an assurance from his client that Burr's expedition has no treasonable intent, Burr hands him substantially the same written statement he sent Senator Smith. Clay is convinced and declares to the court that he pledges his own honor on Burr's innocence. A second grand jury refuses to find a true bill. The Republicans of Frankfort honor the little colonel with another ball.

Wilkinson's turgid declarations startle President Jefferson and his cabinet into activity. Hitherto they seem to have discounted Daveiss' warnings as expressions of the party spite of pestiferous Federalists. Now the Secretaries of War and the Navy send out messengers to arouse their forces, and on November 27 President Jefferson issues his proclamation that "sundry persons are conspiring and confederating together to begin a military enterprise against the dominions of Spain," and enjoining "all faithful citizens who have been led without due knowledge and consideration to participate in the said unlawful enterprise to withdraw from the same without delay."

John Graham, President Jefferson's private investigator, has not been idle during these late fall days. He presents the information he has collected in Pittsburgh and Marietta, and from Blennerhasset's own lips, to Governor Tiffin of Ohio. Governor Tiffin passes it on to the legislature then in session at Chillicothe. A bill is rushed through authorizing the militia to seize Burr's boats and supplies.

Tatterdemalion troops take possession of the boats building on the Muskingum. They descend on Blennerhasset's island paradise, break into the wine cellar, plunder the kitchens, trample the flower beds, slaughter the sheep and break up the fence rails for campfires. Blanny himself escapes by boat into a snowstorm in the night, while the leveled muskets of his recruits hold off the militia officer come to arrest him. Mrs. Blennerhasset follows in a big flat manned by a group of schoolboys from Pittsburgh. From then on the expedition is a race between the speed of the current and the couriers distributing the President's proclamation.

Almost two weeks go by before the Blennerhassets get news of their leader. Taking refuge one late December evening from the chop and the storm in the mouth of the Cumberland, they are met by a skiff with a letter. Colonel Burr is anchored a couple of miles upstream and requests five hundred dollars in paper and fifty in silver. Next day Blennerhasset joins the colonel and the whole flotilla pushes off downstream together.

For Burr it is just in time. A Colonel Hardin of South Carolina is on his way down the Cumberland with the announced intention of shooting him on sight. The President's proclamation has thrown

Nashville into a fury. The citizens have hardly read it before they prepare to burn Burr in effigy. General Jackson dons his uniform and musters his militia. He almost breaks down with patriotic emotion when the elderly veterans of the Revolutionary War, who have formed a corps known as the Invincibles, ride up to tender their lives in defense of the Union. Some days before, Jackson's man John Coffee has returned to Colonel Burr seventeen hundred and twenty-five dollars and sixtytwo cents which represents the unfinished boats which Burr had to abandon in his haste to depart. Accounts are closed between them, except for a note of hand for five hundred dollars the general unwisely put his name to, which eventually will come back protested.

Unopposed except by cold rain and high winds and an occasional sawyer, as they call floating logs in those waters, Burr's flotilla, amounting now to thirteen boats manned by some sixty men, drifts down the Ohio to Fort Massac. The lieutenant in command, who has not heard of the proclamation or of orders to apprehend Burr, exchanges civilities with the little colonel and even gives one of his sergeants a furlough to go along on the pretense of helping the settlers reach the Bastrop lands.

New Year's Day 1807 finds the flotilla comfortably beached at New Madrid in Louisiana Territory. According to one account, forty new recruits join Burr's party. Other witnesses were to speak of cannon, and of two gunboats building there. Some were to accuse Blennerhasset of trying to buy arms and ammunition from the army post. Next morning they push off. Still keeping ahead of the hue and cry, they are borne swiftly southward on the current of the enormous brown river. Blanny and Burr follow their progress on their maps. Blanny is later to confess that it is when the boats go past what seems to him the logical spot from which they should have proceeded overland to the Bastrop grant that he first suspected an imposture.

Burr for his part seems to have forgotten all about the settlement. His talk now is of Baton Rouge. The Spanish post is supposedly so ill defended that even the peaceable Governor Claiborne is said to have suggested, jokingly over the wine after dinner, that he and his guests drive up the levee from New Orleans in their carriages some evening and take it.

The weather has cleared. The little colonel is in high spirits. He appoints officers and noncoms. Muskets are brought out of a packing case. Burr puts some of the boys through the manual of arms on one of the big flatboats as they drift down the river. At his friend Judge Bruin's plantation some thirty miles above Natchez he is confidently expecting a message from General Wilkinson, whom he believes to be waiting in New Orleans for the word.

At Chickasaw Bluffs they spend a whole day while Burr tries to talk young Jacob Jackson, the lieutenant in command of the army post there, into coming along with him. Burr offers him a captain's commission and tells him that though men high in the Jefferson administration are opposed to open war with Spain they favor a filibustering expedition by private persons. He expects assistance from "the present military force." General Eaton is coming around with part of the navy. Burr will be furnished with ten thousand stand of arms in the near future. Lieutenant Jackson is impressed but he refuses to leave his post without orders.

According to Dunbaugh, the sergeant from Fort Massac, Burr tries to get Dunbaugh to suborn some of the soldiers to desert with their arms and ammunition but Dunbaugh thinks it's too risky. After some hesitation Lieutenant Jackson does let Colonel Burr buy thirty pounds of lead and three dozen tomahawks, and suggests that after consulting his friends, he himself might resign from the army to join Burr's expedition.

His troopers help Burr's men repair some broken guns and run off five hundred musket bullets. Burr hands the lieutenant a hundred and fifty dollars in Kentucky bank notes and a sight draft drawn on Senator John Smith at Cincinnati for five hundred dollars towards the expenses of raising a company.

Burr is so anxious to reach Judge Bruin he has himself rowed ahead of the flotilla in a keelboat. He reaches Bayou Pierre the morning of January 10. Judge Bruin has the reputation of being a hard drinker. Burr finds him in a state. Burr is shown the President's proclamation. He is told that acting Governor Cowles Mead of Mississippi has called out the militia with orders to arrest him. He is handed an issue of the *Mississippi Messenger* containing a transcription of his cypher message. Wilkinson has betrayed him.

Burr slips back into the role of injured innocence. Skillfully he fences for terms with Cowles Mead. Mead later declares the man's statements were so strange he doubted his sanity. After surrendering on terms to the civil authority Burr lets himself be taken to Natchez. Friends stand bail.

Again Burr finds himself the toast of Federalist dinners. The ladies ply him with dainties. In Natchez he has a host of defenders. Another grand jury refuses to find him guilty of an indictable offense and furthermore issues a presentment against General Wilkinson's illegal arrests of suspected persons in New Orleans.

The presiding judge, Thomas Rodney, an administration supporter, has a different view. His son Caesar Augustus has just been appointed Attorney General of the United States. Judge Rodney refuses to lift Burr's bond.

News comes of the apprehension of Bollmann and Swartwout. General Wilkinson has offered five thousand dollars for Burr's capture living or dead. Burr knows the general well enough to be sure that, with all Burr knows, Wilkinson would much prefer to have him dead. Panic seizes the imperturbable conspirator. Nothing for it but to jump his bail and to vanish into the wilderness.

From hiding Burr tries to send a message to his men. It is a note stitched into the colonel's old surtout worn by a slave boy.

"If you are yet together keep together and I will join you tomorrow night—in the mean time put all your arms in perfect order. Ask the bearer no questions but tell him all you may think I wish to know. —He does not know this is from me nor where I am."

The boy is apprehended, the note discovered. Immediately the governor spreads a cordon of militia round Burr's camp. Every man they can lay hands on is arrested.

Meanwhile Burr, furnished with a pair of good horses, rides desperately off through the forest towards the Spanish frontier.

10. At the End of His Rope

About eleven o'clock on the night of February 18 or 19, he couldn't be sure of the date when he told the story in court under oath, Nicholas Perkins, a backwoods lawyer who ran the land office for Mississippi Territory, left the group around the fire in Sheriff Brightwell's log tavern where he'd been sitting up to play backgammon with his friend Thomas Malone, clerk of the court of Washington County situated deep in the piny woods along the Tombigbee River, and went to the door for a breath of fresh air.

It was a night of clear frosty moonlight. Perkins could see far down the rutted road. Though he was described as a fearless giant of a man, and a major in the territorial militia, Perkins admitted being startled to see two horsemen come riding up out of the forest.

The smaller of the horsemen rode right past. He was a shabby-looking little fellow lost under a broadbrimmed beaver hat. His companion reined in his horse and asked Perkins the way to Major Hinson's. He turned out to be a New Orleans man named Robert Ashley who had worked for the Philip Nolan who had been General Wilkinson's agent in his dealings with the old Spanish government.

Perkins told him the major was away from home, and added that, on account of the freshet, the flooding of the creeks would make it hard for a stranger to reach the Hinson house that night. The sensible thing would be to put up at the tavern where there was refreshment for man and beast. Ashley insisted they must push on, so Perkins told him the best places to ford the streams. While he was talking to Ashley, Perkins kept staring after the first traveler, who had pulled up his horse thirty or forty yards up the road. The man aroused his suspicions.

That very day Perkins had read the territorial governor's proclamation offering a reward of two thousand dollars for the apprehension of Colonel Aaron Burr, who had forfeited his bond at Natchez two weeks before. Perkins scratched his head as he walked to the fire. These men were up to no good. Mrs. Hinson was alone. Mightn't the little man with the hatbrim flapped over his face be Burr himself?

Right away Perkins routed the sheriff, who was related to Mrs. Hinson, out of bed. They saddled their horses and rode off after the mysterious travelers. They found Ashley in the Hinsons' front room. Mrs. Hinson, who'd been hiding in the back of the house in a fright ever since the strangers walked in, let herself be seen when she heard voices she knew and started to fry up some supper for her visitors.

The small man sat warming himself beside the fire in the kitchen with his hat pulled down over his face. Perkins observed him narrowly. He wore a boatman's ragged pantaloons, and a coarse blanket wraparound belted in by a strap. The hat that had once been white was stained and shabby, but the riding boots on his very small feet were elegant and new. Perkins caught one quick glance of his eyes from under the brim of the hat and was convinced that the man must be Colonel Burr. Everybody spoke of how Burr could look clean through you with his lustrous black eyes.

He took Ashley aside and asked him pointblank if his companion were Colonel Burr. Ashley became agitated and walked out of the house without answering a word.

Perkins began to feel the two thousand dollars almost in the palm of his hand but he had to move with circumspection. The little colonel was held in great respect in the Western country. He was known to be a dead shot. Mumbling a misleading excuse, Perkins rode off in a hurry to Joseph Bates's house at Nanahubby Bluff on the Tombigbee. Bates let him have a canoe and a Negro to paddle it and he went speeding down the flooding river to a palisade named Fort Stoddert which was the last fortification before the frontier of Spanish West Florida.

Arriving there about daybreak, he roused Lieutenant Gaines, who had charge of the federal troops defending the fort, and told him he had the traitor Burr in the palm of his hand. Right at this moment Burr would be starting down the trail to Pensacola. No way to cross the river but by Mrs. Carson's ferry. The lieutenant ordered out a file of mounted soldiers and they galloped off to intercept him.

On the trail they found Burr and his companion. The sheriff, whom Burr had fascinated in a few short minutes' conversation, was acting as their guide to the Spanish border. Colonel Burr took high ground.

He pointed out to the young lieutenant the risk he took making an arrest without a warrant.

The lieutenant brought out the President's proclamation.

Burr declared the proclamation was illegal and unconstitutional. The lieutenant insisted that he was an officer in the United States Army and had to do his duty. Colonel Burr would be treated with all the respect due an ex-Vice President of the United States if he made no effort to escape. The little colonel was conducted back to the fort and shut up in a room where dinner was served him in solitary state. Sentries were posted at the windows and doors.

Ashley meanwhile had managed to disappear into the woods. Lieutenant Gaines and Major Perkins started racking their brains as to how they could get their prisoner safely to Washington City.

The weather was freezing and drizzly. The rivers were in flood. There were no roads yet through the enormous woodlands of Mississippi Territory. The country abounded in Indians of doubtful loyalty. Rumor had enormously magnified Burr's expedition. For all they knew the back country was full of partisans grouping to rescue their leader.

Nothing for it but for Gaines to take the little colonel into his family under a sort of parole. Gaines's brother, who was government factor to the Choctaw nation, was ill in bed. Burr showed himself the soul of tact and courtesy. Explaining that he'd picked up a certain amount of medical information on his travels, he proved a skillful physician and helped nurse the brother back to health. Meanwhile he sat at the man's bedside keeping him amused with sprightly talk about Indian quirks and customs.

At the table he fascinated the family by his knowledge of books and pictures and the great world. He fixed his black eyes on the ladies with respectful attention. He played chess with Mrs. Gaines. So long as he stayed at Fort Stoddert not a word passed his lips about the failure of his Western project, or about his arrest, or his plans.

Lieutenant Gaines was counting the hours until he should see the last of his charming prisoner. Burr's friends had been spreading the story that the aim of Burr's thwarted expedition was to drive the Spaniards out of West Florida. As that was the dearest wish of every settler in the Mississippi Territory expressions of sympathy were heard on every hand. "A week longer," Gaines wrote General Wilkinson, "the consequences would have been of a most serious nature."

At last the floods subsided to the point where Gaines felt it would be safe to try to take his prisoner up the Alabama River. The party was rowed in a government boat. When they stopped at John Mills's house on Tensaw Lake, the ladies of the family all wept over the sorrows of Colonel Burr. Indeed a certain Mrs. Johnson was so moved by his plight that when a boy was born to her some months later she named him Aaron Burr. "When a lady does me the honor to name me the father of her child," Burr was wont to remark, "I trust I shall always be too gallant to show myself ungrateful for the favor."

At the boatyard at the head of navigation of the Alabama River Gaines turned his prisoner over to Major Perkins—to Perkins' friend Malone and to a guard of six men, including two federal soldiers with muskets—to be conducted to Washington City. Gaines sent them off under the strictest injunction not to speak to their prisoner or to listen to his blandishments and to shoot to kill at his first effort to escape.

He found them good horses. Riding thirty or forty miles a day, avoiding the settlements, they hurried their prisoner along Indian traces through drowned woodlands. It was a rainy March. The nights were cold. Wolves howled about their campfires. Half the time they were drenched to the skin. Burr's fortitude amazed his guards. Never a word of complaint. Never a sign of fatigue. He rode his fine horse with as much style, so one of the guards told his friends, as if he were riding at the head of his New York regiment.

They crossed the rivers in Indian canoes, swimming their horses alongside. Line Creek, the Cubahatchee, the Calabee, the Chattahoochee, the Flint, the Ocmulgee. At last on the Oconee River in the state of Georgia they found a ferry and an inn not far beyond. For the first time since leaving the Alabama country they slept under a roof.

When they crossed into South Carolina Perkins redoubled his precautions. He knew that Burr's soninlaw, Joseph Alston, the husband of the colonel's renowned daughter Theodosia, was a member of the legislature and belonged to one of the most influential families in the state. Public sentiment there was supposed to be strong for Burr.

Perkins arranged his cavalcade in a square with Burr in the middle. Two riders went ahead of him, two on either flank, and two behind. They passed through towns and villages at a brisk trot.

In the village of Chester about fifty miles south of the North Carolina border they rode past an inn. From the inn came a sound of music and dancing. A crowd had gathered to look in the windows. The prisoner suddenly jumped from his horse and cried out to the bystanders that he was Aaron Burr under military arrest, and must be taken to a magistrate.

Perkins dismounted at one leap with a pistol in either hand and ordered Burr to remount.

"I will not," cried Burr.

Perkins dropped his pistols and, being a man of enormous strength, grabbed the little colonel round the waist and lifted him back on his horse like a child. Malone grabbed Burr's reins, pulled them over his horse's head, and led him off as fast as he could while the guards formed up about him. Before the astonished villagers could open their mouths the cavalcade was lost in the dust. Colonel Burr broke down. As his guards told the story, he burst into a flood of tears. Malone, who rode beside him, was so distressed at his prisoner's humiliation that he found the tears streaming down his own face as he rode.

It was the man's eyes that moved him so, Malone told his friends afterwards. Burr's eyes were like stars.

At the age of fiftyone Aaron Burr had reached the end of his rope.

CHAPTER III

The Labor and Contentions of Public Life

1. Colonel Monroe's Treaty

After a blustery February the spring of 1807 proved mild. Jefferson was even more restless than usual to break away if only for a few days from the routine of official life to see to his crops and his mill, and to his fruit trees and flower garden at Monticello. Recollection of the successes of his first administration made the frustrations of his second hard to bear.

As the Ninth Congress drew to a close, news from the West had set the President's mind to rest in regard to Burr's conspiracy. He had the satisfaction of feeling that he had judged the situation correctly: the settlers on the Western Waters would have none of the little colonel's castles in the air.

But now new setbacks confronted him. His and Madison's foreign policy had two basic aims: the purchase of the Floridas and the end of the impressment of American seamen by the Royal Navy. Even so sanguine a man as Thomas Jefferson had to face the fact that both policies had gone awry.

The very day that Congress adjourned the British minister handed the President a copy of the treaty which his own envoys James Monroe and William Pinkney had signed at the Foreign Office. Jefferson was aghast at what he read.

Monroe had let himself be talked into putting his name to exactly the treaty Jefferson had instructed him not to sign. William Pinkney, the Annapolis lawyer who was sent over to join Monroe because Jefferson and Madison were impressed by a brief he wrote demolishing the legal arguments on which the British based their harassment of neutral shipping, had fallen into the same error. It was a worse treaty than Jay's.

Jefferson recognized that his friend Monroe had been in for a run of bad luck. His diplomatic tour of duty in Europe, which opened so auspiciously with the Louisiana Purchase, had suffered one discomfiture after another. After weary months of haggling with the Spanish authorities in Madrid, his negotiation for settling the boundaries of Louisiana was completely stalled. Jefferson's secret scheme to bribe the French government to force the Spaniards to give up Florida had proved unworkable. Talleyrand, the skillful corruptionist, was going into eclipse at the imperial court. The victories of the Grande Armée had put all the bullion of Europe at Napoleon's disposal. He no longer felt the need for small change from the Yankees.

Transferred to England at the moment when Fox's taking over the Foreign Office seemed to offer an opportunity for a reasonable settlement of the problems of impressment and neutral shipping, Monroe had found himself, after Fox's death, bucking an upsurge of the war spirit absolutely unprecedented among the levelheaded Britishers. In their quiet backwater on the Potomac Jefferson and Madison could hardly imagine the frenzy for empire which swept through Whigs and Tories alike.

Trafalgar had left Britain seemingly invincible at sea. After Austerlitz Napoleon could indeed harness all the resources of continental Europe for her destruction; but the islanders, safe behind their wooden walls, could trade blow for blow.

Napoleon countered the British blockade of his continental ports with the Berlin Decree, which declared a total blockade of the British Isles. For the British, from the royal dukes to the lowest flunky who opened the coach door, it was a case of who is not for us is against us. That bloody confrontation left no room for the consideration of neutral rights.

When, late on the night of March 3, the joint committee drove in a carriage down Pennsylvania Avenue to carry to the President the formal notification of the recess of Congress, one of its members, Senator John Quincy Adams of Massachusetts, asked Mr. Jefferson if he intended to call a special session to consider the British treaty. The President's answer, in an emphatic tone, was "Certainly not."

President Jefferson had been unable to attend the closing session of Congress, in a committee room at the Capitol, as was his custom, because he was laid up with another of his prostrating migraine headaches. It was days before he could summon the equanimity to write Monroe.

Monroe, after Madison and Gallatin, was the public man in whom he had most confidence. Now Monroe had failed him. Though he admitted freely that Monroe's situation in England was difficult he found it hard to excuse him for acting deliberately against his instructions. In his private meditations Jefferson couldn't help suspecting that presidential aspirations had something to do with it. Could it be that his friend was playing up to the Federalist vote? Ever since he had announced he would refuse a third term, Jefferson had been working quietly to have Madison accepted as his successor. Now a group of Virginia Republicans had begun to clamor for Monroe. A rift in the ranks of the party might have consequences Jefferson didn't care to think of.

He wrote Monroe as kindly as he could that he would have left the discussion of the faults of the treaty to the Secretary of State, "but that I perceive uncommon efforts, and with uncommon wickedness, are making by the federal papers to produce mischief between myself, personally, & our negociators; and also to irritate the British government by putting a thousand speeches in my mouth, none of which I have ever uttered."

He declared he was unalterably opposed to ratification of any treaty which did not provide against the impressment of American seamen. He felt that the British had inadvertently given the U.S. an opportunity to back out of his particular agreement by the declaration which they produced at the last moment that American submission to the French blockade would void any commitment on the part of Great Britain. A treaty only respected by one party wasn't a treaty at all.

"Depend upon it, my dear Sir," he continued, "it will be considered a hard treaty when it is known. the British commisrs appear to have screwed every article as far as it would bear, to have taken everything & yielded nothing."

The President suggested that Monroe try a few more conversations with the British commissioners, and that if they continued to prove obdurate he should use this as a pretext to come home, leaving Pinkney in London, "who by procrastinations, can let it die away and give us time, the most precious of all things to us."

He offered Monroe the governorship of Orleans Territory. This meant more than sugaring the pill of failure for an old friend. The present governor, young Claiborne, though well meaning and a devoted Jeffersonian, was reported to have antagonized both the established Creoles and the recently arrived American settlers. Burr's conspiracy and General Wilkinson's carryings on in New Orleans had brought home to the President the need for a man of Monroe's steadiness in the administration there.

He had already removed Wilkinson as governor of upper Louisiana. One of the Senate's last acts before adjournment had been to confirm the President's appointment of Meriwether Lewis to that post in Wilkinson's place. Captain Lewis had proved his mettle by the success of his expedition to the Pacific. Now if Jefferson could induce Monroe to take over New Orleans, he would not only have a man he trusted in what he assured his friend was "the 2nd office in the U.S. in importance, "but would have Monroe out of harm's way during Madison's campaign for the presidency. Monroe's refusal of the post was to prove a further disappointment.

2. John Randolph's Quids

The prospects for administration policies abroad were becoming more and more stormy as the hundred year old contest between France and England for domination of the world rose to a fresh climax. To make things worse the orderly growth of the Republican party at home, on which Jefferson hung his every hope for the future, had been suddenly challenged.

The challenger was John Randolph. John Randolph was a relative of the President's on his mother's side and a much closer connection of Jefferson's soninlaw, Thomas Mann Randolph, who, as husband of his only surviving daughter, Patsy, and as father of his adored grandchildren, was a most intimate member of his family. Along with Thomas Mann Randolph and with Jack Eppes, Jefferson's other soninlaw, John Randolph had formed part of a sort of family phalanx in the House of Representatives during the early years of the Republican administration. By the caustic brilliance of his speeches as chairman of the Committee on Ways and Means, he had won the leadership of the Republicans in the House and done good service in advancing the Jeffersonian causes. Now he not only rose in opposition on the floor but he held the President's private schemes, such as the intrigue for the purchase of Florida, up to scorn in a pair of the articles signed Decius in the Richmond *Examiner*. What was worse his sayings and writings were being gleefully repeated in the English press and were doing as much damage to the administration's policies abroad as at home.

With Joseph H. Nicholson of Maryland and a couple of others John Randolph was forming a dissident faction in Congress. He called them the party of the *tertium quid*, of the alternative course. Where, before, administration measures had gone smoothly through the House, now the President never knew when the unpredictable John Randolph would rise to his feet and impudently push a spoke into the wheel.

Though he remained friendly with Gallatin, John Randolph now spoke of Madison in terms of abhorrence. Some congressmen claimed that his failure to obtain the legation in London had turned him against the Secretary of State. John Randolph had put in a bid for the mission abroad through a friend soon after his ill success in the impeachment proceedings against Justice Chase temporarily disgusted him with service in the House. The report which came back, that both Jefferson and Madison thought him too erratic for a diplomatic post, was a bitter frustration. Though a passionate Virginian, John Randolph's schoolboy reading had filled him with dreams of the debates at Westminster. Like so many Americans of the new generation, he felt a provincial craving for England as an intellectual home.

The slight rankled. Personal pique turned into political opposition. One of the first symptoms of his dissidence was a quarrel with his cousin Thomas Mann Randolph which nearly ended on the dueling field. The President became convinced that John Randolph was the source of the untimely boom for Monroe which he feared might split the party at the next presidential election.

At thirtyfour John Randolph had reached a point in his development where he could brook subservience to no man. One of the cleverest and stormiest members of a family given to carrying selfindulgence to the point of mania, he was beginning his long and erratic career as a lone voice in Congress.

Pride of family was the besetting sin of the new generation in Virginia. John Randolph eagerly traced his lineage to Pocahontas and through the Randolphs of Turkey Island to dim eminent Randolphs of Elizabethan times in Warwickshire. To distinguish himself from all other John Randolphs living or dead he began to sign his name: John Randolph of Roanoke.

He was the son of a John Randolph who died young, leaving behind a reputation for truculence, broad landholdings in southside Virginia, and a well connected wife with three small children. John Randolph's mother soon married St. George Tucker, who raised the Randolph children and three more of his own on his wife's plantation, Matoax, near Petersburg on the Appomattox River.

St. George Tucker, a Bermudian of great ability, was a student at William and Mary when Jefferson was practicing law in Williamsburg. When the Revolution came he joined the Virginia militia, wrote some graphic letters describing the Yorktown campaign, and as a pupil and successor of George Wythe became one of the luminaries of the Virginia bench. He published an edition of Blackstone renowned in its day, wrote Addisonian essays, and had a neat touch with light verse. His *Probationary Odes* are still amusing to read. His contemporaries considered him one of the most agreeable and learned of men. In the earlier part of his life his stepson was fulsome in his praise. It was not till later, after he had quarreled with his stepfather, as he did with every man of stature who crossed his path, that John Randolph wrote bitterly of Judge Tucker: "The first blow I ever received was from the hand of this man, and not a week after his union with my mother."

One of John Randolph's earliest recollections was the family's winter flight to Bizarre, another Randolph plantation further up the Appomattox River, when the traitor Arnold's raiders occupied Petersburg during Jefferson's unhappy second term as governor. Bizarre, which had been settled on his elder brother Richard by their father's will, was to be John Randolph's home during most of the earlier part of his life.

His schooling was much interrupted by illness. At one point he seemed so wasted by the prevailing ague that his stepfather sent him to the Tucker family in Bermuda for many months. He almost died of scarlet fever. Sometime in adolescence he suffered a crippling attack of mumps. A physician who examined his body after his death discovered that the testes had failed to develop. This accounted for his falsetto voice and the look of withered boyishness his face wore throughout his life. He never grew a beard. His engagement to the reputedly lovely Maria Ward was suddenly broken off with no reason given. "My apathy is not natural but superinduced," he told a friend to explain his lack of relations with women. "There was a volcano under this ice, but it is burnt out."

As a lad he was restless, quarrelsome, embittered. He threw a knife at his brother's head in a fit of ungovernable temper. Though a voracious reader he could never get along with his schoolteachers. He was just on the point of matriculating at Princeton, where he claimed Dr. Witherspoon kept him unduly long in the grammar school—"this subterranean abode of noise and misrule"—in order to embezzle his funds, when he was called home to the bedside of his dying mother.

After her death John and the middle brother Theodorick studied in a desultory way at Columbia College in New York and at William and Mary. His stepfather wanted to send him to Edinburgh to study medicine, but, though he seems to have attended a few lectures at the medical school in Philadelphia, he never could take the medical knowledge of the day seriously enough to go in for it.

He grew up a tall gangling man with a short narrowshouldered body and long legs. His lank hair he considered a heritage of the Powhatans. The eyes in his small boyish face were described as large and searching. His extremities were bulky. A man who remembered seeing him in bed said he looked like a pair of oyster tongs under the covers with his small head and his great length and enormous feet.

He was a dedicated sportsman. As a child he had enjoyed angling in the brown river at Bizarre. He early took to shooting quail and duck. He was passionate for bird dogs and horses. His friends spoke of him as a sort of centaur, never out of the saddle. At family gatherings he was a truculent figure, booted and spurred, thrashing about with his riding crop. In youth he spared some affection from his horses and dogs for a few friends of his own age, and especially for his brothers. Later his love for his nephews became obsessive. When his stepfather remarried he moved in with his elder brother Richard at Bizarre.

When John Randolph was nineteen his brother Richard was the center of a family tragedy that left its mark on every Randolph involved for the rest of their lives. They were still shaken by Theodorick's death of a wasting disease, which was probably tuberculosis, when the family became implicated in a public scandal. A grand jury indicted Richard Randolph for murder.

Richard seems to have been a generous and warmhearted fellow. In his will be manumitted his two hundred slaves, set apart four hundred acres for their support, and delivered himself of a diatribe against the wickedness of slavery. He was married to another Randolph. Her name was Judith. She was the daughter of a crusty old fellow known as Tuckahoe Tom who had been Jefferson's first schoolmate in his early years. One of Judith's elder brothers was the Thomas Mann Randolph who married Jefferson's daughter Martha.

Judith's younger sister Ann Cary, known as Nancy in the family, had been courted by Theodorick before his death. Since her father had other plans for her she left home, after one of the family quarrels so common among the Randolphs, and took up her abode with her sister at Bizarre. The household at Bizarre was a large one and included besides John Randolph and Richard's children a widowed poor relation and her brood.

On the first of October 1792 there arrived on a visit to Glenlyvar, the seat of Randolph Harrison in Cumberland County, Richard Randolph and his wife Judith, her sister Nancy and a couple of other relatives, including an Archibald Randolph described as an admirer of Nancy's. Presumably the ladies drove in a coach and the gentlemen rode horseback. After dinner that afternoon Nancy, who had been complaining of feeling ill, went upstairs. She was not seen again that day. Her room communicated only with the room at the head of the stairs where Richard and his wife slept.

In the middle of the night the Harrisons were awakened by screams which they first thought came from Judith. Their guests asked for laudanum. It was explained that Nancy was taken with a fit of hysterics. After she'd found the laudanum Mrs. Harrison ran upstairs with a candle. Judith was sitting up in bed. The door to Nancy's room was bolted. When Mrs. Harrison knocked the door was opened but she was begged not to bring the candle in as the light would hurt Nancy's eyes. Richard Randolph was in Nancy's room. She was in great pain and had just taken the laudanum. Besides Richard and Nancy there was no one in the room but two young Negro girls.

When she was told that Nancy was feeling better, Mrs. Harrison went back downstairs to attend to a child of hers who was feverish. The Harrisons returned to bed in due course and were just dozing off when they heard a heavy step on the stairs which they supposed to be Richard's. Their first thought was that he was coming down to send for a doctor. When they heard his steps going back upstairs some time later they dismissed the incident from their minds and fell asleep.

Next day they couldn't help noticing bloodstains on the stairs and on the bed where Nancy still lay with the covers pulled tight about her. Later their Negroes told the Harrisons that Nancy had suffered a miscarriage and that something had been hidden in the woodpile. Nancy kept her bed several days.

At the end of the week the Richard Randolphs and Nancy left for home. Neither of the three showed any sign of strain or tension. They seemed the same united happy family they had been when they came. Mrs. Harrison found bloodstains on the mattress after they had left. When Randolph Harrison was shown a bloody shingle in the woodpile he forbore to look further.

The Randolphs settled back into their life at Bizarre as if nothing had happened. Nancy took to horseback riding again. Meanwhile busy tongues were speeding the story through the countryside. John Randolph first heard it at Williamsburg.

The tale that was going around was that Nancy Randolph had given birth to an illegitimate child, that Richard was the father, that he had killed it and buried it in the woodpile at Glenlyvar. The scandalous tongues were so insistent that the Cumberland County grand jury indicted both Richard and Nancy for murder. Richard was lodged in the county jail.

Richard immediately sought out the best lawyers he could find: John Marshall, who was then practicing law in Richmond, Alexander Campbell, and Patrick Henry.

The first messenger who reached old Henry offered him two hundred and fifty guineas. He replied that he was in poor health and that the journey from his comfortable retreat away from the chills and fevers of Tidewater, up on the Staunton River, would be far too tiring for him. It took an offer of five hundred guineas to induce the old orator to stir his stumps.

Men and women of the best blood of Virginia followed each other to the witness stand. The testimony was damaging all round. Neither Richard nor Nancy was called to testify by their lawyers. The testimony left no doubt that Nancy had been with child. Witnesses described Richard's unduly caressing manner to his sisterinlaw. There had been either a birth or a miscarriage. The case for murder fell through for lack of a corpus delicti. The accused were acquitted.

John Randolph noted in his diary: "The trial. Return. Quarrels of the women. I ride postillion with Bill Vaughn's horses."

Nancy's story to her intimate friends was that the child was Theodorick's and was born dead. Neither Richard nor Judith uttered a word. After Richard's own death three years later, ill feeling between Nancy and John soured to virulent hatred. He accused her of incest, called her the murderess of her child, and accused her of poisoning his brother Richard. She claimed that it was his foul tongue that had caused her to be driven out, destitute and homeless, by the Randolph connection.

Indeed many Virginians felt Nancy was more sinned against than sinning. A consoling letter of Jefferson's to his daughter and soninlaw has survived: "Every one at present stands on the merit or demerit of their own conduct. I am in hopes therefore that neither of you will feel any uneasiness but for the pitiable victim, whether it be of error or slander. in either case I see guilt in one person but not in her . . . never throw off the best affections of nature in the moment when they become most precious to their object, nor fear to extend your hand to save another lest you should sink yourself."

John Randolph was enrolled at William and Mary during this trying time. He was then the most Jacobin of Jeffersonian Republicans. He used the French republican names for the months and addressed his friends as Citizen in his letters. His overbearing manner to his mates at the college caused a highflying young Federalist from Norfolk to challenge him to a duel. John Randolph left his opponent with a nasty flesh wound in the hip, was reconciled to him on the field of honor, and ever afterwards spoke well of him.

Dueling was frowned on in Williamsburg. John Randolph had to ride out of town in a hurry.

The oddest part of the story, as related by mutual friends, was that the quarrel, instead of being political, seemed to have been over the pronunciation of the word "omnipotent." John Randolph was a stickler for what he called orthoëpy.

This incident put an end to the young man's formal education. Expelled from college, he lounged away his time at Bizarre, reading, gambling, drinking, hunting, riding from race meet to race meet. When he came of age he found himself the possessor of great estates, but with so many obligations to meet on complicated mortgages in the hands of British tobacco agents that he was always short of funds. After his brother's death, his two preoccupations were freeing his plantations from debt and educating his nephews. The elder was deaf and dumb, but on Tudor, the younger one, he staked great hopes.

His life was solitary. The friends of his youth were moving to Tennessee and Kentucky and to the black lands beyond the Ohio. Even after the abolishing of entail, for which the old families blamed Thomas Jefferson, there wasn't much opportunity for an energetic young man in southside Virginia. John Randolph wrote his stepfather, with whom he was still on good terms, that Bizarre seemed as retired now as the island of Juan Fernández.

Politics came as natural as horseflesh to the Virginia gentry. John

Randolph was induced to run for Congress as a Democratic Republican at the age of twentyfive. Immediately he found himself in debate with the great Patrick Henry before a crowd at Charlotte Court House. The subject was the Alien and Sedition Acts, which Henry, now a Federalist, was supporting.

It turned out to be Patrick Henry's last public speech. The journalists of the time lavished so much rhetoric on the contrast between the rising and the setting sun that it is hard to discover exactly what was said. In spite of a bad cold and the peculiar flutiness of his voice John Randolph held his own. "I'll tell you what," a local farmer was heard to say, "the young man is no bugeater either."

John Randolph first sat in the very Federalist Sixth Congress in Philadelphia during the last year of John Adams' administration. Congressmen were astonished by his smooth cheeks and boyish appearance. From the moment when he answered Speaker Sedgwick's query as to whether he was old enough to be eligible with "Go ask my constituents," John Randolph felt he had found his element. His picturesque expressions and bullying manner often got him into hot water.

In an attack on what the Republicans considered a Federalist scheme to saddle the nation with a standing army on the pretext of the undeclared war with the French Directory he denounced the recruits as ragamuffins. Two officers of the marines jostled him in a theatre soon after in an attempt to provoke a duel. Instead of letting himself fall into their trap John Randolph wrote a testy note to President Adams demanding that the majesty of the people be protected in the person of their representatives.

President Adams huffily returned the letter to the House of Representatives, with the statement that it was up to the House to protect its own prerogatives. Randolph came out of the ruckus that followed with such a reputation for skill in debate that when the Seventh Congress was organized after Jefferson's victory in 1800 he was made chairman of the Committee on Ways and Means.

In spite of his truculence John Randolph had charm. He was an amusing table companion. He became the favorite of the Speaker, an unassuming North Carolina planter named Nathaniel Macon, and struck up a warm friendship with Gallatin's brotherinlaw Joseph C. Nicholson of Maryland. It was not long before he was considered the leader of the administration forces on the floor of the House.

President Jefferson, who knew the irresponsible Randolphs too well to place complete reliance in his young cousin, dealt with him mostly through Gallatin. Gallatin was admittedly fascinated by his madcap reasoning and sarcastic phraseology. The Republican majority remained torn between admiration for his energy in debate and resentment of his overbearing manner when the mood seized him. He was master of the epithet that stuck like a burr. His melodrama delighted the galleries.

3. *John Marshall Takes His Stand*

One of the chief items on the Republican agenda during President Jefferson's first term was to restore the political balance in the federal judiciary. John Adams, before leaving office, did his best to offset the Republican victory by appointing judges he could expect to hold the fort for Federalism. With John Marshall Chief Justice of the Supreme Court he could indeed rest quiet at Quincy, confident that the federal bench would give no ground to the Jacobins and visionaries who were winning at the polls.

As a first move in their war against the Federalist judges the Republicans repealed the Judiciary Act under which Adams made a host of appointments in the last weeks of his administration. To make sure that the Supreme Court should not find the repeal unconstitutional they included a measure postponing its next session. Next they set about to use the Congress' constitutional powers of impeachment to get rid of the more objectionable occupants of the federal bench.

The first case was that of a district judge in New Hampshire named John Pickering who had proved incapable of carrying out the duties of his office. According to some this was due to drunkenness, according to others to progressive insanity. The President reported the facts in a message to Congress and the House appointed John Randolph and his friend Nicholson to manage Pickering's impeachment before the Senate.

While preparations were going on for the impeachment proceedings, John Marshall, having reached the term when he could call his justices together, produced an opinion which was eventually to have momentous consequences. One of Adams' "midnight" appointees, William Marbury, applied for a writ of mandamus to compel the Secretary of State to deliver him his commission as justice of the peace. It was the policy of the administration to consider these appointments null.

In a curiously backhanded opinion, couched in the forceful and repetitious language for which he was becoming famous, John Marshall held, on the one hand, that the validity of a man's appointment to office depended on the President's signature and on the instrument's being countersigned by the Secretary of State. The delivery of the document was a mere formality.

No man knew better than John Marshall that this particular commission had been signed because as acting Secretary of State he had countersigned it himself among many others by candlelight at the

President's house the night before John Adams hurriedly left Washington City to avoid taking part in his erstwhile friend Jefferson's inauguration.

So far the Chief Justice allowed the plaintiff to win his point. Then in the second part of his decision he found that the section of the Judiciary Act of 1789 under which the plaintiff appealed to the Supreme Court was in conflict with the Constitution. Therefore the court did not have the power to issue the requested writ of mandamus. The Constitution was supreme over all legislation. The Supreme Court was empowered to decide whether any law, state or federal, was in accord with it. Hence the Supreme Court had the last word on what was legal and what was not. But Mr. Marbury must apply elsewhere for his writ.

The chessboard was set. With his decision in Marbury vs. Madison John Marshall made the first move in the long contest between the executive and the judiciary.

John Randolph was no lawyer. Even as a debater he hardly proved a match for the Federalist attorneys. Impeaching Judge Pickering turned out deceptively easy. His best friends didn't deny the man's incompetence. He failed to appear to answer charges. In spite of the Federalist plea that, being insane, he was incapable of standing trial, the Republican managers obtained the twothirds vote of the Senate necessary for his removal.

The impeachment of Supreme Court Justice Samuel Chase of Maryland was another matter. Chase was an intemperate Federal partisan and he certainly drank too much, but he was far from being incompetent. A great bear of a man, more than six feet tall and almost as wide, swollen with selfsatisfaction and high living, he was thoroughly steeped in English law and he fought like a wildcat.

John Randolph seems to have felt the difficulty of his task from the moment he began to write up the articles of impeachment. John Quincy Adams, who was all for the counterbalancing judicial power his father had set up, and who felt a supercilious detestation for John Randolph, in his diary described that orator's performance during the trial as "consisting altogether of the most hackneyed commonplaces of popular declamation, mingled up with panegyrics and invectives upon persons; with a few well-expressed ideas, a few striking figures, much distortion of face and contortion of body, tears groans and sobs; with occasional pauses for recollection and continual complaint of having lost his notes."

Although the Federalists were in a cold sweat for fear the impeachment would succeed, the Republican managers felt dispirited from the first. John Randolph's ranting and raving astonished friend and foe. Representative Manasseh Cutler of Massachusetts wrote home of his "outrageous invectives against the Judge . . . in the midst of his harrangue the fellow cried like a baby with clear, sheer madness."

It may have been in sudden reaction to the realization of his own inadequacy for the task of removing Justice Chase that John Randolph turned on another administration measure with all the waspish eloquence which, at his best, he could command.

The Yazoo claims were a problem Jefferson had inherited from past administrations. During the full fury of speculation in public lands in the 1790s investment companies had managed to bribe every member but one of the Georgia legislature, so the story went, to put through what amounted to a steal of vast tracts claimed by that state between its westernmost settlements and the fertile delta formed by the Yazoo River where it emptied into the Mississippi. One of the accomplishments of Jefferson's first administration was to induce the state of Georgia to cede the disputed area to the federal government. The legislature had already rescinded the grant as fraudulent. Gallatin, Madison, and Levi Lincoln, the now retired Attorney General, spent, under the President's direction, many months working out a compromise settlement which they thought would be fair to all concerned: to the squatters on the land, to the Indians who were being dispossessed, and to the speculators, mostly New Englanders and many of them recent converts to Republicanism, whose titles, acquired in good faith, were in danger of extinction.

As the owner of an inherited estate, John Randolph hated speculation in land. As a bigoted Virginian he distrusted New Englanders. When the Yazoo compromise came up in the form of a bill he violently attacked the section which compensated the speculators. His bitter tonguelashing of the Postmaster General, Gideon Granger, who was lobbying for the bill, threw the whole administration phalanx into disarray. He accused Granger of profiting himself from the validation of the Yazoo paper.

The Yazoo bill passed but Justice Chase's impeachment failed. John Randolph went bitterly home to the log house he lived in on the Roanoke River surrounded by his dogs and his horses and his Negroes. When he returned to Washington for the opening of the Ninth Congress he found that Gideon Granger's friends had marshaled the northern Republicans against him. Granger had vowed that either he or Randolph must fall. When Granger was asked whether he meant to call Randolph out, he said he meant fall "as a public man."

Barnabas Bidwell of Massachusetts was now administration floor leader of the House. John Randolph and his quids became an Ishmaelite band. Their hand was raised against every man and every man's hand was raised against them. It was a situation which John Randolph found thoroughly to his liking.

4. *A Family Feud*

Throughout the impeachments of Pickering and Chase the real target of the administration forces was the Chief Justice. If Chase could be removed, John Marshall would be next. No man knew that better than John Marshall. He defended himself by his own peculiar methods, never admitting for a moment that he was engaged in a contest of any kind. Neither Marshall nor Jefferson was allowing the vendetta between them to be seen on the surface.

The Chief Justice's disarming manner was a disappointment to many Federalists who wanted to see him lead the charge against the enemy democrats. Senator Plumer wrote in his notes that he was more impressed by John Marshall's brother William when both men testified at the Chase trial.

The Marshalls were a clan. One of the brothers was clerk of the United States Circuit Court in Virginia where Chase had gone to such extreme lengths to bolster the prosecution against a printer named Callender indicted under the Alien and Sedition Acts.

Plumer noted his admiration for the "frankness, fairness & I will add firmness" of William Marshall's testimony. "His testimony was of it-self . . . a complete defense for the accused.—Unless it can be destroyed." Plumer preferred William to his brother John. "The Chief Justice discovered too much caution—too much fear—too much cunning—He ought to have been more bold—frank & explicit than he was. There was in his manner an evident disposition to accommodate the Managers. That dignified frankness which his high office required did not appear. A cunning man ought never to discover the arts of the trimmer in his testimony."

Like John Randolph and Thomas Jefferson, John Marshall was descended from the Randolphs of Turkey Island. The cousins did not necessarily agree. The incompatibility of temperament between the President and the Chief Justice finally took on the characteristics of a family feud.

There was a great deal that was similar in their bringing up. Like the President's father, Peter Jefferson, the Chief Justice's father Thomas Marshall was a frontiersman of the old school. Both men came from the yeomanry, were selfeducated, acquired large holdings of land, and married into the Tidewater aristocracy. Like Peter Jefferson, Thomas Marshall served in the House of Burgesses and in various county offices. While Jefferson's early associations with the gentry were with the Tuckahoe Randolphs, Marshall's were with the Fairfaxes of the Potomac shore and their dependents the Washingtons.

While Jefferson was raised the oldest of two boys in a family of girls, Marshall had to cope with a great gang of younger brothers. The Marshalls were a lusty crew. All fifteen of them reached maturity. The Albemarle County of Jefferson's early years was somewhat closer to Williamsburg and to the great world than the cove in the Blue Ridge in what was later to be Fauquier where Marshall spent his first nineteen years.

Marshall was twelve years younger. Jefferson's background was more cultivated. There was more of the enlightenment in Jefferson's schooling and more of the expanding frontier in Marshall's. Jefferson's father died when he was fourteen, leaving him a large landowner. Marshall's father lived on vigorously to be the intellectual companion of his adolescent years. It wasn't till Thomas Marshall moved to Kentucky after the peace that he became a man of means.

In the selfdeprecating letter John Marshall as an old man wrote Justice Story in response to a request for some autobiographical notes, he told of his father's setting him to copy out Alexander Pope's *Essay on Man* when he was twelve. Pope, Edmund Burke, Blackstone, and Adam Smith were the whole of his literary education. He picked up the law in court from the pleadings of other lawyers and from the rulings of judges. He developed an extraordinary knack for learning as he went along. The profoundest influence remained Pope's iambic expression of the reasoned pragmatism of the English eighteenth century:

I turned the tuneful art
From sounds to things, from fancy to the heart;
For wit's false mirror held up nature's light,
Showed erring pride—whatever is is right;
That reason, passion, answer one great aim;
That true self-love and social are the same,
That virtue only makes our bliss below,
And all our knowledge is—ourselves to know.

"He was my only intelligent companion," Marshall wrote Story of his father, "and was both a watchful parent and an affectionate and instructive friend. The young men within my reach were entirely uncultivated; and the time I spent with them was devoted to hardy athletic exercises."

Both Jefferson and Marshall were men of rugged physical health. Marshall tended to veil his analytic powers behind the common man pose of a backwoodsman. He was a great jokester. Where Jefferson learned by reading, Marshall learned by his ears. Jefferson, whose upbringing was that of a country gentleman of scientific tastes, tended towards a speculative aloofness. Marshall delighted in cornfield humor. He was raised to the rough and tumble.

As soon as the Revolutionary War began Marshall enlisted in the militia. Soldiering, even in a cause that engaged him passionately, would never have occurred to Jefferson. Thomas Marshall was already lieutenant colonel in a Virginia regiment. Young John, barely turned twenty, first served as a lieutenant in the fighting around Norfolk. After Monmouth Court House two years later he was promoted to captain. He attributed his devotion to the Union to that service. "I found myself associated with brave men from different states who were risking life and everything valuable in a common cause believed by all to be most precious:—I was confirmed in the habit of considering America as my country, and congress as my government."

He came away from his army service one of George Washington's most devoted partisans. His father had known and worked with the general as a youth when they were both surveyors for Lord Fairfax. Personal allegiance to George Washington was strong among the whole Marshall clan.

Back in Virginia, away from the general's personal influence, Captain Marshall soon lost interest in a military career. His father had planned all along to make a lawyer of him. When the enlistments of his militiamen expired he took advantage of a furlough to study law at William and Mary. He was a very plausible young man. He was promptly elected to Phi Beta Kappa. After taking careful notes on George Wythe's lectures for about a month, he got himself admitted to the Virginia bar. Thomas Jefferson, as governor, signed his license to practice.

Arnold's invasion threw him back into the service but it was not long before he resigned his commission. As he put it to Justice Story: "I thought I might without violating the duty I owed my country, pay some attention to my future prospects in life."

John Marshall had a career to make. He was head over heels in love. He was ardently wooing the daughter of a York River magnate whose estates had been devastated by Cornwallis and who was reduced to trying to support his family on his stipend as treasurer of Virginia.

Since the courts were still closed John Marshall turned to politics. Fauquier County returned him to the Assembly. His fellow delegates were so taken with him they elected him to the Executive Council. As a member of the Executive Council, in spite of his mountaineer look, the slouch hat and slovenly dress and the loosejointed lounging stance that had thrown the girls off at first, John Marshall was in a position to ask for the hand of Jacquelin Ambler's daughter. He was twentyeight years old. She was a little more than fifteen.

Now this attractive Polly Ambler, who was to be the center of all the love and affection John Marshall had in him for almost fifty years of married life, was the daughter of the Becky Burwell who was Thomas Jefferson's college sweetheart. After their falling out the fair Rebecca married Jacquelin Ambler on the rebound. Her bitterness against Jefferson was so strong that she passed it on to her children. Since his putting through the law to abolish entail, and his efforts to end slavery, hatred of everything Jefferson stood for was becoming an obsession with the Tidewater gentry. The Amblers had almost split their sides laughing at the story of how Jefferson had to run out of Monticello with Tarleton's troopers on his heels on the last day of his term as governor.

John Marshall settled down with his adored wife to practice law in the raw new town of Richmond. The Richmond bar was a roster of great names: Edmund Randolph, Edmund Pendleton, John Wickham, Alexander Campbell. Without cracking a lawbook, merely by listening to lawyers and jurists arguing in court, Marshall became, in a very few years, the admitted leader of his profession.

From Pope and Blackstone and his own welldeveloped acquisitive instinct, he imbibed an enthusiasm for property rights. He defended the legality of the Fairfax proprietorship of the Northern Neck against the sequestrations carried out by wartime Virginia legislatures.

When Gouverneur Morris and Robert Morris turned up in Richmond in the course of their campaign to monopolize the tobacco trade with France, he became the lawyer for the Morris interests. His brother James married Robert Morris' daughter Hester. The Marshall brothers joined with Robert Morris in a syndicate to take over the Fairfax claims once they could be extricated from the depredations of voteconscious legislatures who wanted to extinguish the British quitrents forever. Their struggle to build themselves a fortune out of the Fairfax properties was to have a profound influence on the course of John Marshall's thinking.

John Marshall was a convivial young man. His account book abounded in expenditures for wines, whiskey, and punch. He was fond of whist and backgammon. He was a member of both the aristocratic Cincinnati and of the more popular Society of St. Tammany. He subscribed to balls and horse races and to the club at Formicola's Tavern. He was an active parishioner of St. John's Church. He was fond of the theatre.

His best friend in those days was a young lawyer from the Northern Neck, Jefferson's protégé, James Monroe. When Albert Gallatin frequented Richmond, while he was searching the wilderness for a place to found a settlement of Swiss, Marshall offered to take the shrewd young foreigner into his law office.

Though he was an enthusiastic Federalist from the first days of the Constitutional Convention, it was as a man of the people that he campaigned for a limitation of popular rule. When, during the impassioned campaign for ratification, he was elected to the legislature from Henrico County, he was seen dancing with his supporters round a bonfire which they stoked with the opposition ballots in front of the polling table.

At the Virginia convention John Marshall was closely associated with the spokesmen for the settlers on the Western Waters. His father, a couple of brothers, and Humphrey Marshall, the cousin who had married one of his sisters, were all prominent in the affairs of what was still the District of Kentucky. He backed up Pendleton, Wythe, and Madison in their arguments for ratification. His particular task was to elaborate in a series of speeches the theory of the division of power. He urged with particular energy the need for independence in the judiciary.

George Washington, from his retirement at Mount Vernon, was exerting all the influence he could muster with his fellow Virginians to defend the Constitution against Patrick Henry's oratory and the scholarly libertarianism of George Mason. John Marshall took upon himself the role of Revolutionary veteran calling on good patriots to support their Commander in Chief.

When party lines hardened between Jeffersonians and Hamiltonians during Washington's second administration John Marshall found himself the chief defender of the President's policies in Virginia. He spoke out for the Jay treaty. On a trip to Philadelphia to argue a case before the Supreme Court he became friendly with such extreme New England Federalists as Fisher Ames, George Cabot, and Theodore Sedgwick.

In spite of his unpopular views John Marshall remained one of the most popular men in Richmond. He early served as city recorder. He was appointed major general of the militia. It was on the recommendation of the New England Federalists that John Adams chose him to join Charles Cotesworth Pinckney and Elbridge Gerry on the mission to France that blew up in the XYZ scandal. Marshall explained to his friends quite frankly that he accepted the job, which was uncommonly well paid for a diplomatic appointment, because he needed the money.

Robert Morris' unexpected bankruptcy left the Marshall brothers facing the alternative of promptly raising a large sum in cash or losing their investment in the Fairfax properties. After the failure of the mission to France he landed in Philadelphia with his knowledge of the world much extended and with nineteen thousand dollars in his pocket. His notes on the doings in Paris remain an amusing and lighthearted commentary on that odd episode. He was greeted as a conquering hero by the Federalists from South Carolina to Maine.

It was at George Washington's insistence that he entered national politics by running for Congress in 1799. It fell upon him, as Washington's leading representative in Virginia, to announce the general's death to the House and to move the famous resolution, which Harry

Lee had written: "expressive of the profound sorrow with which Congress is penetrated on the loss of a citizen, first in war, first in peace, and first in the hearts of his countrymen."

Serving in Congress was a sacrifice in many ways. It meant giving up a lucrative legal practice in Richmond. His investments in the Fairfax lands and the estate his father gave him in Fauquier County and his military claims in Kentucky needed tending. His dear Polly was almost an invalid. Though she was to bear him ten children, six of whom survived to grow up, she suffered from what was described as a nervous disorder that made her pathetically dependent on her husband's tender attentions. Already they had two boys of school age and a five year old girl.

In Congress Marshall sided with the Federalists, but Sedgwick and Cabot complained in their letters to New England that he was too much of a Virginian to be a perfect Federalist.

His Federalism, like Washington's, was a development of the nationalism which had animated the Continental troops. He envisaged the federal government as the upholder of contracts and treaties, and the protector of the citizen's right to the quiet enjoyment of his property.

To the annoyance of the New Englanders he voted for the repeal of the Alien and Sedition laws. At the same time he opposed a resolution which would reopen the question of abolishing slavery. The transatlantic slave trade was already on the way to being outlawed in spite of the arguments of some New England shipowners that by so doing Congress abandoned to foreigners the profits of a lucrative traffic.

Marshall's most remembered speech in Congress was in defense of John Adams' surrendering to the British, under the extradition clause of the Jay treaty, a mutineer accused of murder who claimed to be a citizen of Connecticut. The Robbins case continued to furnish campaign ammunition to the Republicans even after it was pretty well proved that the man really was a British subject as the Royal Navy claimed. Albert Gallatin, who, as floor leader for the Republican minority, was expected to produce an answer, exclaimed that the points Marshall made in favor of strict observance of the treaty were unanswerable.

At the close of the session, writing to Rufus King, the Newburyport lawyer whom Washington had appointed minister to England, Speaker Sedgwick summed up his impressions of the Virginian: "He is a man of very affectionate disposition, of great simplicity of manners and honest & honorable in all his conduct. He is attached to pleasures with convivial habits strongly fixed. He is indolent therefore, and indisposed to take part in the common business of the house. He has a strong attachment to popularity but indisposed to sacrifice to it his integrity: hence it is that he is disposed on all popular subjects to feel the public pulse and hence results indecision and an expression of doubt."

Sedgwick could not approve Marshall's courting popularity. "He is disposed," he complained, "to express great respect for the sovereign people. . . . The latter is of all things the most destructive of personal independence & of that weight of character which a great man ought to possess."

President Adams appreciated the "weight of character" behind Marshall's disarmingly lackadaisical manner. Marshall had been proving his personal loyalty by continuing to support the President after Adams' break with the Hamiltonians and the extreme New England Federalists.

He did refuse to replace his good friend McHenry when John Adams suddenly blew up in the face of that amiable Baltimorean and summarily dismissed him as Secretary of War; but when Adams removed Pickering for good cause Marshall felt in duty bound to take over the Department of State.

During the stormy last weeks of his presidency Adams failed to convince John Jay that he should accept appointment as Chief Justice. Marshall called on the President to suggest the choice of William Paterson, the esteemed New Jersey jurist who had proved himself a zealous Federalist during the prosecutions under the Alien and Sedition laws. Adams, possibly because Judge Paterson was such a good friend of Hamilton's, wouldn't hear of him.

As Marshall remembered the interview in his letter to Story, "he said in a decided tone: 'I shall not nominate him.' After a moment's hesitation he said 'I believe I must nominate you.' . . . I was pleased as well as surprized, and bowed in silence."

When Thomas Jefferson strolled over to the Capitol for his first inauguration it was Chief Justice John Marshall who handed him the Bible and administered the oath of office. Though Marshall had not openly favored Burr during the period of the contested election, he had let it be known through the columns of the *National Federalist* that he considered his cousin Jefferson the worst possible choice for the presidency. When Marshall's own name was suggested as temporary President, if the tie in the House of Representatives could not be broken, he did nothing to discourage the idea. As Chief Justice and acting Secretary of State, and as John Adams' private adviser, he was already wielding what little executive power remained in the breakup of John Adams' administration.

When Jefferson was declared elected Marshall accepted the situation with his usual air of good nature. Though he was dead set on supporting the system he believed in through the exercise of the judicial power, he was in no hurry to show his hand.

His chief preoccupation during the first years of Jefferson's administration was with the state of his own private finances. His salary was only four thousand a year. As Secretary of State he had been able to continue his law practice, but as Chief Justice that was impossible. He and his brother still owed over thirty thousand dollars on the Fairfax deal. His domestic expenses were high because he didn't dare for the present expose his ailing wife to the dangers of the Washington climate, and riding circuit and attending sessions at the national capital would force him to be much away from home. He hit upon a scheme which he hoped would bring him in a pile of money. He would write a life of George Washington.

George Washington's lawyer nephew, Bushrod Washington, was an associate justice and a sincere friend. He had charge of the general's letters and papers. Washington suggested to Marshall that Marshall was the man to write his uncle's biography. He would thereby bolster the cause of Federalism and good government and net them both a handsome profit.

After some correspondence with publishers and printers Marshall and Bushrod Washington convinced themselves that a life of the father of his country in five volumes would bring in one hundred and fifty thousand dollars which they would divide, share and share alike. The Philadelphia Quaker named C. P. Wayne who secured the copyright as publisher soon convinced them that their expectations were fantastic. He did promise to pay them a dollar a volume for every volume he sold of the fivevolume work. John Marshall, who had at first suggested that one year would be ample, now contracted to dash off his hero's biography in two.

When Jefferson got wind of the enterprise he immediately wrote Joel Barlow, who was still in Paris making his fortune in French funds, begging him to come home to write the true history of the United States. "your residence here is essential, because a great deal of the knowledge of things is not on paper, but only within ourselves"—he was speaking of himself and Madison—"for verbal communication." His opinion was that Marshall's book would be written "principally with a view to electioneering purposes."

John Marshall meanwhile was finding the work heavy going. He had no training as a historian. He was not a man of letters. He became so entangled with the early history of the colonies that George Washington's name barely appeared in the first volume. The publisher complained bitterly of the intolerable length of the second. Marshall went on writing and writing. Events he had experienced or felt deeply like the Battle of Monmouth or Arnold's treason he described with zest, but in most of the thousands of pages his admiration for the hero of his youth smothered in a morass of verbiage.

It was only in the final volume, which he wrote after the failure of the impeachment proceedings against Justice Chase had freed his mind from the fear of being removed from the office which was now his only steady source of livelihood, that he reached a narrative stride.

Marshall's *Life of Washington* was sold by subscription. Wayne had hoped the postmasters would secure subscribers as a public service, but most of the postmasters turned out to be Republicans and offered little cooperation. Marshall and his friends ascribed this lack of enthusiasm to the personal malignity of President Jefferson.

One of Wayne's principal book agents to drum up subscriptions was the inimitable Parson Weems. Weems's own *Life of Washington* sold exceedingly well. The Reverend Mason L. Weems was a Marylander from Anne Arundel County who was ordained an Episcopal minister in England. With the Church disestablished he found it impossible to support his large family by preaching so he turned to biography and to peddling books.

Besides his successful primer on Washington he produced edifying sketches of Benjamin Franklin and William Penn, devotional tracts, and temperance pamphlets such as *The Drunkard's Looking Glass*. He traveled the length and breadth of the land from New England to Georgia, his saddlebags stuffed with sample books, selling subscriptions and pamphlets. Wagonloads of books lumbered after him. He preached at camp meetings. He played the fiddle at country dances. He delivered patriotic addresses to state legislatures. He was the most successful book agent of his time.

Although personally a Republican, breathing out brotherhood and love, Parson Weems was a conscientious salesman. He did his best with Marshall's *Washington* but his enthusiasm soon cooled. The first volume raised a storm of protest from the subscribers. They had paid their money to read about George Washington, not for a rehash of colonial history. The second gave them the impression that the great man's life "would be prostituted to party purposes," Weems wrote Wayne. "Give old Washington fair play and all will be well," he exhorted. "Let but the Interior of the Work be Liberal and the Exterior Elegant, and Town House and a Country House, a Coach and a Sideboard and Massy Plate shall be thine."

Marshall finished the fifth volume in the summer of 1806. He had at first been reluctant to allow his name to appear on the title page. He admitted suffering many a pang when discrepancies and errors were brought to his attention. Subsequently he spent years of his life trying to revise the biography for later editions.

Financially the publication proved a disappointment. Though the publisher was an honest man and did his best, all he was able to squeeze out for his authors was around ten thousand dollars to be divided between them.

As the years went on Jefferson continued to view Marshall's efforts as a historian with the same hostility with which he regarded the Chief

Justice's judicial opinions: "The sufferings inflicted on endeavors to vindicate the rights of humanity are related with all the frigid insensibility with which a monk would have contemplated the victims of an auto da fe," was how he summed up his feelings. "Let no man believe that Gen. Washington ever intended that his papers should be used for the suicide of the cause, for which he had lived, and for which there never was a moment in which he would not have died."

5. The Chief Justice Rules on Treason

The spring of 1807 found John Marshall freed at last from the drudgery of historical writing. For better or worse the stacks of sheets closely written in violet ink, which finally amounted to more than half a million words, were in the hands of the publisher. While he worked, the tide of democracy, which he was hoping to stem, rose and rose. Thomas Jefferson's popularity had never been so high.

It was the explosion of the Burr conspiracy, after it had smoldered in rumor and gossip for months, that gave the Chief Justice his first opportunity to exhibit "that weight of character" Theodore Sedgwick claimed "a great man ought to possess."

His decision in Marbury vs. Madison had been a theoretical exercise with no immediate effect on events. Now an appeal to the Supreme Court for a writ of habeas corpus presented the occasion to exhibit the judicial power in its most popular light as protector of civil liberties, and at the same time to administer a rebuke to President Jefferson's administration.

January 21 Dr. Erick Bollmann, the German adventurer whose misfortunes were well known in Philadelphia, and young Sam Swartwout of New York were brought to the marine barracks in Washington and there detained under heavy guard.

These were the first of several batches of prisoners whom General Wilkinson was arresting as implicated in Burr's schemes and shipping north from New Orleans. From the moment the vainglorious general decided to turn in Aaron Burr the desperate need to clear his own name kept him in a tantrum. He puffed up the conspiracy out of all reason. In his letters he ranted and stormed of dangers by sea and land. When he reached New Orleans he brushed Claiborne aside, disregarded the courts, and set himself up as a military dictator. He sent out squads to arrest anyone suspected of dealing with Burr they could lay their hands on. He showed himself particularly zealous to implicate in Burr's plot anybody who might have damaging revelations to make about his own connection with the little colonel.

Two days after the arrival in Washington of Swartwout and Bollmann, the Republicans, catching some of the contagion of the panic Wilkinson was promoting in New Orleans, introduced a bill in the

Senate temporarily to suspend the right of habeas corpus in cases of treason. In the debate as recorded by Senator Plumer, it transpired that the aim of the measure was to hold Bollmann and Swartwout until they could be induced to testify against Burr. John Quincy Adams, who was no friend of Jefferson's, was among its adherents. The bill passed the Senate by a large majority.

Meanwhile Swartwout and Bollmann were indicted on the charge of treason before the district court and held without bail in the custody of the marines. Bollmann was in a blue funk. He asked to see the President and in a long interview with Jefferson and Madison poured out all he knew of Burr's dealings with Merry and Yrujo. He offered to turn state's evidence. Jefferson promised him a pardon if he did so.

By the time the bill for suspending habeas corpus reached the House such circumstantial accounts of Burr's failure to engage any large force in his undertaking had reached Washington that, undoubtedly at Jefferson's suggestion, Jack Eppes led the opposition. The bill was overwhelmingly defeated and its adherents in the Senate made no effort to revive it. "I hope I shall never again consent," noted Plumer, who had voted yea, "to the passage of an important law in haste."

Jefferson wrote immediately to Wilkinson in a tone calculated to coax the general off his high horse: "Your belief that Burr would really descend with six or seven thousand men, was no doubt founded on what you knew of the numbers which could be raised in the Western country for an expedition against Mexico, under the authority of the government; but you did not calculate that the want of that authority would take from him every honest man, and leave him only the desperadoes. . . . in approving, therefore, as we do approve, of the defensive operations for New Orleans, we are obliged to estimate them, not according to our own view of the danger, but to place ourselves in your situation, and only with your information."

The implication was that, seen from Washington, Wilkinson's dictatorial measures were hardly justified by the danger; but that, seen from New Orleans, they possibly were. The same day the President wrote Claiborne that "every good officer must be ready to risk himself in going beyond the strict line of law, when the public preservation requires it."

Jefferson added to Wilkinson that public opinion would approve the arrest of Swartwout and Bollmann and would certainly approve any measures necessary to send Burr, Blennerhasset, and Comfort Tyler north for trial. "I hope however, you will not extend this deportation to persons against whom there is only suspicion. . . ." He went on to tell Wilkinson that the general was getting a bad press but that the administration would see to it that his conduct should appear in a better light.

"Burr and his emissaries found it convenient to sow a distrust in your mind of our dispositions towards you; but be assured that you will be cordially supported in the line of your duties."

Wilkinson was the commander of the only military force the administration had at its disposal on the Mississippi and Jefferson had made up his mind, in spite of the clamor in Congress, where Wilkinson was taking Burr's place as the villain of the piece, that this was too ticklish a time to try to replace the General in Chief of the Army of the United States.

The same group of Maryland Federalist lawyers who had defended Justice Chase hurried to the assistance of Bollmann and Swartwout. They appealed to the Supreme Court for a writ of habeas corpus.

At noon on February 21 John Marshall delivered the opinion of the majority of the court. He began by enlarging on the definition of treason which the Constitution described as consisting "only of levying war against them, and adhering to their enemies, and giving them aid and comfort. . . . If a body of men be actually assembled for the purpose of effecting by force a treasonable purpose," explained the Chief Justice, "all those who perform any part, however minute or however remote from the scene of the action, and who are actually leagued in the general conspiracy, are to be considered as traitors."

This pronouncement, taken at face value, seemed to support the actions of the administration in allowing Wilkinson to stretch the law a little in order to deliver the malefactors to the courts. But Marshall promptly brought up the question of whether Burr's enterprise was actually treasonable. He analyzed Wilkinson's version of Burr's cypher epistle, which the Attorney General had included in the government's brief, and decided, on no particular evidence but his own personal opinion, that the wording would apply better to an expedition against Mexico than to an expedition against New Orleans. Even the reported remarks about Burr's intention to do "some seizing" at New Orleans indicated a design to rob and not necessarily a design to commit treason.

He found the evidence against Bollmann far weaker than that against Swartwout. Even if both men had been engaged in "a culpable enterprise against the dominions of a power at peace with the United States," the crime had not been committed in the District of Columbia.

Had there existed a tribunal in New Orleans, concluded Justice Marshall, sarcastically referring to the resignation of federal Judge Workman, who had disbanded his court rather than countenance Wilkinson's illegal arrests, it was in New Orleans the defendants should have been tried.

Unanimously the justices granted the writ and Bollman walked out a free man amid the congratulations of the Federalist crowd.

Congressional interest in the case had been so great that neither the Senate nor the House was able to secure a quorum while the hearing went on. As soon as the Republican representatives were back in their chamber there was loud talk of impeaching the entire court or at least of securing a constitutional amendment to take jurisdiction away from the Supreme Court in criminal cases; but the tide of opinion shifted with every dispatch from New Orleans.

Soon many Republicans were approving John Marshall's decision. John Randolph attacked Wilkinson's arrests as "the most daring usurpation which ever did, will or can happen in this or any country."

Anger against Burr was quite forgotten in the indignation lashed up against Wilkinson's illegal acts. When another group of Wilkinson's victims, General John Adair, Peter V. Ogden, and James Alexander, were landed on the Baltimore dock they were freed by the first court they applied to.

Leaving the clamor of Washington behind him, John Marshall was already making his way in a leisurely fashion through the early spring countryside to preside over the summer term of the district court of the United States in his home city of Richmond.

CHAPTER IV

Confrontation at Richmond

1. The Cast Assembles: Burr's Examination

On March 27 Aaron Burr wrote from Richmond to his daughter Theodosia, who had hurried back to South Carolina with Mari and little Gamp as soon as it became clear that her father's castle in the air had collapsed: "My military escort having arrived at Fredericksburg on our way to Washington, there met a special messenger, with orders to convey me to this place. . . . I am to be surrendered to the civil authority tomorrow, when the question of bail is to be determined. In the mean time I remain at the Eagle Tavern."

Burr spent the next three days under guard at that respectable hostelry. While all Richmond buzzed with the excitement of his arrival he was busy with the tailor rigging him more suitable apparel than the boatman's trousers and floppy felt hat which were already notorious. The consummate actor was preparing to play his greatest role.

During those days he managed somehow to secure funds and to get in touch with wellwishers who would be willing to stand bail. Then, around noon on March 30—so David Robertson, an attorney who knew shorthand and who stepped forward to record the proceedings, described the scene—"The United States Marshall for the District of Virginia, attended by two of his deputies, waited on Colonel Burr at his lodgings . . . and, after informing him in the most respectful manner of the nature and object of his visit, conducted him through an awfully silent and attentive assemblage of citizens to a retired room in the house where he was brought before Chief Justice Marshall for examination."

Since the room was small the initial stages of Burr's examination were carried on in private. The government's case was in the hands of George Hay, United States district attorney for Virginia, because Blennerhasset's island on the Ohio, the chief scene of the alleged crimes, was within the confines of that enormous commonwealth.

George Hay, then a little over forty, was the son of Anthony Hay, the popular host of the Raleigh Tavern in Williamsburg in pre-Revolutionary days. He was raised in the full fervor of Virginia libertarianism, studied law, and made a name for himself by a tract in favor of the liberty of the press during the agitation against the Alien and Sedition laws, and by vigorously Jeffersonian articles signed Hortensius in the Richmond *Examiner*. A blunt downright man, full of fervor for the Republican cause, he was married to Monroe's elder daughter.

On behalf of Burr appeared two of the most esteemed members of the Richmond bar: portly Edmund Randolph, onetime governor of Virginia, whose misadventures as Secretary of State under Washington had been forgotten in his success as an advocate in later life; and John Wickham, a Long Island man, reputed to have come from a family of Tories, whom William Wirt in his *British Spy* essays found "distinguished by a quickness of look, a sprightly step, and that peculiarly jaunty air which I have mentioned as characterizing the people of New York." Besides the lawyers no one was admitted except "a few friends invited by counsel for Colonel Burr."

George Hay presented a copy of the evidence on which the Attorney General had based his charges against Bollmann and Swartwout. Nicholas Perkins told what seemed a plain tale of Burr's arrest, though Robert Ashley later categorically contradicted some of the details. Hay moved forthwith that the prisoner be committed first on the charge of high misdemeanor in preparing a military expedition against the dominions of the King of Spain. Further he contended that there was cause to believe that the prisoner had committed acts of treason. He referred to the broad interpretation of the constitutional definition which had been promulgated by the Supreme Court in the Chief Justice's own words only a month before in the case of Bollmann and Swartwout. Since argument by counsel would be necessary on this motion, all parties agreed to move the proceedings up the hill from Main Street, where the Eagle Tavern with its stables and yards occupied an entire block, to the courtroom in Thomas Jefferson's new Ionic Capitol.

Next morning the Chief Justice appeared betimes on the bench. William Wirt, who was soon to appear in the case himself, had described him a couple of years before as "in person tall, meagre and emaciated; his muscles relaxed and his joints so loosely connected, as not only to disqualify him apparently for any vigorous exertion of body, but to destroy anything like elegance and harmony in his air and movements. . . . He is as far removed from the idealized graces of Lord Chesterfield as any man on earth. . . . His head and face are small in proportion to his height, his complexion swarthy, the muscles of his face relaxed . . . his countenance has a faithful expression of great good humor and hilarity; while his black eyes . . . possess an irradiating spirit which proclaims the imperial powers of his mind. . . . Without the aid of fancy, without the advantages of person, voice, attitude, gesture or any of the ornaments of an orator, he deserves to be considered one of the most eloquent men in the world; if eloquence may be said to consist in the power of seizing the attention with irresistible force. . . . His voice is hard and dry; his attitude . . . often extremely awkward; as it was not unusual for him to stand with his left foot in advance, while all his gesture proceeded from his right arm, and consisted merely in a vehement perpendicular swing of it, from about the elevation of his head to the bar, behind which he was accustomed to stand. . . . All his eloquence consists in the apparently deep self-conviction, and emphatic earnestness of his manner."

Caesar Augustus Rodney, the recently appointed Attorney General of the United States, who had allowed George Hay to conduct the opening proceedings, was now preparing to speak up for the prosecution. Burr's lawyers were eager to begin the defense. The crowded courtroom waited breathless. A half an hour late Colonel Burr appeared, announcing with a confident smile that he had mistaken the time.

Since the stairways and lobbies were packed with Richmonders trying to get in, proceedings were adjourned to the hall of the House of Delegates. Randolph and Wickham launched into their argument. Intent was no basis for a charge of treason. Colonel Burr rose and in his most courtly manner pointed out that he had already been acquitted of these charges in Kentucky and Mississippi, that in each case he himself had sought an investigation: that he had forfeited no recognizance but had merely retired to avoid the illegal seizure of his person and property by a military force. His role was still injured innocence. He asked why the guards who conducted him to that place avoided every magistrate on the way, unless from a conviction that they were acting without lawful authority. "Why had he been debarred from the use of pen, ink and paper, and not even permitted to write to his daughter?"

William H. Cabell, then governor of Virginia, was one of the spectators. He wrote his brother Joseph, Jefferson's lifelong friend, a couple of days later: "I have not been able to think of anything but Colonel Burr for several days. . . . The public anxiety was greater than I ever saw it. . . . Burr made a short speech after his lawyers had finished but it was very inferior to my expectation. Those who knew him formerly say he is much broken, but he has still the finest eye I ever saw, and during the trial, looked as little like a criminal as any man in the room—on this trying occasion he conducted himself with infinite dignity & propriety."

Burr had failed as a revolutionist, but he remained matchless as a courtroom lawyer. As the proceedings advanced he regained all his aplomb. This was a world he knew how to deal with. Attack was the best defense.

He knew that Thomas Jefferson was personally directing the prosecution from Washington. The prosecution's case must rest on Wilkinson. Burr now felt that the ranting General in Chief, whom a few weeks back he had relied on as his partner in high adventure, would be the easiest man in the world to discredit. He knew that the Chief Justice hated Jefferson as hard as he did. If he could attack Jefferson through Wilkinson, he could not help winning John Marshall's sympathy. On the whole he held a good hand of cards.

Burr must have listened with a certain relish to Caesar Augustus Rodney's rambling address. The Attorney General was almost apologetic. He spoke of the high offices Colonel Burr had held and of his transcendent talents and declared that he himself had considered him a friend and treated him as such in his own house. Now Aaron Burr stood charged with the most heinous crime. The chain of circumstances showed that without doubt he was guilty and must be put on his trial. Rodney added haltingly that if Burr should be acquitted by a jury of his countrymen it would give nobody more pleasure than himself, the Attorney General.

Argument followed about the amount of bail. The Chief Justice declared that on the motion to commit and on the amount of bail he preferred to submit a written opinion, "to prevent any misrepresentations of expressions which might fall from him." Court was adjourned and everybody went home to dinner. The Attorney General departed for Washington and took no further part in the proceedings.

Next morning the Chief Justice read a declaration which the prosecution heard with dismay. After quoting Blackstone's remark that in such high crimes, unless the suspicion against the accused seemed totally groundless, he must be held for trial, he capped it with a comment which was repeated gleefully at every Federalist dinner table. He did not understand Blackstone as meaning to say "that the hand of malignity may grasp any individual against whom its hate may be directed, or whom it may capriciously seize, charge him with some secret crime, and put him on the proof of his innocence."

The Chief Justice declared that he was unwilling, at this point, to commit Burr for treason, but that he felt the evidence sufficient to commit him for high misdemeanor. In explaining this decision he outlined what was to be the keynote of the defense. Reiterating his interpretation of the cypher letter, he insisted that that mysterious document pointed to an attack against the Spanish dominions instead of to a treasonable enterprise against New Orleans. Robbing the banks was no act of treason. Therefore, until the government presented more cogent evidence he would hold Colonel Burr for misdemeanor only. As to the proof of treason: "five weeks have elapsed since the opinion of the Supreme Court has declared the necessity of proving the fact if it exists. Why is it not proved?"

Treason would not have been a bailable charge, but misdemeanor was. Bail was set at ten thousand dollars, and later in the afternoon Colonel Burr presented five securities to the court, entered into recognizance for that sum to appear before the circuit court on May 22, and walked out a free man.

As soon as he rose from the bench a friend pointed out to John Marshall that the Chief Justice's remark about malignity might be interpreted as a slur on Jefferson's administration. The Chief Justice immediately explained in his genial offhand manner to Mr. Robertson, who sat with a sheaf of notes before him, that of course he meant no allusion to the conduct of the government, but merely to elucidate Blackstone's doctrine.

Aaron Burr found himself the hero of all the Federalist mansions scattered along the hilltops of Richmond, where detestation of Jefferson was becoming the password to social acceptance. Invitations poured in. The afternoon he dined with John Wickham in celebration of the initial victories of the defense, John Marshall was of the party. Wickham and the Chief Justice were warm and confidential friends. Wickham had been thoughtful enough to warn Marshall that the dinner was for Aaron Burr. Marshall, who loved a good dinner, said he'd come anyway. According to his friends, he did sit at the other end of the table, had no direct communication with the accused man, and left early.

This incident did not pass unnoticed by the Republican press. "Let me inform the conscience of the chief justice," wrote someone, possibly Thomas Ritchie himself, under the signature of "A Stranger from the Country," in Ritchie's *Enquirer* on April 10, "that the public does not view his dining with Burr as a circumstance so trivial as he himself may incline to consider it." He characterized the Chief Justice's conduct as "grossly indecent" and added: "It is impossible to separate the judge from the man."

Jefferson was anxiously studying every letter and newspaper that came in from Richmond. News of the inauspicious beginning of the prosecution's case reached him just as he was taking off for a much-needed rest at Monticello. He could see right away that the Attorney

General and George Hay were no match for the astute Federalist lawyers Burr had marshaled in his behalf. Besides Randolph and Wickham, the little colonel had been angling for the services of the Charles Lee who had been Attorney General under Washington and had helped Luther Martin defend Justice Chase, besides appearing for Marbury in Marbury vs. Madison. He had already engaged two of the brightest of the young Virginia attorneys, Benjamin Botts and John Baker. The President had heard too that Luther Martin, himself a bitter personal enemy—"an unprincipled & impudent federal bulldog," Jefferson called him—was on his way from Annapolis to join the defense.

The unhappy outcome of Chase's impeachment had proved that the ablest lawyers tended to be Federalists. The President had to make do with what Republicans he could collect. He arranged to have Alexander McRae, a gruff Scot who was lieutenant governor of Virginia, assist in the prosecution, and got off an express to William Wirt, who was trying a case in Williamsburg, engaging him for the government. Young Wirt was generally thought of as a coming man.

He was another innkeeper's son. His father was a German Swiss who kept a public house in Bladensburg on the Baltimore–Washington road. Left an orphan at an early age, Wirt was brought up to the law in the Edwards family, prominent in Virginia and Kentucky, and although barely thirtyfive had already made himself a reputation in the Virginia courts. A good Republican, he was the sort of lawyer with literary tastes Jefferson approved of. Already the author of *Letters of a British Spy*, which had turned out to be a very popular little volume, he was now devoting his spare time to a life of Patrick Henry. The President's request reached Wirt a few days before an urgent invitation arrived from Aaron Burr, still tirelessly combing the countryside for legal talent, to join his own battery of counsel. Though Wirt was admired as an orator in the florid style of the day, he still lacked the experience and scholarship needed to cope with the redoubtable talents Burr had assembled.

Jefferson was exasperated by the difficulties the Chief Justice was putting in the way of the prosecution. From Monticello he wrote William B. Giles, the administration leader in the Senate, commenting testily on "the newborn zeal for the liberty of those whom we would not permit to overthrow the liberties of their country." He riposted bitterly against John Marshall's reproach that sufficient proof of Burr's guilt had not been presented. "As if an express could go to Natchez or the mouth of Cumberland, and return in five weeks, to do which had never taken less than twelve. . . . if there had ever been an instance in this or the preceding administrations, of federal judges so applying principles of law as to condemn a federal or acquit a republican offender I should have judged them in the present case with more charity. All this however, will work well," he added with his inexhaustible optimism, "the nation will judge both the offender and the judges for themselves. . . . they will see then and amend the error in our Constitution, which makes any branch independent of the nation. . . . if their protection of Burr produces this amendment it will do more than his condemnation would have done. against Burr personally, I never had one hostile sentiment. I never indeed thought him an honest frank-dealing man but I considered him as a crooked gun, or other perverted machine, whose aim or shot you could never be sure of."

2. *The Curtain Rises: Preparations for the Trial*

Burr took high ground in his letters to Theodosia: "Was there in Greece or Rome a man of virtue and independence, and supposed to possess great talents, who was not the object of vindictive and unrelenting prosecution?" He suggested, tutorwise, that she look up the instances in ancient history and send him an essay on the subject by May 22. "I promise myself great pleasure in the perusal, and I promise you great satisfaction in the composition."

For her benefit he surveyed the scene from a far different angle from the prosecution. "The most indefatigable industry is used by the agents of government and they have money at command without stint. If I were possessed of the same means I could not only foil the prosecutors but render them ridiculous and infamous."

He complained that the grand jury was composed of twenty democrats and four Federalists. At the same time William Wirt, still stoutly maintaining to his friends that John Marshall was a fairminded man, was facing the fact that, by insistence on a technicality, the court had limited the number of grand jurors to sixteen; "and consequently the chance of the concurrence of 12 in finding a Bill was reduced to a minimum." When he got time to write an account of the proceedings to his foster brother Ninian Edwards in Kentucky he declared, "Burr and his counsel were filled with triumph at the prospect that there would be no Bill found—they displayed their triumph very injudiciously."

Duly sworn, after all challenges were exhausted, the list of the grand jurors turned out to be a roster of some of the ablest men in Virginia. When the court chose John Randolph as foreman, the Federalist dinner tables rocked with satisfaction. Nobody could accuse the Chief Justice of bias; he had chosen a Republican; but of all Republicans, John Randolph was the least friendly to Jefferson. The erstwhile administration leader in the House was making a career of opposition to the man he was coming to jeer at as St. Thomas of Cantingbury.

May 1 Burr slipped out of town, unobserved except by the vigilant eye of the Richmond *Enquirer*, on the northbound stage. A few days later the Philadelphia papers reported his arrival in that city. He was in Philadelphia to raise money. He was keeping up the pretense that he really held title to the Ouachita lands. The Republican journalists were making great sport of the number of protested notes with Burr's name on them that flowed back and forth across the country.

Pestered by Burr's creditors who held a mass of paper which he had endorsed, and in a blue funk for fear his political career was hopelessly compromised, Joseph Alston was writing President Jefferson, the governor of South Carolina, and everybody he could think of, to repudiate any connection with Burr's schemes.

In Natchez, overwhelmed by a backwash of unpaid bills, Harman Blennerhasset was using up the last remnants of his fortune to stave off debtors' prison. Soon Blanny would be reminding Alston of his promise to stand behind Burr's paper.

As May wore on Richmond filled with curious visitors. The proceedings against Aaron Burr proved the greatest show in the history of the commonwealth. Every bed in every inn was taken. Every house was stuffed with guests sleeping on truckle beds in the attics. Every stable and shed had its complement of horses and gigs. Coaches and carriages encumbered the innyards. Families of country people came in covered wagons and camped in the open lots. The streets were brilliant with uniforms of the army and navy and of various militia organizations. The ladies all wore their best. Among the men every costume was represented, from oldfashioned kneebreeches and cocked hats to nankeen pantaloons and tight tailcoats in the French style, and homespun and linseywoolsey, and fringed buckskins from the Western Waters.

Attracted by the concourse, showmen and hucksters turned up in quantity. Special horse races and wrestling matches were arranged. An enterprising dentist named John de Tellier set up shop at the Eagle Tavern and advertised his "Patent Perpendicular Extraction Instruments . . . which take out the teeth without the possibility of fracturing the jaw or bruising the gums, and with much less pain than the instruments that are generally used by surgeons and dentists."

Though many Republicans were wagering that Aaron Burr would jump his bail again, on the morning of May 22 the little colonel was seen flitting among his lawyers, cool and collected, wearing a neat suit of black silk, with his hair carefully powdered and tied in a queue. Judge Cyrus Griffin, George Washington's appointee to the Virginia District Court, joined the Chief Justice on the bench. Judge Griffin, a native of Farnham in the Northern Neck, was a modest and

competent jurist who had served on the Court of Appeals in Cases
of Capture during the war and as last president of the Continental
Congress. Though Justice Marshall was seen occasionally to consult
him sotto voce, Judge Griffin hardly opened his mouth during the
whole course of the proceedings.

The government had collected so many witnesses, there was hardly
room for the spectators. Among the witnesses was Andrew Jackson,
tall, rangy, and profane in his improvised uniform of general of the
Tennessee militia. His hair, hastily tucked into an eelskin behind, was
described as floating wildly in the breeze.

An enormous youth, standing six feet five in his stocking feet and
correspondingly broad, was prominent among the spectators. It was
Winfield Scott of Petersburg, who at that time was hopefully trying
to study law and who listened attentively to the arguments of counsel
as part of his education.

Another young attorney who attended was Washington Irving of
New York. He came as a journalist. Irving had already made himself
a name with a series of essays gently spoofing the rustic follies of his
fellow citizens. He was paid a retainer by one of Burr's Little Band
so that he could report the proceedings for the *Morning Chronicle*.

From day to day the crowds were disappointed. The proceedings
marked time. The Chief Justice would not allow the grand jury
to start its examination of witnesses until General Wilkinson should
arrive. Burr's friends scoffed loudly as May passed into June. The
general would never dare show his face. While the grand jurors sat
idle, deploring their wasted days, counsel for both sides entertained
the courtroom with a rambling and recurrent argument over the nature
of treason and on the amount of the prisoner's bail.

On May 28 the session was enlivened by the appearance of Luther
Martin on behalf of Colonel Burr. Luther Martin had been carrying
on a vendetta with Thomas Jefferson for years. He was a farmboy
from New Jersey who had moved to the Eastern Shore of Maryland.
As a young country attorney he showed himself a fanatical patriot
and a great persecutor of Tories during the Revolutionary War. He
served in the Continental Congress and signed the Declaration of Independence but vigorously opposed ratification of the Constitution.
For twentyseven years he held the office of attorney general of
Maryland. A great wassailer and brandy drinker, he was a lifelong
crony of Samuel Chase's.

His private and personal antipathy to Jefferson sprang from the
fact that his wife, who died young and to whose memory he was
devoted, was the daughter of Michael Cresap. When Jefferson published his *Notes on Virginia* he included an account of the murder
on the Ohio of the Indian chief Logan's family by a band of white
traders under Cresap's orders. The accusation was denied by the

whole Cresap clan. Jefferson collected all the facts he could. Luther Martin published an abusive pamphlet in rebuttal. The final evidence collected by Jefferson's friends on the Ohio showed that Michael Cresap was at least partly responsible. The result was bad blood between the Cresaps and Thomas Jefferson so long as Jefferson lived.

Luther Martin was further embittered by unhappiness over the misfortunes of his two daughters. A lonely rancorous man, fast drifting into helpless alcoholism, he was a prey to violent hatreds and affections. Wirt described him as "a most loose careless, slubbering speaker . . . the style very coarse . . . a blackguard of the lowest order & his rudeness seems to be now the only quality which keeps him up in the public eye." While he roared down the Republicans during the Chase trial he took a fancy to Aaron Burr. As soon as he caught sight of Theodosia she became the apple of an old man's eye.

When Burr did the handsome thing to end the dispute over bail by offering to raise his security to twenty thousand dollars "so that the court should not be embarrassed" Luther Martin stood up and offered himself as one of the sureties.

On May 25 John Randolph appeared and asked, in the sarcastic tone he was such a master of, that the grand jury be dismissed for lack of business. George Hay in great embarrassment assured the court that General Wilkinson was on his way. The sessions of the grand jury were adjourned first for a week and then from day to day.

June 9 Colonel Burr brought the spectators scurrying back into the Hall of Delegates when he rose with a motion to subpoena the President of the United States. He claimed he needed for his defense the orders sent out by the Secretaries of War and of the Navy and the original of Wilkinson's cypher letter which was in Thomas Jefferson's possession. Counsel for both sides argued the subpoena in high style for several days while the listeners sat on the edge of their chairs.

Luther Martin who, drunk or sober, was a hard man to put down rose in a fine frenzy. "All we want is the copies of some papers and the original of another. This is a peculiar case, sir. The President has undertaken to prejudge my client by declaring that 'of his guilt there can be no doubt.' He has assumed to himself the knowledge of the Supreme Being, and pretended to search the heart of my highly respected friend. He has proclaimed him a traitor in the face of that country which has rewarded him. He has let slip the dogs of war, the hellhounds of persecution, to hunt down my friend."

Four days later John Marshall granted the subpenoa, *duces tecum*, to be served on the President and the heads of departments, but when he drew up the writ the wording was: "The transmission to the Clerk of this Court of the original letter of General Wilkinson and of copies duly authenticated of the other papers and documents described in the annexed process, will be admitted as sufficient observance of the process, without the personal attendance of any or either of the persons herein named."

As the documents mentioned were already in Richmond at the disposal of the court, the motion was purely for effect.

3. *The General Puts in an Appearance*

On June 13, a Saturday, the news spread about the Capitol that General Wilkinson, with a suite of witnesses, had disembarked from a U. S. Navy schooner and was on his way to Richmond. The *Enquirer's* correspondent in reporting the general's arrival observed that the schooner saluted the frigate *Chesapeake*, outfitting off Norfolk for a Mediterranean station, before coming to anchor, and that the salute was duly returned. In the same issue the editor apologized to his subscribers for the poor quality of the paper on which the *Enquirer* was printed. He had published so many extras keeping the public informed of the course of the trial that his good newsprint had run out. Fine white paper was on its way from Philadelphia.

George Hay promptly reported to the court that only the fatigue of the journey prevented General Wilkinson from presenting himself that very day.

Immediately the court began to swear witnesses for the grand jury. Two veterans of the naval war with France, Commodore Truxton and Captain Decatur, led the way, along with Benjamin Stoddeart, who had been John Adams' very diligent Secretary of the Navy.

When Erick Bollmann's turn came George Hay tried rather clumsily to hand him the presidential pardon he had so eagerly sought during his interview with Jefferson and Madison back in Washington. Bollmann had changed his mind. He had been feted by the Richmond Federalists as a minor hero of Burr's odyssey. Emboldened by the atmosphere of success in Burr's camp, he refused to accept any pardon. Luther Martin explained that he preferred to rely on the constitutional guarantee that no man could be forced to testify against himself. The court sent him to the grand jury anyway.

Monday, June 15, the halls and lobbies of the Capitol were jammed with people. Crowds stumbled panting up Shockoe Hill. Men and boys hung from the window ledges and climbed the great trees on the eroded slope, craning their necks for a glimpse of the principal actors in the grand confrontation about to take place.

Men's accounts of the encounter in the Hall of Delegates varied according to their political persuasions. Washington Irving, writing a friend, said Wilkinson "strutted into court . . . swelling like a turkey cock." David Robertson, the stenographer, described the general's countenance as "calm, dignified and commanding, while that of Colonel Burr was marked by a haughty contempt."

Wirt's description in his letter to Ninian Edwards was possibly more discerning: "In the midst of all this hurlyburly came Wilkinson and his suite, like Pope's fame 'unlooked for,' at least by Burr's partisans. It was curious to mark the interview between Burr and Wilkinson. There was no nature in it—they had anticipated the meeting and resolved on the countenance which they would wear—Wilkinson had been some time within the bar before Burr would look towards him, affecting not to know he was there until Hay introduced him by saying to the court: 'It is my wish that General Wilkinson, who is now before the court, should be qualified and sent up to the Grand Jury.' At the words 'who is now before the court,' Burr started in his chair, turned quickly and fastened a look of scorn and contempt on Wilkinson—Wilkinson bowing to the court on his introduction did not receive Burr's first glance; but, his bow finished, he turned his face down on Burr and looked with all the sullenness and protervity of a big black bull—Burr withdrew his eyes composedly and that was the end of it."

Wilkinson himself described the scene in a letter to President Jefferson in his own inimitable style. "I saluted the Bench & in spite of myself my eyes darted a flash of indignation at the little Traitor on whom they continued fixed until I was called to the Book—The Lyon hearted Eagle-Eyed Hero, sinking under the weight of conscious guilt, with haggard Eye, made an Effort to meet the indignant salutation of outraged Honor, but it was in vain, his audacity failed Him, He averted his face, grew pale & affected passion to conceal his perturbation."

As soon as Wilkinson had taken the oath he was sent to the grand jury.

The past months had been the worst in James Wilkinson's life. After years of ill health his wife, whom he loved and depended on, had sunk into her last desperate illness. Humphrey Marshall's newspaper in Kentucky had been dragging out all the old scandals about his subsidy from the Spaniards.

From the moment that Wilkinson decided to turn state's evidence against Burr, with characteristic gall he began to cast about for ways of making a cash profit out of his treachery. He hit on a dodge that he thought would produce a bonus from his Spanish employers and at the same time keep him in good odor with the administration. He knew that President Jefferson was avid for exploration of the West. He already had Lieutenant Pike, the discoverer of the headwaters of the Mississippi, searching out the trails to Santa Fe. Now he sent off an agent named Walter Burling, ostensibly to buy mules, on a mission to the Spanish Viceroy in Mexico City. For Jefferson's ear his story would be that Burling was spying out the roads and mountain passes. The President would be made to understand that this expedition had put Wilkinson to great personal expense. For the Viceroy he drafted a letter, picturing himself, again like Leonidas holding back the Persian hordes, as averting an attack on Mexico. In payment for this service he respectfully demanded the sum of one hundred and twentyone thousand pesos.

He blew up such a bogy out of Burr's schemes that he ended by frightening himself. He put the city under martial law. He set his troops to digging earthworks and building palisades without regard for the ownership of the land he requisitioned. His squads arrested everybody suspected of associating with Burr.

Even the hardened frontier intriguers among Wilkinson's old associates were appalled. From New Orleans Thomas Power wrote Stephen Minor, the Spanish officer whose guest Wilkinson had recently been outside of Natchez: "I have seen the mad dog several times—I was never less pleased with him in my life than I am at present—I dare not commit my sentiments and opinions to paper. Suffice it to say that I am horribly disgusted—selfishness is undoubtedly inseparable from the heart of man, but carried beyond a certain degree, it is highly criminal and hateful. I leave you to make your own comments—I see that the . . ." (Power left a word blank. He meant Minor to fill in "plot" or "conspiracy") "of the little Prince" (he meant Burr), "the mad dog etc. is all fudge. . . . Nay it is more—I take it to be imposture and knavery."

In February Mrs. Wilkinson died at the house of a hospitable Creole planter who was serving as the general's aide. Shattered with grief, Wilkinson lingered for three months more in New Orleans, in spite of insistent requests from Washington that he come north immediately to testify. Meanwhile he tried to distract the administration from the clamor against his arbitrary acts, by blood and thunder about the torrent of Burrites that was about to descend on him. In a letter to Senator Smith he ranted that no matter at what cost to himself he would expose the little arch traitor, "that damned and pickled villain," before the grand jury. He further declared that he was composing, so that the whole world should know the truth, a book of three hundred pages quarto.

That hot June morning Colonel Wilkinson dressed carefully in the rooms that had been engaged for him at the Eagle Tavern. He donned the general's uniform with sash and epaulets of his own designing, his famous gold spurs, and a great encrusted sword that clanked on the ground behind him.

The general strutted into the grand jury room. The minute John

Randolph caught sight of this warlike regalia he shrilly ordered the marshal to take that man out and disarm him. He would not be allowed to intimidate the grand jury.

He had discovered that the copies of Burr's and Dayton's cypher messages which had been in the general's hands had been tampered with. Phrases had been erased. Words written in.

With Randolph in the lead the jurymen gave the general a hard time. They kept asking him why, since he claimed he first learned of Burr's plot from Swartwout in October, he had let a whole month go by before warning Governor Claiborne that an attack was imminent on New Orleans. When they came to vote on the indictments, a motion to add Wilkinson's name to the list was only lost by seven to nine. John Randolph was furious. "But the mammoth of iniquity escaped," he wrote his friend Nicholson; "not that any man pretended to think him *innocent*, but upon certain wire-drawn distinctions that I will not pester you with. W——n is the only man I ever saw who is from the bark to the very core a villain."

While the grand jury was closeted in one part of the Capitol, at the public sessions in the Hall of Delegates Burr and his lawyers hammered on their theme that Wilkinson was the true traitor of the piece. Instead of witness for the prosecution he should be in the prisoners' dock.

"While the grand-jury were engaged in examining the evidence, Burr amused us with a series of interludes in court," William Wirt wrote Ninian Edwards. "Motion upon motion, argument upon argument for upwards of thirty days, the principal policy of which was to turn the current of popular indignation from Burr against the administration, by representing Burr as the victim of envy, malignity and persecution. These arts had no effect beneficial to Burr, except upon a few federalists who were predisposed to believe anything and everything dishonorable to the administration—but upon the community at large, from whom Burr's jury must come, the effect was not inauspicious. . . ."

On Monday, June 22, Burr's attorney brought in a motion for the attachment of the person of General Wilkinson. While the motion was being argued before an interested audience an event occurred off the Virginia Capes which was to switch public attention from Burr and his problems to a more pressing danger.

4. A Broadside Interrupts the Pleading

The American frigate *Chesapeake*, which the Richmond newspapers mentioned as anchored off Norfolk when General Wilkinson arrived on his schooner, put to sea that same morning. Her departure was long overdue. She had been delayed three months by the inefficiency of the Washington navy yard. Under orders to relieve the *Constitution* as flagship of the Mediterranean fleet, she sailed with Commodore James Barron aboard. She had just made sail after heaving to off Cape Henry to wait for the pilot boat when the British frigate *Leopard*, which had been seen in company with two British ships of the line anchored in Lynnhaven Bay to take on provisions, bore down on her. Signals fluttered from her yardarm: a message for the commodore.

Unsuspecting, since, being at peace, British and American ships occasionally carried each other's dispatches, the skipper of the *Chesapeake* hove her to again. A lieutenant came aboard in a jolly boat with a note from the *Leopard's* captain.

He informed Commodore Barron that he had orders from his admiral to search the American ship for deserters. Barron read the words with stupefaction. His guns were loaded but no powder was ready. His decks were encumbered with sick men on stretchers; it would take hours to clear his ship for action. He answered that the only men aboard who might fit such a description were American citizens who had been wrongfully impressed. He would not allow his crew to be mustered except by their own officers.

The boat carrying the commodore's reply had hardly left the *Chesapeake's* side before the *Leopard*, which had been maneuvering for position, appeared close to windward. Her captain shouted that he was going to carry out his orders. To gain time Barron pretended not to understand. He quietly passed along the word to prepare for action. Before the gunner had a chance to unlock the doors of his magazine, the *Leopard* discharged her broadside pointblank into the *Chesapeake*. Barron was wounded in the first discharge. After two more broadsides, since no lighted matches were available to fire his guns with, he struck his colors. The only gun the Americans managed to fire was touched off by the third lieutenant, who brought a live coal up from the galley in his fingers.

Three men had been killed outright, eighteen wounded, and the masts and rigging severely battered. The British boats came promptly alongside. British tars swarmed aboard brandishing their cutlasses. The officers, brushing aside Barron's statement that he had surrendered and that the ship was a British prize, mustered the crew and arrested three Americans who had fled from a British man of war. They dragged off another poor wretch they found hiding in the coalhole, whom they claimed was an Englishman named Jenkin Ratford and who was soon after hanged from the yardarm for desertion.

Humiliated and disgraced, the crew of the *Chesapeake* made what sail they could. The ship limped back to Norfolk. When the dead and wounded were landed there the people of Norfolk ran riot. Not finding anything else to attack, they vented their rage on the water casks of the British fleet.

The mayor and city councilmen cut off all communication with the British ships in Lynnhaven Bay. Indignation spread like a brush fire from city to city throughout the United States. Public meetings flamed with patriotic fervor. In Washington President Jefferson published a proclamation requiring all armed British vessels to leave American ports and forbidding any sale of supplies to them. Burr's bogus conspiracy lost its primacy in the press dispatches.

5. The Grand Jury Finds True Bills

News of this most crushing national humiliation since St. Clair's rout on the Wabash had not yet reached Richmond when word went around that the grand jury was about to bring in an indictment. Every man who could puffed up the hill to the Capitol. At two o'clock that afternoon, while young Botts was still arguing for the attachment of General Wilkinson, who sat brazen with selfrighteousness among the government lawyers, John Randolph led his soberfaced jurors into court and laid several indictments on the clerk's table.

The clerk read out the endorsements: true bills against Burr and Blennerhasset for treason and misdemeanor.

In his letter to Ninian Edwards, Wirt described with some relish the consternation in the camp of the defense caused by Burr's indictment: "When the grand-jury came down with the Bills against Burr and Blennerhasset, I never saw such a group of shocked faces. The chief justice, who is a very dark man, shrunk back with horror upon his seat & turned black. He kept his eyes fixed on Burr with an expression of sympathy so agonizing and horror so deep & overwhelming that he seemed for two or three seconds to have forgotten where & who he was. I observed him & saw him start from his reverie under the consciousness that he was giving away too much to his feelings and look around upon the multitude to see if he had been noticed. . . ."

Wirt caught himself. He was still full of admiration for John Marshall. "He is, I believe it," he added, "one of the greatest & best of men. Some of our political friends, warped by their own prejudices, think him too much warped by his:—if he is so, he does not know it; for never did I know a man more solicitous to cast away bias from his mind & decide every proposition on its abstract merits: I think he has sometimes decided wrong, but it is much more probable that I myself am wrong."

The Chief Justice had no choice but to order Burr to the public jail. The following day Burr's lawyers presented an affidavit to the effect that confinement in the filth and promiscuity of the jail would injure the prisoner's health and that the jail afforded no private room for consultations with his lawyers. The court decided the little colonel might be returned to his lodgings at the Eagle Tavern and deputed Benjamin Latrobe, Jefferson's Surveyor of Public Buildings, present as a witness for the prosecution on account of his friendship with Bollmann, to judge whether the rooms could be made secure. Latrobe seems to have reported adversely because a day later the shutters of the diningroom windows of the house where Luther Martin lodged were fitted with bars and the prisoner was conducted there under a guard of seven men.

While the grand jury was deliberating further indictments John Randolph appeared in court and asked the court's assistance in obtaining a copy of a letter postmarked May 13, 1806, written by James Wilkinson, to which Burr's cypher letter was thought to be an answer. The members of the grand jury were aware that they could not ask the accused to present material which might incriminate him but hoped he would facilitate their inquiry into the facts. John Randolph was hinting that the letter might incriminate General Wilkinson.

The Chief Justice replied dryly that the jurymen were quite right in their opinion as to incriminating materials.

Colonel Burr rose and in his most selfrighteous manner declared that it would be impossible for him "to expose any letter which had been communicated to him confidentially." He added, with that suggestion of the steel claw under the velvet glove of which he was such a master, that he was not then prepared to decide "how far the extremity of circumstances might impel him to such action."

Mr. McRae interposed that the general had informed him that he wished to have the whole of the correspondence between Aaron Burr and himself exhibited before the court. Wilkinson was referring to other letters he had in his possession even more damaging to Burr.

Burr replied, with elaborate sarcasm, that the general was "welcome to all the éclat which he may expect to derive from his challenge," but that the letter postmarked May 13 would not be produced. "The letter is not at this time in my possession and General Wilkinson knows it."

Even in their deadly grapple a certain intimacy persisted between the two men. Each knew how the other's mind worked. Each was telegraphing to the other that he held in his possession the evidence needed to convict him. Whoever produced any more damaging correspondence would do so at his own risk.

The grand jury returned with a new set of indictments presenting Senators Jonathan Dayton late of New Jersey and John Smith of Ohio, along with Comfort Tyler, Israel Smith, and David Floyd, who had been Burr's agents in organizing the expedition, as guilty of treason and of levying war against the United States on Blennerhasset's island in Wood County, Virginia, on December 13, 1806.

William Wirt wrote Ninian Edwards that Dayton was skulking around Richmond incognito and that the wily ex-senator had invited two eminent Rhode Island lawyers to defend him. The prospect pleased Wirt. "We shall have the grand climacteric characters of the American bar to cope with." He indulged himself in a burst of professional vanity as he added:

> O the blood more stirs
> To rouse a lion than to start a hare.

6. Guest of the New Penitentiary

A few days later Burr was removed to the new penitentiary which Latrobe had designed and recently completed for the commonwealth of Virginia. Jefferson made the preliminary sketches for this edifice which he hoped would incorporate all the features of the new penology aimed at reforming the criminal as well as punishing him. A great arcaded stone building in the shape of a horseshoe on a hill overlooking the James, it was recognized as the most modern prison and as one of the grandest public buildings in the young Republic.

Burr seems to have been happy under the cool vaulted ceilings of his new quarters. Since his tacit agreement with Wilkinson that neither of them would play his trump card he was convinced that he would be acquitted. Meanwhile being in the custody of the federal marshals was at least a protection from his creditors. The countinghouses of the whole eastern seaboard resounded with the clamors of the holders of protested notes for tens of thousands of dollars who were getting ready to place the little colonel in debtors' prison whenever they could lay their hands on him.

"I have three rooms in the third story of the penitentiary," he wrote Theodosia, "making an extent of a hundred feet. My jailer is quite a polite and civil man—altogether unlike the idea one would form of a jailer. You would have laughed to have heard our compliments last evening."

The jailer apologized for having to keep the door locked after dark. Burr replied that he would prefer it, to keep out intruders. When the jailer told him lights would have to be extinguished at nine, the little colonel exclaimed that was quite impossible because he never went to bed before midnight. "As you please, Sir," said the jailer.

"While I have been writing different servants have arrived with messages, notes and inquiries," Burr continued in cheerful vein to his daughter, "bringing oranges, lemons, pineapples, raspberries, apricots, cream, butter, ice and some ordinary articles."

He enjoyed boasting to Theodosia about what good care the ladies of Richmond took of him. "My friends and acquaintances of both sexes are permitted to visit me without interruption," he explained in his next letter, "without enquiring their business, and without the presence of a spy. It is well that I have an antechamber or I should often be gêné with visitors. . . . If you come I can give you a bedroom and parlour on this floor. The bedroom has three large closets and it is a much more commodious one than you ever had in your life. . . . Remember no agitations, no complaints, no fears or anxieties on the road, or I renounce thee."

The trial proper began on August 3. Under the plea that traveling back and forth between the penitentiary and Richmond would be too great a tax on the accused and on his lawyers, Burr, accompanied by his seven guards, was removed to a private house. His suite at the penitentiary was promptly occupied by the chief victim of his impostures, Harman Blennerhasset.

Poor Blanny had been taken into custody by the federal marshal in Kentucky, where he had already fallen into the clutches of Burr's creditors, bent on attaching his person and property. He called in Henry Clay as his counsel and with his help held off the bailiffs by producing a letter from Joseph Alston which promised to assume at least part of the indebtedness. Mrs. Blennerhasset meanwhile was eking out an existence with their two boys in a house she had managed to purchase in Natchez. Blanny arrived in Richmond worn out by two weeks of hard riding. His chief worry was how to support his family. He noted in his journal the consoling fact that during his detention as prisoner of the United States his board and lodging would be free. He was planning to conduct his own defense, in the hope that his legal talent would be so brilliantly revealed that a career in the law would open up for him.

When the Alstons arrived they took over Burr's old quarters in Luther Martin's house. "I want an independent and discerning witness to my conduct and to that of the government," Burr had written Theodosia when he asked her to come. ". . . I should never invite anyone, much less those so dear to me, to witness my disgrace. I may be immured in dungeons, chained, murdered in legal form, but I cannot be humiliated or disgraced. If absent you will feel great solicitude. In my presence you will feel none, whatever be the malice and power of my enemies."

In spite of the scandal Joseph Alston was still a member of the South Carolina legislature. He was recovering from his fright. When he called on Blanny the nearsighted Irishman couldn't help noting that Alston's "great solicitude" seemed to be to crawl out of the promises, written and verbal, he had made to guarantee his fatherinlaw's paper. Other emissaries of Burr's and soothing notes in the colonel's own hand kept arriving at the penitentiary. Thoroughly disillusioned, Blanny was coming to the conclusion that the colonel was more intent on staving off inconvenient disclosures than in coming to the assistance of the family he had ruined. Blanny was beginning to wonder if Cowles Mead hadn't been right when he said he thought Burr was mad. He noted wryly in his diary that there was method in his madness.

No more than Burr could Blanny complain of the conditions of his imprisonment. Friends were allowed to visit him. His meals came from the Washington Tavern. He had a servant he could send out for books and papers. The Richmond ladies showed their detestation of Jefferson by sending him jams and jellies. He even had a personal barber from among the convicts, a free Negro named Vaun, who, he noted quaintly, was serving a twentyeight year term for cutting his wife's throat with a razor.

7. The Trial Proper: Anticlimax

The heat of the Richmond summer had driven away the spectators. The government witnesses had scattered to the hills. Andrew Jackson rode back to Tennessee convinced that all Burr intended was an expedition against the dons. He had decided that General Wilkinson was the villain and President Jefferson a sniveling coward. Profoundly shocked by Jefferson's temperate response to the unprovoked attack of the *Leopard* on the *Chesapeake,* he delivered himself of an impassioned speech from the steps of the Capitol long remembered by the inhabitants of Richmond: "Mr. Jefferson has plenty of courage to seize peaceable Americans . . . and persecute them for political purposes. But he is too cowardly to resent foreign outrage on the Republic. An English man of war fires on an American ship . . . so near his capital he can almost hear the guns and what does he do? . . . A year or more ago I gave at a dinner to Aaron Burr the toast 'Millions for defense and not one cent for tribute.' . . . They change the tune on this side of the mountains. Millions to persecute an American and not one cent to resist England."

When the court assembled in the Hall of Delegates at noon on August 3, George Hay was forced shamefacedly to admit that he had not the witnesses on hand he needed to present his case. Court was adjourned from day to day, while Hay's postriders combed the country for witnesses. It was not till the following Monday that enough government witnesses were assembled to justify impaneling the jury.

The Chief Justice presided over the selection of the jurors with a great air of impartiality. A number of veniremen were rejected because they admitted having formed an opinion, like a certain Mr. Bucky, who declared that whether treason were proved or not he thought Burr ought to be hung.

From the first words of the trial the defense held its advantage. George Hay's prosecution never recovered its impetus. In spite of William Wirt's flights of oratory, his fanciful description of the beauties of Blennerhasset's island before Burr arrived like the serpent to ruin that Eden, which every schoolchild was soon to be reciting, Burr and his lawyers retained the offensive. Though the people in general agreed with Mr. Bucky and with Ritchie's *Enquirer* that Burr ought to be hung, Richmond high society applauded every telling point made by the defense.

President Jefferson was desperately preoccupied with finding means short of war to counter the aggressions of the Royal Navy. He could only give half his mind to the Burr trial even though the conviction of Burr had become an idea so fixed that it clouded his judgment. At one point he wrote Hay, after reading of particularly intemperate remarks by Old Brandy Bottle, as Luther Martin was popularly known, that if Luther Martin was such a good friend of Burr's, why couldn't he be indicted for misprision of treason himself?

The administration was in a painful dilemma. To make a proper case against Burr the prosecution would have to incriminate Wilkinson. Yet the President and his chief advisers, Madison and Gallatin, had decided that the state of affairs in New Orleans demanded that, come what may, they support the General in Chief.

The prosecution's case for treason against Burr—though a procession of witnesses from the rank and file of those whom the little colonel had deceived were ready to testify to a variety of other crimes —depended on John Marshall's broad definition of treason in the habeas corpus proceedings of Bollmann and Swartwout. Relying on that decision, George Hay made no effort to prove that Aaron Burr was present when the overt acts were committed. The prosecution rested and the defense rested without adding much to the arguments which had been aired in court before the formal trial began.

8. *The Chief Justice Deals a Trump*

On August 31 John Marshall read a long decision. He blandly withdrew his previous definition of treason with the admission that there were times when the Supreme Court might be called upon to reconsider its judgments.

"The present indictment charges the prisoner with levying war against the United States, and alleges an overt act of levying war. That overt act must be proved, according to the mandates of the constitution and of the act of congress, by two witnesses. It is not proved by a single witness."

The Chief Justice furthermore ruled that since the overt act had not been proved "corroborative or confirmatory testimony" was not admissible. As was his custom he handed his opinion in writing to the lawyers.

The court adjourned to give the district attorney time to read it over. Next morning George Hay threw up the case.

The testimony of his witnesses had been ruled out unheard. Wirt exclaimed to Hay that at last he was convinced that John Marshall was a prejudiced man. The prosecution decided to leave the case to the jury.

The jury returned after twentyfive minutes. The verdict was read by the foreman, the muchrespected Colonel Carrington. "We of the jury say that Aaron Burr is not proved to be guilty under this indictment by any evidence submitted to us."

Aaron Burr immediately objected to the wording of the verdict. Luther Martin asked if the jury intended to censure the court for suppressing irrelevant testimony. Members of the jury, as politely as they could, made it clear that that was just what they did intend. The Chief Justice, in high good humor, ended the imbroglio by suggesting that the verdict stand as the jury had written it but that plain "not guilty" be entered in the record.

The little colonel was no sooner freed of the indictment for treason than he found himself attached for debt in a civil suit. Somehow he managed to find surety to the amount of thirtysix thousand dollars.

Emboldened by the favorable verdict in Burr's case, Jonathan Dayton, whom Blanny now called "Old Slyboots," emerged from hiding and appeared in court with an affidavit to the effect that he had not been on Blennerhasset's island in December 1806. Hay entered a *nolle prosequi*.

When Harman Blennerhasset was brought in the next day his case was treated in the same way. Blanny was disappointed. He had been working for a month on a brief in his own defense. He was confident that he would so shine among the legal talents assembled that he would win a place among the lights of the Virginia bar.

Blanny was admitted to bail on the misdemeanor charge along with Burr and the rest.

Immediately he started to dog Burr's footsteps. The little colonel became very hard to see. Blanny kept writing him begging for an explanation. He and his family were penniless. Colonel Burr must propose some plan for repaying the money he owed him. Whenever he got to see Burr, the colonel was surrounded by friends. He was remarkably inattentive to requests for a financial settlement. Blennerhasset then sought out Alston. All Governor Alston would talk about was how he himself was fifty thousand dollars in the hole.

When at last Blanny was granted an interview with Burr alone, it turned out that Burr wanted to question him about what men of influence he could introduce him to in England.

Blennerhasset confided to his diary the sudden hope that in exchange for some letters Burr might be induced to repay a little of the money he owed, but when Blanny hinted a *quid pro quo* Burr would only talk of his projects. Not for a minute had he given up his castles in the air. The new aggressive mood of the administration at Westminster might provide just the climate he needed for getting backing for his plan of disunion. "He is as gay as usual," Blanny noted, "and as busy in speculations on reorganizing his projects for action as if he had never suffered the least interruption."

Burr tried to fob him off by an invitation to dinner. "The dinner was neat," noted Blanny, "followed by three or four kinds of wine. Splendid poverty!"

The Richmond hostesses showed Blennerhasset some attention as another victim of the administration's malignity. Being a fair musician, he comforted himself by taking part in the concerts of the Richmond Harmonic Society.

The misdemeanor trial proved to be more a trial of General Wilkinson than of Aaron Burr. The lawyers for the prosecution had lost heart. Important papers were mislaid. They had only the most perfunctory assistance from the Attorney General.

After another verdict of not guilty, the Chief Justice scandalized the Federalist faction by holding the accused to their bail in spite of their acquittal until they should be tried on the same charge in the state of Ohio. They were indicted in Chillicothe but the charges were never pressed.

Aaron Burr departed for Philadelphia. Already he was trying to recruit young men to form his suite on his projected journey to England. He kept begging Blennerhasset, who, now a thoroughly disillusioned man, still followed in his trail in hope of a settlement of his claims, for letters to friends of noble birth. A threat of tar and feathers caused them both to hurry through Baltimore. The democratic mob had to content themselves with burning the two of them in effigy, along with John Marshall and Luther Martin, thrown in for good measure.

In Philadelphia Blanny found Burr moving as usual in the best circles. He never got the slightest satisfaction of his claims from either Alston or Burr.

The little colonel's mind was set on getting out of the country. After several months dodging bailiffs and creditors, traveling under assumed names and hiding out under strange disguises, he managed to smuggle himself aboard the packet for England.

One of his last acts in New York was to borrow a few dollars from his German cook who, knowing his master, made him leave a trunkload of personal effects as security.

CHAPTER V

All the Odious Passions

1. An Adams Changes Parties

Jefferson was at the President's house in Washington City when news reached him on June 25, 1807, of the *Leopard's* attack on the *Chesapeake*. He had come back four weeks before much refreshed by a busy month at Monticello where he planted paper mulberries, horse chestnuts, purple beech, locusts, and a row of white Antwerp raspberries, laid out thorn hedges; and saw to the digging of flower beds around the open lawn behind the house which his masons and carpenters were at last completing in its final form. His granddaughter Anne Randolph was to superintend the planting of a long list of perennials and flowering shrubs during his absence. With real glee he was planning the delights of retirement.

After all these pleasant outofdoor occupations in the delicious Albemarle spring the torments of office weighed heavily upon him. Earlier that winter he had unburdened himself to his venerable friend John Dickinson: "I am tired of an office where I can do no more good than many others who would be glad to be employed in it. to myself, personally, it brings nothing but increasing drudgery and daily loss of friends. every office becoming vacant, every appointment made, me donne un ingrat et cent enemies. my only consolation is the belief that my fellow citizens at large give me credit for good intentions. . . ."

Though he could see clouds gathering about his administration, he could still feel that up to now his good intentions had been rewarded with a fair amount of success. The good sense of the people in which he had so much confidence had thwarted the schemes of the disunionists in New England and beyond the mountains. With a Republican governor in the Boston State House, the tide of Republicanism seemed on the flood in the Northeast. His favorite design for a national university was still to be launched, but he hoped that the even more grandiose schemes that he and Gallatin were assembling under the head of "internal improvements" were on the way to being implemented.

In January the plan for the Cumberland Road, later known as the National Turnpike, was laid before the House. In February Congress appropriated fifty thousand dollars for a survey of the Atlantic shoreline. The establishment of lighthouses was clearly federal business.

This survey went far beyond spotting aids to navigation. Jefferson thought of it as the first step towards accomplishing vast projects Gallatin had already sketched out with the help of a corps of surveyors. An inland waterway along the coast from New York to Georgia was to include George Washington's canal through the Dismal Swamp. These waterways were to be paralleled by a post road running from Maine to Georgia. Further canals were planned to connect the Hudson River with Lake Champlain and Lake Ontario, and to bypass Niagara and the falls of the Ohio. Roads were to be built through the mountains linking the heads of navigation of the Susquehanna, the Potomac, the James, and the Santee with the Allegheny, the Monongahela, the Kanawa, and the Tennessee rivers. The roads to Detroit, St. Louis, and New Orleans were to be made more passable. Gallatin figured that these improvements could be accomplished over a tenyear period at a cost of around two million dollars a year.

This was all a far cry from Jefferson's old theory of limited federal powers. He now felt that expenditure on roads and canals was justified by the solvency of the national government. He felt that roads and canals would link the states together in such a way as to forever disrupt the plans of the disunionists. These internal improvements would demand an amendment to the Constitution. Jefferson was confident he could find enough friends in the state legislatures to ratify it. He envisaged an "empire for liberty" which would occupy the entire continent north of Mexico. He still hoped for peaceable acquisition of the two Floridas, and occasionally included Cuba in his plans as a southeasterly outpost. The threemile limit should be extended to take in everything west of the Gulf Stream as American waters.

As it became obvious that the dominant faction at Westminster wanted to use the revived Rule of 1756 (by which no wartime trade by a neutral with a belligerent would be allowed beyond the trade that had been carried on in peacetime) not only to counter Bonaparte's Berlin Decree but to destroy the competition of American shipping on the high seas, Gallatin settled down to figure how a war with Great Britain, if it should become necessary, could be financed. He reported to the President that it would cost ten millions a year.

Two years of war would eat up the twenty millions they were counting on for internal improvements.

From the depth of his soul Jefferson believed that war was no solution for international conflicts. In spite of the successful outcome of his small war against the Barbary pirates he distrusted navies. In his gunboat program which had become such a bone of contention with the Federalists, he had tried to work out a system of harbor defense that would make a navy unnecessary. He had hoped that Fulton's torpedoes might prove effective. Although he believed in a welltrained militia and wanted to institute an annual conscription by age groups on the Napoleonic model, he had little confidence in professional soldiers.

His first thought, when news came of the British attack on an undefended American frigate, was that it made war inevitable. War with the greatest naval power that had ever sailed the seas was frightening to contemplate. As always when faced with an important decision he waited to consult his entire cabinet. He looked upon the executive as a directory where the President was first among peers. Particularly he relied on Madison and Gallatin. When he wrote of the presidency as "we" in his letters he was thinking of his peculiarly intimate collaboration with those two men.

While they waited for Gallatin to arrive from New York, where he'd been politicking at the home of his wife's family, the very political Nicholsons, Jefferson and Madison went to work to draft a proclamation.

At the same time the President headed a subscription for the benefit of the wounded seaman and kept in constant communication with Governor Cabell of Virginia about measures to enforce the boycott of the British fleet established by the Virginians. This had been countered by a threat by the British commanders to blockade Hampton Roads. The governor had called out a very considerable body of militia. Jefferson saw two dangers to be faced: a British attack on Norfolk and the infection of the troops by the malaria he knew was rampant in the swamps back of Cape Henry.

As soon as Gallatin had approved of the text the proclamation was published. Armed British ships were ordered to leave American ports. Citizens of the United States were required to have no intercourse of any sort with the Royal Navy. Except in the case of ships in distress taking refuge from storms or enemy action the President forbade any furnishing of supplies or aid to their crews. This interdiction was to be in effect until the British government made "honorable reparation of the wrong which had been done and exercised effective control of its naval commanders."

Only Congress could declare war. In calling a special session of Congress for late October, the President was playing for time. He wanted to give the British government a chance to disavow the outrage. He wanted to give American shipowners time to get their ships into home ports. He wanted to give the states and the War Department time to prepare. Furthermore he didn't dare ask the members of Congress to face the Washington fevers during the sickly season.

As soon as the administration had set its course, Gallatin wrote his wife a long letter. Possibly under the influence of her fireeating father, Hannah Gallatin had been clamoring in her letters for an immediate declaration of war: "To spurn negotiation and tremble for the fate of New York are not very consistent. But every person not blinded by passion and totally ignorant of the laws of civilized nations knows that whenever injuries are received from subordinate officers, satisfaction is demanded from the government itself before reprisals are made; and that time to receive our property from abroad and to secure our harbors as well as we can is of importance to us can anyone doubt in New York? It is our duty to ask for reparation, to avert war if it can be done honorably, and in the meanwhile not to lose an instant in preparing for war. On the last point I doubt, between ourselves, whether everything shall be done which ought to be done. And for that reason alone I wish that Congress may be called somewhat earlier than is now intended. . . . The principal objection will not be openly avowed, but it is the unhealthiness of this city."

Gallatin had reason to know; one motive for his trip to New York was to recover from an intermittent fever that had attacked him unusually early that year.

"I think I increased my sickness by intensity of thinking and not sleeping nights," he wrote Hannah. "I certainly grew better as soon as my plans were digested, and, except as to New York, I feel now very easy, provided that our recourses shall be applied with ability and in the proper direction." He added a postscript. "I have seen Mr. Erskine"—the British minister still generally credited with good intentions towards the United States—"whom I treated with more civility than cordiality; but I could not help it. I believe that he is much embarrassed between what is right and his fear of the naval officers of his own government."

The first result of the news from the Virginia Capes was an outburst of patriotic emotion which united Federalists and Republicans behind the administration. Mass meetings in all the large cities endorsed the President's proclamation. Volunteers stood in line at army recruiting stations. Only in Boston, where the Essex Junto had great influence on the town government, was there a conflict of opinion.

Timothy Pickering had left Washington when Congress adjourned, thoroughly convinced that Jefferson's administration was in secret alliance with Bonaparte:

"I cannot turn my eye to the situation of our country," he wrote home, "without feeling all the uneasiness which results from the knowledge of its defenceless condition and the want of spirit and the indisposition to put it in a safe state. Our Chief Magistrate seems to be absorbed in what would amuse a minute philosopher, but which is a reproach to one who holds the reins of an empire. And the whole band who now govern are apparently more occupied in plans for securing themselves in place and power than in studying to render the country safe and prosperous. . . . If Great Britain be overthrown or forced to make peace, the United States will lie at the mercy of France . . . after all the examples of Europe the president affects to think—in fact he says—we have nothing to apprehend from the French. But Bonaparte will have no occasion to make war upon us: let him demand tribute and it will be paid. . . . Should he take pity on us and give us a king, as he has done to so many nations around him, he will then send an army . . . having made no preparation for war, we shall of course submit without a blow. . . . Such is my disheartening view of the miserable situation of our country."

Family misfortunes added to Pickering's gloom that summer. He had just returned to his farm at Wenham from the burial of his eldest son Timothy, who had been his companion in his pioneering venture on the Susquehanna and was in many ways his favorite. Two of his younger boys, who showed signs of nervous disorders from childhood, were on their way to hopeless insanity. He was a man of fervid family affections. Grief and anxiety at home tended to sharpen the violence of his political opinions. As soon as he heard of the *Leopard-Chesapeake* encounter he declared that the British captain was in the right. The Americans were encouraging British sailors to desert. The British had a right to search for deserters. George Cabot and John Lowell agreed with him.

For a few days they effectually blocked the calling of a town meeting in Boston, but they had reckoned without John Quincy Adams. The extreme Federalists had helped send John Adams' eldest son to the Senate, but he was not a party man. Devotion to the United States was bred in his bones. He often said his political principles were union at home and independence abroad. On July 9 he made a terse entry in his journal: "I had this day a somewhat warm debate with Mr. John Lowell at the Suffolk Insurance Office."

During the session of Congress which had closed in March, the opinions of the younger Adams had undergone an evolution similar to those of his friend Senator Plumer of New Hampshire. Plumer admired young Adams and reported his speeches with particular care in his memorandum. "He is a very honest man—though a man of violent prejudices," he noted. Riding home on the stages from Washington together, Senator Adams entertained Plumer with stories of his upbringing in Europe. "He is a man of information—but too formal, his manners are too stiff and unyielding—he is too tenacious of his opinions."

John Quincy Adams was a chip off the old block. Now approaching his fortieth birthday, he already thought of himself as a middle-aged man. Some of his father's friends declared that even as an infant John Quincy had shown no sign of youth. A prodigy from the time he could toddle, the center of the amazed affection of John and Abigail Adams' very special household, his education had been different from that of any of his contemporaries. He absorbed Whig politics with his ABCs. His primer was the learned conversation of his father and his father's friends, somewhat seasoned perhaps by his mother's shrewd remarks. He was brought up in an atmosphere of fervid patriotism. His mother taught him to recite, every night after the Lord's Prayer, Collins' ode to the fallen Jacobites:

> How sleep the brave who sink to rest
> By all their country's wishes blest.

His first formal schooling was at Passy when his father was envoy to the court of Louis XVI. At eleven he was attending a Latin school in Amsterdam. Soon after he sat in on courses at the University of Leyden.

At fourteen he went off to St. Petersburg as secretary to his father's friend Francis Dana, who was sent by Congress to try to persuade the Empress Catherine to join with the new American states in promoting freedom of the seas for neutral commerce. He lived a year in St. Petersburg, spending his time reading everything he could lay his hands on from Cicero to Hume. When it became obvious that the Empress was not to be induced to negotiate with the upstart nation in the west, the sixteen year old John Q. made his way alone across all of northern Europe in the middle of winter. He rejoined his father in time for a short course of study at The Hague with the editor of Vattel's treatises on international law. After that he served as his father's secretary during the peace negotiations at Versailles. When the treaty was signed there was some discussion among the Adamses: should John accompany his father's legation to London or sail home to enter Harvard College?

The young gentleman made up his own mind: "After having been traveling for these seven years almost all over Europe," he ruminated in his diary, "and having been in the world, and among company for three; to return to the pale of a college, subjected to all the rules which I have long been freed from; then to plunge into the dry and tedious study of the law for three years and afterwards not expect (however good an opinion I may have of myself) to bring myself into notice under three or four years more; if ever. It is really a prospect somewhat discouraging to a youth of my ambition (for I have ambition though I hope the object is laudable)—" He was eighteen; though there was great mutual affection and admiration between them, he had enough of secretarial jobs under his father's wing. "I am determined that so long as I shall be able to get my living in an honorable manner I will depend on no one."

He graduated from Harvard in two years and moved to Newburyport to study law with Theophilus Parsons, who was a paladin of the Essex Junto. Burke's reaction against Jacobin excesses in France was laying the intellectual foundation for extreme Federalist opinions in America. Under that influence John Q. published a violent attack under the name of Publicola on Thomas Paine's *Rights of Man*. This publication, which was generally attributed to his father, the Vice President, did a great deal to embroil John Adams in the quarrel which estranged him for so many years from his old friend Jefferson. George Washington read the articles, approved, and appointed the young Adams minister to the Netherlands. Since the Netherlands had unfortunately been occupied by the armies of the French Republic he was sent on to Berlin.

When his father was elected President, John Quincy retired from the diplomatic service, and after marrying the daughter of a Marylander who was United States consul in London, came home to Boston to raise a family and practice law. The townspeople spoke of him as prickly as a porcupine, but his anti-Jacobin opinions and his erudition endeared him to the Federalist politicians. Harvard endowed him with the Boylston professorship. There was prestige in the Adams name. The Massachusetts legislature sent him to the Senate in 1803. In spite of his crabbed independence his politics remained tolerably acceptable to his colleague Timothy Pickering until they collided head on over the *Chesapeake* affair.

Thwarted in their efforts to call a town meeting, indignant Bostonians met at the State House. There John Quincy Adams joined with Elbridge Gerry, the Jeffersonian leader of the Marblehead Republicans so detested by all good Essex County men, to draft a resolution approving the President's proclamation. The resolution received such popular acclaim that the extreme Federalists were forced to allow a similar resolution to be passed a few days later at a proper town meeting at Faneuil Hall. From then on all the rancor of Timothy Pickering's political partisanship was aroused against both Adamses. He was already feuding with the father. His war of words against the son was to go on so long as he lived.

2. The Argument by Congreve Rocket

As soon as Jefferson and Madison could agree on the phrasing of the message dispatches were sent off to Monroe by the fast schooner *Revenge*, then refitting in Hampton Roads after having brought General Wilkinson and his suite up from New Orleans. Monroe and Pinkney were instructed to carry the protest of the American government to Mr. Canning, the new Foreign Minister. They were instructed to insist on a disavowal of the outrage, on reparations, and on a pledge from the British government that impressment of American seamen would cease forthwith.

Through that sultry July Jefferson and Madison and Gallatin met almost daily. It would be fall before they could expect an answer by the *Revenge*. Meanwhile they pored over each fresh batch of dispatches to arrive from Europe. It was hard to develop a consistent policy when every mail brought news of some new cataclysm. Bonaparte was at the peak of his power. Kingdoms were knocked over at his slightest whim. Redrawing the map of Europe had become a sort of game. He had fallen out with the Czar Alexander of Russia, who was now trying to back up the Prussians in the defense of eastern Germany. This encouraged Jefferson to hope that Alexander might unite with the Scandinavian countries to set up a northern confederacy which would defend the rights of neutral shipping against both the French and the British. From the days of Dana's mission to Russia a league of northern neutrals to insure the freedom of the seas had been one of the fundamental aims of American diplomacy.

With the imperial French government the President's tactics were unchanged; he was still waiting for the moment when Bonaparte would find it to his advantage to sell, or to force the Spaniards to sell, Florida to the United States. At the same time he could hardly have been unaware that Bonaparte, who had mischievously insisted, in the terms of the original cession, that the boundaries of Louisiana be left vague—so that there would be cause for friction, whenever he should find friction useful to his purposes—was dangling Florida as a bait. Every time the Emperor sensed that French seizures of American ships might push the Americans into an alliance with England, his Foreign Minister would encourage fresh hopes of a Florida settlement.

When Monroe received his new instructions by the *Revenge* he was appalled. He couldn't help suspecting he was being placed in a false position for political purposes at home. By linking impressments with the *Chesapeake* affair Jefferson and Madison were making negotiation impossible.

Canning had already disavowed the attack on the *Chesapeake* and had seen to it that Admiral Berkeley, on whose orders the commander of the *Leopard* had acted, should be recalled. The Foreign Secretary had further let it be known that he was planning to send a special mission to Washington to discuss the matter of a modest indemnity "adequate to their respective situation and condition in life" to be paid to the families of the American seamen killed or disabled by the *Leopard's* broadsides; but when Monroe tried to follow his instructions by bringing up the question of impressment he was met by one of Canning's scornful stares.

Neither Monroe nor Pinkney was a match for the man who now occupied the Foreign Office. William Pinkney was a stately Marylander, a man of parts but still somewhat the provincial attorney in spite of his English education. Monroe had developed into a slow, plodding, rather solemn diplomat. Jefferson used to say you could turn James Monroe inside out without finding a spot of deception in him. He was solid and incorruptible but his best friends admitted that he lacked mental agility. These two wellmeaning Americans were dealing with one of the sharpest wits developed by Pitt's own private nursery of political brains in the British Parliament.

George Canning was the son of a thirdrate actress and a disinherited barrister who died when the boy was still in arms. His mother had the ill luck to take on a second marriage with an actor who was such a ruffian that another member of the troupe, knowing that young Canning had wealthy connections, wrote to the boy's uncle that George was a likely lad but that, if something were not done for him, the boy would certainly be headed for the gallows.

The uncle took over his education. George responded handsomely. At Eton he distinguished himself by bringing out a literary magazine called the *Microcosm* which a London publisher found so entertaining that he paid fifty pounds for the copyright. George's uncle was a fashionable Whig, an intimate of Devonshire House and of Sheridan and Fox. At Oxford Canning showed himself such a francophile that the story went around, when he went down to study law at Lincoln's Inn, that Godwin was grooming him to lead the revolution of the British radicals. The Terror turned Canning into a conservative. Like many another young Englishman, he found his political ideas boxing the compass. He had a knack for ridicule. His lampoons in the *Anti-Jacobin* did as much as Burke's philippics to speed the conservative reaction that Pitt built his politics on. Pitt took the young writer up and saw that he was elected to Parliament.

Having put his political career on a solid basis by marrying the daughter of a major general said to be worth a hundred thousand pounds in her own right, George Canning was ready to take over the leadership of the Tories after Pitt's death. His rival was an Ulsterman with a prodigious number of Irish titles, Lord Castlereagh. In the Tory ministry under Lord Portland which extinguished the last dying flicker of Charles James Fox's liberal policies after the collapse of the Ministry of All the Talents, Canning was Secretary of Foreign Affairs and Castlereagh Secretary of War.

In the summer of 1807 neither Canning nor Castlereagh had time to worry over the silly pretensions of the Americans. While Canning kept Pinkney and Monroe at arm's length by a few languid sarcasms, the cabinet was planning, amid desperate secrecy, a naval expedition against Denmark.

After Bonaparte whipped the allied army at Friedland on June 14, the Czar Alexander, leaving the Prussians to their fate, retreated into Lithuania. The two Emperors and the Prussian King met three weeks later on a raft anchored in the river Niemen near Tilsit, to discuss peace terms. Bonaparte imposed an immense indemnity on the Prussians and somehow extracted from Alexander a secret agreement by which, if the British should refuse to make peace with the French, Alexander promised to join him in an alliance to bar the Baltic to British shipping.

These secret articles of the Treaty of Tilsit were to prove the ruin of Jefferson's strategy of encouraging a league of northern neutrals. Bonaparte was in funds. He had no need to raise money by selling the Floridas. Jefferson's whole foreign policy seemed about to go by the board.

The Scandinavian peoples had managed to keep out of the Napoleonic wars. Like the Americans they had profited greatly from the wartime carrying trade. Now with Prussia at his feet, Bonaparte began his customary campaign of threats and cajolery to soften up the Danes, whose islands dominated the narrow sea lanes into the Baltic. The Danes had built up not only a merchant marine but a fairly formidable navy. Bonaparte, whose fleet had been swept from the seas after Trafalgar, saw a nucleus there for a fresh challenge to the British on their own element. The Danish court tried desperately to maintain neutrality.

George Canning had a firstrate intelligence service. Two weeks after the treaty was signed at Tilsit the secret articles were laid on his desk. The Tory cabinet, buoyed up by an election in which the opposition lost two hundred seats, decided to grab the Danish ships before Bonaparte did. All through July a British squadron of overwhelming firepower was being assembled off Yarmouth. News came to Downing Street that Bonaparte had ordered thirty thousand men to be collected at Hamburg under Marshal Bernadotte.

The British cabinet had to move fast. Postriders went all over England quietly alerting men chosen for the expedition. One very surprised young diplomat was routed out of bed in a country house and told to report immediately to Mr. Canning for a secret mission. Francis James Jackson was a cocky careerist with no compunctions whatsoever about Mr. Canning's highhanded methods. In his letters to his family he left a very personal record of the attack on Copenhagen. On July 18 he wrote his brother George, who was also in the foreign service, that after a long hurried journey he was at that moment sitting in Mr. Canning's room at Downing Street, waiting for the Foreign Secretary to return from a cabinet meeting. Rumor went that he was to be sent with an expedition to "cover the retreat of a large body of English troops who had gone to the assistance of Prussia."

Canning sent him galloping off to Yarmouth to join the fleet. Accompanied by transports carrying a body of troops, seventeen line-of-battle ships sailed from the Downs on July 27. Two weeks later Jackson was put ashore at Kiel to present Canning's demands to the Danish Foreign Minister. He presented these demands so crudely that crazy old George III remarked, in a lucid interval, that his envoy ought to have been kicked downstairs. Jackson demanded an immediate "junction" of the Danish navy with the British. His Majesty was offering a hundred thousand pounds yearly rent as balm for the hurt feelings of the Danes. Count von Bernstorff lectured Jackson like a Dutch uncle for his impudence. The Prince Royal declared he was ready to die in defense of his country's neutrality.

Neutrality had become as much a dirty word to the British as to the French. Jackson wrote his mother in high spirits that negotiations had failed. "Everything promises a successful enterprize."

He traveled overland to Copenhagen to give the Danes a few hours more to ponder his ultimatum and to spy out what he could of their defenses. The roads were full of refugees hurrying out of the city. Others were hurrying in to take refuge behind the walls.

The Danes refused to be browbeaten. August 16 Jackson asked for his passports. A boat put him aboard one of the British ships anchored in battle array off the city. He reported gleefully to the admiral that the Danes had no means of resistance. There were no guns on the ramparts. The city's water supply could easily be cut off. The British outnumbered them five to one. All he'd seen was four thousand wretched peasants of the Landwehr and a few praams and floating batteries. "If the Danish gov't," he wrote, "contrary to reason and common sense, persist in incurring the evils of war, the responsibility must rest on their own heads."

Meanwhile the redcoats were landing. The investment of the city had begun. "The sailors are most eager," Jackson noted, "I saw them the other day in action with the gunboats and they reminded me of a pack of foxhounds dashing into cover. . . . I remain afloat because it is more entertaining to be in the center of things. . . . I make my home aboard for we live admirably here; on shore they don't know how to make themselves comfortable."

It was all a great lark. While preparations were being made to bombard the city Jackson sailed over to Stockholm for a sightseeing trip. He got back to his ship just in time. The cannonade had begun. Fires had started ashore. He found his brother George with the admiral, watching the burning of the city from the stern gallery of the flagship.

George Jackson described the scene in a letter home: "I never saw nor can well conceive a more awful yet magnificent spectacle. It was the beginning of the bombardment *in forma*. We saw and heard it going on till daylight as we lay in our cots. . . . I cannot describe to you the appalling effect it had upon me. Our cabin was illuminated by an intensely red glow, then suddenly wrapped in deep gloom, as the flames rose and fell while the vessel quivered and every plank in her was shaken by the loud reverberation of the cannon. Alas, poor Danes I could not but feel for them. . . . Lord Cathcart"—the British military commander—"told me next morning that he had thrown 2000 shells into the town, besides the fire from our gunboats and the famous catamaran rockets."

After a couple more days of bombardment George Jackson was sent off to England on a sloop with dispatches announcing that resistance was at an end. "Ere I left," he wrote, "the fire had increased to a prodigious height. The principal church was in flames looking like a pyramid of fire and the last I saw and heard of the illfated city was the falling of the steeple with a tremendous crash and the loud huzzahs it occasioned along our line."

Francis James Jackson remained to take part in the capitulation. The Danish fleet was carried off to England. The British had suffered less than a hundred casualties; but the bodies of near two thousand noncombatants, men, women, and children, were found in the ruins. "There seems to be a disposition to commiserate the Danes," he noted in a puzzled way when he got back to England. "The fact is the magnitude of our achievement startled the public, though they will enjoy the benefit of it."

The magnitude of the British achievement so startled Bonaparte that he went off into one of his famous rages. Thrashing around for some ally of Britain's to attack, he ordered Portugal invaded. He announced that the Portuguese and Danish flags had ceased to exist. "The House of Braganza shall reign no more," he declared at a fulldress court function which the American minister, John Armstrong, attended at Fontainebleau. The result was the flight of the Portuguese regent and the entire Braganza court, in what was described as a flotilla of a thousand ships, under the protection of a British squadron, to establish a new empire in Brazil.

Canning had settled the Danes. He now turned on another troublesome set of neutrals who were trying to profit by the war. The carrot and the stick. He had already intimated to the American envoys that there would be no more searching of American warships. He picked a civilspoken gentleman named George Henry Rose, the son of a prominent Scottish Whig who was vice president of the Board of Trade, to negotiate a settlement of the *Chesapeake* business.

Rose embarked for America on the frigate *Statira* on November 14. On the same day Monroe sailed home on the *Augustus*. Neither of them was aware of the contents of an order in council, promulgated on November 11, which was printed in the London *Gazette* the very day they sailed. Canning seems intentionally to have kept them in the dark.

According to this order, any American ship was liable to capture, no matter what its cargo was, which sailed for any port in Europe from which the British flag was excluded. Bonaparte sewed the matter up a month later by decreeing in Milan that any neutral ship that had touched at an English port, or had been searched by a British warship, was fair prize for the French. There were to be no more neutrals.

3. *Jefferson Answers with an Embargo*

Congress meanwhile had assembled in Washington. The House for the first time met in its handsome oval chamber, girdled by fluted sandstone columns and lit by skylights from above, which had resulted from the combined architectural inventiveness of Jefferson and Latrobe. The debate dealt with measures of coercion short of war. In the face of the realities of British power martial fervor was subsiding. Congress had no stomach for war. The country was too obviously unprepared even for defense. On December 14 the act passed during the spring session of the previous year forbidding the importation of a long list of English goods, which had been suspended to give the English government time to see the light of reason, was allowed to go into effect.

Two days later Secretary Madison received a copy of a royal proclamation which had preceded the order in council. English seamen serving in foreign bottoms were ordered home and officers of the Royal Navy were expressly required to exercise the right of impressment over neutral ships. Private messages were arriving by a flock of vessels putting into American ports, warning of even more stringent measures to come against neutral shipping. Canning had entrusted Rose with the carrot. Now the cabinet was using the stick.

December 17 Jefferson called his heads of departments together. All agreed to follow the precedent set in 1794 under somewhat similar circumstances. An embargo must be imposed on American shipping. Gallatin had one of his sleepless nights. Next day he wrote the President that he felt there should be a time limit on the embargo. "In every point of view—privations, sufferings, revenue, effect on the enemy, politics at home etc—I prefer war to a permanent embargo. Governmental prohibitions do always more mischief than had been calculated; and it is not without much hesitation that a statesman should hazard to regulate the concerns of individuals, as if he could do better than themselves."

At a second cabinet meeting Gallatin was overruled. American ships must be kept in port until measures could be taken to get their neutrality respected. The President's message as presented to Congress asked for an embargo without time limit, on the theory that this would give Secretary Madison more leeway in dealing with the British envoy, whose arrival was daily expected.

Senator Pickering jumped at the conclusion that the secret aim of the administration's embargo was to back up Bonaparte's blockade of the British Isles. Pickering and his friends opposed the bill vehemently but it passed after a day's debate in each house. John Quincy Adams was for it. Years later Pickering wrote accusingly that Adams had cried out: "The President has recommended the measure on his high responsibility. I would not deliberate. I would not consider; I would act."

President Jefferson had barely time to affix his signature to the first Embargo Act before news came that the frigate *Statira*, with His Majesty's envoy Mr. George Henry Rose aboard, had dropped anchor in Hampton Roads.

That gentleman's instructions were hardly as conciliatory as Canning had pretended to Pinkney and Monroe.

He was instructed not to set foot ashore before insisting on some modification of the President's proclamation of nonintercourse with the Royal Navy. Furthermore he was to protest strongly against the American practice of enticing British seamen into their ships. Canning's claim was that the *Chesapeake* affair resulted from the refusal of the American authorities to give up British deserters. There followed an exchange of notes and messages with the Secretary of State, all at crosspurposes. It was not until January 14, 1808, that Rose, finally tired of his confinement on the frigate, deigned to allow himself to be set ashore at Washington City.

The President received him politely, but he found the Americans very lowerclass. In one of his first dispatches to Canning he deplored the presence in Congress of a tailor, a weaver, four notorious swindlers, six or seven tavernkeepers, a butcher, a grazier, and a curer of hams, as well as a crowd of schoolteachers and Baptist ministers. Tradespeople! In Washington Mr. Rose kept these sentiments to himself. The British legation was well informed on American politics. Rose hadn't been in the city fortyeight hours before he was dining at a Georgetown dinner table in company with Senator Pickering, who had been described to him as the head of the pro-English party.

Pickering found Canning's envoy all sweet reasonableness. "Mr. Rose's face is indicative of a placid temper and his conversation confirms it," he wrote his nephew Tim Williams, who was a merchant in Boston. "He possesses good sense and a virtue perfectly conciliatory. Such is also the disposition of the minister Canning, by whom he was selected. Canning was his schoolfellow and intimate friend. It seemed to me a sort of friendly compulsion that sent him hither. . . . He manifested a solicitude even to anxiety for a pacific adjustment of our difficulties."

Pickering remarked on Mr. Rose's surprise that the terms of the Monroe treaty had been kept secret. No British minister would have been guilty of such concealment. "What our Government will demand as a reparation for the attack on the *Chesapeake* I do not know, nor what Mr. Rose is authorized to concede; but I run no hazard in saying that nothing will in reality be denied, and that if after all a war with England should ensue, the fault will be our own."

He went on to surmise that the President was waiting for news of some British measure in retaliation against Bonaparte's paper blockade which would give him an excuse to make exorbitant demands on Rose. "He will doubtless be thoroughly disappointed."

The day after Pickering sent off his letter the *American Intelligencer* printed the full text of the order in council of November 11. The popular reaction was as vigorous as to the attack on the *Chesapeake*. Even the New Englanders admitted the need for an embargo. The hope was that it would be of short duration. Though he was determined to support the administration, John Quincy Adams, like Gallatin, had his doubts about its efficacy. On January 21 he offered a resolution to the Senate that a committee be appointed to consider whether the arming of merchant ships would not be a more effective measure. The resolution was lost seventeen to ten.

Rose's negotiation dragged on till spring. The Federalists crowded around him begging him not to do or say anything that would give the President an opportunity to arouse popular feeling against England. Spokesmen for the administration whispered in his ear that Mr. Jefferson was ready to withdraw his proclamation, which was causing real inconvenience to British warships on the prowl off the coast for French privateers, if Mr. Rose would offer some concession in return. Secretary of State Smith told him outright that he was authorized by the President to say that if American shipping were exempted from the orders in council a rupture with France was a distinct possibility.

Rose was a conciliatory gentleman, but whenever he wanted to concede something he came up against the peremptory nature of Canning's instructions. When he finally had to admit that, in return for the recall of Admiral Berkeley, the American government was expected to disavow Commodore Barron's harboring of deserters, Madison closed the discussion by telling him that the United States could not be expected to make "an expiatory sacrifice to obtain redress."

The alternatives left were war or an embargo sustained long enough to bring the British to terms. Jefferson considered war wasteful, uncivilized, and ineffective. He had been determined all his life to find some other means of coercion. The invention of a bloodless method of solving international differences would be the crowning glory of his Republican administration. Enforcement of the embargo became for him a crusade for human betterment.

Such a measure could only be carried out by universal consensus. The President was so convinced of the rightness of his stand that he took it for granted that the citizenry in general would go along with him as they had in the Burr conspiracy. Shipowners, seafaring men, mechanics, merchants, fishermen would cheerfully submit to the sacrifices necessary to make the embargo effective.

The opposite happened. Overnight Pickering and his extreme Federalists found in the embargo a popular issue. Closing down the shipping industry threw men out of work by the thousands in the seaport towns. The New England fisheries became unprofitable for lack of a market for salt cod. The Federalists began to be listened to. They lashed up regional prejudices; they linked the administration with the tyrant Bonaparte in a plot to destroy New England. Merchants and working people and tradesmen who had been eager recruits of the Democratic Republicans began to have their doubts.

Pickering kept the presses steaming with remonstrance and vituperation. A flock of pamphlets from the pens of his Essex County friends appeared on the bookstalls. These writings were enthusiastically reprinted in London and encouraged Canning to persist in his policy. With the States split into wrangling factions he had nothing to fear from the Americans. After Rose sailed home with his mission a failure Pickering kept up a correspondence with him full of assurances that Britain would have, "among the righteous of the land," support of any measures necessary to defeat the French.

Pickering's old notion of a Northern confederacy, linked perhaps with New Brunswick and Nova Scotia, began to take shape again. He wrote earnestly from Washington to Rufus King, who had been John Adams' minister to England and was now "cultivating his garden," as he put it, in retirement on Long Island: "We must have a union of

Northern Interests to control the predilections & the fears of Jefferson & overthrow Virginia domination."

Revived tension between Federalists and Republicans was reflected in animosities in Congress. One of the leading orators in the House, the Adamses' old family friend Josiah Quincy, never lost an opportunity to denounce the embargo system. In the lobbies of the Senate, Pickering startled all who would listen with hints of Napoleonic influences. A Federalist representative from New York State named Barent Gardinier, who was a warm friend of Pickering's and King's, went so far, in attacking the embargo, as to declare that "there is an unseen hand which is guiding us to the most dreadful destinies . . . we know nothing . . . we legislate without knowing. We are told what we are to do, and the Council of Five Hundred do it."

This reference to Bonaparte's puppet legislature brought three Republicans to their feet demanding that the speaker be held in contempt. In the resulting fracas Gardinier challenged George W. Campbell of Tennessee. A crowd of more than a hundred gathered at the spot chosen across the District line for the encounter. The contestants allowed themselves to be separated by the local magistrates but a few days later they met in secret and Gardinier was so badly wounded that for days his friends despaired of his life.

4. Jefferson's Longest Year

In the cabinet room at the President's house enforcing the embargo became an obsession. Though Gallatin never ceased to consider war a better measure he loyally carried out every galling detail of the President's instructions. In the Senate John Quincy Adams, who was personally in favor of arming merchant ships and letting them sail, went along with the administration measures. The Republican majority put through act after act tightening and strengthening the restrictions, but to no avail.

Smuggling and evading regulations had been second nature to New England seafaring men in colonial times. In recent years skippers had become adept at all sorts of dodges to circumvent the rules laid down by the British authorities. They found the wartime carrying trade, though risky, immensely profitable. Shipowners showed zest and enterprise in finding ways to get around the embargo. Fresh restrictions were laid down almost daily. Coastwise shipping had to be regulated, trade with Canada laid under an interdict. Jefferson's administration found itself in the position of having to enforce martial law along every river and in every harbor on the Atlantic coast.

Early in the winter Jefferson wrote his old Philadelphia friend, Mrs. Trist, that he looked forward to 1808 as the longest year in his life. It proved not only the longest but the bitterest. He had to lay aside the planning of the national capital, the sketching out of an educational system, of canals, and postroads; all the great projects for the national future he enjoyed putting his mind on. Instead his days were filled with restrictive measures he had to concert with the ever loyal indefatigable Gallatin. They found themselves relying on the commerce clause of the Constitution so to control international trade that in the end they were suppressing it altogether.

The details were excruciating: ". . . For Passamaquoddy and St. Mary's, and the secret coves and inlets of the coast.—And be it further enacted, &c, that wheresoever in any port or on the coasts and shores of the United States elsewhere, a collection of provisions or of lumber shall be made or making which is suspected to be intended for exportation contrary to the provisions of the said laws for laying an embargo, it shall be lawful for the collector of the same port, or of the nearest port, by any agent to be appointed by him, to have the same deposited, if provisions, in warehouses to be approved by him, and to be duly secured by lock, the key of which shall remain with such an agent; or if lumber, then to be placed under a sufficient guard by day and night, the expense of which shall be paid by the owner of such lumber. . . ."

Jefferson was never one to spare himself paper work. He sat at his desk drafting in his small neat hand page after page, that his pantograph copied off, of measures which became month by month less enforceable. The migraine headache hardly ever left him. "I have but one hour in the morning," he wrote Gallatin, "in which I am capable of thinking, and that is too much crowded with business to give me time to think."

There were other worries besides the embargo. The Republican majority in Congress was restless and disoriented. A resolution to abandon Washington and move the capital back to Philadelphia reached the point of being referred to a House committee before it was squelched by a hasty mobilization of the President's supporters.

Building a splendid national capital had been Jefferson's pride and care through all the years of his administration. The President's house and the Capitol were still incomplete, but under Latrobe's management they were well on their way. Jefferson was impressing the seal of his renovated classical style, which he felt would furnish the proper frame for the selfgoverning institutions of free men, on every pediment and column of the new buildings.

Among his accomplishments there had been, as always, frustrations. He was disappointed in his hopes of planting parks and avenues. The poplars on Pennsylvania Avenue were about all he had to show for his efforts. He was not even able to save the magnificent forest growth that had so delighted him when he first visited the site of the city.

"How I wish I possessed the power of a despot," Mrs. Harrison Smith quoted him as crying out to a shocked company at his dinner table one afternoon. "Yes, I wish that I was a despot that I might save the noble, the beautiful trees that are daily falling sacrifice to the cupidity of their owners and the necessities of the poor." The cutting down of a fine tree, he told his dinner guests, was akin to murder. Every day he remained in office he felt the frustrations more keenly than the satisfactions of power.

The long session of Congress ended in late April. By that time, so the President wrote his Attorney General, he had been reduced by constant headaches "to almost total incapacity for business."

5. Jefferson Heals a Break

As usual his headaches ceased and his spirits revived as soon as he found himself on the Georgetown ferry and jouncing over the rutted roads through the Maytime woods towards Monticello. Amid the ruin of so many hopes he had one solid cause for rejoicing. He had managed a reconciliation with his old friend Monroe.

Monroe landed in Virginia smarting over his ill success in England and over Jefferson's preference for Madison for the presidency. He was immediately beset by emissaries from John Randolph and his quids urging him actively to seek the nomination.

"I see with infinite grief a contest arising between yourself and another," Jefferson immediately wrote him, "who have been very dear to each other and equally so to me. I sincerely pray that these dispositions may not be affected between you; with me I confidently trust they will not. for independently of the dictates of public duty which prescribe neutrality to me, my sincere friendship for you both will ensure its sacred observance. . . . I already perceive my old friend Clinton"—the Vice President who in spite of his age still aspired to the presidential nomination—"estranging himself from me. no doubt lies are carried to him as they will be to the other two candidates. . . . I know too well from experience the progress of political controversy, and the exacerbation of spirit into which it degenerates, not to fear for the continuation of your mutual esteem. one piquing thing said draws on another, that a third, and always with increasing acrimony, until all restraint is thrown off and it becomes difficult for yourselves to keep clear of the toils in which your friends will endeavor to interlace you. . . . a candid recollection of what you know of each other will be the true corrective."

Jefferson kept recurring to the agonies of office in his letters that year: "My longings for retirement are so strong, that I with difficulty encounter the daily drudgeries of my duty but my wish for retirement itself is not stronger than that of carrying into it the affections of all my friends. I have ever viewed Mr. Madison and yourself as two principal pillars of my happiness. were either to be withdrawn, I should consider it as among the greatest calamities which could assail my future peace of mind."

It took considerable correspondence, but in the end Jefferson won him back. Monroe was no man to hold a grudge. He made a clean breast of his hurt feelings, declared that he had overcome them, and even seemed ready for a reconciliation with Madison.

On the road up to Monticello Jefferson's overseer, Edmund Bacon, met him with the tales that beset the returning landowner. The dam that furnished water for his mill on the Rivanna, from which he had hoped for a sorely needed income, had not yet been properly rebuilt after its destruction by a freshet. The miller was incompetent and possibly a thief. Work was lagging on his fishpond. Frosts had killed many plants in his nursery plot. The sesame seed he was experimenting with as a new source of eating oil had come up few and far between.

Still Jefferson found his house habitable if unfinished. The views of the mountains were as magnificent as ever. His *Magnolia glauca* was in bloom. He counted a hundred and seventyfive artichokes in his vegetable garden and three hundred and thirtyseven roots of Cooper's pale green asparagus. His daughter and grandchildren came over from Edgehill to visit him and, as usual, were a sheer delight.

After a bare month he had to tear himself away from the fresh airs of his hilltop, from his drafting board where he was projecting a new manor house in a novel octagon shape, from his farmlands and his flower beds and his grandchildren. Back in the muggy heat of Washington he plunged again into the miseries of office. In spite of the vindictive opposition of the Federalists he was determined to give the embargo a full trial. Privately he admitted that Gallatin might be right; war might be preferable.

6. *Who Says A Must Say B*

Congress had doubled the regular army and had appropriated funds for more gunboats and for the commissioning of several frigates. Instead of deploying the new forces at the disposal of the national government for defense against the foreign enemies, Jefferson and Gallatin found themselves, by the hideous logic of the embargo, compelled to put them to use against their fellow citizens.

Gallatin summed up the situation with his usual disenchanted clarity: "If the embargo must be persisted in any longer two principles must necessarily be adopted. . . . 1st that not a single vessel shall be permitted to move without the permission of the Executive. 2nd that the collectors be invested with the general power of seizing property anywhere, and taking the rudders or otherwise effectually preventing the departure of any vessel in harbor . . . without being liable to personal suits. I am sensible that such arbitrary powers are equally dangerous and odious."

The ramifications were endless. The Vermonters were moving raftloads of supplies up Lake Champlain for sale in Canada and daring the federal troops to stop them. To prevent the export of flour Jefferson and Gallatin had to decide how much flour the city of Boston needed for its own use. There was the case of a Chinese mandarin who asked permission to remove his effects from New York to Canton; was he a bona fide alien or was he cover for a mercantile speculation?

7. An Appeal to a Liberal Czar

No matter how great the emergency, it had become the custom to suspend the operation of the federal government during the sickly season. In late July Gallatin retired to New York, and Jefferson and Madison to their estates in the Virginia hills. Since Montpelier was only a day's ride from Monticello and the mails took a week to New York, that summer the President put in more time on foreign than domestic affairs.

In August Madison joined Jefferson, and their congenial mutual friends Joel and Ruth Barlow, at Monticello. The Department of State went into permanent session.

Jefferson, who was still ignorant of the secret part of the Treaty of Tilsit, had been carrying on a correspondence with the Czar Alexander. He and Madison decided that the time had come to send a special mission to St. Petersburg to win the liberal Emperor to active neutrality.

For a year Jefferson had been trying to find the proper niche for his old friend William Short. Short was one of his Virginia law pupils for whom he felt a truly fatherly affection. Short had developed into an accomplished diplomat. Jefferson remembered with gratitude his able collaboration as secretary of the legation in Paris. Jefferson convinced Madison that Short was the man to deal with the Russian court.

Madison dispatched his appointment, subject to senatorial approval, to Philadelphia where Short was waiting for orders to sail. The mission was to be secret. There had been much fruitless consultation about the proper person for Short to take along as secretary: the President insisted that he be a loyal Republican. Meanwhile Jefferson and Madison concocted an epistle to Alexander. "Great and good Friend" was the style of republican simplicity they used in addressing foreign potentates. They respectfully requested the Czar to come to the assistance of the United States by enforcing "by the high influence of your example the respect due to the character & rights of a peaceable nation."

8. *The Freedom of the Press*

Jefferson was tormented by the rising opposition to his policies. In his note bidding Short goodbye, he unburdened himself on the subject of the Federalist press. Even after thirtyfive years of public life he had not learned to steel himself against newspaper criticism. The struggle to enforce the embargo had left every nerve raw.

He referred Short to the third and fourth columns on the third page of the Philadelphia Federalist journal, the *United States Gazette*, for August 31 as an example of "daring and atrocious lies."

"The papers have lately advanced in boldness and flagitiousness even beyond themselves. . . . however I have from the beginning determined to submit myself as the subject on whom may be proved the impotency of a free press in a country like ours, against those who conduct themselves honestly and enter into no intrigue."

The letter was dated September 6 so the offending journal must have just arrived in the mail. The columns Jefferson referred to claimed to quote a remark of his to an unnamed correspondent: if we had to fight the British, American seamen could man ships furnished by the French. Mr. Madison was quoted as saying: "France wants money and we must give it."

If Jefferson's feeling had not been exacerbated out of all proportion he could hardly have helped smiling as he read further down the column. A gentleman from Caracas was quoted as saying that in a popular rising against the French invasion the Spaniards had destroyed every Frenchman in Spain and that Bonaparte had been so badly wounded by the Duke of Infantado during an engagement under the walls of Bayonne that he had had to have his arm amputated. An unlikely tale on the face of it.

If Jefferson wasn't amused by the ironies implicit in these columns in the *United States Gazette*, Short, a less partisan observer of the international scene, undoubtedly was. Bonaparte, on his long rampage set off by the British coup at Copenhagen, had overturned the Bourbon monarchy in Spain and crowned his brother Joseph King of the Spaniards. The Spaniards revolted against alien rule with desperate violence, defeated a French army, and engaged Bonaparte in the Peninsular War which was the beginning of his undoing. The British were preparing to help the Spaniards, so the British cabinet and the American Federalists now found themselves on the libertarian side, while the American Republicans, during the present summer at least, were giving only lukewarm response to this revival of the spirit of 1776 by the patriots of Spain.

In spite of his breadth of view and the variety of his interests Jefferson never in his life could abide criticism of his motives. During the agonizing struggles of his last months in the presidency he became more sensitive than ever. Many years before he had written Edward Carrington that if he had to choose between a free press and a free government he would choose the free press. As recently as his first administration, when Humboldt visited him on the way back from Mexico, he boasted gaily to the great geographer of his indifference to slander. Humboldt, who had the run of the President's house during his stay in Washington—so Mrs. Harrison Smith told the anecdote in her journal—found a scurrilous sheet in the cabinet room and asked the President why he didn't suppress the libels being circulated against him. "Put that paper in your pocket, Baron," cried Jefferson, "and should you hear the reality of our liberty, the freedom of our press questioned, show this paper and tell where you found it."

No matter how bold a front he could occasionally put on, the libels so tortured him that he began to find an insult under every mention of his name on the printed page. Morbidly reticent about his private and family life, Jefferson had already suffered more than any man living from the freedom of the press.

The scandalous stories started with a burst of ingratitude on the part of a drunken printer named James Callender during the first year of Jefferson's presidency. Callender was a Scottish Jacobin who escaped from the clutches of Pitt's catchpoles and took refuge in Virginia. He made himself useful to Jefferson's adherents in their campaign against the Federalists. Justice Chase jailed him under the Sedition Act for a piece of Republican propaganda called "The Prospect Before Us." Jefferson bought his publications and helped him out with small sums of money. As soon as he became President he pardoned the man and tried to get his fine remitted. Callender insisted that the only fit reward for his services was the job of postmaster at Richmond. Jefferson, who by this time had discovered that Callender had a thoroughly bad character, would not hear of it. Callender retaliated by publishing in a Richmond sheet, the *Recorder and Ladies' and Gentlemen's Miscellany*, of which he was part owner, a piece of scandal about Jefferson's early life.

This tidbit had been circulated during the 1800 presidential campaign by "Light Horse Harry" Lee, who, after brilliant exploits during the Revolutionary War, had been leading a checkered and frustrated life in politics and land speculation. Henry Lee was a devoted partisan of Washington's. At the time of Jefferson's estrangement from the old Commander in Chief, Lee turned on Jefferson with violent hatred. Somehow he got a story out of a friend of Jefferson's schooldays,

Jack Walker, to the effect that Jefferson had made adulterous advances to his wife. Whatever happened had happened when they were all very young, years before Jefferson's tragically happy marriage. The Federalist journals repeated the tale enthusiastically. Along with even more scurrilous material, it was printed in the *New England Palladium* and so bandied about the press that Jefferson felt he owed an explanation to the members of his cabinet.

He wrote his Secretary of the Navy, at that time, Robert Smith: "I plead guilty to one of their charges, that when young and single I offered love to a handsome lady. . . . It is the only one founded on truth among all their allegations against me." At the same time he sent private assurances to Walker, who was being stirred up by Lee to demand public reparation, that Mrs. Walker had never responded to his advances.

Callender's other story was that Jefferson had a mulatto mistress at Monticello who had borne him numerous children. Jefferson never opened his lips on that subject either in public or in private. The scandal was widely circulated in prose and verse. Thomas Moore incorporated it into the poem he wrote after his tour in America to express his disgust with American democracy:

> *The Patriot, fresh from Freedom's council come,*
> *Now pleased retires to lash his slaves at home.*
> *Or woo perhaps some black Aspasia's charms,*
> *And dream of Freedom in his bondmaid's arms.*

The topic was irresistible. Both William Cullen Bryant and John Quincy Adams touched on it in satirical verses. There was a popular song about "Dusky Sall." Legends of the libertine philosopher's orgies with mulatto wantons up on the hill were handed down from generation to generation of students at the University of Virginia. Mrs. Trollope elaborated them with relish in her *Domestic Manners of the Americans*. To this day there are families in the United States who believe themselves descended from Jefferson's mulatto mistress.

The story had a kernel of truth. That truth was so painful to Jefferson that he never would speak of it. His daughter Martha Randolph told part of it to her children before she died. Her son Thomas Jefferson Randolph, after making him promise not to publish them, gave further details to Henry S. Randall when Randall was collecting materials for his *Life of Jefferson*. Randall passed the facts on, still insisting on secrecy, to James Parton, who was at work on a new Jefferson biography, in a letter which finally came to light among Parton's papers at the Harvard University Library.

"Walking about mouldering Monticello one day with Col. T. J. Randolph (Mr. Jefferson's eldest grandson)," Randall wrote, "he showed me a smoke-blackened and sooty room in one of the col-

lonades and informed me it was Sally Hemings' room. He asked me if
I knew how the story of Mr. Jefferson's connexion with her originated. I told him I did not. 'There was a better excuse for it,' said
he, 'than you might think; she had children that resembled Mr.
Jefferson so closely that it was plain that they had his blood in their
veins.'"

Indeed they did, and blood even more precious to Jefferson than
his own.

"The secrets of an old Virginia manor house were like the secrets
of an old Norman castle," wrote Randall to Parton. This secret extended over several generations.

By his marriage to Martha Wayles Skelton, Jefferson acquired some
valuable parcels of land, an encumbrance of debt which was to plague
him all his life, and a number of slaves who had been the property of
his wife's father, John Wayles.

Among these slaves was a mulatto family named Hemings. They
were the children of a Betty Hemings who, according to the testimony
of old Isaac, for years blacksmith at Monticello, was the daughter of
an English seacaptain and of one of John Wayles's own slaves. She
was reputed to be startlingly handsome. John Wayles was married
three times to wellconnected Virginia ladies. After his third wife
died he lived with Betty Hemings as his concubine and had six
children by her. When he died this family formed part of Martha
Jefferson's inheritance. Furthermore—though of course such relationships were never spoken of—they were her half brothers and sisters.
Sally, the "Dusky Sall" of the legend, was the youngest, born the
year of John Wayles's death.

The Hemingses were treated as house servants at Monticello.
After Martha Jefferson's death Sally helped take care of the orphan
girls and in 1787 went along with Polly Jefferson, then eight, when
she was shipped overseas to rejoin her father at the legation in Paris.
Five years after the Jefferson family returned home Sally had a child
by a white man. Four others followed. Years later she boasted to
these children that Thomas Jefferson was their father and that he
had first taken up with her when she was his daughter's maid in
Paris.

The eldest boy, Madison, who was said to bear a distinct resemblance to the Jeffersons, believed all his life that he was Thomas
Jefferson's son. Jefferson had him trained as a carpenter. He was
freed when he was twentyone, along with his mulatto brothers and
sisters, according to the terms of Jefferson's will, and moved, like
so many free Negroes, to Ohio. When he was sixtyeight he published the story of his life in the *Pike's County Republican*.

Not long before she died, Jefferson's only surviving daughter,
Martha Randolph, called two of her sons, Thomas Jefferson and

George Wythe Randolph, to her bedside and proved to them, by the dates of the slaves' births in the Farm Book, that President Jefferson could not have been the father of Madison Hemings, because he was away from home for fifteen months preceding his birth. Randall added in his letter to Parton that he had checked the dates in Jefferson's account books and that Mrs. Randolph's statement was correct.

Randall went on with his report of his conversation with Jefferson's grandson: "He said Mr. Jefferson never locked the door of his room by day & that he (Col. R.) slept within sound of his breathing at night. He said he never had seen a motion or a look, or a circumstance that led him to suspect for an instant that there was a particle more of familiarity between Mr. Jefferson & Sally Hemings than between him & the most repulsive servant in the establishment—& that no person ever living at Monticello dreamed of such a thing. With Betsey Hemings, whose children also resembled him, his habitual meetings, were less frequent. . . . Col. Randolph said that he had spent a good share of his life closely about Mr. Jefferson—at home & on journeys in all sorts of circumstances and he fully believed him chaste & pure—as immaculate a man as God ever created."

Several nephews grew up as part of the family circle at Monticello. They were the sons of Dabney Carr, the promising young orator who was Thomas Jefferson's best friend in his early days at the Virginia bar, and of Jefferson's sister Martha. After Dabney Carr's untimely death in 1773 Jefferson buried him at the spot on the hilltop which they both had picked for their graveyard and took his sister and her six children to live with him. Two of the boys, Sam and Peter, were his particular favorites and, as he had no boy of his own, were raised by him as his sons.

". . . Colonel Randolph said that a visitor at Monticello dropped a newspaper from his pocket or accidentally left it. After he had gone he (Col. R.) opened the paper and found some very insulting remarks about Mr. Jefferson's Mulatto Children. The Col. said he felt provoked. Peter & Sam Carr were lying not far off under a shade tree. He took the paper and put it in Peter's hands, pointing out the article. Peter read it, tears coursing down his cheeks, & then handed it to Sam. Sam also shed tears. Peter exclaimed 'aren't you & I a couple of —— pretty fellows to bring this disgrace on poor old uncle who has always fed us. We ought to be—by ——.' "

Colonel Randolph explained to Randall that Sally Hemings was Peter Carr's mistress, and her sister Betsey, Sam's. It was through them that the Jefferson strain was transmitted to the Hemings children. "Their connexion with the Carrs was perfectly notorious at Monticello & scarcely disguised . . . never disavowed. Mr. Jefferson was deeply attached to the Carrs—especially to Peter. He was extremely indulgent to them & the idea of watching them for faults or vices probably never occurred to him.

"I asked Col. R. why on earth Mr. Jefferson did not put these slaves that looked like him out of the public sight by sending them to his Bedford estate or elsewhere. He said Mr. Jefferson never betrayed the least consciousness of the resemblance—and although he (Col. R.) & he had no doubt his mother, would have been very glad to have them thus removed, that both he & all venerated Mr. Jefferson too deeply to broach the topic to him. What suited him suited them."

Callender got drunk, fell into the James River one winter night and drowned in two feet of water, but the calumnies he launched spread far and wide. Timothy Pickering laid his hands on Jefferson's letters to Callender encouraging him to pamphleteer for the Republicans, and published them in every Federalist journal. In New England, where denunciations of slavery were becoming a commonplace of pulpit and press, the philosopher President's licentious hypocrisy became a household word.

The venomous partisan strife produced some strange associations. In 1806 one of Jefferson's appointees, federal Judge Pierpont Edwards, a cousin of Aaron Burr's, induced a grand jury to indict Tapping Reeve for libel at common law. Reeve was Burr's tutor and married his sister. He became one of the leading jurists of New England and judge of the Superior Court of Connecticut. His crime was vituperation of the President in the Litchfield *Monitor*. Two preachers and the editors of the *Connecticut Courant* were further indicted for printing and disseminating Callender's defamatory stories. Though Jefferson's theory was at this time that legal action might be "salutory" to restrict newspaper publication to the provable truth, the resulting prosecutions were later dropped at the President's own request. The stories meanwhile became part of the political mythology of the Jeffersonian era.

Poplar Forest, the Bedford County estate Jefferson's grandson referred to in his talk with Randall, was the only one of his wife's plantations Jefferson still retained in 1808. It was situated in the hills west of the James beyond Lynchburg. As he became more and more beset with visitors at Monticello Jefferson formed the habit of riding over there for a couple of weeks of quiet every summer. As soon as he completed his business with James Madison in the summer of 1808 he set off for Poplar Forest, but this year he had time for only a glimpse. Possibly he spent a day laying out the ground plan of the new house on which he had started to exercise his architectural hobby even before he completed Monticello. By October 1 he was spending the night with the Madisons on his way back to Washington.

9. Essex vs. Marblehead

All the news they had was bad. Public meetings in the seaport towns were denouncing the embargo. The settlements around Lake Champlain were in a state of insurrection. Judges and juries were refusing to convict offenders against the regulations. Governor Sullivan of Massachusetts, a good Democrat, was pronouncing the embargo unenforceable. Local elections were going against the Democratic Republicans. Madison had a letter from Gallatin, who was still in New York:

"You have heard that New England is lost. If there was an election tomorrow here it would I think be no better. Of New Jersey I know nothing & therefore fear the event. . . . The people have been taught to view the embargo, less as a shield protecting them against the decrees and orders of foreign powers, than as . . . the cause of the stagnation of commerce & depreciation of products. Nor have we been defended on proper grounds nor with sufficient ability."

Jefferson and Madison had formed the habit of making the journey to Washington together. The moment they arrived in the unfinished capital they went to work on the President's eighth and last annual message to Congress. As soon as Gallatin reached town from New York he pitched in on the financial section. It was a rather wordy message, explaining in vague terms the failure of the embargo thus far to bring the belligerent powers to terms and the necessity for its continuance. Meanwhile harbor defenses were on the way at New York and New Orleans, one hundred and three gunboats had been completed, and recruiting was going on for the national army. Jefferson considered a welltrained militia "the best security for a free people." "It is incumbent on us, at every meeting, to revise the condition of the militia," he wrote, "and to ask ourselves if it is prepared to repel a powerful enemy at every point."

The President was able to speak with satisfaction of the boom in manufactures encouraged by the cutting off of imports from Europe. Everything was being done to encourage the manufacture of arms, both in government arsenals and in private factories. He could report with pride that, in spite of the losses from the embargo, Gallatin's Treasury had taken in eighteen million dollars that year, that another two million three hundred thousand had been paid off the national debt, and that after the next payment on the debt due on January 1 there would still be a surplus of nine million dollars. He tactfully suggested that Congress, "whenever the freedom and safety of our commerce shall be restored," consider "the improvements of roads, canals, rivers, education, and other great foundations of prosperity and union, under the powers which Congress may already possess," or which were to be granted by amendment to the Constitution.

In a final paragraph he thanked Congress and his fellow citizens for their "repeated proof of confidence. . . . in the transaction of their business I cannot have escaped error. it is incident to our imperfect nature. but I may say with truth, my errors have been of the understanding: not of intention."

As soon as the members of Congress retired to their respective chambers Hillhouse of Connecticut took the floor of the Senate with a motion to repeal the Embargo Act. Pickering, tall, cadaverous, his lanky black hair pulled back off his domed bald head, followed with a blistering speech declaring that the embargo was in exact conformity with the wishes of the French Emperor. He painted a lurid picture: having defeated the British, Napoleon would use the English fleet to transport his army across the Atlantic "in order to add to his titles that of Emperor of the Two Americas."

Pickering was riding high in Massachusetts. The Essex Junto was more of a state of mind than a political machine but it was powerful nonetheless. Essex men saw to it that John Quincy Adams should be superseded in the Senate for the next Congress. Adams resigned in a huff, announcing that he would devote himself henceforth to his law practice and to his Harvard College lectures. The Essex men further used their influence in the legislature to change in their favor the rules for the picking of presidential electors.

When Canning in London trapped Pinkney into making him, confidentially, a written offer from the Washington government to repeal the embargo if Britain would lift the orders in council in so far as they applied to American ships, Canning's sarcastic letter of rejection, which Madison was keeping under his hat, appeared in print, no one knew how, in the *New England Palladium*. Canning's indelicacies had less support in his own country than among the New England Federalists. The Essex Junto was on the way to out-Tory the Tories.

The people of Massachusetts were not yet entirely converted to these sentiments. At a town meeting in Salem, the heart of Essex County, held on October 28 the vote was 570 for continuing the embargo to 490 against. The Marblehead fishermen continued to observe the embargo at such great sacrifice that during the winter of 1808–9 sympathizers in Norfolk County sent them twenty barrels of salt pork, thirty barrels of meal, and other supplies in a train of wagons "to eat with their dry fish." A few months before Dr. Nathaniel Ames of Dedham, an outspoken Republican, refused to attend the funeral of his brother Fisher Ames when he found the Essex Junto politicians turning the burial of that brilliant paladin of Federalism into what he termed "a political pageant."

From Quincy old John Adams, who, though still at odds with Jefferson, could not stomach Pickering, shot off an occasional booming remark to encourage the patriots. "Our Gazettes and Pamphlets," he wrote Dr. Rush, "tell us that Bonaparte will conquer England . . . and send I know not how many hundred thousand soldiers here and conquer from New Orleans to Passamaquoddy. Though every one of these Bugbears is an empty Phantom, yet the People seem to believe every article of the bombastical Creed and tremble and shudder in Consequence. Who shall touch these blind eyes?"

The year 1809 dawned amid mounting political hysteria. These "bugbears," as John Adams called them, had begun to haunt even the Unionist faction of Federalists.

Humphrey Marshall wrote Pickering approvingly from Kentucky and his cousin the Chief Justice, who was now heart and soul with New England in everything except secession, applauded his speeches and writings. "I thank you sincerely," John Marshall wrote Pickering, "for the excellent speeches. . . . If sound argument & correct reasoning could save our country it would be saved. Nothing can be more completely demonstrated than the inefficacy of the embargo, yet that demonstration seems to be of no avail. I fear most seriously that the same spirit which so tenaciously maintains this measure will impell us to a war with the only power which protects any part of the civilized world from the despotism of that tyrant with whom we shall then be ravaged." In the House John Randolph echoed Marshall's warning with a denunciation of what he claimed was the administration's intention to declare war on England.

In spite of the Federalist furor voting had been going quietly forward for the election of James Madison as fourth President. His presidential electors were chosen before the agitation against the embargo carried the Northern state legislatures into the Federalist camp. Now a Republican revival in Pennsylvania made his election sure. The vote turned out to be a hundred and twentytwo for Madison against fortyseven divided between George Clinton and Charles Cotesworth Pinckney of South Carolina, an estimable gentleman whom the Federalists settled on for want of a better candidate.

The Enforcement Act, signed by President Jefferson on January 9, 1809, proved to be the embargo's last gasp. The measure followed the specifications of Gallatin's desperate report of the preceding July by putting trade and commerce under martial law. Its administration was to be in the hands of the armed forces.

The new rules for enforcement were met by a fresh outbreak of seditious oratory. General Benjamin Lincoln, an elderly Revolutionary hero who had been collector of the port of Boston, resigned rather than carry them out. The Massachusetts legislature denounced the measure as unconstitutional. Governor Trumbull of Connecticut refused to call out his state militia.

The moderate Federalists were calling for repeal but Pickering's cry, not to wait for repeal but to "defeat the accursed measure now," rang through the New England town meetings. The town of Bath in the province of Maine voted to set up a committee of correspondence in the Revolutionary model. Gloucester and Newburyport followed suit. A crowd of four thousand citizens at Faneuil Hall demanded the interposition of the General Court between the national government and the citizenry of that state. The Massachusetts Senate passed a resolution declaring that the commonwealth was ready to cooperate with other legislatures "to concur in measures to rescue our common country from impending ruin."

10. British Agent

In Pickering's addresses and in the townmeeting orations he inspired there appeared so strong an undercurrent of secessionist talk that Sir James Craig, the governor of Lower Canada, seated at Quebec, felt that the time had come to win New England away from the American Union. His secretary had for some time been in communication with a gentleman named John Henry who claimed to be intimate with men of prominence throughout the New England states.

John Henry was an Irishman who landed in America as a youth and was apprenticed to a New York merchant. After serving as an artillery officer in the Army of the United States under John Adams, he somehow got admitted to the bar. Failing as a lawyer, he went to work in Montreal for the fur traders of the Northwest Company. On a visit to the United States in 1808 he wrote back letters to the governor's secretary which Sir James Craig found so interesting that he forwarded them to Castlereagh and, receiving some encouragement from the War Office, he appointed Henry his secret agent to treat with certain New England leaders he believed were planning secession.

Early in February of 1809 Henry traveled over frozen roads down through Vermont to Boston, noting signs of disaffection as he went. He carried credentials, with the governor's signature and a red seal affixed, but was instructed not to show them unless absolutely necessary to obtain some public man's cooperation.

A detailed plan was forming among British colonial officials for the reunion of the states of Massachusetts, Connecticut, Vermont, New Hampshire, Rhode Island, and New York with New Brunswick and Nova Scotia. The new colony was to have a capital of its own and was to be called New Britain. A program was laid out to encourage emigration of farmers and artisans from the rest of the United States and for the education of young people of mark in Canadian schools. Shipping was to be attracted to New Britain by encouraging trade with the West Indies from which the rest of the American ports were to be excluded. In case of war, Washington, as national capital of the United States, was already marked for destruction.

It is hard to see how Mr. Henry made much headway. He was able to assure the British authorities that in case of a war with Great Britain the governor of Vermont would declare that state's neutrality; and that, if a proper effort were made, the four northern states might possibly be induced to place themselves under the protection of Great Britain. His final report stated candidly: "I can assure you that they do not at this moment fully entertain the project of withdrawing the Eastern States from the Union, finding it a very unpopular topic."

While Mr. Henry was conferring with New England secessionists, President Jefferson was trying to hold his crumbling administration together long enough to hand it over intact to James Madison on March 4.

His heart was no longer in his work. "I have thought it right," he wrote his old Philadelphia friend Dr. Logan, "to take no part in proposing measures the execution of which will devolve on my successor. I am therefore an unmeddling listener to what others have to say." The Federalists saw a different motive in Jefferson's restraint. "Fear of responsibility."

What came to be known as the Force Act had not been on the books for a month before the revulsion against the embargo, and everything connected with it, now sweeping Federalists and Republicans alike, reached Congress. After a fruitless debate on whether the arming of merchant ships or a declaration of war should be substituted, the Embargo Act was repealed. A tepid measure which pleased no one, cutting off commercial intercourse with both France and England, was substituted. Pickering's Massachusetts Federalists and Canning in England meanwhile exerted every effort to make the world believe that repeal meant submission to the orders in council. President Jefferson resignedly signed the bill on March 1.

11. *The Unkindest Cut*

He had to suffer one further humiliation. He had held back William Short's appointment as minister to Russia, in the hope that his friends could get it through the Senate without arousing too much Federalist rancor during the legislative scramble which always accompanied the last days of a Congress. In response to a thoroughly specious Federalist objection that intercourse with Russia could be carried on just as well through diplomats at present in Europe, the Senate unanimously rejected Short's confirmation.

"This reception," wrote Jefferson to his old friend, whose diplomatic career was thus being brought to an abrupt end, "of the last of my official communications to them could not be unfelt."

It was a bitter understatement.

The morning of Madison's inauguration Jefferson refused a seat in the carriage of the President elect. He rode alone to the Capitol through a crowd estimated at ten thousand and hitched his horse to a post. After walking into the Hall of Representatives he declined to be placed on the dais. "This day I return to the people," he was heard to say, "and my proper seat is among them."

Mrs. Samuel Harrison Smith, who was devoted to both Madison and Jefferson, watched the proceedings with an anxious eye. Mr. Madison was not an impressivelooking man. She noticed that he was "pale and trembling" when he embarked on his inaugural address. Hardly anybody could hear a word he said.

Mrs. Madison, on the other hand, ravished all hearts. She was dressed in a plain cambric dress with a long train and wore a bonnet of purple velvet with white plumes. Mrs. Smith found her "all dignity, grace and affability." Mrs. Smith's husband in his account of the affair in the *National Intelligencer* described Mr. Madison as wearing a full suit of cloth "of national manufacture."

After the ceremony Mr. and Mrs. Madison, having passed a troop of militia in review, returned to their own house. Mr. Jefferson promptly arrived to congratulate them. When the Smiths went to call on Mr. Jefferson at the President's house, where it had been arranged for him to remain for a few days more while he saw to the packing of his papers and scientific collections, they found him quite alone.

After dinner Jefferson attended the dance at Long's Hotel. "You must tell me how to behave," he said to a friend. "It's forty years since I've been to a ball."

John Quincy Adams, in Washington to argue a case before the Supreme Court, also attended. "The crowd was excessive, the heat oppressive, the entertainment bad," he noted tersely in his diary.

Mrs. Smith, quite the contrary, enjoyed the inaugural ball. Mrs. Madison wore bird of paradise plumes and behaved like a queen. Mrs. Smith did remark on the heat. The glass had to be broken out of the transoms for ventilation. Everybody noticed the sparkle in Mr. Jefferson's eye. It was Mr. Madison who looked solemn. Somebody asked Mr. Jefferson why that was. No wonder Mr. Madison looked serious, was his reply. "I had the burden on my shoulders and now he's got it on his."

Later in the evening Mrs. Smith found herself standing beside Mr. Madison. When he made a move to leave, everybody insisted he must stay to supper. He let himself be prevailed upon but whispered in Mrs. Smith's ear, "I'd much rather be in bed."

CHAPTER VI

From the Groves of Monticello

1. Shaking off the Shackles

Thomas Jefferson left Washington for the last time on March 11, 1809. Edmund Bacon, his overseer, had already set off with two heavy wagons loaded with furniture and boxes, each hauled by a sixmule team. Two pairs of sorrel Chickasaw horses were hitched to another wagon weighted down with shrubs from Maine's nursery. Eleven servants perched wherever they could find room on the wagons. The overseer followed with the carriage.

Bacon told the story to the Reverend Mr. Pierson years later: "On the way home we had a tremendous snowstorm. It snowed very fast and when we reached Culpeper Court House it was half a leg deep. A large crowd of people had collected there expecting that the President would be along. When I rode up, they thought I was the President and shouted and hurrahed tremendously. When I got out of the carriage they laughed most heartily at their mistake. There was a platform along the whole front of the tavern and it was full of people. Some of them had been waiting a good while, and drinking a good deal, and they made so much noise that they scared the horses, and Diomede backed, and tread upon my foot, and lamed me so that I could hardly get into the carriage the next morning. There was one very tall old fellow that was noisier than any of the rest, who said he was bound to see the President—'Old Tom,' he called him. They asked me when he would be along, and I told them I thought he would certainly be along that night, and I looked for him every moment. The tavern was kept by an old man named Shackleford. I told him to have a large fire built in a private room, as Mr. Jefferson would be very cold when he got there, and he did so. I soon heard shouting, went out, and Mr. Jefferson was in sight. He was in a one-horse vehicle—a phaeton—with a driver, and a servant on horseback. When he came up, there was great cheering again. I motioned to him to follow me; took him straight to his room, and locked the door. The tall old fellow came and knocked very often, but I would not let him in. I told Mr. Jefferson not to mind him, he was drunk. Finally the door was opened, and they rushed in and filled the room. It was as full as I ever saw a bar-room. He stood up, and made a short address to them. Afterwards some of them told him how they had mistaken me for him. He went on next day, and reached Monticello before we did."

"I had a very fatiguing journey," Jefferson wrote President Madison, "having found the roads excessively bad, though I have seen them worse. the last three days I found it better to be on horseback, and travelled eight hours through as disagreeable a snowstorm as I was ever in. feeling no inconvenience from the expedition but fatigue, I have more confidence in my vis vitae than I had before entertained." He was nearing his sixtysixth birthday. "The spring is remarkably backward," he added—Madison was a fellow farmer: "no oats sown, not much tobacco seed, and little done in the gardens. wheat has suffered considerably. no vegetation visible yet but the red maple, weeping willow and lilac." Always optimistic, he noted that the price of wheat in Richmond was on the rise.

He was met at Monticello by his daughter Patsy and the young Randolphs and ranks of cheering slaves and a cavalcade of Albemarle County neighbors. "I retire to my family, my books and farms," he wrote his French philosopher friend Du Pont de Nemours. ". . . never did a prisoner, released from his chains, feel such relief as I shall on shaking off the shackles of power. . . . should you return to the United States perhaps your curiosity may lead you to visit the hermit of Monticello. . . ." He added a postscript. "If you return to us, bring a couple of pair of truebred shepherd's dogs. You will add a valuable possession to a country now beginning to pay great attention to the raising of sheep. . . ." "Safe in port" was a phrase he often used in his letters in those days. So long as he lived he never left his native Virginia.

2. The Burden on His Shoulders

While Jefferson was reveling in the outdoor life at Monticello, riding his farms on his favorite horses, planting his experimental garden, setting out hedges and fruit trees, and seeing to his nailery and his mill, his friend Madison in Washington was struggling with far thornier problems. His selection of a cabinet proved a hornet's nest.

The President's first choice for Secretary of State was known to be Albert Gallatin. Even before Madison's inauguration such a cabal against Gallatin reared its head in the Senate under the leadership of

Gallatin's erstwhile friend General Samuel Smith, the bumptious Baltimore shipping magnate, that it became evident that the appointment would fail of confirmation. When Madison sought to satisfy the Smith faction by offering the Treasury to Robert Smith, Gallatin remarked bleakly that in that case he would be handling both departments. Wasn't that too much to ask?

Madison decided to let Gallatin remain in the Treasury and to appoint Robert Smith to the State Department. Madison doubted Smith's competence, but he was intending, anyway, to keep foreign affairs in his own hands. Dearborn had already resigned from the War Department and was being rewarded for his services there by the more lucrative and less arduous position of collector of the port of Boston. For War and the Navy Madison picked William Eustis, a retired military surgeon from Massachusetts, and Paul Hamilton, who had once served as governor of South Carolina, two inoffensive gentlemen whom nobody would oppose because nobody knew anything about them.

During the weeks before his inauguration Madison's mail had been full of unsolicited advice as to cabinet appointments. Robert Fulton sent in the naïve suggestion that Madison appoint their mutual friend, the poet Joel Barlow, as Secretary of the Navy to facilitate the installation of Fulton's harpoon torpedoes for harbor protection. He further invited Mr. Madison to attend a demonstration of his torpedoes at Kalorama, where as usual he was being put up by his beloved Barlows while he lobbied around Washington trying to interest Congress and the departments in various inventions.

"Toot," as Fulton was known in the Barlow family, was in fine fettle that winter. His joint steamboat experiment with Robert R. Livingston on the Hudson was proving an overwhelming success.

Though the steamboat, still vaguely referred to as the *North River*, was described as looking like "a saw mill set on fire and mounted on a scow" she had reached Albany without a hitch in thirtytwo hours from New York. She had carried passengers and freight regularly back and forth for six weeks. Fulton was planning to institute a scheduled service between New York and Albany at seven dollars a head as soon as the ice broke in the spring. His portfolios were full of plans for improved steam vessels. If Jefferson's internal improvements could be put into effect the canals would prove ideal for steam navigation. The war talk excited him. He saw a chance for his submarine which he'd worked on in France for so many years. He was projecting a steampropelled floating battery which would put Jefferson's derided theories of harbor protection on a really practical basis.

President Madison had more pressing matters on his mind than steam navigation or experiments with torpedoes. Months before his retirement Jefferson had lost control of Congress. The Democratic

Republican majority had split into cliques. Now Gallatin, that astute manipulator of parties and men, was losing his authority.

The President saw the breach between Gallatin and the Smith brothers becoming irretrievable. Gallatin, to whom order and rectitude in financial matters was a consuming passion, had been shocked by the defalcation of a naval agent at Leghorn. The man was intercepted by John Armstrong in Paris and forced to disgorge most of the funds he had embezzled, but in the resulting investigation it transpired that Robert Smith had been using his brother's firm's bills of exchange to finance naval expenditures in the Mediterranean. It looked to Gallatin as if the firm of Smith & Buchanan were being allowed to use government funds for commercial transactions. He protested vigorously to Samuel Smith and received a tart letter in return. To make matters worse the controversy was dragged into the Baltimore newspapers in the course of General Smith's campaign for reelection to the Senate.

Madison's administration was showing every sign of getting off to a bad start when Fortune seemed suddenly to smile. Negotiations with the British took a new turn. David Erskine, His Majesty's minister, was, after all, his father's son. He was married to an American lady. His dearest ambition was to effect a reconciliation. A month after Madison's inauguration Erskine received fresh instructions from Canning which he felt might be made, by stretching a point here and there, the basis for an accommodation. He called on Robert Smith and made a suggestion: if the President would drop a condition he kept harping on, that Admiral Berkeley should be courtmartialed as part of the reparations for the attack on the *Chesapeake*, his government would do the handsome thing. The President consented. There followed an exchange of letters disposing of that grievance.

A few days later Erskine agreed that His Majesty would modify his orders in council if the President would withdraw his proclamation of nonintercourse in so far as it related to Great Britain. The President complied and David Erskine promptly announced that he was authorized to declare that "the orders in Council of January and November 1807 will have been withdrawn as respects the United States on the 10th of June next."

The Republican newspapers burst into thanksgivings. As soon as he heard the news the governor of Upper Canada recalled his secret agent from Massachusetts. On May 1 Sir James Craig's secretary, Herman Ryland, wrote John Henry in disgust: "I am cruelly out of spirits at the idea of Old England truckling to such a debased and accursed government as that of the United States."

Enthusiasm for Madison swept the seaport towns. Without waiting for June 10 several hundred ships hastily stowed their cargoes and put out from American ports. President Madison found himself, somewhat prematurely it turned out, the toast of the Eleventh Congress called that spring in special session.

The Federalists were confounded. John Randolph and his quids turned to blaming Jefferson for the misunderstandings of the past year. Military appropriations, which all congressmen hated, were suspended, and a mere seven hundred and forty thousand dollars was set aside for fortifications. Madison was able to revive Jefferson's plan for a Russian mission. The day before Congress adjourned in an atmosphere of almost lyrical good feeling, Madison put through his nomination of John Quincy Adams as minister to the court at St. Petersburg.

3. Pavel Petrovich Svinin

It was mid-July before the Madisons were ready to leave for Montpelier. Their last official act was to receive the chargé d'affaires sent by the Czar Alexander to inaugurate formal diplomatic relations between the two great sprawling nations that had for the moment the common aim of keeping out of Europe's wars.

The Russians soon made themselves very much at home in the United States. The consul general's secretary was a romantic young painter named Pavel Petrovich Svinin. When he went back to St. Petersburg he published an illustrated volume describing the American scene with great enthusiasm and inaccuracy. Niagara Falls, the Natural Bridge, and Jefferson's and Latrobe's new hall for the House of Representatives impressed him particularly.

He was enraptured by the beauty of Fulton's new Hudson River steamboat, the *Paragon*. The passenger quarters were luxurious. "Gleaming silver and bronze, shining mirrors and mahogany are everywhere, and the most fastidious person of the most refined taste can find here everything to his liking: the best wines, all manner of dainties, and even ice cream in the hot season." Cooking was done by steam from the boiler. Cabins, berths, sofas were all order and cleanliness.

The cleanliness impressed him in Philadelphia. In spite of the monotony of the architecture he found that city almost comparable to St. Petersburg, and as recently carved out of the wilderness. He pointed out that every house had a water tap and that even the porches and sidewalks were scrubbed with soap Saturday afternoons.

As well as being a watercolorist of considerable charm Svinin was a critic and connoisseur. He wrote discerningly of the painting of Benjamin West, and John Trumbull, and Sully and Vanderlyn and the Peales.

While preparing his volume to make Western democracy known to the Russians, he published sketches of life in Moscow and St. Petersburg and an engraving of the Czar Alexander in the Philadelphia *Port Folio*. He shrewdly explained how the scarcity of labor was pressing the Americans towards the invention of mechanical devices.

He was carried away by the skillful construction of the covered bridges. "No two countries," he wrote in a final accolade, "bear a more striking resemblance than Russia and the United States."

4. *Summer Capital*

When the Madisons reached Montpelier they found the house torn up. Madison had caught the contagion of Jefferson's mania for classical porches and columns. With advice from Thornton and Latrobe, he was completing his remodeling of his paternal mansion, which he had started from a sketch of Jefferson's some years before. As soon as he could spare them from Monticello Jefferson had sent over his brickmaker and Dinsmore, his best carpenter and cabinetmaker, to help the Madisons. Notes and messages traveled in a continuous stream between Montpelier and Monticello that summer.

Visitors from Washington trod a path between the two plantations. Mrs. Samuel Harrison Smith left a record in her diary of her visits in the first days of August. She and her husband went first to Monticello. She described their day there. The guests were out on the terrace at dawn admiring the view of the mountains. Mr. Jefferson had a passionate enjoyment of weather and landscape. She never forgot how vividly he described the beauty of a snowstorm he had seen some winters before pouring over the Blue Ridge. Mr. Jefferson took her for a ride with his granddaughter Ellen in a little chair he called "the sociable." She was in a fright for fear they would tip over because he took them around the lower unfinished circuit of the hilltop, driving over fallen trees and great rocks. He seemed to be looking more at the view than at the road.

The hilltop air gave everybody an appetite. Breakfast was simple, muffins and hot breads with butter and ham, but there was a folded napkin at every plate. Mr. Jefferson took Mrs. Smith and her husband, who was one of the few journalists he confided in, to visit his library. He showed them a set of views of ancient villas around Rome. He read them a page of *Piers Ploughman*. Mrs. Smith admitted she found it as unintelligible as Hebrew. Then he showed her some Greek romances and loaned her a French translation of one of them. He opened the little cabinet where he kept his garden seeds in glass vials. Big seeds like peas and beans were in tin canisters. Mrs. Smith was disappointed in the appearance of the library. She found it too cut up by walls and arches.

Dinner, in the beautiful whitepaneled dining room, she found simple and abundant. She had described his table at the President's house as combining republican simplicity with aristocratic refinement. Dishes were presented in the French style. Mr. Jefferson had taken his two Negro cooks to Washington with him to learn cookery from Monsieur Julien. After tea the ladies were served the most delicious figs, all Monticello grown.

The household was somewhat out of kilter during the Smiths' visit because Mr. Jefferson's daughter, Mrs. Randolph, who usually acted as hostess, was indisposed, and his granddaughter Anne, only recently married, was laid up by a miscarriage. In the late afternoon Mrs. Smith found Mr. Jefferson arranging a race on the lawn for his smaller grandchildren. They made him run too. When they came back tired and hot from running the little girls threw themselves into their grandfather's arms. He sat on the grass with the children lolling about him. "It is only with them," he told Mrs. Smith, "that a grave man can play the fool."

This was the life Jefferson described a year later with such relish to his old friend Kosciusko, the Polish patriot who had presented him some years before with a sable cloak, acquired when he was a prisoner at the court of the czars, in which Jefferson bundled up when he was writing at his desk in cold weather. "in the bosom of my family and surrounded by my books. I enjoy a repose to which I have long been a stranger. my mornings are devoted to correspondence. from breakfast to dinner I am in my shops, my garden, or on horseback among my farms; from dinner to dark I give to society and recreation with my neighbors and friends; and from candlelight to early bedtime I read. my health is perfect, and my strength considerably reinforced by the activity of the course I pursue; perhaps it is as great as usually falls to the lot of near sixty-seven years of age. I talk of plows and harrows, seeding and harvesting with my neighbors, and of politics too if they chose, with as little reserve as the rest of my fellow citizens and feel at length the blessing of being free to say and do what I please."

Mrs. Smith confided in her diary that she was "sad to tears" when she and her husband rode down the hill from Monticello on their way to Montpelier, but Mrs. Madison's cheerful greeting made her feel "all warm again." They arrived at the Madisons' late in the afternoon. They found the President with a group of gentlemen still "smoking segars and drinking wine" in the dining room. Elevation to the presidency hadn't changed Mr. Madison's manners. Mrs. Smith found him as "plain, friendly, communicative, and unceremonious as any Virginia planter."

Over the wine and pineapples Mrs. Madison scolded Mrs. Smith a little for not bringing her small daughters. Mrs. Smith said she had been afraid of incommoding her friends. Dolley Madison laughed and flashed her dark eyes. She only had twentythree guests in the house, she exclaimed. She wouldn't have known the Smith children were there. At that point Mr. Madison and Mr. Smith "peeped in on them" and suggested they come out on the piazza. They walked and talked until tea "or rather supper" was served. At table they found President Madison's brother William and his family and several other relatives, "all plain country people."

When bedtime came Mrs. Madison and her lady's maid, Nany, helped Mrs. Smith undress. It was Nany who called her next morning "to a late breakfast & brought me ice and water (this is universal here even in the taverns) & assisted me to dress. We sat down between fifteen and twenty persons to breakfast & to a most excellent Virginia breakfast; tea, coffee, hot wheatbread, light cakes, a pone or cornloaf, cold ham, nice hashes, chicken, &c &c."

A couple of mornings later Mr. Madison had to tear himself away from his guests and hurry back to feverhaunted Washington. Urgent messages had been arriving from Gallatin. Canning had repudiated David Erskine's agreement. Erskine was ordered home and was to be replaced by none other than Francis James Jackson, the man who'd shown such zest in delivering the ultimatum to the Danes which was followed by the bombardment of Copenhagen.

Canning found himself a pretext for his repudiation of his minister. His Majesty George III (now a fuddled old man in a last lucid interval before his final plunge into incurable dementia) had taken umbrage at a phrase in the note forwarded to Westminster by the American Secretary of State.

Madison had indeed laid himself open to this charge by indulging in a petulant sentence which he added to Robert Smith's draft. "While he (The President) forbears to insist on the further punishment of the offending officer (Admiral Berkeley) he is none the less sensible of the justice and utility of such an example, nor the less persuaded that it would best comport with what is due from his Britannic Majesty to his own honor."

This wasn't the sort of talk any Briton would put up with from an American. Canning jumped to his sovereign's defense, secure in the support of every Tory squire in the kingdom, and of every London merchant who profited from the smuggling trade through Heligoland to the Continent, which was so strangely tolerated by the British authorities.

Canning at that moment needed all the political support he could get. Lord Portland's cabinet was in difficulties. His lordship was bedridden. The British expeditionary force, sent to back up the Spanish revolt against Napoleon under the younger Wellesley, who was soon to attain fame as Lord Wellington, won victories but lost ground. The money marts of the City were showing the strain of wartime expenditures. The interruption of the cotton trade was bringing starvation to textile workers in the Midlands.

Canning was trying to take advantage of the hard times to force a reorganization of the Tory government. By ousting his colleague Castlereagh he hoped to get himself appointed Prime Minister. Putting their transatlantic cousins in their place would do him no harm with his constituents.

President Madison spent four days in Washington drafting a proclamation which restored the provisions of the Non-Intercourse Act with regard to Great Britain. Then he hurried back to the purer air of Montpelier. Gallatin and his wife followed. By the end of August both families were being entertained at Monticello, eating Mr. Jefferson's figs and his Roman broccoli, and French dishes flavored with the particularly excellent onions he'd harvested from his soninlaw Tom Randolph's seed. While they admired the view from the Monticello terraces they discussed the difficulties foreign and domestic that faced Madison's administration.

Gallatin was no longer on speaking terms with Robert Smith or his brother the general. He had made up his mind to resign from the cabinet, and to try to get back his old seat in the House of Representatives. Jefferson wouldn't hear of it. Without Gallatin their mutual project to pay off the national debt and to establish a massive program of internal improvements would never be accomplished. Jefferson was casting around for ways to strengthen his friend Madison's administration.

Though Madison and Monroe were outwardly reconciled, he found each of them still fretful about the political activities of the other. Working as usual by indirection, he was planning to induce Madison to make Monroe Secretary of State. First he had to get Monroe away from the Southside quids and the Richmond Federalists. Monroe would arrive in Albemarle any day now. His small plantation house, Ashlawn, which Jefferson himself had helped him rebuild in his favorite style, was in sight of Monticello. Jefferson was confident he could talk Monroe around as soon as he got him within earshot. Meanwhile he exerted all his powers of persuasion to keep Gallatin from resigning.

There were other topics to be discussed. Nonintercourse might keep the British and French at bay long enough to give John Quincy Adams time to reach St. Petersburg. Perhaps the Czar Alexander could be induced to throw his weight on the side of neutral shipping. Jefferson and Madison both felt that if war with England should become inevitable Canada would fall into the American Union. Madison felt that no coercion would be necessary: "When the pear is ripe it will fall of itself." Any convenient pretext would suffice for the occupation of the Floridas. They had long since convinced themselves that West Florida, at least, was rightfully United States territory as part of the Louisiana Purchase.

Madison and Jefferson shared a blind spot on military affairs. Though Gallatin urged more energy in preparing the army for war, Madison and Jefferson still viewed the ambivalent and dilatory activities of their General in Chief, James Wilkinson, with a vague complacency.

Wilkinson came out of the Burr trial tarnished but as brazen as ever. As soon as he finished testifying for the prosecution he sent a challenge to John Randolph, who had made no secret in and out of court of the fact that he considered the general a thief and a rogue. "I cannot descend to your level" was Randolph's answer.

As soon as Congress met Randolph moved that a House committee be appointed to investigate Wilkinson's dealings with the Spaniards. Daniel Clark produced letters that would have damned any other man, but Wilkinson, strutting around Washington in the famous uniform of his own design, shrugged them off. He countered each accusation with a cloud of verbiage.

When Randolph refused a second time to meet him on the field of honor, the general published a handbill, denouncing "John Randolph, M.C.," to the world "as a prevaricating, base, calumniating scoundrel, poltroon and coward."

Jefferson, while he was still President, had turned the evidence against the general over to a military court. Now, to the amazement of the informed public, the court found that Brigadier General Wilkinson had behaved "with honor to himself and fidelity to the country."

Meanwhile the general was sedulously attentive to every whim of Dearborn's War Department. He labored to build up the armories at Harper's Ferry and Springfield. As long as the embargo lasted his troops tried to enforce it. At the same time he carried on a correspondence with his old crony, Governor Folch of West Florida, trying to chivvy him into giving up Mobile. Madison and Jefferson were convinced that if any man could take advantage of the breakup of the Spanish dominions in America which resulted from Napoleon's overthrow of the Bourbons in Spain, that man was Wilkinson. Wilkinson talked himself up as the intimate friend of the various Spanish governors and political chiefs. With time and encouragement he would get possession not only of Mobile but maybe of the Texas plains, without firing a shot.

The administration gave him every facility. When in the winter of 1809 he started off on a schooner to take command of the defense of New Orleans, the War Department advanced him half a year's pay and furnished him a license to export fifty barrels of flour and twelve barrels of apples. The general always enjoyed a little trading on the side. Crisp Northern apples would help win the hearts of the Spanish authorities.

He was tendered a seventeengun salute at Annapolis and public dinners in Norfolk and Charleston. He visited Havana and Pensacola on the way to the Mississippi. The splendors of a welcoming banquet in New Orleans were somewhat marred by a challenge to fight from the general's erstwhile friend John Adair, whom he had tried to implicate in the Burr conspiracy. It was Wilkinson's turn to declare that his high position made a duel unbecoming.

New recruits for the augmented army were drinking and carousing in the stews of New Orleans. It was up to Wilkinson to whip them into shape. As usual he disregarded the orders of the War Department. Instead of taking his troops upriver, as Secretary Eustis directed, to the high ground back of Fort Adams, he encamped them among the swamps in the malarial delta. Tales of the dreadful sickness and mortality in the Army of the United States were beginning to reach Jefferson and Madison when they met at Monticello.

Somehow neither of them could quite put his best mind on the army and navy. Gallatin wrung his hands. Waste and inefficiency were sopping up the appropriations, which were already endangering his financial system. Neither on land or sea, he pointed out, were the forces of the United States as ready to face an enemy as they had been the year before.

The chills and fevers of Washington were thought to abate by late September. Returning grimly to face the burdens of office, Madison and Gallatin made their way through the late summer dust to the capital. They left Jefferson convinced that the one thing he could do to help them was to induce Monroe to accept a post with the administration.

5. "Copenhagen" Jackson

When the Madisons arrived at the President's house they found that the new British minister had been cooling his heels for a month at Anthony Merry's old residence overlooking Rock Creek. Unlike Merry, Francis James Jackson enjoyed himself in Washington. "I am surprised," he wrote home, "that no one should before have mentioned the great beauty of the neighborhood." He got hold of some good saddle horses. He and his wife rode around the country and found it of a "beautifully picturesque appearance." It amused him to flush a covey of partridges within three hundred yards of the Capitol.

When he presented his credentials to President Madison the new British minister found him "a plain and rather mean-looking little man" but he enjoyed the punch and seedcake that a Negro servant brought in. At dinner three weeks later Jackson was gratified by Mr. Madison's observance of protocol. The President gave his arm to Mrs. Jackson, while Mr. Jackson had the satisfaction of leading the congenial Mrs. Madison to the table.

Jackson was not so happy in his formal dealings with the Department of State. After a couple of conversations with Robert Smith, who gave him the impression of being puzzled and scatterbrained, he found himself treating directly with the President through communications which Madison wrote in his Secretary's name. At Canning's insistence Jackson took the attitude that the United States Government had tricked Erskine into making unauthorized concessions. His tone was bullying. It became clear at once that he himself had no concessions to offer. After a short exchange of notes, Madison let him know the United States Government refused to consider "this gross insinuation" of trickery and delivered his ticket of leave: "It only remains, in order to preclude opportunites which are thus abused, to inform you that no further communications will be received from you."

The hero of Copenhagen took his rejection with ill grace. In defiance of diplomatic propriety he furnished the newspapers with columns of expostulation. He ostentatiously shook the dust of Washington from his feet. The government there was a mere "mob of savage Democrats." He would seek support from the better element to the northward. Mrs. Jackson, a Prussian baroness who yearned for the courts of Europe, would have been delighted to cut short their stay in the wilderness, but Jackson wanted to see the country. He had promised the Foreign Office he would spend a year in America and he was determined to stay out his time.

The Federalists took up Jackson's quarrel with gusto. The wealthy Baltimoreans showed the pair every attention. Mrs. Jackson to be sure found "their cuisine detestable; coarse table linen, no claret, champagne and madeira indifferent." During the month they spent in Philadelphia, "we have dined at home" wrote Jackson, "but twice." In his opinion New York was unique in America, "resembling more the best of our country towns, with the additional advantage of the finest water that can be imagined . . . as much life and bustle there as at Liverpool."

The Jacksons spent an agreeable spring in a country house overlooking the Hudson. One of the sights from that house was the view, every three or four days, of Fulton's steamboat advancing "against wind and tide at a rate of four miles an hour. . . . There is a general rush of our household to watch and wonder until it disappears. . . . I doubt if I would be obeyed were I to desire any one of them to take a passage on her."

In June the rejected British envoy was officially invited to Boston. The Massachusetts legislature passed a resolution declaring that there was no cause for a rupture with Great Britain. "In Boston, the head-quarters of most good principles, I was feasted most famously. . . . After living nine days in clover at about eighteen of the principal houses . . . they gave me . . . a public dinner, at which near three hundred persons were present, and where we had toasts and cheer-ing and singing in the best style of Bishopsgate Street or Merchant Taylor's Hall." Towards the end of the wine drinking Timothy Pickering rose and gave the toast which was to become the Federalist rallying cry: "The world's last hope, Britain's fast-anchored isle."

Francis James Jackson needed all the encouragement his Boston friends could offer. He was soon to find that not only had he been turned down by the government he was accredited to, but that the man who accredited him had lost the Foreign Office. When the British cabinet broke up in confusion after Lord Portland's fatal stroke and the ill success of an attempted invasion of the Netherlands, Canning re-fused to serve under Spencer Perceval. Treating Castlereagh as a friend whenever they met, he had been busily intriguing to get him dropped from the administration. When Castlereagh learned of Can-ning's double dealing he called him out. They met on Putney Heath. Canning was shot through the thigh. So Jackson's patron was *hors de combat* and in deep disgrace besides. The Marquess of Wellesley, the Duke of Wellington's older brother, took over as Foreign Secretary. Instead of demanding Jackson's reinstatement, as Jackson had hoped, the marquess imperiously ordered him home.

6. *Monroe's Honor and Grade*

While Madison was reporting his discomfiture of "Copenhagen" Jackson, in his message to the first regular session of the Eleventh Congress assembling in November, Jefferson rode over to Ashlawn for a long quiet talk with Monroe. Both men had been encouraged by Republican victories in Maryland and Vermont. They were pro-foundly saddened by the news which had just reached them of the mysterious death of Governor Lewis of Louisiana.

Meriwether Lewis was a man in whom Jefferson had invested great hopes for the future. He loved him with the fatherly affection he lavished on the younger men to whose training and education he de-voted so much thought. Lewis was dead. Others would have to finish his report on the exploration of the northwest country which he had carried out with such skill.

He had been on his way to Washington from his post in St. Louis to explain alleged irregularities in his accounts as governor. He was found shot to death in a lonely shelter on the confines of the Mississippi Territory.

Some said he had been murdered, others that he had shot himself. Knowing that Lewis was subject to fits of extreme depression, Jefferson tended to the opinion that his friend had indeed taken his own life.

"The catastrophe of poor Lewis," Jefferson wrote Madison when he reported the conversation with Monroe, "served to lead us to the point intended." That was that Monroe thought the post of governor of Louisiana, which Jefferson offered him while he was still in England, "incompatible with the respect he owed himself."

Monroe would have taken a cabinet post if Madison had offered it when he first took office. Now he felt he needed three years to straighten out his personal affairs. His uncle Joseph Jones had recently died and left him executor of his very considerable estate. Monroe's years abroad had reduced his own plantations to a state of dilapidation; it would take time to make them productive again. Jefferson tried to interest him in a military office. General Hampton, second in command in the national army, had just died. Monroe cried out that he'd sooner be shot than accept a command under Wilkinson.

If a real crisis should occur, wrote Jefferson, Monroe was ready to be called on; "he is satisfied that such is the deadly hatred of both France and England, and such is their self-reproach and dread at the spectacle of such a government as ours; that they will spare nothing to destroy it; that nothing but a firm union among the whole body of Republicans can save it."

The respect Monroe owed himself was sorely bruised. He had encouraged the campaign to run him for President largely because he needed to be reassured that, in spite of the humiliations that brought his diplomatic career to an end, he still had the confidence of his fellow citizens. Jefferson concluded that Monroe would accept any military or civilian post directly under the President. "Everything from him breathed the purest patriotism, involving, however, a close attention to his own honor and grade."

Jefferson ended his letter to Madison in a tone of unusual fervor: "God bless and carry you safely through all your difficulties."

7. The Emperor's Little Game

Throughout the Madison regime Jefferson's hilltop was close to being the summer capital of the United States. Hardly an important visitor to Montpelier failed to pay his respects to the hermit of Monticello. Through the *National Intelligencer* and the Richmond *Enquirer* Jefferson followed the debates in Congress and in the Virginia State Capitol. Through his correspondence with the Republican leadership he exercised more influence in his retirement that he had during his last painful year in office. He remained a quiet partner in the old triumvirate.

Madison's policy towards Bonaparte, in particular, was affected by Jefferson's confidential correspondence with Lafayette and Du Pont de Nemours and with Jefferson's fellow members of the Institut de France. Though Jefferson had retired as President of the United States, he remained president of the American Philosophical Society. He clung to the eighteenthcentury notion of a republic of letters which transcended national boundaries. In spite of the forced subservience to the Emperor of Jefferson's friends among the erstwhile French republicans, and for all of his castigation of Bonaparte as "the Attila of the age," he never got over his fellow feeling for them. He retained respect for the opinions of Du Pont and Lafayette, whom he considered as American democrats *in partibus infidelium*.

No matter how much they sympathized with Jefferson's grand design, Du Pont and Lafayette remained Frenchmen. They couldn't help being stirred by the victories of the Grande Armée, and by Bonaparte's effective modernization of French society. Jefferson had such sanguine hopes of their eventual influence on the French administration that he failed at times to understand to what extent Bonaparte used the philosophical republicans as decoys, in the cat and mouse policy he developed towards American shipping.

Notwithstanding the pleas of some of Bonaparte's most trusted advisers the Emperor could not get it through his head that there were real benefits for France in neutral commerce. All he could see was that foreigners who refused to accept his authority were getting rich from the carrying trade. Furthermore, with French shipping driven off the seats, they were helping enrich his enemy England. Though he never wanted to push the Americans so far as to drive them into a British alliance, whenever he needed a few extra million francs for the imperial treasury, the rich neutral cargoes of cotton and sugar and rum and salt fish and hides, tied up in French and Spanish and German ports by the endless chicanery of his customhouses, were the first things he thought of. He justified his seizures by a series of trading-with-the-enemy laws, decrees and counterdecrees, some secret and some published in the *Moniteur*.

Bonaparte enjoyed deception for its own sake. Somehow he managed to convince the Madison administration that he had promised, if only Great Britain would revoke its orders in council, to drop his restrictions against American ships entering continental ports. Veiled hints were forwarded to Washington through gruff General Turreau, who was rapidly outstaying his welcome as French minister, and through "frank" conversations between officials of the Napoleonic court and John Armstrong in Paris, that an unpublished decree to that effect already existed, signed and sealed.

When hard pressed to defend Madison's policies against attacks by Pickering and Josiah Quincy and John Randolph, administration orators in Congress occasionally alluded to a diplomatic contract with France which precluded any concessions to Great Britain. Like a heavily laden ship trying to beat out of some bay against wind and tide, the administration zigzagged between British aggression and French spoliation. Every tack found the President's policy nearer the rocks on one shore or the other.

This was all grist to the Federalist mill. Pickering insisted that a secret agreement existed between Jefferson and the French usurper. The weakness of the Federalist position lay in the fact that, though their press could always stir up dissatisfaction among the shipping interests, the voters were deserting them with each succeeding election.

8. *American Manufactures*

Looking out from Monticello, Jefferson could see the year 1810, which was a bleak year indeed for Albemarle County crops, turning out favorably on the whole for the Republican administration. Prosperity came back fast after the repeal of the embargo. Farm products became salable again. Shipyards throve up and down the coast. Gallatin reported almost a million and a half tons under the American flag. Another nine hundred thousand tons of foreign shipping registered in American ports was largely American built. With the commerce of the belligerents strangled by blockades and exclusions, a large part of the trade of the world was carried in American bottoms.

United States territory had more than doubled since Jefferson took office in 1801. The population had increased by a little more than a third. The census takers discovered that the population of the United States was now more than seven million. New York and Philadelphia were the two largest cities, with nearly a hundred thousand each. Baltimore was forging ahead of Boston. The Western settlements had not grown so fast as the land speculators expected. Ohio reported less than a quarter of a million, Indiana twentyfour thousand, Illinois twelve thousand. In Michigan Territory they found only five thousand settlers. Even Kentucky and Tennessee showed only gradual growth.

The Western Waters were waiting for steamboats to move their produce. Livingston and Fulton already had the *New Orleans* under construction at Pittsburgh. Five steamboats plied the Hudson River between New York and Albany. Fulton's twinhulled steam ferry was in service between New York and Paulus Hook on the Jersey shore.

There was a steamboat on Lake Champlain, another on the Delaware, and another on the St. Lawrence. America's vast mileage of inland waterways was on the edge of awakening to the thump of walking beams and the splash of paddlewheels.

The embargo, so ruinous to the carrying trade, had proved a stimulus to manufacturing. Looms multiplied in New England cotton mills. Seventyfive million yards of linen, cotton, and woolen goods were reported as household production. A new factory was turning out cotton prints. Iron furnaces, forges, and blooming mills were operating throughout the States. Pittsburgh turned out claw hammers, hatchets, shovels, pots, and skillets. There were tanneries and distilleries everywhere. Lynn, Massachusetts, was already preeminent in shoes. Danbury was producing hats. Philadelphia was the printing and publishing center, reporting an annual production of half a million volumes. A hundred and seventynine mills produced various kinds of paper. Kentucky and West Tennessee made cordage and duck. Steam engines were multiplying. Factories were transforming the country towns. Mills were damming the rivers for water power.

Even Jefferson, who in his earlier days was suspicious of factories as unbalancing the agricultural economy he felt essential to a self-governing society of free men, was now for encouraging "manufactures to the extent of our own consumption of everything of which we raise the raw material." He was enthusiastic for homespun and for the production of every useful article that could be made on the farm or plantation. He was beginning to call for "a due balance between agriculture, manufacture and commerce."

While Jefferson still dreaded the appearance of the sort of urban proletariat he'd seen in England and France as the byproduct of mass manufactures, he greeted with enthusiasm every advance in technology. "The basis of household manufacture is now so established," he wrote Kosciusko, "that the farmer & laborer clothes himself entirely. the rich alone use imported articles, and on these alone the whole taxes of the general government are levied. the poor man who uses nothing but what is made in his own farm or family, or within his own country, pays not a farthing of tax to the general government but on his salt: & should he go into that manufacture also, as is probable, he will pay nothing."

In spite of the threat of war Jefferson was still looking hopefully to Madison and Gallatin to extinguish the national debt; "our revenues," he went on in his most sanguine vein, "liberated by the discharge of the public debt & its surplus applied to canals, roads, schools &c, the farmer will see his government supported, his children educated, and the face of his country made a paradise by the contribution of the rich alone, without his being called to spare a cent from his earnings."

This preview of the later Democractic theorem: tariff for revenue only, he called "our Quaker system."

He was mechanizing the handicrafts of his Monticello work force wherever he could. "every family of any size is now getting machines on a small scale for their household purposes," he wrote. He had built into his flour mill Oliver Evans' system of belts and conveyers which made American milling the first automated industry. In his nailery he was using a nailcutting machine invented fifteen years before by a Newburyport man. He described to Kosciusko his carding machine which cost only sixty dollars and which could be worked by a girl of twelve. He had spinning machines for wool and cotton and a new loom with a flying shuttle which would weave two hundred yards a day. Two women and two girls, operating machines which cost only a hundred and fifty dollars, could easily produce the two thousand yards of linens, cottons, and woolens he needed to clothe his servants. He was particularly enthusiastic over the quality of the cider he made in his cider press. Besides spinning and weaving and nailmaking, he had wheelwrights, carriage builders, blacksmiths, shoemakers continually at work on Mulberry Row. Five moldboard plows of his own design were facilitating the cultivation of his farms. He himself worked a small forge in his study where he turned out the delicate brass fittings needed for his "mathematical instruments."

He was looking to his household manufactures to produce the hard cash he had to have now that he no longer received the presidential salary. Though many eminent men with legal training added to their income by collecting fees from pupils and apprentices they took into their offices, it never occurred to Jefferson to charge for his services of that sort. He described to Kosciusko the informal school he conducted at Monticello. "a part of my occupation & by no means the least pleasing, is the direction of the studies of such young men as ask it. they place themselves in the neighboring village, and have the use of my library & counsel & make a part of my society. in advising the course of their reading I endeavor to keep their attention fixed on the main objects of all science, the freedom & happiness of man. so that coming to bear a share in the councils & government of their country they will keep ever in view the sole objects of all legitimate government."

9. Jefferson's Private Affairs

The burst of national prosperity that followed the repeal of the embargo was far from being reflected in Jefferson's own finances. He had left the presidency somewhere around twenty thousand dollars in debt. Interest charges kept inflating the old indebtedness which he never quite managed to extinguish on his wife's properties. The twentyfive thousand dollar salary, lavish for the day, had never been quite sufficient to pay for his entertaining in Washington and his expenditures on his plantations.

He had sunk nearly thirty thousand dollars in his fourstory stone gristmill, and in the long canal that brought the water down from his dam on the Rivanna. His continual brickmaking and building at Monticello and Bedford Forest took hands away from productive work. His indulgence towards the people who worked for him cut down on the efficiency of his farming. He was all too prone to put his name on the notes of impoverished relatives and friends. Even while President he had occasionally to borrow from more thrifty associates such as Madison and Short.

He even managed to borrow from the absent Kosciusko. In a section of the letter he wrote his Polish friend during the winter of 1810 which Jefferson's early biographers went to some pains to suppress, he apologized for the reinvestment he'd made of part of the funds which Congress had voted Kosciusko for his services in the Revolutionary War.

Jefferson described his "thralldom of mind" when he discovered the weight of the indebtedness he had to cope with when he left the public service. "a friend accommodated me readily with a considerable part of the deficiency to be reimbursed out of the first proceeds of my estate." To cover the rest he and the man in charge of Kosciusko's holdings had a proposal to which he hoped Kosciusko would not object. It was with "mortification" and "affliction" that he made the suggestion that the fortyfive hundred dollars' worth of stock in the Bank of the United States which was held in Kosciusko's name and which would have to be reinvested when the national bank was liquidated might be used to pay off some of Jefferson's own indebtedness. He had set apart the proceeds of an estate worth three thousand dollars a year for repayment, and he would pay the same interest that the bank had paid. Kosciusko could not lose by the arrangement, and when he returned to the United States on his promised visit the sum would be ready to reinvest as he thought best. As an earnest of good intentions Jefferson included a bill of exchange for a year's interest in his letter.

Sanguine as ever, Jefferson had no inkling of the fact that the whole plantation economy of Virginia was in decline. It was only the high wartime prices of wheat and flour, and to some extent of tobacco, which were keeping the Virginia planters solvent. Though they made less noise over it, the southern agriculturalists had suffered more from the embargo than the New England merchants. The surplus crops they depended on for cash had been unsalable for two years. It would take them several seasons to recoup their losses.

For Albemarle 1809 had been a poor year for crops. Eighteen ten was nearly as bad.

Thomas Mann Randolph, Jefferson's soninlaw who kept an eye on the farms while Jefferson was in Washington, was an eager naturalist and an excellent farmer. He was reputed to be the first man to introduce contour plowing. But he was an even worse manager than Jefferson was. "No man," so a neighbor put it, "ever made better crops or sold them at worse prices." The erratic, irresponsible strain that ran through the whole Randolph family showed itself in him in a reckless incurrence of debt. His own property at Edgehill was already mortgaged to the eyes. The Randolphs had nine children to launch in the world. Jefferson had been paying for the education in Philadelphia of the eldest boy, who was his namesake. Now, to his great delight, his daughter and soninlaw with their entire family were cutting expenses by taking up their permanent residence at Monticello.

Jefferson had about ten thousand acres left from his father's and his wife's extensive estates. Roughly half was around Monticello where he raised wheat, and half in Bedford County where tobacco was still the cash crop. He felt his farms had an assured income of five or six thousand dollars. He looked forward to raising stock which would be fed the oats, barley, and corn he could grow on the place. There would be an added cash profit from his flour mill and nailery. He had the finest horses in Virginia. He had imported an improved strain of hogs. He expected great returns from his sheep with improvement of the breed.

The American consul in Lisbon had managed to ship two pair of particularly fine merino sheep from Europe to Alexandria. Jefferson and Madison were each to have a pair. Merino sheep were the rage among Virginia farmers. Jefferson wrote Madison that he was disgusted with the high price importers were charging the farmers for merino rams.

He felt it was up to Madison and himself to raise as many rams as they could and to distribute them free to improve the breed of sheep in every county in Virginia. "no sentiment is more acknowledged in the family of agriculturalists than that the few who can afford it should incur the risk & expense of all new improvements & give the benefit freely to the many of more restricted circumstances."

Furthermore he was spending lavishly to import fattailed sheep from North Africa. Ever since he took over Shadwell after his father's death Jefferson had thought of his resources as inexhaustible. It never occurred to him to shirk "risk & expense" for the public good.

Though he had written abundantly to his friends about the frugal life he would lead as the hermit of Monticello, entertaining his guests cost almost as much at home as in Washington. There were times when Mrs. Randolph had to find beds for as many as fifty people. Families of cousins stayed for weeks and months. In search of advice and support, members of Congress, heads of departments, political appointees streamed in continual procession through Monticello. Thirtyseven house servants were normally engaged in waiting on this household.

"After Mr. Jefferson returned from Washington, he was for years crowded with visitors," was how Bacon described the situation to the Reverend Mr. Pierson, "and they almost ate him out of house and home. They were there all times of the year; but about the middle of June the travel would commence from the lower part of the State to the Springs, and then there was a perfect throng of visitors. They travelled in their own carriages, and came in gangs—the whole family, with carriage and riding-horses and servants; sometimes three or four such gangs at a time. We had thirty-six stalls for horses, and only used about ten of them for the stock we kept there. Very often all of the rest were full, and I had to send the horses off to another place. I have often sent a wagon-load of hay up to the stable, and the next morning there would not be enough left to make a hen's-nest. I have killed a fine beef, and it would all be eaten in a day or two. There was no tavern in all that country that had so much company. Mrs. Randolph, who always lived with Mr. Jefferson after his return from Washington, and kept house for him, was very often greatly perplexed to entertain them. I have known her many and many a time to have every bed in the house full, and she would send to my wife and borrow all her beds—she had six spare beds—to accommodate her visitors. I finally told the servant who had charge of the stable, to only give the visitors' horses half allowance. Somehow or other Mr. Jefferson heard of this; I never could tell how, unless it was through some of the visitors' servants. He countermanded my orders."

As if his affairs were not involved enough, Jefferson was threatened with a lawsuit which he feared might destroy him financially. During his last year in the presidency a complicated dispute arose between the city of New Orleans and Edward Livingston over the ownership of a sandbank known as the Batture. The Batture was flooded at high water, but at low water was used as a natural dock for loading and unloading boats and small vessels. In the course of the speculations through which Livingston was trying to raise the money to pay off his debts so that he could rehabilitate himself in New York, he acquired the riparian rights of a Creole who claimed the Batture as an extension of his property. With the growth of the city after incorporation into the American Union, waterfront lands were becoming immensely valuable.

When Livingston started dyking the sandbank to reclaim it from the river the municipal and territorial authorities declared the Batture to be, according to French and Spanish law, in the public domain. Jefferson, who hated land speculation, backed them up. After taking the advice of his heads of departments and of the Attorney General he ordered a federal marshal to drive off Livingston's workmen. To him it was a clear case of private greed against the public weal. He himself prepared a brief for the use of the federal attorneys in New Orleans.

Livingston, who saw the chance of fortune and vindication slipping through his fingers, bestirred himself amazingly. An act of despotism had infringed his liberties as a citizen. He appealed to the public with a pamphlet; he petitioned Congress for relief; and he brought suit, personally and individually, against the marshal who dispossessed him and against ex-President Jefferson. For damages he claimed the full value of the land he'd been deprived of.

Jefferson immediately engaged George Hay and William Wirt to defend him. Livingston, besides being a member of one of the most powerful families in New York, was a man of swashbuckling energy and an able lawyer. Jefferson was haunted by the fear that he would somehow manage to get his suit considered by the Supreme Court of the United States, where Jefferson would find himself at the mercy of his affectionate cousin, John Marshall. He was convinced that Marshall would find some way to ruin him if he could.

10. *A New Race of Heroes*

It was a period of speculation and landgrabbing all down the lower Mississippi. Cotton was proving every year more profitable. Investors were bidding up the price of land. In midsummer of 1810 the American planters in the district around Baton Rouge decided to take matters into their own hands. They were tired of paying taxes to the dons. Every post was bringing fresh news of the disintegration of the Spanish dominion. Miranda at long last was successful in Caracas. Mexico was in revolt. With some help from British warships the local inhabitants had driven the Spanish troops out of Buenos Aires. Rebel generals were mustering troops to liberate South America. Now the inhabitants of West Feliciana, having assembled in convention, declared the independence of West Florida "before the Supreme Ruler of the World." They requested annexation to the United States but wanted to reserve the granting of lands to themselves. To show they were in earnest they stormed the fort at Baton Rouge. The garrison ran, except for one young officer, a Creole named Louis Granpré, who attempted resistance and was shot down in the scuffle.

Madison had to move fast. Ignoring the West Feliciana convention, he instructed Governor Claiborne to take over the territory. Writing Jefferson in October, he explained that even at the risk of straining his executive authority he had to take action for fear the British would try to reimburse themselves with the two Floridas for the immense sums they had spent in Spain financing resistance against the French. "The country to the Perdido River, being our own, may be fairly taken possession of, if it can be done without violence."

As soon as Congress met in the fall Timothy Pickering startled the Senate by reading a letter out of its secret files, written when Talleyrand was Foreign Minister under the Consulate, which denied that the Floridas were part of Louisiana. An uproar ensued. Samuel Smith moved that the senator from Massachusetts was "in palpable violation of the rules." Young Henry Clay defended President Madison with a carefully documented history of congressional legislation on the Louisiana territories.

Henry Clay, now senator from Kentucky, was assuming the leadership of a group of restless young congressmen from the South and West who were becoming known as the War Hawks. In his maiden speech a few months before he had expressed a state of mind which was soon to drive Jefferson's pacifism out of the councils of the Democratic Republican party.

Clay wanted expansion, not only to the south but to the north. "The conquest of Canada is in your power," he cried. "I trust I shall not be deemed presumptuous when I state that the militia of Kentucky are alone competent to place Montreal and Upper Canada at your feet. . . . The withered arm and wrinkled brow of the illustrious founders of our freedom are melancholy indications that they will shortly be removed from us. Their deeds of glory and renown will then be felt only through the cold medium of the historic page: we shall want the presence and the living example of a new race of heroes to supply their places."

11. Gallatin's Difficulties

Far from showing themselves a "new race of heroes," the factions in the Eleventh Congress vied with each other to table legislation which either of the belligerents might consider aggressive. They were particularly chary with military appropriations. Against Federalist opposition administration supporters did manage to put through two measures which endorsed President Madison's Florida policy. One was a bill setting Louisiana up as a state and incorporating in it most of the occupied Spanish territory. The other was a secret measure authorizing the President to seize East Florida whenever such a course might seem necessary.

Though Madison's Florida policy was approved in Congress, Gallatin found himself in difficulty. Deeming war with Great Britain inevitable, he was already at work on plans to finance the expenditure that war would make necessary.

The national bank formed the hub of his projects, but the charter was about to expire. The question of renewal came up while Congress was debating the Florida and Louisiana bills. Opposed to renewal were Samuel Smith and his followers (whom John Randolph had labeled "the invisibles"), the Clinton group from New York, backed by a flock of local financiers who wanted federal funds invested in their state banks, and Duane's vociferous *Aurora* in Philadelphia. Their argument was that the bank was staffed by Federalists, that it paid profits to British investors, and that it was unconstitutional to boot.

For years William Duane had been consumed with hatred for Gallatin. Duane came of an Irish family. Though American born he learned the printer's trade in Ireland. After suffering some persecution for outspoken publishing in India and in London he arrived in America, like many another immigrant printer-journalist, with a chip on his shoulder and an exaggerated sense of the power and privileges of the press. He went to work with Benjamin Franklin's grandson on the *Aurora* and, when young Bache died, married his widow and took over the paper. An enthusiastic Republican and an able editor, he earned Jefferson's gratitude by his services in the campaign of 1800. Duane was duly arrested under the Alien and Sedition laws, and when Jefferson assumed the presidency the charges against him were duly dismissed. Though not quite such a blackguard as Callender he had as inflated notions as Callender of what his reward should be out of the spoils of victory.

Duane first ran afoul of Gallatin in the early days of Jefferson's administration when he conceived the idea that it was Gallatin who stood in the way of his getting his proper share of government printing. Gallatin's associates in Pennsylvania politics opposed some of Duane's friends, and Duane began to broadcast a picture of Gallatin as the crafty Genevan who had enmeshed Jefferson and Madison in his intrigues and was using the Treasury to make himself millions by speculating in public lands.

Duane had a veneration for Jefferson that amounted to awe. He knew very well that Jefferson's countenance was necessary for his bread and butter. So long as Jefferson remained in office he kept his malice within bounds, but as soon as Madison became President the columns of the *Aurora* began to fill up with slanders against Gallatin. Knowing that Jefferson, like many pious Republicans, was suspicious of a national bank, Duane let himself go in a virulent campaign against renewal of the charter. In the course of it he wrote of Madison as a puppet in the Genevan's hands.

Gallatin's chief defender in Congress was, like Clay, a newcomer.

Senator William Harris Crawford was a broadshouldered mountaineer from the Georgia hill country. While he lacked the silver tongue of the new young orators like Clay and Representative Calhoun of South Carolina, there was a sober thoughtfulness about his massive presence that made him listened to. He reiterated Gallatin's arguments that partisan considerations had played no part in the bank's policies. A central bank was essential for sound government finance and a stable currency. It didn't matter who the investors were if the bank were properly managed. Liquidating the bank would mean handing back to the British several million dollars which would furnish capital for waging war if war should become unavoidable.

In the House the bill to renew the charter was tabled by one vote. In the Senate the vote was seventeen for to seventeen against. Samuel Smith, who counted Baltimore banks among his commercial ventures, raged against Gallatin. The onslaught on the bank became a personal onslaught on the character of the Secretary of the Treasury.

It was generally believed that the House would reconsider if the Senate voted the bank. The decision lay with "the withered arm and wrinkled brow" of the Vice President, the aged George Clinton. The Clintons were up to their necks in New York banking. The Vice President lost no time in declaring that the Constitution had never granted Congress the power to set up commercial corporations. He voted nay. The first United States Bank was dead.

Gallatin immediately sent in his resignation to President Madison. Jefferson, thoroughly alarmed by the threatened breakup of the cabinet, wrote far and wide from Monticello to drum up support for Gallatin. He defended the Secretary of the Treasury to William Wirt in a letter intended for the eye of Thomas Ritchie, who owned and edited the Richmond *Enquirer*.

Jefferson didn't need to explain that he himself didn't believe in a national bank. His views were well known. He pointed out that Gallatin had no part in setting up the bank but that as Secretary of the Treasury "he derived immense convenience" from its various branches "because they gave the effect of ubiquity to his money wherever deposited. money in New Orleans or Maine was at his command and by their agency turned into money in London, Paris, Amsterdam or Canton . . . and if he was in favor of the bank, what is the amount of that crime or error in which he had a majority save one in each House of Congress as participators? yet on these facts endeavors are made to drive from the administration the ablest man except the President who was ever in it."

He remonstrated with Duane. He told the editor of the *Aurora* he was making himself unpopular in Virginia and, so Jefferson surmised, in "other respectable portions of the union," by his attacks on the administration. He wanted Duane's services on the Republican side; "after so long a course of steady adherence to the general sentiments of the republicans, it would afflict me sincerely to see you separate from that body, become auxiliary to the enemies of our government, who have to you been the bitterest enemies, who are now chuckling at the prospect of division between us, and, as I am told, subscribing to your paper. the best indication of error which my experience has tested, is the approbation of the federalists."

Jefferson backed up his arguments by pointing out some practical results of Duane's stand. Jefferson was interested in helping Duane set up as a publisher of books as well as newspapers. He had only recently induced him to undertake the printing of a translation of a commentary on Montesquieu by Lafayette's dear friend, Destutt de Tracy, a member of the Académie Française whom Jefferson had nominated for the American Philosophical Society. This was a complicated project because the translation had to be presented in such a way that Napoleon's police could have no suspicion of the author's real identity. Destutt's ideas on government were very close to Jefferson's. Jefferson wanted Destutt's *Commentary* read as a way of counteracting the monarchical and anglophile side of Montesquieu's teaching. Duane was as usual in need of funds. He needed new fonts of type. His printers were striking for arrears in pay. Jefferson had been helping him finance the publication of Destutt's book by suggesting to Virginia friends that they subscribe five hundred dollars each to furnish Duane capital to enlarge his publishing business.

Most of these men were administration supporters. They were disgusted by Duane's attacks on Gallatin and by his slurs against the President. Jefferson quoted to Duane a letter from one of them, who was trying to raise money in Richmond: "D's three or four last papers contain such paragraphs in relation to Mr. Madison, that even your letter cannot now serve him."

Jefferson knew his Duane.

He sent a copy of his remonstrances along with his letter to Wirt, who was the friend he referred to without naming him. He told Wirt he'd done his best to straighten Duane out. "It is possible Duane can be reclaimed as to Mr. Madison but as to Mr. Gallatin I despair of him."

Madison refused even to consider Gallatin's resignation. Instead he asked for the resignation of Robert Smith. He had felt for some time that Smith was involved in his brother's cabal against Gallatin and in the hue and cry against the entire administration on the part of the dissident Republicans. Madison had taken the precaution of previously sounding out Monroe, who, when John Tyler resigned to accept a federal judgeship, had been elected to serve his unexpired term as governor of Virginia. Monroe passed the word along that he was now ready to become Secretary of State in Madison's cabinet.

As balm for hurt feelings Madison offered Robert Smith the lega-tion to Russia. This offer nearly involved him in another chapter of misunderstandings. Some time since, the President had received a letter from Mrs. Abigail Adams which led him to believe that her son John Q. wanted to be relieved from his post at St. Petersburg, so when a vacancy occurred on the Supreme Court he sent off a formal appointment to the younger Adams. Prickly John Q. replied somewhat tartly that he didn't consider himself qualified for the supreme bench but that he wanted to stay on at St. Petersburg where he considered himself on the verge of certain accomplishments.

Madison was extricated from his dilemma by Robert Smith himself. Smith at first seemed gratified and affected to consider the appoint-ment a sort of promotion. Jefferson wrote Smith a discreet note insinuating that his retirement was of his own choosing. After a few days of cogitation Robert Smith blew up. Political intriguers were telling him he'd been unceremoniously fired. He declined the Russian legation, refused an invitation to dinner at the President's house, and in spite of his brother's advice to keep quiet, relieved his hurt feelings by turning over to the press a rambling diatribe against Madison.

Only the most extreme antiadministration Republicans took up his cause. Even the Federalists said he'd made a fool of himself. This publication wrote finis to Robert Smith's political career.

12. *To Enforce Neutrality*

John Quincy Adams was indeed on the edge of accomplishments in St. Petersburg. He had sailed into the Baltic in the fall of 1809 and found the Norwegian and Danish harbors full of captured Amer-ican merchant ships. The Danes, under pressure from the French, had seized fifty vessels as prizes, with cargoes valued at five million dollars. After protesting to the Danish government and condoling with the dispossessed skippers, Adams continued on to Kronstadt. At his first interview with Count Roumanzoff, the Czar Alexander's Foreign Minister, the count was sympathetic but spoke of the allevi-ation of the plight of neutral shipping as a lovely dream; the French alliance was still in the ascendant. John Q., who liked to consider him-self plagued by ill luck, was knuckling down to the miseries of a frustrating Russian winter when suddenly the diplomatic weather cleared.

Two days after the American envoy arrived in St. Petersburg Alexander kicked over the Napoleonic traces. At their next interview in late December, Count Roumanzoff, admitting his own amazement at the turn of affairs, announced that the Czar had ordered him to demand the restitution of American property from the government in Copenhagen.

Though he had no funds to match the lavish entertaining and the gorgeous equipages of the French ambassador, who was the able and scholarly Caulaincourt, the dour little New Englander found himself a person of consideration at the Russian court. The Czar had decided that the health of his empire demanded foreign trade. Napoleon was blockading the Baltic to keep him from it. When the ice broke in the following spring Napoleon added insult to injury by revoking the licenses he had already granted to neutral carriers. He claimed they were all Englishmen in disguise. He caused Denmark, Holstein, Prussia, and Mecklenburg to close their ports to the American flag, and demanded that the Russians do the same.

The Czar protested to Caulaincourt. To avoid war with France he had been willing to break off relations with the English but he must be allowed to trade with the Americans. After a summer of claims and counterclaims the Czar announced he would encourage neutral shipping and published a ukase against the importation of "French luxuries."

Caulaincourt was recalled. Before leaving he ruefully congratulated stubby little Adams. "It seems you are great favorites here." Indeed from Archangel to Riga American ships were being given every facility by the Russian officials. Jefferson's Russian policy was bearing fruit. "You have found powerful protection," added Caulaincourt with a mysterious smile.

When James Monroe took over the State Department in April 1811, among the first dispatches that met his eye were reports from Adams of the widening breach between Napoleon and the Czar. The protection of American shipping was among the chief causes. War was imminent between the two Emperors.

New patterns were forming in the diplomatic kaleidoscope. William Pinkney was on his way home from England, leaving Samuel Smith's levelheaded son, who'd been snatched from a continental grand tour, as chargé d'affaires in London. Pinkney had waited long enough to see the supposedly Whiggish Prince of Wales established as Regent, when George III was at last declared incompetent, without bringing about any change in Tory policies. In spite of bankruptcies in the City, famine and disaffection in the Midlands, and a general disruption of commerce, Spencer Perceval still ruled England. Almost the same day that Pinkney sailed, Augustus John Foster, who had served in the British legation under Merry, was dispatched to the United States instructed to protest nonintercourse and the occupation of Florida.

John Armstrong had come back from Paris the autumn before, all puffed up with presidential aspirations. Now Joel Barlow, Madison's and Jefferson's confidential friend, appointed minister in his stead, was waiting for the proper moment to sail for France. He was renting his lovely Kalorama estate during his absence to the new French envoy, a career diplomat named Louis Serurier.

As if to emphasize the continuation of the Tory policy of harassment of the American carrying trade, the old watchdog of the British fleet, the *Melampus*, began cruising again off Sandy Hook. In her company appeared a formidable new frigate, the *Guerrière*. While Foster was crossing the ocean, boats from the British warships were arrogantly boarding American vessels, examining manifests, and carrying off likely seamen on the pretext that they were British subjects.

When the *Guerrière* boarded a coastwise brig off Sandy Hook and impressed an apprentice named Diggio in spite of the skipper's declaration that the boy was an American citizen, raised in his own home, resentment flared up as it hadn't since the attack on the *Chesapeake*. Even in Washington a little of the spirit of the War Hawks appeared in the departments.

The War Department was still paralyzed by the vast extent of the problems facing the Secretary and his eight clerks, but the Secretary of the Navy was doing his best to revive the fleet after so many years of neglect. His task was made easier by the fact that he had at his disposal firstrate officers who could rely on skillful crews trained in seamanship by years of blockade running. Though the active navy consisted only of eight frigates, a half a dozen brigs, and the rotting gunboats left over from President Jefferson's experiments in harbor defense, officers and men were spoiling to avenge the *Chesapeake*.

One of the few American warships ready for sea was the fifteen hundred ton *President*, fortyfour guns. She was one of three splendid frigates laid down under John Adams. With the *United States* and the *Constitution* she represented the keenest marine design of the time. In rigging and firepower these vessels somewhat outclassed corresponding British frigates. The *President* lay at anchor off Annapolis, with John Rodgers of Tripolitan fame, in command. She was reputed to be the smartest sailor of the lot. Her figurehead was carved with the likeness of George Washington.

Secretary Hamilton promptly ordered John Rodgers to cruise off the coast and to try to protect American shipping from these searches and impressments. His orders read that he must "be determined at every hazard to vindicate the injured honor of our navy and revive the drooping spirits of our nation."

About thirty miles off the Virginia Capes Commodore Rodgers

spied a ship under full sail. He could tell she was a warship from her rigging. Thinking she was the *Guerrière*, he made sail in pursuit, intending to hail her and to demand that Diggio be given up. The chase went on all day. At dusk he caught up with the supposed *Guerrière*, maneuvered to windward, and hailed her. His hails were answered by the flash from a gun. No more nonsense like the matches not being lit on the *Chesapeake*. The *President* let the strange ship have two broadsides which disabled her completely.

Rodgers cruised all night around the wallowing hulk. In the morning he learned that she was the *Little Belt*, a British corvette carrying only twenty guns. Her captain refused his proffered assistance. He admitted to having more than thirty men killed and wounded. On the *President* only one boy had been hurt by a splinter. Commodore Rodgers reported that the knowledge that there were so many men killed "would cause him acute pain all his life" but that his orders were to fire when fired upon.

The Royal Navy published its own version of the engagement in which the *Little Belt*, outmanned and outgunned, had fought a noble battle for three quarters of an hour when set upon without provocation. A courtmartial was demanded for the commander of the *President*. Rodgers himself requested a court of inquiry.

In spite of a paragraph in the *National Intelligencer:* "We understand that the conduct of Commodore Rodgers in repelling and chastizing the attack so causelessly and rashly made on the United States frigate *President* by the British ship of war *Little Belt* has the approbation of the President of the United States, and that the request of the commodore for an investigation of his conduct on the occasion has not been acceded to, his known candor and honor precluding any doubt of the correctness of his statement of the circumstances of the affair," a court of inquiry was held in New York where Commodore Rodgers' report was verified and confirmed.

"You see the new shapes our foreign relations are taking," President Madison wrote Jefferson. "The occurrence between Rodgers & the British ship of war, not unlikely to bring on repetitions, will probably end in an open rupture, or"—he added with his characteristic balancing of one possibility against another—"in a better understanding, as the calculations of the B. govt. may prompt or dissuade from war."

Indeed, relations with Great Britain continued to drift in the doldrums between war and peace. Foster, as Madison had suspected he would, refrained from making too much of the *Little Belt* affair. He tried to convince Monroe that Napoleon's decree removing restrictions from American ships was a hoax. Privateers and blockading cruisers were making communication with France almost impossible. Monroe was continually pressing Serurier for some tangible evidence of the change in imperial policy. When news came that some American ships had actually been released from French ports Madison and Monroe judged that the favorable moment had come to launch Barlow's mission.

13. Poet and Diplomat

Joel Barlow's fitness for a diplomatic post had been the cause of considerable debate in the Senate the preceding winter. He was denounced as a poet and an atheist, and for having made a fortune in France by dubious practices. Samuel Smith was described as "raving like a madman" against him. Barlow was defended, and ably, by Henry Clay, and to everyone's amazement by Timothy Pickering.

Pickering declared that he'd known Mr. Barlow when he was a chaplain with the Connecticut troops in the Continental Line and had found him a young man of good character. He made sport of those who denounced Barlow in the same breath as an impractical poet and an unscrupulous moneygrubber. He admitted that Barlow was a Deist, but after all, he pointed out sarcastically, there were Deists in more exalted positions. No man knew the French better or was more appropriate for the mission.

In the course of a varied career since he emerged from Yale College in the early days of the Revolution as a rawboned young parson with a taste for versifying, Barlow had indeed learned to know the French. After editing the first *American Mercury* among the Hartford Wits, who most of them turned out later to be Federalists, Barlow, an enthusiastic Republican, first went to France to sell land for the ill-fated Scioto Company. When that project failed he made his reputation as a political pamphleteer in the battle of words between Edmund Burke on one hand and Paine and the British radicals on the other over the crimes and glories of the French Revolution. Pitt's England became too hot for the author of *Advice to the Privileged Orders* but the pamphlet made him famous among the French.

Like Jefferson, who had only recently left the legation to France to become Secretary of State, he urged his French friends to adopt American constitutional methods. The Convention named him, along with Washington, Madison, Hamilton, and Paine, a citizen of France. In that capacity he was induced to stand for election as delegate from Savoy. Instead of electioneering he got snowbound in a mountain inn and wrote, in a fit of homesickness for his native Connecticut, *The Hasty-Pudding*, one of the few American poems of the time which still makes good reading.

Barlow's relapse into versifying very likely saved his head. Tom Paine barely escaped with his life after voting against Louis XVI's execution. It was Barlow who saved Paine's papers when the author of *The Rights of Man* was led off to the Luxembourg.

The collapse of revolutionary hopes in the carnage of the Terror left Barlow stranded in Paris with his beloved Ruth to support. There was a shrewd Yankee streak in the poet pamphleteer. He went into business as broker and agent for American shipowners, profited by the neutral trade, bought French government bonds when they were low and, with the rise in national prosperity under the Directory and the Consulate, found himself becoming a man of wealth.

When Monroe succeeded Gouverneur Morris as minister to France, Barlow once more found the American legation the congenial home for literary republicans it had been in Jefferson's day. Like his Connecticut contemporary, John Ledyard, Joel Barlow was a man who never could turn down a trip. His French Jacobinism had been a passing phase. He was a patriot eager to be of use to his countrymen. Monroe didn't have too much trouble inducing him to accept a really hazardous mission. This was to go as American consul to Algiers, to ransom the American seamen held there as slaves, and to get a treaty out of the ruling Dey.

The business took the better part of two years. To keep Ruth from worrying he narrated each chapter of accidents in mockheroic style in his letters. It was a question whether he was in greater danger from the plague that raged through the city or from the murderous whims of the Dey, whom he described as "a huge shaggy beast, sitting on his rump . . . with his hind legs gathered up like a tailor or a bear."

After a number of hairbreadth escapes and endless waiting for remittances from the Department of State Barlow managed to pull a Yankee trick on the Dey. He induced the Dey's private financier to advance him the ransom money out of the Dey's own funds. The surviving prisoners were sent home.

Pickering, then Secretary of State under John Adams, approved the transaction. After twelve more months of haggling over the treaty Barlow not only won the friendship of the old brute of a Dey but managed a private investment in Mediterranean shipping on the side. He landed in Marseilles about ten thousand dollars richer than he'd left it and wearing a pair of resplendent black mustachios. He'd had to cultivate a ferocious look, he wrote Ruth, to deal with the Barbary pirates. Their motto was "Who makes himself mutton the wolf eats."

The Barlows were childless. When an engaging young painter with a taste for mechanics named Robert Fulton turned up in Paris, fresh from Benjamin West's London studio, the Barlows took him in and mothered him. During the years he worked on his submarine, "Toot" was one of the family. Barlow financed Fulton's early experiments. When Bonaparte turned down the submarine, Fulton and Barlow made plans for a prototype steamboat. When Robert R. Livingston arrived as Jefferson's envoy to the French, Barlow interested him in the scheme.

Meanwhile Barlow had been busy on an essay on the rights of neutral shipping and had completed Jefferson's translation of Volney's *Ruines*. Jefferson admired Barlow's writing and kept teasing him to go to work on his long promised history of the Revolutionary War.

Barlow and Fulton collaborated in literary as well as mechanical projects. When Barlow went to work to revise his early *Vision of Columbus* into the grandiose *Columbiad*, Fulton drew the illustrations. They both admired Benjamin West. The *Columbiad* was Benjamin West's painting set to verse. When the rhetorical epic was published in Philadelphia it was Robert Fulton, now in the money from the success of his steamboat, who designed the opulent volume and paid the printing costs.

Jefferson had long been urging Barlow to settle in Washington. During Jefferson's second administration Barlow's Kalorama and the President's house were the two poles of a lively intellectual life such as the national capital was rarely to enjoy. Barlow had barely finished his prospectus describing Jefferson's project for a national university when Madison and Monroe decided he was the one man who could make Napoleon see reason.

Napoleon by this time was almost as mad as the old Dey of Algiers. President Madison had pledged his political integrity on Napoleon's contract to open his ports to American shipping. The credit of his administration depended on the success of Barlow's mission. Even at fiftyseven, Barlow was no man to turn down a trip.

They sent him off in style. Joel and Ruth Barlow and Ruth's sister Clara, who was recovering from an unhappy marriage, and Joel's nephew Tom, whom he was taking along as secretary, and a couple of American consuls who were old friends drove down to Annapolis and went aboard the United States frigate *Constitution*, Captain Issac Hull commanding.

Benjamin Latrobe came from Washington to see them off. Joel's last letter to Fulton, entrusted to the pilot off the Capes, described the excellent accommodations. The frigate was a model of cleanliness and discipline. Fulton had recently married Harriet Livingston, a cousin of the chancellor, so that now he had personal as well as business ties with the Livingston clan. "God bless our dear friends Harriet & Fulton," wrote Barlow. "Our health & spirits are pretty good. I wish the prospects of success in this mission were as good as the prospects of a fine passage."

14. *Tippecanoe*

Barlow had reason for misgivings. The end of 1811 was disturbed by rumblings and premonitions of the stormy year to come. The Atlantic seaports stirred restlessly under spoliation and impressment.

In Baltimore the British were the popular bugaboo. In Norfolk a mob of seamen evened the score for the Royal Navy. They retaliated against some knifings by French sailors by boarding and burning a French privateer. In Savannah they burned two. There were killed and wounded on both sides. The American seafaring man was as ready to fight the French as the British.

Governor William Henry Harrison of Indiana was heard to say that he could tell the state of relations between Washington and Westminster by the behavior of the Northwest Indians. That fall there was panic on the frontier. Rumors of a coming war were stirring hopes among the dispossessed Indian tribes that the British might help them regain their lost hunting grounds. The Canadians from the British outposts along the Great Lakes were, like the French voyageurs before them, mostly traders in furs: the Indians saw no threat in them; but the intruders from the United States cleared land, laid out towns, exterminated the game; they were the enemy.

The settlements north of the Ohio were alarmed by reports of a strong new Indian leadership. A Shawnee named Tecumseh and his twin brother, a medicine man known as the Prophet, were collecting remnants of broken tribes into a militant organization and were building a town, like a white man's town, where Tippecanoe Creek forked with the Wabash.

Tecumseh was a leader. His tragedy was that he was trying to take Jefferson's advice. As President, Jefferson had lectured the Indians against fighting among themselves, against drinking the white man's firewater, and had urged them to till the soil. The twins urged their supporters to follow that advice. They set them to farming, forbade the use of whiskey, and especially forbade the chiefs to take it upon themselves to sell Indian lands to the United States Government.

The rush of western settlement had introduced a certain ambivalence into Jefferson's attitude towards the Indians. As a natural philosopher he regarded them with enthusiastic curiosity but as a practical politician he put the interests of the white settlers first. He had laid down his policy as clearly as he could in a private paragraph in an official letter to Governor Harrison some years before; "Our system is to live in perpetual peace with the Indians, to cultivate an affectionate attachment from them, by everything just and liberal which we can do for them within the bounds of reason, and by giving them effectual protection against wrongs from our own people. the decrease in game rendering their subsistence by hunting insufficient, we wish to draw them to agriculture, to spinning and weaving, the latter branches," he added—he knew the temperament of the Indian braves —"they take up with great readiness, because they fall to the women, who gain by quitting the labors of the field for those which are exercised within doors. when they withdraw themselves to the cul-

ture of a small piece of land they will perceive how useless to them
are their extensive forests, and will be willing to pare them off from
time to time in exchange for necessaries for their farms and families."
Jefferson was not too squeamish about means. "to promote this disposition to exchange lands, which they have to spare and we want, for
necessaries, which we have to spare and they want, we shall push our
trading houses, and be glad to see the good and influential individuals
among them run in debt, because we observe that when their debts get
beyond what the individuals can pay, they become willing to lop them
off by cession of lands. . . ."

In spite of Jefferson's scientific interest in the Indians and his admiration for some of their qualities, his heart was with the settlers; it was
the frontiersmen who carried with them the seeds of a free society. It
was they who were building an empire for liberty. He relied on his
system of responsible federal agents in charge of government trading
posts to give the Indians the best treatment compatible with the acquisition of their lands.

"At our trading houses," he wrote Harrison, "we mean to sell so
low as merely to repay us cost and charges . . . this is what private
traders cannot do, for they must gain; they will consequently retire
from the competition, and we shall thus get clear of this pest without
giving offense or umbrage to the Indians. in this way our settlements
will gradually circumscribe and approach the Indians, and they will
in time either encorporate with us as citizens of the United States, or
remove beyond the Mississippi. the former is certainly the termina-
tion of their history most happy for themselves; but in the whole
course of this, it is essential to cultivate their love."

Jefferson had no illusions as to what the result must be if his system of peaceful penetration and absorption should fail: "Should any
tribe prove foolhardy enough to take up the hatchet at any time, the
seizing the whole country of that tribe, and driving them across the
Mississippi, as the only condition of peace, would be an example to
others, and a furtherance of our final consolidation."

Gallatin was as keen as Jefferson about Indian lore; in fact he was to
become in later life the founder of the science of Indian ethnology.
His boyhood friend, Jean Badollet, who had been his partner in early
pioneering ventures, had been appointed land officer at Vincennes.
Badollet, who had something of the European cult of the noble savage,
was convinced that the Indian leaders would respond to tactful and
sympathetic treatment. He was all for "cultivating their love." He believed this to be the policy of President Madison. His letters kept
Gallatin informed of the growing tension along the Wabash.

Governor Harrison was under continual pressure from the settlers
to take aggressive action. Badollet was present at several arguments

between Tecumseh and Harrison about cessions of Indian lands. Badollet felt that reason and justice were on the side of Tecumseh. He wrote desperate letters trying to warn the administration of what would be the result of Harrison's obsessive fear of British intrigues. Harrison was yielding to the universal hysteria by calling out the militia for an expedition up the Wabash which Badollet feared would set the whole Northwest frontier on fire. "If all this is not imposition on the administration," he wrote Gallatin, "say that I have become a knave. All I fear is that such a madman will goad the Indians into some act of despair to make good all he has got published of their bloody views."

Badollet was right. To overawe the Indians and their British allies Governor Harrison marched his militia up the Wabash. After a number of inconclusive parleys in the line of march, when Harrison's column reached the vicinity of Tecumseh's town Harrison's bivouac was suddenly attacked before dawn one November morning. After fighting the Indians off with considerable loss of life, Harrison's militia burned Tecumseh's settlement and then retired with somewhat indecent haste to Vincennes. From then on the Shawnee brothers threw themselves into alliance with the British.

The hero of the occasion was John Marshall's brotherinlaw, Joseph H. Daveiss, who, after his removal as district attorney, published a pamphlet attacking President Jefferson's handling of the Burr affair, and added his voice to the grand chorus of denunciation of Wilkinson's treasons. Daveiss was mortally wounded repelling an Indian breakthrough into Harrison's camp.

Humphrey Marshall in his *History of Kentucky* called Harrison "a little selfish intriguing busybody" and held him responsible for Daveiss' death.

Tippecanoe thereafter became a strictly partisan affair. The Federalists denounced the battle as a disgrace and the Democratic Republicans turned it into a political rallying cry.

When the Twelfth Congress assembled in Washington in early November the gaunt figure of Timothy Pickering, holding forth with dank hair and scornful eye; was no longer seen in the Senate. He had been defeated by Speaker Varnum of Massachusetts. The Bay State had gone Republican. Elbridge Gerry was already serving his second term as governor. The Federalists were reduced to a Gideon's band. Since George Clinton's death Madison's reelection to the presidency was considered a foregone conclusion. The House of Representatives elected Henry Clay speaker. The War Hawks took over the organization of the House.

Congress set to work to prepare for war. Freedom of the seas was becoming a national battle cry. The British minister made an effort to divert public indignation from England to France by settling the *Chesapeake* dispute. A few days before Congress met Foster wrote Monroe formally disavowing Admiral Berkeley's act and promising to restore the two impressed seamen who still survived after three years' imprisonment on a hulk in Halifax Harbor, to the deck of the *Chesapeake*.

This tardy reparation had little effect. The newspapers seemed to have forgotten the *Chesapeake*. So far as the public mind was concerned, Commodore Rodgers' trouncing of the *Little Belt* had wiped out that affront.

Foster was a puzzled man. He knew his government wanted to avoid war with the United States. A group of new men were raising their voices in Parliament for conciliation. Starvation, sedition, and riot among millhands and laborers thrown out of work by the interruption of trade were making the orders in council unpopular in England. Petititions for their repeal were producing angry debates. The press was divided. A change of policy seemed imminent, but no fresh instructions reached Foster from the Foreign Office, where Castlereagh still presided.

In Washington the War Hawks from beyond the Alleghenies were for the conquest of Canada. It mattered little to them whether the pretext were war with England or with France or with both.

The administration, still under the influence of Jefferson's pacifism, was going through the motions of continuing Madison's threadbare French policy. The theory was still held that Napoleon was about to desist from seizing American property, and that the British would be forced to corresponding concessions. An able representative like Pinkney in London with full powers might have been able to take advantage of the turn of the tide in British politics. Though the theory of a contract with France had long been discredited, for want of an alternative, Madison and Monroe, just at the moment when war with France would have proved more advantageous, drifted towards war with England.

In the early winter of 1812 a series of almost farcical events in Washington turned that drift into a settled course.

15. *The Count de Crillon*

There appeared one February day at the State Department a personage representing himself to be Count Eduart de Crillon, the scion of a French noble family known to be prominent at the imperial court. He carried a letter of introduction from Elbridge Gerry. This pretended Count de Crillon, described by Foster in a dispatch home as a thickset darkcomplected man "with monstrous thick legs" and a scar on his forehead, turned out to be a gambler and confidence man named Soubiron from some village in the Ile de France. The authorities in Washington were quite taken in by him.

The bogus count had cottoned up to John Henry, Sir James Craig's secret agent among the New England Federalists, at a London dinner table. John Henry had been in England for two years, importuning the Foreign Office for a suitable recompense for his services to the Crown. The British officials differed with Mr. Henry about the value of these services.

Henry confided in the count, who spoke and wrote a tolerable English. The count suggested to Henry that since he had been despitefully treated by His Majesty's Government his only recourse was to make the documents relating to his travels in New England available to the Americans. The Americans would certainly pay a hundred and twentyfive thousand dollars for them. The count was a man of honor and understood these things. Leave it to him.

The count and John Henry set sail. When they landed in Boston they sought an interview with Governor Gerry, and intimated that they had information very damaging to the Federalists which they must impart to the Secretary of State. The count didn't deny the possibility that he might be a secret envoy from the Emperor Napoleon. He dressed in ducal style, sported the Legion of Honor, and showed all and sundry an autograph letter purporting to be from Marshal Bessières, the hero of Austerlitz. He told a harrowing tale of having displeased the Emperor by a peccadillo and being intent on performing some service which would restore him to the imperial favor. Gerry swallowed the story and introduced him as the son "of the besieger of Gibraltar."

In Washington Henry kept out of sight while the count ingratiated himself with the administration and with the French minister. The Federalists endeared him to the Republicans by denouncing him as a French spy. Both Madison and Serurier, though faintly suspicious, treated him with wary civility on the chance that he might be some sort of secret agent. When the President invited him to dinner, Serurier took him up. The count showed considerable skill in using his standing with the administration to build up his standing with the French minister and vice versa. For a full month he was the lion of Washington society.

Meanwhile he was driving the hardest bargain he could with Monroe for Henry's papers. Neither the President nor his Secretary of State could resist what seemed to be a prime opportunity to dispose of the Federalists, who had been making negotiations impossible by encouraging British intransigence, and at the same time to unite the country for the war that seemed inevitable. The count and Monroe finally agreed that Henry was to be paid fifty thousand dollars, but that the papers were not to be published until Henry was safe aboard ship for France.

While he was selling Henry's papers to Monroe the count was making sure that most of the fifty thousand dollars should stay in his own pocket. From the beginning of their friendship he had been regaling Henry with tales of his beautiful castle of St. Martial in the Pyrenees near the ancestral Château de Crillon. Out of sheer friendship he would part with his castle, and would hasten home to set Henry up in the most aristocratic circles in France. He just happened to have the title papers with him. In return for most of the loot he delivered a deed to St. Martial, duly notarized and witnessed, to Henry and saw him aboard the United States sloop *Wasp*. Needless to say no such castle existed.

On March 9, 1812, President Madison forwarded the Henry papers to Congress with a special message. The Federalists were in a stew until they discovered that Henry had scratched out the names in his report of conversations with New England leaders and replaced them with asterisks. Indeed it later turned out that the letters were practically fraudulent. Most of them were mere paraphrases of the originals as preserved at the Record Office in London. Still the evidence was overwhelming that Sir James Craig had dickered with disaffected New Englanders and joined in their plan to detach the Eastern states.

The War Hawks took the bit in their teeth and put through a new thirtyday embargo on shipping. Foster warned the Foreign Office that this was the prelude to a declaration of war.

16. *The War That Need Never Have Been Declared*

The slowness of transatlantic communications played hob with Anglo-American diplomacy. Accounts of the disclosure of the Henry papers reached London in time to give momentum to the opposition's efforts to repeal the orders in council. The story helped discredit Castlereagh and the Tory system. Just as the opposition was on the point of upsetting the Tory administration the British government was thrown into confusion by the assassination of the Prime Minister. Spencer Perceval was shot to death on May 11 by a demented bankrupt as he was stepping into the lobby of St. Stephen's.

As soon as a new government was formed under Lord Liverpool, the opposition continued to press for the repeal of restrictions on neutral shipping. The Tories were in complete disarray. On June 16 Castlereagh rose in the Commons to announce that the government had decided to suspend the orders in council.

Jefferson's policy of coercion short of war had succeeded, but no one in Washington knew it.

A month earlier Henry Clay headed a delegation to wait on the President for the purpose of assuring him that Congress was ready to vote a declaration of war whenever he requested it. Madison decided to give the British one more chance. He would wait for the arrival of the fast sloop *Hornet* with dispatches from Joel Barlow. The *Hornet* duly arrived but brought nothing new. Foster showed Monroe his latest instructions from Castlereagh, which Monroe found highly unsatisfactory. On June 18 the war declaration passed the House and was signed the same day by President Madison.

Rumors had obsessed Washington during the three weeks the Senate and House were debating Madison's war message behind closed doors. The declaration of war was received with enthusiasm. Martial music was heard on Pennsylvania Avenue. A company of militia paraded before the President's House. President Madison went so far as to give a military touch to his costume when he rode out in his coach. Richard Rush, the comptroller, wrote his father, the beloved Philadelphia physician, faddist, and patriot of the old school, Dr. Benjamin Rush, "He visited in person—a thing never known before—all the offices of the departments of war and the navy, stimulating everything in the manner of a little commander in chief, with his little round hat and huge cockade."

The same issue of the Richmond *Enquirer* in which Jefferson, at Monticello, read the news of the declaration of war carried a dispatch from Gothenburg in Sweden: War declared by the Emperor Napoleon on the Czar Alexander. The Grande Armée was on the march against Moscow.

Jefferson's policy towards England was wrecked at the point of fruition by accidents of time and space. Now his diplomatic maneuvering to create a league of neutrals was producing unexpected results. Alexander's espousal of the cause of American shipping was starting a train of circumstances which would result in the undoing not of the British Empire but of the French.

"Nous voilà donc," Jefferson breezily wrote Kosciusko on July 28, "en guerre avec l'Angleterre." He proceeded to make a series of prognostications: "our present enemy will have the sea to herself, while we shall be equally predominant on land, and shall strip her of all her possessions on this continent. she may burn New York, by her ships and congreve rockets, in which case we must burn the City of London by hired incendiaries, of which her starving manufacturers will furnish abundance. . . . hunger will make them brave every risk for bread. . . . I hope we shall confine ourselves to the conquest of their possessions, & defence of our harbors, leaving the war on the ocean to our privateers. these will immediately swarm on every sea, & do more injury to British commerce than the regular fleets of all Europe would do. . . . I know your feelings on the present state of the world, & hope that they will be cheered by the successful course of the war and the addition of Canada to our confederacy. the infamous intrigues of Great Britain to destroy our government (of which Henry's is but one sample), and with the Indians to tomahawk our women and children, prove that the cession of Canada, their fulcrum for these Machiavellian levers, must be a sine qua non in a treaty of peace."

Jefferson shared the delusion of most of his countrymen in the South and West that the Canadian pear was ripe for the picking. It seems to have occurred to no one that the small British regular forces north of Lake Erie had the advantage of inside lines and of the skill and training that came from twenty years of almost continuous warfare.

Writing President Madison to thank him for the documents relating to the declaration of war, Jefferson described the declaration to be "entirely popular here, the only opinion being that it should have been issued the moment the season permitted the militia to enter Canada. . . . the federalists indeed are openmouthed against the declaration: but they are poor devils here, not worthy of notice. a barrel of tar to each state south of the Potomac will keep all in order . . . to the north they will give you more trouble," he added in an effort to pump a little steel into mild little Madison: "you may there have to apply the tougher drastics . . . hemp and confiscation."

Jefferson had his ruthless side. If war it had to be he was shelving his pacifism for the duration. Tales of the massacres of outlying settlers were already coming in from the Northwest. He urged the immediate conquest of Canada to stop Indian barbarities.

In spite of his grim mood, Jefferson believed that, in war and peace, national policy should continue. He concluded his letter with some suggestions about keeping up the export trade in spite of hostilities: "The great profits of the wheat crop have allured every one to it: and never was such a crop on the ground as that which we generally begin to cut this day. it would be mortifying to the farmer to see such a one rot in his barn. it would soon sicken him of the war. . . . for carrying our produce to foreign markets, our own ships, neutral ships and even enemy ships under neutral flag, which I would wink at, will probably suffice."

He wrote Duane in particularly sanguine vein later in the summer— Duane was taking advantage of the war spirit to market a new edition of his military manual—"as far as the neighborhood of Quebec will be a mere matter of marching and will give us experience for the attack of Halifax the next, and the final expulsion of England from the American continent. Halifax once taken every cockboat of hers must return to England for repairs."

Jefferson saw the interruption of trade with America and the closing of the Baltic as bringing England to financial collapse. All the best English would have to emigrate. Duane had expressed the suspicion that immigration from England would bring with it Tory prejudices likely to encourage the Federalists. "Still I agree with you that these immigrations will give strength to English partialities, to eradicate which is one of the most consoling expectations from the war, but probably the old hive will be broken up by a revolution, and a regeneration of its principles render intercourse with it no longer contaminating."

Most Republicans agreed that the invasion of Canada had first priority. To accomplish it, Secretary Eustis, with his incompetent staff and multifarious duties which ranged from those of quartermaster general to commissioner of pensions, had at his disposal the militia of the various states and ten regiments of the Army of the United States, all under strength and scattered over an immense territory. The thirteen new regiments Congress had voted existed only on paper. For commanders he had Henry Dearborn, whom Madison appointed major general in charge of the Northern Department; and Thomas Pinckney, a moderate Federalist from South Carolina, who had proved his ability as a diplomat under Washington and Adams, holding similar rank in the Southern Department. Dearborn and Pinckney were both in their sixties. Neither of them had seen service in the field since they were boys in the Revolutionary War.

The ranking brigadier was still James Wilkinson. General Wilkinson had recently emerged from a long courtmartial at Frederick Town, Maryland, where he managed to brazen out a second acquittal on the old charge of having been in the Spanish pay, and to repel charges of insubordination, wastefulness, neglect of duty, and corruption which grew out of the tragic loss of life among his troops on the Mississippi. Wilkinson as usual defended himself with vigor and skill, but he left Frederick Town in worse repute than ever, in spite of the fat volume of autobiographical apologetics which he was preparing for publication.

While President Madison felt he had to approve the decision of the courtmartial, he couldn't help appending a spiteful reprimand which only served to embitter the vainglorious general.

When Secretary Eustis started drafting his plans in the early spring of 1812, it was well understood at the War Department that the crucial command was the Northwest. The frontier was barely defended. To oppose the threatened avalanche of Indian hordes, a hundred and twenty troopers garrisoned the old British fort at Detroit and tiny detachments occupied stockades on the Wabash, on Michili-mackinac Island, and at Fort Dearborn on the Chicago River.

Another politician in his sixties, a New Englander named William Hull, also reputed to have served with distinction during the Revolution, was governor of Michigan Territory. He was placed in command of the armies on the frontier. As soon as he received this appointment Hull hastened to Washington and there, along with Dearborn and Eustis, helped President Madison concoct a plan of campaign. A powerful expeditionary force was to attack Montreal through Lake Champlain. Three other armies were to invade simultaneously through Niagara, Sackett's Harbor at the eastern end of Lake Ontario, and Detroit.

It was essential to reinforce Detroit before the news of the declaration of war reached the British outposts. Hull rode back to Dayton, Ohio, and there took command in early June of one national regiment, various groups of militia, and some grenadiers, amounting in all to a couple of thousand men, and marched them so briskly across country to the mouth of the Miami River at the western end of Lake Erie that the commander of the British forces north of the lakes was thoroughly alarmed.

Major General Isaac Brock, a thoroughly competent officer, was receiving intelligence daily through Indian runners. He could count on a little more than two thousand regulars along his entire frontier. Both he and the governor general of Canada were squeamish about arming the militia for fear that the Ontario farmers might sympathize with the Americans.

By the first of July Hull had not yet received official notice of the declaration of war. To save space in his wagon train, he loaded his entrenching tools, his personal baggage, his hospital stores, and a trunk containing his muster rolls, along with the latest plan of campaign forwarded him by the War Department, on a schooner bound for Detroit.

The British got notice of the declaration of war before the American commander did. The same day the official notification reached Hull from Secretary Eustis, the British captured his schooner.

General Dearborn, meanwhile, who was supposed to be in charge of the eastern prongs of the offensive, was in Albany building a recruiting center. Dearborn was preoccupied by a constitutional question raised by the Federalist governors of Massachusetts and Connecticut: did the President have the right to order out the state militia since no actual invasion had taken place? The New Englanders denied he had such a right and blocked every move to raise troops for the war. Theophilus Parsons, the Federalist Chief Justice of Massachusetts, backed them up by a decision from the bench.

Madison wrote despondently to Jefferson on August 17 from Washington, where the war situation was forcing him to expose himself to the bilious fevers of the season: "The seditious opposition in Mass. & Cont. with the intrigues elsewhere insidiously cooperating with it, have so clogged the wheels of the war that I fear the campaign will not accomplish the object of it. . . . We just learn . . . that the important post of Michillimackinac has fallen into the hands of the Enemy. If the reinforcement of about 2000 ordered from the Ohio, and on the way to Hull, do not enable him to take Malden"—Fort Malden was the British post across from Detroit—"and awe the Savages emboldened by the British success, his situation will be very ineligible."

There was worse news to come. Hull's situation was ineligible indeed. Two days before Madison sent off his letter to Jefferson from the President's house, Hull surrendered Detroit. Hull had arrived in good order and crossed the St. Clair River to Sandwich where he published a proclamation inviting the Canadians to flock to the American standard. He lost his nerve at the prospect of storming Fort Malden, which was known to be thinly manned, and hesitated so long that he gave Brock time to throw in reinforcements and to hold a grand council of a thousand Indian warriors.

"He who attracted most my attention," Brock wrote Lord Liverpool, "was a Shawnee chief, Tecumset, brother to the prophet who for the last two years has carried on, contrary to our remonstrances, an active warfare against the United States. A more sagacious or more gallant warrior does not, I believe, exist. He was the admiration of everyone who conversed with him."

Hull was an elderly man in ill health. He had his wife and daughter with him. He was taken with such panic at the thought of being cut off by the Indians that he hurried his army back across the river. When Brock pressed his advantage by crossing the river after him and investing Detroit, Hull raised the white flag without allowing any proper resistance to be made. The same day an Indian party overran Fort Dearborn on the Chicago River, burned it, and butchered the major part of the garrison. The whole Northwest seemed lost to the United States.

The expeditions planned to nip off the Niagara peninsula did not fare much better. Alexander Smyth, who was inspector general of the United States Army, had his command in Buffalo, while Stephen Van Rensselaer, who was running for governor of New York on the Federalist ticket, headed the militia of that state at Fort Niagara. Both generals were supposed to cross the river simultaneously to catch a British force, again under the command of Isaac Brock, in a pincers movement.

Instead Smyth and Van Rensselaer had a falling out and Van Rens-

selaer tried to storm Queenston Height, on the north shore of the
Niagara River, on his own. In spite of the bravery of his troops the
operation failed. Craven boatmen left them without means of retreat.
Some ninety were killed and nine hundred taken prisoner.

It was mountainous Winfield Scott, now a lieutenant colonel, who
braved the Indian snipers to make his way through the British lines to
arrange the terms of surrender. The British did suffer one severe loss.
Major General Brock was shot dead leading his men in a counterat-
tack.

Van Rensselaer resigned his commission in disgust and was replaced
by Brigadier General Smyth. Smyth's orders were to cross by night in
boats and to seize Fort Erie, at the western entrance of the Niagara
River, as soon as the force under his command should amount to
three thousand men. Smyth was strictly an armchair general. Recruits
came in, but he never could muster the necessary three thousand. He
contented himself with sending messages to the fort under a flag of
truce, demanding its surrender "to avoid effusion of blood," until his
army disbanded in frustration and shame. Homebound militiamen
amused themselves by taking pot shots at General Smyth's tent.

News of these disasters was received with as much incredulity as
indignation. "The detestable treason of Hull has indeed excited a deep
anxiety in all breasts," Jefferson wrote Duane on October 1, ". . . but
it has been succeeded by a revived animation, and a determination to
meet the occurrence with increased efforts; and I have so much confidence in the vigorous minds & bodies of our countrymen, as to be
fearless as to the final issue."

He concurred with Duane that Monroe should be Secretary of War.
"I clearly think with you on the competence of Monroe to embrace
great views of action." All he knew of Eustis was that he was "a
pleasant gentlemanly man." Jefferson added that he had so much confidence "in the wisdom and conscientious integrity of Mr. Madison as
to be satisfied, that however torturing to his feelings, he will fulfill his
duty to the public and to his own reputation by making the necessary
change."

To Madison himself he wrote consolingly: "the seeing whether our
untried generals will stand proof is a very dear operation. two of them
have cost us a great many men. we can tell by his plumage whether a
cook is dunghill or game. but with us cowardice & courage wear the
same plume. Hull will of course be shot for cowardice & treachery, and
will not Van Rensselaer he broke for cowardice & incapacity?"

The "vigorous minds & bodies" of his countrymen in which the
sanguine Jefferson found such encouragement were more engaged in
partisan conflicts during the first months of the war than in coopera-

tion against the enemy. Instead of uniting the country the declaration of war seemed to widen the breach between Federalists and Republicans. Massachusetts now had a Federalist governor. Members of Congress who voted for war were hissed when they showed their faces on the Boston Stock Exchange. The Republican member for Plymouth was manhandled and literally kicked out of town. The lower house of the Massachusetts General Court issued an address to the people of the state: "Express your sentiment without fear and let the sound of your disapprobation of this war be loud and deep. . . . If your sons must be torn from you by conscription consign them to the care of God: but let there be no volunteers except for defensive war."

Timothy Pickering, who had retired to his farm back of Salem, presided over a public meeting and put through a resolution calling for state conventions to debate on the crisis in affairs. Pickering right along had urged state conventions as the first step in his plan for the secession of the eastern states.

The Federalists were encouraged in their opposition to hostilities on the Canadian border by negotiations for an armistice. The governor general of Canada had in August sent an officer to General Dearborn in Albany for that purpose, and a parallel parley was going on in London between the American chargé d'affaires and the Foreign Office. Meanwhile, though insisting on the right of impressment, British naval officers were treating Yankee skippers with indulgence and tact. Licenses were being freely granted to American vessels to carry foodstuffs to Spanish and Portuguese ports, where they were needed to provision Wellington's armies. Even Jefferson's hatred of the British was strangely tempered when it came to selling them wheat.

He explained his theory of wartime commerce at some length to the Philadelphia type founder, James Ronaldson. Ronaldson was in France, carrying a letter of introduction from Jefferson to Du Pont de Nemours, who Jefferson, always deeply interested in the encouragement of printing, hoped would help him find the supply of antimony he needed for the casting of his types. He was answering a letter of Ronaldson's reporting complaints heard in Paris of American trading with the British enemy. "You doubt," Jefferson wrote, "whether we ought to permit the exportation of grain to our enemies; but Great Britain with her own agricultural support, and those she can command by her access into every sea, cannot be starved by withholding our supplies. and if she is to be fed at all events, why may we not have the benefit of it as well as others? I would not indeed feed her armies landed on our territory . . . but this would be my only exception. and as to feeding her armies in the peninsula, she is fighting our battles there, as Bonaparte is in the Baltic. if we could, by starving the English armies, oblige them to withdraw from the peninsula, it would be to send them here; and I think we had better feed them there for pay, than feed and fight them here for nothing. . . . no country can pay war taxes if you suppress all their resources. to keep the war popular, we must keep open the markets."

Jefferson was not alone. War hatred of the British was tempered, during the year 1812 at least, by all sorts of considerations, of which the complications of international trade were not the least weighty. No such restraint showed itself in the virulent partisan strife between Republicans and Federalists. The Republicans called the Federalists traitors: the Federalists pinned on the Republicans every crime which could be attributed to the French Jacobins or to the armies of Napoleon. Their press excoriated the military bungling of Madison's administration at the same time as it called for the immediate cessation of a war which benefited no one but the French. Their arguments were strengthened by an exhibition in Baltimore of mass brutality that shocked the country.

Baltimore was a boom town. Shipbuilding, warehousing for the foreign trade, and the fitting out of privateers attracted an unruly brawling population. The working people were ardent Republicans. At the same time the wealth and fashion of the city had retained, since the days of Luther Martin and Justice Chase, a strong Federalist hue. Their mouthpiece was the *Federal Republican*, a newspaper edited by Jacob Wagner, who had been chief clerk of the State Department under Pickering. In spite of his having been retained in office by Jefferson, when Wagner resigned in 1807 he used his knowledge of the inner workings as the basis for a series of slanderous attacks on the Republican administration. He had been set up in his newspaper by the Federalists. The Baltimore mob celebrated the declaration of war by pulling down Wagner's printing shop.

Wagner moved his presses to Georgetown in the District of Columbia and shipped his paper into Baltimore to be distributed from his house on Charles Street. The Federalists, damned if they'd be dictated to by a Jacobin mob, spread the word that the paper was actually being printed at Wagner's house. When it was bruited abroad that the Republicans were planning to close down that press too, General Henry Lee, of Light Horse fame, Jefferson's mortal enemy, hotheaded and scatterbrained as ever, collected a band of Federalist stalwarts to defend the house.

The mob advanced. Shots were fired from the windows. There were a number of wounded. Two bystanders were killed. Militiamen were hauling up a cannon to shoot the door down when Mayor Johnson arrived with a troop of cavalry and persuaded the Federalists to submit to civil authority and to allow themselves to be conducted to the city jail. The streets were in an uproar. Violent men stormed the jail next morning. The mayor was overpowered when he tried to intervene. They beat the prisoners so hideously that one Revolutionary veteran was killed and General Lee so badly injured he was a cripple for the rest of his life. The magistrates stood by helpless. The rioters would not allow the wounded to be attended to. Eight bodies lay in a bloody heap on the prison steps until noon.

The Federalists were reminded of the worst excesses of the French Revolution. The New England Republicans found no word of defense. Boston town meeting passed a resolution declaring that the riot was "the first fruits of the unnatural and dreadful alliance into which we have entered in fact if not in form."

The Baltimore riot, followed by Hull's surrender and Smyth's fiasco, came near destroying the Republican party. In Massachusetts John Lowell stimulated a resurgence of Federalist activity by a scathing pamphlet called *Mr. Madison's War*. Pickering was triumphant.

To add to the difficulties of the administration the oncoming presidential election was splitting the Republicans. Madison's reelection was thrown into jeopardy when De Witt Clinton, the aggressive new leader of his father's old faction in New York, started campaigning for the Republican nomination. A young man named Martin Van Buren, reputed to be the illegitimate son of Aaron Burr, managed his campaign.

Though Van Buren was no kin of Burr's he did have something of Burr's political skill and of his utter lack of political scruple. The Federalists were encouraging the Clintonians. A situation was developing somewhat like the state of affairs in 1801 when Burr came within a hairsbreadth of the presidency.

Doughty old John Adams, disgusted by the unpatriotic policy of the Federalists, allowed himself to be listed as an elector on Madison's ticket, but the Federalists swept Massachusetts. In New England only Vermont went for Madison and Gerry. The Clinton-Federalist combination carried New York, New Jersey, Delaware, and half of Maryland. The final vote in the electoral college was 128 for Madison to 87 for De Witt Clinton.

It was the navy that saved the day for the Jeffersonian Republicans. Jefferson and Madison during their whole public life had shared a vehement distrust of vessels of war. Jefferson was enthusiastic for gunboats, and suggested to Madison the arming of fast pilot boats, which would outsail and outmaneuver the lumbering British ships of the line, but to his mind there was something Federalist about a frigate. He was repelled by the gory pomp of the formalized sea battles of the time. He was for militia on land and privateers on the sea. "The partisans of England here," he wrote Kosciusko, "have endeavored much to goad us into the folly of choosing the ocean instead of the land for the theatre of war. . . . I hope we shall confine ourselves to the conquest of their possessions, and the defence of our harbors, leaving the war on the ocean to our privateers."

All through 1812 it was on the ocean that the Americans excelled. Even on Lake Erie, Smyth's disgrace had been alleviated by a brilliant nautical operation. A navy lieutenant with a force of fifty seamen and fifty soldiers recaptured the brig *Adams*, which had fallen into Brock's hands with the surrender of Detroit. The *Adams* and a smaller vessel named the *Caledonia* were cut out by a party in boats from under the guns of Fort Erie. The *Adams* had to be blown up but the *Caledonia* was sailed to the American shore to be added to the nucleus of an American flotilla.

The American fleet on the ocean was so outnumbered that the British could muster more ships than the United States had guns. Soon after war was declared Captain Hull, who had taken Barlow to France the year before on his *Constitution*, managed to avoid an overwhelming British squadron and to catch the British frigate *Guerrière* on her own. In thirty minutes' combat he left her without a spar standing. When she surrendered she was found to be so badly damaged she had to be sunk. When Hull landed the surviving officers and crew prisoners at a Boston wharf one Sunday morning, partisan rancor was forgotten in a burst of patriotic enthusiasm. Isaac Hull was a nephew of the unfortunate General Hull. His victory helped atone for his uncle's defeat and brought it home to the lords of the Admiralty that they were facing a formidable opponent.

Soon after, the small frigate *Essex*, Captain David Porter, after scooping up a transport full of redcoats bound for Canada, worsted the British sloop of war *Alert*. The American sloop of war *Wasp*, one of Jefferson's few additions to the navy, disabled and boarded the British brig *Frolic* but was in turn captured with her prize by a British 74. On a cruise in Brazilian waters the *Constitution*, Commodore Bainbridge in command, reduced the powerful British frigate *Java* to a hulk and forced her surrender.

The naval victories united all factions as nothing had since the humiliation of the *Chesapeake*. Even President Madison became navy-minded. On December 10 Federalists and Republicans alike celebrated the victories with a naval ball at Marine Headquarters. Washington City was illuminated. The colors of the *Guerrière* and the *Alert* were featured among the decorations. In the middle of the festivities young Lieutenant Hamilton, Secretary Hamilton's son, arrived with dispatches from Commodore Stephen Decatur. His *United States* had captured another British frigate. The colors of HMS *Macedonian* were added to the decorations on the wall.

The *National Intelligencer* featured a squib which circulated far and wide through the press: "G.B. *stamped* us into independent states, *counciled* us into a manufacturing people, she is now *fighting* us into a maritime power."

CHAPTER VII

The Sevenfold Wonders of the Time

1. Two Pieces of Homespun

For all his misgivings about the navy Jefferson, following the fortunes of war from Monticello in alternating moods of philosophical aloofness and acute personal concern, could not help kindling to the exploits of the American fighting ships. On May 27, 1813, he made honorable amends in a letter to John Adams. "I sincerely congratulate you on the successes of our little navy; which must be more gratifying to you than to most men, as being the early and constant advocate for wooden walls."

Their tenyear feud had come to an end the year before when John Adams celebrated New Year's Day by forwarding to Jefferson "two Pieces of Homespun lately produced in this quarter by One who was honored in his youth with some of your Attention and much of your kindness."

The two pieces of homespun turned out to be two volumes of John Quincy Adams' *Lectures on Rhetoric and Oratory*, but Jefferson, being a literalminded man, and not waiting for the arrival of the package to take up a correspondence with his old friend, answered with a short disquisition on the state of spinning and weaving in Virginia. Household manufacture was among his favorite topics. "The economy and thriftiness resulting from our household manufactures are such that they will never again be laid aside: and nothing more salutary has ever happened than the British obstructions to our demand for their manufactures.

"A letter from you," Jefferson went on, "calls up recollections very dear to my mind. It carries me back to times when, beset with difficulties and dangers, we were fellow laborers in the same cause, struggling for what is most valuable to man, his right of self-government."

He evoked the immense growth of the country: ". . . and so we have gone on; and so we shall go on, puzzled and prospering beyond example in the history of man. and I do believe we shall continue to grow, to multiply and prosper, until we exhibit an association, powerful and wise and happy, beyond what has yet been seen by men."

They brought each other up to date on the state of their health and of their families. Jefferson couldn't help boasting that in spite of being a greatgrandfather he enjoyed "considerable activity of body and mind." He spent three or four hours a day on horseback, but he confessed that (since a violent attack of muscular rheumatism the summer before) he wasn't as much of a walker as he used to be. Adams, who was eight years Jefferson's senior, bragged a little about being able to walk three or four miles every fair day, or to ride ten or fifteen if he had to, but admitted to suffering from a complaint "that nothing but the Ground can cure . . . a kind of Paralytic Affection of the Nerves, which makes my hands tremble, and renders it difficult to write at all, and impossible to write well."

Soon they were lamenting the death of the mutual friend who had worked so hard for a reconciliation between them. Benjamin Rush, one of the most warmhearted, exuberant, precipitate, and occasionally one of the most injudicious of men, had managed, through a stream of cajoling letters, to bring them together. When Jefferson got news of Dr. Rush's death in Philadelphia he wrote Adams: "Another of our friends of 76, is gone, my dear Sir, another of the Cosigners of the independence of our country, and a better man than Rush, could not have left us, more benevolent, more learned, of finer genius or more honest. we too must go; and that ere long."

For all his large family and the swarms of visitors and friends at Monticello, Jefferson was experiencing something of the lonesomeness of old age. Only a rough half dozen were still alive out of the generation of 1776. He put it this way in another letter: "Like a tree standing solitary in a field, I view myself almost singly surviving the multitude of cotemporaries who formerly occupied the space around me."

The feeling that they were among the last men living who still spoke the language of the Revolutionary years added to the zest with which Jefferson and Adams plunged into their renewed correspondence. They were nine days apart; they never again met face to face, yet their conversation immediately became indispensable to them. They answered each other's epistles as eagerly as young people building up a new friendship. They jotted down every random notion that came into their heads. They indulged in anecdotes and digressions. They ranged through the whole experience of their lives. Now and then they contradicted themselves as well as each other. Their letters were drafted with special care. They left wide margins for notes and afterthoughts. Though they disclaimed any idea of publication, in the back of both men's minds was the thought that someday somewhere somebody would be interested in what they had to tell each other. They exchanged notions about Priestley's ideas of religion, and about prophets and impostors white, black, and red; about Morton of Merrymount who so shocked the godly in New England; and about Genghis Khan's methods of hunting and the possible Siberian origin of the American Indians. Adams described his row with Pickering and Jefferson bewailed his difficulties with Edward Livingston. They came to the edge of a quarrel in retrospect over the Alien and Sedition Acts. Adams pointed out that Jefferson had put his name to the acts as Vice President and was as responsible for them as he was. Jefferson poured healing oil by blaming Pickering and the Essex Junto for his disagreements with Adams, and Adams sought Jefferson's indulgence by roasting the clergy. On this topic they found themselves in heartwarming agreement.

"I wish You could Live a Year in Boston," exclaimed Adams, "hear the Divines, read their Publications. . . . You would see how spiritual Tyranny and ecclesiastical Domination are beginning in our Country. . . . No I have not done with spiritual Pride in high places and in low. I would trust these liberal Christians in London and in Boston with Power, just as soon as I would Calvin or Cardinal Lorrain. . . . Checks and Ballances, Jefferson, however you and your party may have ridiculed them, are our only security for the Progress of Mind, as well as the Security of Body. Every species of these Christians would persecute Deists as soon as either Sect would persecute another, if it had unchecked and unbalanced Power. Nay the Deists would persecute Christians, and Atheists would persecute Deists, with an unrelenting Cruelty as any Christians would persecute them or one another. Know thyself human Nature!"

Jefferson in reply quoted three lines of Theocritus about a woodsman in the mountains who couldn't decide which tree to start cutting. "And I too, my dear Sir, like the woodcutter of Ida, should doubt where to begin should I enter the forest of opinions, discussions and contentions which have occurred in our day. . . ." He switched from religious intolerance to political intolerance: "the same political parties which now agitate the U.S. have existed thro' all time . . . and in fact the terms of Whig and Tory belong to natural, as well as to civil history. they denote the temper and constitution of mind of different individuals."

Adams' mind occasionally boggled at the immensity of the task that faced them. "I cannot write Volumes in a Single Sheet: but these Letters of yours require Volumes from me." He reaffirmed a statement of his in an address to a meeting of Boston young men, which Jefferson had criticized as conflicting with his own belief in the perfectibility of man: "without wishing to damp the Ardor of curiosity, or influence the freedom of inquiry, I will hasard a prediction that after the most industrious and impartial Researches, the longest liver of you all will find no Principles, Institutions, or Systems of Education, more fit *in general* to be transmitted to your Posterity, than those you have received from your Ancestors. . . . Now I will avow," insisted Adams, "that I then believed and now believe, that those general Principles of Christianity, are as eternal and immutable, as the Existence and Attributes of God; and that those Principles of Liberty are as unalterable as human Nature."

"You and I ought not to die," Adams cried out again, "before We have explained ourselves to each other."

Through forty years of political struggle Jefferson had promised himself many pleasures in retirement. Now, in spite of his anxiety for the American cause, his financial worries, his dismay at the mounting infirmities of old age, beyond the pleasure he took in his grandchildren, in his garden and experimental farm, and in his drafting board, he found real joy in explaining himself to John Adams.

2. *The Horrors and Perils of the War Office*

Jefferson's position as silent partner in the old triumvirate kept him in constant communication with Madison and Gallatin, and now with Monroe.

Madison had undergone his second inauguration under painful circumstances. He found more obstruction than cooperation from the outgoing Congress for the war measures he presented. In spite of the Republican victory in New York his prospects for the Thirteenth, soon to be called into special session, were not much brighter. Massachusetts had elected Timothy Pickering to the House.

His cabinet was in disarray. Dr. Eustis retired from the War Office in the face of the disasters of 1812. Monroe took over his department. Paul Hamilton's drinking had become a public scandal. When he made an exhibition of himself at the Navy Ball celebrating the victories of Hull and Bainbridge and Decatur, Madison was forced to ask for his resignation as Secretary of the Navy. In his place he appointed the man Jefferson had first thought of for the post in 1801, a Philadelphia sea captain and shipowner named William Jones.

Though his state papers were often as clear and logical as his Federalist essays had been twenty years before, Madison as President failed to develop the administrator's flair for picking the right man for the right place. He worked out excellent plans without finding ways to force them through. While he could be waspish when things went wrong he was timid about hurting people's feelings. He failed to command men's loyalties as Jefferson had. In trying to replace Eustis in the War Office he met with a series of frustrations.

His first choice, as it was Jefferson's, was Monroe, now serving pro tem without giving up the Department of State. Monroe, who was already dreaming of the presidency in 1816, stood off and let it be known that an overall military command in the field would suit him better. Crawford of Georgia refused. Dearborn would not give up his general's uniform for the drudgery of a Washington office. The situation became so bad that Gallatin, the only man in Madison's cabinet who served, with selfless devotion, offered to take the office himself: "If the choice is to fall on a man non-professional, I will be ready (Mr. Monroe still refusing) to accept the War Department with all its horrors and perils."

Monroe meanwhile was developing energetic plans for the summer campaigns of 1813. Just when he began to show signs of letting himself be cajoled into accepting the War Office, Madison entered into negotiations with John Armstrong of New York.

John Armstrong was chiefly known for having, as a young officer, been the author of the "Newburgh Addresses" that caused George Washington so much embarrassment when he was presiding over the demobilization of the Continental Army. After a period of politicking in Pennsylvania as a Federalist, Armstrong had married a sister of Robert R. Livingston's and settled at Red Hook on the Hudson. He switched to the Republicans with the rest of the Livingston clan in 1800, and after a term in the Senate was appointed by Jefferson to replace his brotherinlaw, the chancellor, as minister to France. Napoleon described him as "a morose man with whom one cannot treat."

He came home in 1810 with a higher opinion of his performance at the imperial court than was entertained by either Madison or Monroe. Having made himself useful to the Madison faction against the Clintonians in the election of 1812, when war became imminent Madison appointed him, largely to please the Livingstons, a major general.

General Armstrong was a pugnacious and illtempered man of fifty-five. His presidential ambitions conflicted with Monroe's. It was Gallatin who, as a specialist in New York politics, had convinced Madison that, take it all in all, Armstrong was the best man available. Monroe, back at the Department of State, immediately began to complain that Armstrong was muddling up the military plans he had put so much work into preparing.

As soon as he heard of the nomination Jefferson, in the interests of concord, wrote Armstrong a congratulatory note from Monticello in which he regretted the administration's bad luck with its generals. "it is unfortunate that heaven has not set its stamp on the forehead of those whom it has qualified for military achievement. that it has left us to draw for them in a lottery of so many blanks to a prize, and

where the blank is to be manifested only by the public misfortunes.
. . . I hope you will be ready," he added, "to act on the first breaking
of the ice, as other wise we may despair of wresting Canada from our
enemies."

During his first days in the War Office Armstrong managed to draw
not a few of the blanks Jefferson had so deplored in his letter. Furthermore he alienated the two ablest members of the administration. He
insulted Monroe by offering to make him a major general, when he
knew Monroe wanted the top position or nothing, and insisted on
keeping Dearborn as chief of the Northern Department. He disgusted
Gallatin, to whom he owed his appointment, by making the virulent
and unreliable Duane, Gallatin's most vociferous critic, adjutant general.

Meanwhile the news that came into the War Office was all of fresh
disasters in the winter fighting at Fort Meigs on the river Raisin at
the western end of Lake Erie where William Henry Harrison was
squandering lives and equipment in an illfated effort to recapture
Detroit.

3. *General Winter*

President Madison was having as bad luck with his foreign diplomacy as with his military campaigns. The almost simultaneous declarations of war by Napoleon against Russia and by the United States
against Great Britain temporarily paralyzed John Quincy Adams'
effort at St. Petersburg to keep the Baltic open to neutral shipping.
Even before he started his second term Madison received the news
that Joel Barlow, the warm personal friend he'd counted on to handle
Napoleon, was dead.

In Paris Barlow and his family had settled into the same fine mansion on the Rue Vaugirard where he happily worked on steamboat
projects with Fulton years before. Profiting from his knowledge of
the language and from the assistance of French friends who loved the
eternal boyishness of his nature and who admired him as the leading
American poet, it hadn't taken Barlow long to discover that the Emperor was willing to resort to every type of trickery to involve
the United States in war with England. Since Barlow wanted to avoid
war with either France or England all he could do as minister was to
smile and to keep his ears open.

He went through the pretense of discussing with the Emperor's
Foreign Minister a project for a commercial treaty which they both
knew the Emperor had no interest in whatsoever. Napoleon was too
busy with his Russian campaign to pay attention to the complaints of
Yankee traders even if they were fighting his old enemy. But all at
once, when the Russian campaign began going badly in the fall of

1812, it occurred to the Emperor and his advisers that the Americans might prove useful after all.

Joel Barlow received an urgent invitation to proceed to Wilna in Lithuania where the Emperor was planning to establish winter quarters. There His Majesty would have leisure to listen to the grievances of American shipowners and to discuss a commercial treaty.

At the end of October Barlow left Paris accompanied only by Tom Barlow, his nephew, and by his coachman Louis. His spirits were high at the prospects of another trip. Changing horses at the post stations, they drove night and day across Germany. Heavy rains and military traffic had churned the roads into quagmires. Resting two days in Berlin, Barlow admired the neatness of the Prussian capital. He was a tireless traveler. He and Tom were happy as a couple of boys out to see the world for the first time. "I enjoy an impudent vulgar health," he wrote his anxious and devoted Ruth, "fit for a woodcutter or maple sugar maker."

After Königsberg the roads were frozen. Signs of ruin and carnage were everywhere. Barlow reached Wilna on November 18. Napoleon was already in full retreat. Ten days later the Grande Armée made its last stand in the bloody crossing of the Beresina. The defeat became a rout. The Emperor was soon speeding back to Paris as fast as the horses would carry his traveling carriage.

For the court and the *corps diplomatique* stranded at Wilna it was a case of devil take the hindmost. No food, no lodging, only frozen wastes piled here and there with frozen corpses of horses and men. Driving through snow and sleet across Poland, Barlow caught cold. His cold became feverish. He came down with pneumonia and died in a rickety hovel in the village of Zarnovic.

Among his uncle's papers that Tom brought back to Paris was the draft of some verses which had been going through Joel Barlow's head during the dreadful drive. *Advice to a Raven in Russia* was possibly the most effective poem he ever wrote. The last lines are an excoriation of Napoleon:

> *War after war his hungry soul requires,*
> *State after state shall sink beneath his fires,*
> *Yet other Spains in victim smoke shall rise*
> *And other Moskows suffocate the skies,*
> *Each land reeking with its peoples slain;*
> *And not a stream run bloodless to the main.*
> *Till men resume their souls, and dare to shed*
> *Earth's total vengeance on the monster's head,*
> *Hurl from his blood-built throne this king of woes,*
> *Dash him to dust and let the world repose.*

4. *Britannia Rules the Waves*

Napoleon's defeat in Russia had graver connotations for Madison than his personal grief over the loss of a friend. It meant the frustration of the chief purposes for which war had been declared. With Britain triumphant and all Europe rising against the tyrant, it meant that war with England, instead of being the technical state of hostilities to be settled by negotiation which Madison had envisioned, was now war in earnest. The British government would be able to detach powerful forces from the army and navy to crush once and for all these upstart Americans who had challenged the ruler of the waves in her hour of victory.

All that was left viable of the foreign policies of the Republican administrations was Jefferson's project for a rapprochement with Russia and the Baltic neutrals. When four days after Madison's second inauguration the Russian envoy, André Dashkoff, called at the State Department with a proposal from the Czar Alexander that he use his good offices to restore peace with Great Britain, Madison and Monroe were hard put to it to conceal the enthusiasm with which they accepted the offer.

Immediately it became necessary to appoint a proper delegation to treat with the British. John Quincy Adams, already in St. Petersburg, was an obvious choice. To make the mission bipartisan, James A. Bayard of Delaware, a moderate Federalist who was a relation by marriage of the very Republican newspaper editor Samuel Harrison Smith, was chosen to join him. Albert Gallatin offered his services as the third member.

After his twelve years of hard work in the Treasury as the indispensable hub of the Jefferson and Madison administrations, Gallatin felt he had a right to a change. To finance the war he had had to resort to every bit of prestige he had acquired among the money men. With the help of his friend John Jacob Astor, the immigrant fur trader from Waldorf in Germany who had become one of the financial powers of New York, Gallatin was arranging an internal loan which should see the government through a year of wartime expenditure. The Treasury accounts were all in order. All the papers, including the draft of a bill setting up a new national bank, were ready for the mere signature of a deputy. Gallatin didn't want to spend a day longer in Madison's cabinet as it was at present constituted.

After years of vituperation from the *Aurora*, Armstrong's appointment of Duane was the last straw. Gallatin could hardly have helped feeling miffed with President Madison for submitting to it. When he told Madison that at this juncture he felt he would be more useful abroad, Madison gratefully sent him off to negotiate the peace, with the reservation that he would not allow him to resign from the Treasury. Leaving Mrs. Gallatin and the younger children with the Nicholsons in New York, Gallatin joined Bayard at New Castle, Delaware. They sailed for Sweden in early May of 1813 on the United States ship *Neptune*.

With them went four secretaries: a Colonel Milligan; Gallatin's oldest boy, the sixteen year old James; Dolley Madison's bibulous and dandified son, John Payne Todd; and George Dallas, the son of Gallatin's old friend, Alexander Dallas, who led the Pennsylvania Republicans opposed to Duane and his group around the *Aurora*. So that they could shine at the Russian court the young men were decked out with military titles and resplendent uniforms. Gallatin himself took along a glittering costume considered suitable for the head of a diplomatic mission.

Before the *Neptune* dared sail, the skipper, who was a brother of Secretary of the Navy Jones, had to undergo the humiliation of procuring a pass from the British admiral. The Delaware was under strict blockade by the Royal Navy.

As Jefferson had feared, the American frigates were hopelessly outnumbered. The Chesapeake was a British lake. A British admiral established his naval base in Lynnhaven Bay. Except for an occasional privateer that ran the gantlet out of Baltimore the trade of the Middle Atlantic states was paralyzed. The fine frigate *Constellation* was bottled up above Norfolk in the Elizabeth River.

Soon the blockade was enlarged to include Charleston, Savannah, and the mouth of the Mississippi. British ships were already harassing traffic through Long Island Sound and outside of the harbor of New York. At the same time the Yankee skippers were allowed to come and go freely from New England ports. The British admiral was lavish with licenses for them to trade with the West Indies. It was the Jacobinical Republicans the British government was fighting, not the amenable Federalists of New England.

With each reinforcement of the British fleet rendered possible by Napoleon's difficulties in Europe, it became harder for American ships to take the sea. Decatur was bottled up in New London with the *United States*, the *Macedonian*, and the sloop *Hornet*. The *President*, the *Congress*, the *Constitution*, and the *Chesapeake* were in Boston Harbor under surveillance by a British squadron.

The *Essex* had already fled around the Horn to plunder the British whalers in the Pacific. Commodore Rodgers slipped away to sea with the *President* and the *Congress*, but Captain Lawrence, recently promoted to the *Chesapeake* after a brilliant cruise to the Spanish Main on the *Hornet*, let himself be tempted out to fight by the captain of the British frigate *Shannon;* and, as a result of a series of mischances, lost his frigate and his life and more than a hundred men killed and wounded. The *Chesapeake* had always been rated an unlucky ship.

5. Blockade and Blockade Runners

With the American frigates, for all their proud pennants proclaiming "A Free Trade and Sailors' Rights," cooped up in port, the squadrons of the Royal Navy roamed unhindered through the great inland waterways of the Atlantic coast. The only hazards they encountered were shoal water and an occasional musket shot from militia units hidden on the forest fringed beaches.

Rear Admiral Sir George Cockburn took leisurely soundings in the Potomac River and the upper bay in preparation for attacks on Baltimore and Washington. He burned some settlements on the Sassafras River and wrecked a foundry where cannon were being cast opposite Havre de Grace. Where he met no opposition he paid for his supplies in good English currency.

Cockburn's chief, Admiral Warren, meanwhile tried to invest Norfolk, in order to get at the *Constellation* anchored up the river, but the Virginia militia proved too strong for him; so he sailed across the roads to Hampton, where a shore battery had caused him some annoyance. When the militia retired he landed a force of French Canadian auxiliaries who overran the town, looted and burned, raped any woman who fell into their hands, and behaved with such brutality that a storm of indignation went through Atlantic states. The British officers themselves were shocked.

Jefferson wrote from Monticello that it was hard for him to believe these atrocities. "This is a trait of barbarism, in addition to their encouragement of the savage cruelties"—of the Indians—"& their brutal treatment of prisoners of war, which I had not attached to their character."

1813 was a year of disaster for the Virginia plantations. Winter kill followed by drought, the Hessian fly, and now the British blockade. "We have never seen such an unpromising crop of wheat as that now growing," Jefferson wrote Madison, "the winter killed an unusual proportion of it and the fly is destroying the remainder. we may estimate the latter loss at one third at present and fast increasing from the effect of the extraordinary drought. with such a prospect before us the blockade is acting severely on our past labors. it caught nearly the whole wheat of the middle and upper country in the hands of the farmers and millers."

The failure to sell his last year's flour was making Jefferson's financial situation desperate. His nailery was shut down for lack of nail rod. Obligations kept coming due that he saw no way of meeting. He wrote his agent in Richmond to sell his flour for any price he could get.

Jefferson's private worries were nothing to his anxiety over the conduct of the war. Admitting that he was no military man, he wrote Madison and Monroe offering carefully detailed suggestions for measures of defense. Wouldn't it be possible to build a canal through the sandy land south of Norfolk linking Lynnhaven Bay with the Elizabeth River, through which gunboats could make hit and run attacks on the British fleet? Why couldn't a fortress be built to command the entrance to Hampton Roads? He urged on Monroe the need for universal military training. At a certain age each man should serve for a year. Officers' training should be part of the college curriculum. In his first administration he had sponsored the establishment of a military academy at West Point.

While the bottling up of the American fleet, in spite of the courage and skill of officers and men and the fine sailing qualities of American ships, confirmed his forebodings of the inefficacy of frigates, Jefferson took pleasure in the exploits of the privateers. As he had expected they proved the chief arm in the struggle against Britain.

The first privateers had been pilot boats. A type of sharp fast schooner with a light delicately designed hull and shallow draft had been developing for years in and out of the Chesapeake. These were the Virginia pilot boats which had so aroused Jefferson's enthusiasm that he had suggested them as a substitute for the expensive frigates. In proper ballast they carried an enormous press of canvas and could outrace anything that sailed. The first batch of privateers were pilot boats, fitted with a long Tom—a swivel gun named after Tom Jefferson, so some sailors claimed—and a few carronades. Their best cruising ground was the West Indies where, skimming out of range of the bluff-bowed British warships, they swept the seas of merchant vessels.

Shipyards in Baltimore, New York, and Boston had been busy all winter building larger and sturdier brigs and schooners which, while still fast enough to run away from British ships of the line, could carry enough guns to cope with any armed merchant ship they could cut out from a convoy. During the year 1813 perhaps a hundred American privateers of various types were to capture about three hundred and twenty British ships. Naval vessels accounted for about eighty in the same period. About half of the privateers were eventually taken or destroyed by superior British forces. For American letters of marque it was a short life and a gay one.

American seamen from ship's boy to skipper had been raised on smuggling and the running of blockades. The chief hazard the privateers faced was getting their prizes safe to port. In the end they proved unprofitable because so many of their prizes were recaptured, but all in all they did more to disgust the British shipping interests, who instigated the conflict in the first place, with the American war than any other factor.

"Let nothing be spared to encourage them," Jefferson wrote Monroe of the privateers in a burst of enthusiasm. "they are the dagger which strikes at the heart of the enemy, their commerce. frigates and seventyfours are a sacrifice we must make, heavy as it is, to the prejudices of a part of our citizens. they have indeed, rendered a great moral service, which has delighted me as much as anyone in the United States, but they have had no physical effect sensible to the enemy; and now, while we must fortify them in our harbors and keep armies to defend them, our privateers are boarding and blockading the enemy in their own seaports. encourage them to burn all their prizes and let the public pay for them. they will cheat us enormously. no matter; they will make the merchants of England feel and squeal and cry out for peace."

6. This Damnable Rivalry Between Virginia and Massachusetts

Jefferson protested that he had given up reading the newspapers because they contained so many falsehoods they were a waste of time. John Adams, continually torn between touchy personal feelings and bluff common sense, tried manfully to remain above the battle. Still the contest between Massachusetts and Virginia, which underlay all the politics of the day, kept breaking through the urbane surface of their discussions.

Jefferson claimed that only his Republican party had been the victim of political terrorism. Adams declared no man in political life had had to combat more terrorism than he. "On this subject," cried Adams, "I despair of making myself understood by Posterity, by the present Age and even by you."

After listing the insurrections and seditions the federal administration had to contend with during the period when he had a share in the government Adams suddenly came out with one of his candid admissions: "The real terrors of both Parties have always been and now are, The fear that they shall lose the election, and consequently the Loaves and Fishes. . . . Where is the Terrorism now my Friend? There is now more real Terrorism in New England than there ever was in Virginia. The Terror of a civil War, a La Vendee, a division of the States, etc etc etc. How shall we conjure down this damnable rivalry between Virginia, and Massachusetts?"

John Adams took everything personally. "I thank God that Terror never Yet seized my mind. . . . I have been disgraced and degraded and I have a right to complain. . . . The amount of all the Speeches of John Randolph in the House for two or three Years is, that himself and myself are the only two honest and consistent men in the United States. Himself eternally in Opposition to Government, and myself as constantly in favor of it. He is now in Correspondence with his friend Quincy"—Josiah Quincy's intemperate speeches always seemed just about to advocate the secession of New England without ever quite going over the edge. "What will come of it, let Virginia and Massachusetts Judge."

In an earlier letter Jefferson had tried to steer Adams away from political arguments. "The renewal of these old discussions, my friend, would be equally useless and irksome. . . . my mind has long been fixed to bow to the judgement of the world, who will judge me by my acts, and will never take counsel from me as to what the judgement shall be." He urged Adams to leave a written explanation of his "objects and opinions," adding somewhat pointedly, "I will add that it has been hoped you would leave such explanations as would place every saddle on its right horse."

Their first letters had been guarded. Neither man had wanted to touch off a fit of hurt feelings in the other. But now they wrote with more confidence. Even Abigail had joined in the amnesty. The occasion was the painful death by cancer of the Adamses' daughter, Mrs. William Stephens Smith. Jefferson wrote Mrs. Adams with great tenderness that he understood a bereaved parent's feelings only too well, having suffered them himself.

He was referring to his daughter Polly's death during his first administration. This had been the occasion of a letter of condolence from Abigail. Mistress Abigail had taken a great fancy to Polly when she mothered her, a puzzled little nineyearold on her way to join her father in Paris, at the legation in London. Jefferson answered effusively and was thoroughly miffed to receive a scolding in return. Mistress Abigail's chief complaint was that Jefferson had ousted John Quincy Adams as commissioner of bankruptcy in Boston. Jefferson was touchy about political appointments; and besides he felt he'd been extremely longsuffering about that young man's attacks on him in the matter of Tom Paine and his writings. Mistress Abigail ought to know that Jefferson had early expressed admiration for the precocious abilities of her son, and had always been willing to serve him when opportunity offered. The sense of injustice so rankled that, in his correspondence with Dr. Rush, Jefferson expressly left out Abigail when he consented to a reconciliation with her husband. Now this fresh grief in the Adams family became the occasion for lasting concord between the household at Quincy and Monticello.

As their correspondence developed, John Adams kept coming back to religion. Jefferson was a man to whom he could unburden himself frankly without running the risk of being misunderstood. He explained that he had never considered Jefferson an unbeliever. "Will you please to inform me what matter is and what Spirit is? Unless we know the meaning of Words we cannot reason in or about Words."

Jefferson answered by quoting Adams back to himself: "The human understanding is a revelation from it's maker." He drew the analogy of Socrates and his daemon: "He was too wise to believe, and too honest to pretend that he had real and familiar converse with a superior and invisible being. he probably considered the suggestions of his conscience or reason as revelations, or inspirations from the Supreme mind, bestowed on important occasions by a special superintending providence."

From religion they switched to aristocracy. What did the word mean? Out of a cloud of Greek and Latin quotations, Adams emerged with a definition: "The five Pillars of aristocracy are Beauty, Wealth, Birth, Genius, and Virtues."

He gave Emma Hamilton as a characteristically down to earth example of the aristocracy of beauty: "A daughter of a green Grocer, walks the Streets of London daily with a baskett of Cabbage, Sprouts, Dandelions and Spinage on her head. She is observed by the Painters to have a beautiful Face an elegant figure, a graceful Step and a debonair. They hire her to Sitt. She complies and is painted by forty artists in a Circle around her. The scientific Sir William Hamilton outbids the Painters, sends her to Schools for a genteel Education and Marries her. This Lady not only causes the Tryumphs of the Nile, Copenhagen and Trafalgar, but separates Naples from France and finally banishes the King and Queen from Sicilly. Such is the Aristocracy of the natural Talent of Beauty."

Jefferson, in more prosaic vein, agreed that there was "a natural aristocracy among men. the grounds of this are virtue and talents. formerly bodily powers gave place among the aristoi. but since the invention of gunpowder has armed the weak as well as the strong with missile death, bodily strength, like beauty, good humor, politeness, and other accomplishments, has become but an auxiliary ground of distinction. there is also an artificial aristocracy founded on wealth and birth, without either virtue or talents; for with these it would belong to the first class."

He never could get very far from the problem of government. "May we not even say," he added, "that the form of government is the best which provides the most effectively for a pure selection of these natural aristoi into the offices of government? the artificial aristocracy is a mischievous ingredient in government, and provision should be made to prevent its ascendancy. on the question, What is the best provision, you and I differ, but we differ as rational friends, using the free exercise of our own reason, and mutually indulging it's errors. you think it best to put the pseudo-aristoi in a separate chamber of legislation where they may be hindered from doing mischief by their coordinate branches, and where also they may be a protection to wealth against the Agrarian and plundering enterprises of the Majority of the people. I think that giving them power in order to prevent them from doing mischief is arming them for it . . . mischief may be done negatively as well as positively"—he was thinking of Madison's frustration at the hands of Sam Smith's invisibles and the *Aurora* clique. "of this a cabal in the Senate of the U.S. has furnished many proofs, nor do I believe them necessary to protect the wealthy; because enough of them will find their way into every branch of the legislature to protect themselves. . . .

"I think the best remedy is exactly that provided by all our constitutions, to leave to the citizens the free election and separation of the aristoi from the pseudo-aristoi, of the wheat from the chaff. in general they will elect the real good and wise. in some instances wealth may corrupt or birth blind them, but not in sufficient degree to endanger the society.

"It is probable," Jefferson went on, "that our difference of opinion may in some measure be produced by a difference of character in those among whom we live." He recalled the curious combination of townmeeting democracy in New England with their "traditionary reverence for certain families." He described how the Virginia laws abolishing entail and primogeniture had, in his opinion, "laid the axe to the root of pseudo-aristocracy. and had another which I prepared been adopted by the legislature, our work would have been compleat."

This was the project which Jefferson had felt all his life to be essential to the establishment of a true selfgoverning democracy in Virginia. He had never managed to get enacted, even at the moment when his influence was greatest with the legislature, his Bill for the More General Diffusion of Learning.

"The proposal was," he explained to Adams, "to divide every county into wards of 5. or 6. miles square, like your townships, to establish in each ward a free school for reading, writing and common arithmetic; to provide for the annual selection of the best subjects from these schools who might receive at the public expense a higher degree of education at a district school; and from these district schools to select a certain number of the most promising subjects to be compleated at an University, where all the useful sciences should be taught. worth and genius would thus have been sought out from every condition of life, and compleatly prepared by education for defeating the competition of wealth and birth for public trusts.

"My proposition had for a further object," Jefferson went on, "to impart to these wards those portions of self-government for which they are best qualified, by confiding to them the care of their poor, their roads, police, elections, and nomination of jurors, administration of justice in small cases, elementary exercises of militia, in short to have made them little republics, with a warden at the head of each, for all those concerns, which, being under their eye, they would better manage than the larger republics of the county or state. a general call of ward-meetings by their Wardens on the same day thro the state would at any time produce the genuine sense of the people on any required point, and would enable the state to act in mass, as your people have so often done and with so much effect, by their town meetings."

This was Jefferson's philosophy of government, reduced to a paragraph. He had begun to reconcile himself to the thought that he would never see such a government take form in his lifetime.

"You suppose a difference of Opinion between You and me," answered Adams. ". . . I can find none. I dislike and detest hereditary honors, Officers, Emoluments established by Law. So do you. . . . I only say that Mankind have not yet discovered any remedy against irrisistable Corruption in Elections to Offices of great Power and Profit, but making them hereditary.

"But you will say our Elections are pure? Be it so; upon the whole. But do you recollect in History a more Corrupt Election than that of Aaron Burr to be President, or that of De Witt Clinton last year. By corruption, here, I mean the sacrifice of every national Interest and honour, to private and Party objects.

"I see the same Spirit in Virginia, that you and I see in Rhode Island and the rest of New England. In New York it is a struggle of family feuds. A fewdal Aristocracy. Pennsylvania is a struggle between German, Irish and old English families. When Germans and Irish unite they give 30,000. majorities. There is virtually a Red Rose and a White Rose a Caesar and a Pompey in every State in this Union."

7. Poor Little Withered Apple-John

While the two retired statesmen were carrying on their leisurely colloquy between Quincy and Monticello, Madison in Washington was hard pressed by the Caesars and Pompeys in the Thirteenth Congress. He had weakened the administration's position in the Senate by appointing Senator Crawford to succeed Joel Barlow as minister to France. Crawford was one of the few politicians who properly appreciated the importance of Gallatin's accomplishment at the Treasury. He was the administration's most powerful voice in the Senate. When he resigned to take the Paris appointment, the Smith faction and the *Aurora* faction had their way with Madison's wartime legislation.

Under their lead the Senate refused to ratify the President's appointment of Jonathan Russell, who had been chargé d'affaires in London, as envoy to Sweden. What was worse, the senators by a single vote turned down Gallatin's appointment to the peace mission, on the theory that no man should hold two offices at once. The Senate chose a committee to confer with the President on the subject of declaring the Treasury, where Secretary Jones was presiding on a temporary basis, vacant.

Faced by an acute constitutional problem, Madison announced that he was unable to receive the delegation because he was sick in bed. This was no diplomatic illness. The President was prostrated by one of the malarial fevers that made a nightmare of Washington summers. Dolley Madison nursed him night and day for five weeks. "Even now I watch over him as I would an infant, so precarious is his convalescence," she wrote Hannah Gallatin when he was on the way to recovery. The publisher of the *Federal Republican* could hardly conceal his glee at the prospect of the President's death. Washington Irving was describing President Madison to a Federalist friend as a "poor little withered apple-John."

Monroe wrote a worried letter to Jefferson towards the end of June describing the President's condition as slightly improved. "The Federalists, aided by the malcontents, have done and are doing all the mischief they can. The nominations to Russia and Sweden (the latter made on an intimation that the Crown Prince would contribute his good offices to promote peace on fair conditions) they have embarrassed to the utmost of their power."

With the election as Crown Prince of the highly resourceful Marshal Bernadotte, one of Napoleon's generals who had thrown him over, Sweden became the most important of the northern neutrals. Rumors of a coming armistice between the French and Russian Emperors, which might well turn the British against Russian mediation, made diplomatic representation in Stockholm particularly necessary at that moment.

Monroe confided to Jefferson that, in his opinion, by appointing a committee to confer with the President on executive appointments the Senate faction was aiming to usurp the executive power. He had insisted that such a committee should confer with the Secretary of State as the President's representative, but the committee had refused to meet him. Vice President Gerry's health was poor. "These men," added Monroe, "have begun to make calculations and plans founded on the presumed death of the President and Vice President, and it has been suggested to me that Giles is thought of to take the place of President of the Senate as soon as the Vice President withdraws."

Senator William Branch Giles of Virginia had been a longtime friend and supporter of Jefferson's but his acute dislike of Gallatin had alienated him completely from Madison's administration. He was reputed to suffer from the presidential ambitions which were wreaking havoc among Washington politicians.

8. *Tecumseh*

Madison's frustrations in the presidency kept reminding Jefferson of the failure of the great plans for a democratic republic he and Madison and Gallatin had formulated among themselves after the Republican victory. He had relinquished the presidency far more impressed with the limitations than the opportunities of power. Through no fault of his own he had failed to accomplish so many of the things he had set his heart on. Long ago he had admitted defeat in his hope for the early abolition of Negro slavery. Now in the summer of 1813 his project for the gradual absorption of the Indians into republican civilization was swept away by the tide of events.

Ever since George Washington appointed Benjamin Hawkins Superintendent of Indian Affairs for the vast region south of the Ohio and east of the Mississippi the Creeks and Choctaws and Chickasaws who occupied a large part of Mississippi Territory had been the prime examples of the ability of Indian nations to assimilate the white man's ways. They had taken to farming and stock raising. They had ceased fighting among themselves and intermarried with the Scotch-Irish of the frontier populations.

Jefferson gave Benjamin Hawkins much of the credit for these developments. Hawkins came of a family of North Carolina planters. As a young man he was described as aristocratic, conservative, proud and wealthy. Graduating from Nassau Hall at the outbreak of the Revolution, he showed a knack for languages and became George Washington's French interpreter. He served in the Continental Congress and as one of the first United States senators from North Carolina. Washington employed him to negotiate some Indian treaties. After having been defeated for a second term in the Senate Hawkins accepted the agency to the Creeks. He threw up what seemed to be a handsome political career to live a backwoods life among the Indians on the Chattahoochee River. There he conducted for their benefit a model farm which he turned into an agricultural school. As the Creeks became civilized Hawkins became Indianized. He sat as a chief at the council fires of the Creek nation and did his best to defend their hunting grounds from the inroads of the whites.

The Creeks became the chief furnishers of food for Spanish Mobile. Those of them who didn't like the settled life drifted off into Florida where they became known as Seminoles. The Creek towns progressed smoothly towards civilization until, after the burning of

Tippecanoe drove Tecumseh and his brother Tenskwatawa onto the warpath, Tecumseh's oratory, in his wild drive to unite all the Indian tribes, stirred the younger Creeks into warrior frenzy.

Jefferson described the Shawnee Prophet to Adams as "more rogue than fool. . . . he pretended to be in constant communication with the great spirit, that he was instructed by him to make known to the Indians that they were created by him distinct from the Whites, of different natures, for different purposes: that they must return from all the ways of the Whites to the habits and opinions of their forefathers. They must eat venison instead of pork, or beef; corn meal instead of wheat bread. They must not drink spirits."

The Prophet claimed to have attained supernatural powers. He brewed strong medicine which would make his followers invincible in war. Wherever he went he started the young men singing the song and dancing "the dances of the Indians of the Lakes."

The Prophet was a dumpy illfavored oneeyed man, but Tecumseh, reputed to be his twin, was tall, with clear aquiline features and a stately carriage. While the Prophet brewed spells and incantations and became the center of a cult, Tecumseh planned a confederation, like the American confederation, of all the Indian nations from the Gulf of Mexico to the Great Lakes. The land would belong to all the Indians in common.

This was the root of Tecumseh's dispute with Governor Harrison which led to the fighting on the Wabash. Not even Harrison could help a certain admiration for the Shawnee chief. He wrote of him as "one of those uncommon geniuses which spring up occasionally to produce revolutions and overturn the established order of things. Were it not for the vicinity of the United States," Harrison added, "he would perhaps be the founder of an Empire which would rival in glory Mexico and Peru."

Embarking on a great journey to unite the Indian nations, Tecumseh went down into the Creek country and traveled from town to town carrying his gospel and his brother's rites to the peaceful dwellers in the Mississippi Territory. "Our fathers from their tombs reproach us as slaves and cowards" was reported to be the burden of his discourse. "I hear them now in the wailing winds." His followers must be secret. For eighteen months certain of the young braves among the Creeks practiced the song and the dances of the Indians of the Lakes without a whisper of it getting through to Hawkins and his council of old chiefs.

As soon as news reached the British commanders in Canada of Madison's declaration of war they encouraged Tecumseh's scheme in every way possible. It fitted exactly with the project entertained by Anthony Merry in the days of Burr's conspiracy and by Lord Dorchester and his successor Sir James Craig as Governor General of Canada to form an Indian buffer state along the Mississippi to block the westward advance of American settlement.

At Fort Malden Tecumseh's followers were furnished with arms, ammunition, and clothing. The British commanders admired him inordinately. To give him belligerent status he was named a brigadier general in the British army.

Contingents from the Creeks joined Tecumseh's men in the fighting on the river Raisin. Against Tecumseh's orders they took part in the butchery of stragglers from the militia who fell into their hands. After this baptism in blood, the Creek warriors homeward bound couldn't help slaughtering the men, women, and children they found in two cabins they surprised in a settlement on the Ohio River. The old chiefs immediately ordered the murderers punished. Most of them were killed but a blood feud ensued which amounted to a civil war between the two halves of the Creek nation.

The Tecumseh faction of the Creeks under a halfbreed named McQueen surprised a huddle of loyal Creeks, halfbreeds, and white refugees in a stockade known as Fort Mims. They tomahawked every man, woman, and child, except for a handful who ran off into the woods and some Negroes they saved for slaves. McQueen's Indians went off boasting that they had taken two hundred and fifty scalps that day. After the massacre at Fort Mims it was war to the death with most of the Creek nation.

Jefferson unflinchingly described the failure of his Indian policy in a letter to Humboldt: "You know my friend the benevolent plan we were pursuing here for the happiness of the aboriginal inhabitants in our vicinities"—this was one of the projects Jefferson had talked over enthusiastically with the Prussian geographer when he visited him in Washington a decade before. "we spared nothing to keep them at peace with one another. to teach them agriculture and the rudiments of the most necessary arts, and to encourage industry by establishing among them separate property. in this way they would have been enabled to subsist and multiply on a moderate scale of landed possession. they would have mixed their blood with ours, and been amalgamated and identified with us within no distant period of time. on the commencement of our present war we pressed on them the observance of peace and neutrality, but the interested and unprincipled policy of England has defeated all our labors for the salvation of these unfortunate people. they have seduced the greater part of the tribes within our neighborhood, to take up the hatchet against us, and the cruel massacres they have committed on the women and children of our frontiers taken by surprise, will oblige us now to pursue them to extermination or drive them to new seats beyond our reach."

9. Some Military Blanks

Perry's victory on Lake Erie ruined Tecumseh's design.

Oliver Hazard Perry came of a family of seafaring Rhode Islanders. His father had won distinction in the abortive war with France. He and his brother had seen naval service in the Mediterranean. At twentyeight he was pining with boredom on the gunboats at Newport, and managed to get himself transferred to Isaac Chauncey's command at Sackett's Harbor. Chauncey put him in charge of the flotilla under construction at Presque Isle on the south shore of Lake Erie. Young Perry was an active fellow. He saw to it that the brigs and sloops were outfitted in record time.

Early in September he managed, after incredible exertions by officers and men in moving cannon and ballast, to get his ships across the bar at the mouth of the harbor in time to meet a British fleet off the mouth of Put In Bay. When Perry's flagship the *Lawrence* was shot to pieces by British broadsides, he performed the legendary feat of transferring his flag to the undamaged *Niagara* in the midst of the battle and forced every one of the British ships to surrender.

With control of Lake Erie assured William Henry Harrison's expedition, which had been marking time around Seneca, was ferried across the lake to Fort Malden. At the same time a troop of volunteer cavalry, equipped and organized by Congressman Richard M. Johnson of Kentucky, which had already caused consternation among the Indians of the Lakes, advanced briskly towards Detroit. Johnson was one of Henry Clay's War Hawks who not only voted for the war but fought it. The dash and spirit of his volunteers proved decisive in clearing the Northwest of Indian raiders.

Major General Proctor, in charge of the British forces, seemed bent on proving to the world that the Americans had no monopoly of military incompetence. In spite of Tecumseh's crying out in a council of war that the Indians would call Proctor a fat dog running away with his tail between his legs if he gave up the posts without a fight, Proctor announced the evacuation of Detroit and prepared to pull out of Fort Malden. In the resultant collapse of British prestige Tecumseh saw the end of any hope of keeping the Indian tribes united.

Proctor's retreat was interrupted by an American attack. Johnson's mounted Kentuckians charged through the British line along the Thames River and came within an inch of capturing Proctor himself. Proctor's Indian allies melted into the forest. When he mustered his force at Ancaster, a hundred miles to the east, two weeks later Proctor could barely count a couple of hundred men. Some four hundred British regulars had surrendered to five hundred of Johnson's volunteers. Tecumseh did not survive the ruin of his cause. His dead body was found on the field. Some of the Kentuckians cut strips of skin off his thighs to make themselves razor strops.

The summer campaign on Lake Ontario was less successful. Armstrong's plan was to sweep down the St. Lawrence to Montreal. Since the Canadian settlements barely produced enough food for themselves, the British armies were supplied, at considerable profit to the New Englanders, by the farmers of New Hampshire and Vermont. A campaign down the St. Lawrence would cut these supply lines.

Dearborn and Commodore Chauncey, putting their heads together at Sackett's Harbor, decided instead on a pincers movement against the Niagara peninsula. Their first move was to land a force at York, then the capital of Upper Canada, where the British were building a large vessel to challenge Chauncey's command of the lake.

The troops were disembarked under General Dearborn's direction, though that worthy, who invariably sickened when action impended, was too ill to leave his bunk aboard one of the ships. The very enterprising Zebulon Pike, recently promoted to brigadier general, led the assault, which was immediately successful. In the confusion of victory the long log building that was used by the two houses of Parliament was set on fire and the explosion of a powder magazine raised havoc with the American troops. Zebulon Pike was among the dead. His loss far outweighed any advantages gained by the occupation of York.

Emboldened by this exploit, Dearborn's troops occupied Fort George on the Canadian shore of the Niagara River and from there conducted a series of forays that ended disastrously. Meanwhile the British took advantage of the fact that the American forces, naval and military, were busy at the western end of Lake Ontario to stage an attack on their base at Sackett's Harbor. The attack was beaten off by Jacob Brown of the New York militia, but some idiot, thinking all was lost, set fire to the naval barracks. With them burned the navy yard and most of the stores collected for the campaign against Montreal. President Madison screwed his courage up to the point of letting Armstrong request Dearborn's retirement "until your health be reestablished and further orders."

Dearborn's retirement left General Wilkinson in line for the Northern command. Ever since he had emerged from his latest courtmartial he had been in charge at New Orleans. He had married a Creole lady and found the society there delightful. Furthermore, since Gallatin, who had always opposed adventures in the Floridas, was retiring from the administration, Madison and Monroe agreed that spring to let Wilkinson carry out his longplanned seizure of Mobile.

Everything went smoothly. The Spaniards surrendered their fort in an amicable way and Wilkinson's reputation recovered a little in the estimation of the War Office. Now, since the Russian offer to mediate the conflict with Britain seemed to make further military action in the Floridas unwise, Armstrong wrote Wilkinson that his services were needed in the north.

The two men had known each other since they were both on Horatio Gates's staff in the days of the Conway Cabal. Armstrong regarded Wilkinson with a combination of affection and distrust. He seemed more anxious to get him out of New Orleans, where he might cause mischief, than to engage him in the invasion of Canada. To sweeten the pill Armstrong put through Wilkinson's promotion to major general. As always, when his orders were distasteful, General Wilkinson took his time in complying.

It wasn't till August that he arrived with his wife and family in Washington. There he made himself agreeable to President and Mrs. Madison. Dolley Madison, always warmhearted, set about finding Frenchspeaking associates for the new Mrs. Wilkinson. The general's discussions with Armstrong at the War Office revolved more about the problem of who outranked whom than about the ways and means of conquering Canada. Wilkinson discovered that he was expected to cooperate with another major general with seniority that dated from the Revolutionary War, Wade Hampton of South Carolina. The two men were personal enemies.

The headquarters at Sackett's Harbor had not recovered from the British assault. When Wilkinson arrived there he found a third of the troops down with "lake fever," which seems to have been a form of typhoid, and dysentery. Signs of fall were already in the air. The only uniforms were of a paradeground type, entirely unsuited for a winter campaign in those latitudes. Preparations dragged. The officers in the higher echelons were mostly New York State politicians anxious to make careers for themselves. Active soldiers like Jacob Brown and Winfield Scott found themselves continually outranked. When Secretary Armstrong arrived, to give the expedition against Montreal his personal supervision, he merely added to the confusion.

It was early November before the boats and barges of Wilkinson's command were ready to start down the St. Lawrence. The general had Armstrong's assurance that Wade Hampton, who commanded some regiments at the head of Lake Champlain, would march overland to meet him opposite Montreal.

The weather caused Wilkinson more trouble than the enemy. The general himself had barely recovered from a fit of chills and fevers. Sickness was general. Now he was laid low with dysentery. Opium in various forms was considered the prime remedy for this disease.

Wilkinson took liberal doses which, added to his customary potations of wine and spirits, caused him to be more or less out of his mind most of the time. His second in command, Morgan Lewis, Armstrong's brotherinlaw and one of the political powers of the Livingston clan, was as sick as he was, but General Lewis had the advantage of using blackberry jelly instead of opium for his dysentery.

When they were set upon, at a place called Chrysler's Farm, by a small British contingent, and by a group of gunboats that Commodore Chauncey had somehow allowed to slip past him down the river, the two commanders, both so sick they couldn't stand, added to the confusion caused by the rain and sleet by issuing contradictory orders. The result was that this large wellarmed American force was driven off with heavy losses by a small body of British and a scattering of Indians.

A few days later a messenger arrived announcing that Wade Hampton's column had been intercepted by a British force far from his objective and that, instead of reinforcing Wilkinson, Hampton was resigning his commission in disgust. Wilkinson's army dug itself in at a place called French Mills while the ailing generals tried to make up their minds what to do next. Rations gave out. Dysentery and typhoid carried off hundreds. There were mass desertions. Deep in the winter orders arrived from Secretary Armstrong to burn the boats and to retreat overland to Sackett's Harbor and Plattsburg.

With the pressure reduced on Montreal the British pulled themselves together on the Niagara peninsula. Early in December they forced the Americans to evacuate Fort George. In retreating a New York militia general ordered the adjacent town of Newark burned. In retaliation the British crossed the river and burned Buffalo and Black Rock. Disgusted with the way the war was being managed, the New York militia started to pack up and go home. All Armstrong could think of was to write pleading letters from the War Office requesting reinforcements from Albany.

December 18 a force of five hundred British regulars surprised Fort Niagara at night, while the commander was lying drunk in his bed, and captured the entire garrison and a vast quantity of stores. Meanwhile their Indians burned and scalped at will among the settlements on the American shore.

Wilkinson went into winter quarters near Plattsburg. When he failed again, this time in a small operation against a stone mill held as an enemy outpost, it was too much even for the longsuffering administration in Washington. He was relieved of his command for the last time, and retired to his family to await another courtmartial.

Armstrong may have remembered how Jefferson wrote him months before that it was too bad that heaven had not set a mark on men qualified for military achievement, "that it has left us to draw for them in a lottery of so many blanks to a prize, and where the blank is to be manifested only by the public misfortunes."

10. Traffic with the Enemy

News spread slowly in winter. When it reached Albemarle it was all of public misfortunes. November 30 Jefferson had written cheerfully to Lafayette that the stimulus to the production of textiles in the United States was probably worth the cost of the war. He ascribed the early losses on the Canadian frontier to cowardice, foolhardiness, and "sheer imbecility in the commanders." The American troops would show their mettle if properly led. He wrote in sanguine terms of Wilkinson's expedition, then drifting on the rapid current down the St. Lawrence. General Wilkinson would be in Montreal "in three or four days" and was prepared to winter there. Quebec would not be worth the cost in lives of storming it. "Cut off from subsistence by the loss of the upper country, it must be evacuated by its inhabitants." On December 14 Jefferson entered a melancholy postscript. Another failure of a general. Wilkinson's expedition was stalled at the entrance to Lake St. Francis.

Madison meanwhile was back in Washington, after a short respite at Montpelier, preparing his annual message to the Thirteenth Congress. After allowing himself a certain flattering unction in describing the victory on Lake Erie and the liberation of the Northwest from the depredations of the savages he expressed his regret that the British had refused to accept the mediation of the Emperor of Russia.

He went on to describe a new case of British intransigeance. They were refusing to recognize the American citizenship of twentythree Irishmen captured with an American force in Canada and were sending them back to England to be tried for their lives as traitors. The American command had retaliated by isolating the same number of British prisoners as hostages. Sir George Prevost had immediately placed double that number of American officers and noncommissioned officers in close confinement, and the Americans had riposted by imprisoning the same number of British officers. The United States, President Madison pointed out, had entered "this deplorable contest" only "with the humane purpose of effectuating a return to the established usages of war."

Two days later the President sent a private message to the two houses recommending an immediate embargo on imports and exports. The present situation favored the enemy. Though he did not mention the New England states by name, he made it clear that their supplying of the armies in Canada and of the blockading fleets must be put an end to, and that measures must be taken to stop the importation of rum and textiles from Great Britain and her colonies. "These restraints," he wrote in conclusion, "will be borne with the greater cheerfulness by all good citizens; as the restraints will affect those most, who are most ready to sacrifice the interest of their country in pursuit of their own."

Within a week the bill passed the House and Senate, with only the Federalists and the "malcontents" voting against it, and received the President's signature. In essence this bill amounted to a declaration of war against the New England states. The Federalists who controlled the flourishing New England banks, which were gradually attracting all the specie in the country, retaliated by refusing to join in loans to the national government.

The conflict between Massachusetts and Virginia became as bitter as the conflict between the national government and the British administration.

11. *Negotiation under Fire*

The machinery for enforcing this last embargo had hardly been set in motion before news arrived that called for the revision of every administration policy. The British schooner *Bramble*, operating under a flag of truce, brought into Annapolis an offer from Castlereagh to initiate peace negotiations at Gothenburg in Sweden. In the same mail came European newspapers describing Napoleon's defeat in the threeday Battle of Leipzig in the middle of the past October.

Madison and Monroe accepted Castlereagh's offer, and in January the President appointed John Quincy Adams, James A. Bayard, Jonathan Russell, and Henry Clay as ministers plenipotentiary to meet the British negotiators. When fervid young Clay resigned as Speaker of the House to join the peace mission all the starch went out of the war party in Congress. For a few weeks the President was in doubt as to whether Albert Gallatin would prefer to return to his Treasury post or to remain in the diplomatic service. When he received word from Gallatin, who was spending an interesting few weeks in England, where he was already being treated as an unofficial envoy, that he wanted to remain in Europe, the President appointed George W. Campbell of Tennessee to the Treasury and added Gallatin to the peace mission. This time the nominations were confirmed.

Congress settled down to the uncongenial task of raising an army large enough to defend the country. With Napoleon's empire shattered and the armies of the Grand Alliance pursuing the French across the Rhine, the governing powers in Great Britain could embark for America as large a veteran force as they cared to engage. To encourage recruiting Congress voted a bonus, payable in advance, to every man who enlisted, of one hundred and twentyfour dollars. Furthermore an appropriation was made to build one or more "floating batteries operated by steam" for harbor defense, and a committee was appointed which immediately accepted the plans presented by Robert Fulton of New York. Within weeks, under Fulton's eager supervision, the keels were laid at Adam Browne's shipyard on the East River for his twinhulled warship, propelled by an interior paddlewheel, which he named the *Demologos*.

Armstrong, in the War Office, was proving himself in every emergency to be a smallminded man with ambitions too big for his abilities, but at least he was running out of the blanks Jefferson had spoken of in his letter. Hull was under house arrest, about to go on trial for his life. The elderly incompetents, Dearborn, Hampton, and Wilkinson, were all in retirement, awaiting courtsmartial or boards of inquiry. Armstrong scoured the militia for fresh talent.

He looked for men of ability, but they had to be men he would find useful politically. He was figuring that he had a chance of getting the next presidential nomination away from Monroe if the New Yorkers, who were coming to misprize the Virginians as much as the New Englanders did, would unite with the Eastern Republicans behind his candidacy. Monroe kept warning Madison against Armstrong's appointments; he claimed the man wanted to set himself up as military dictator.

Madison personally revised Armstrong's list before sending it to Congress. For major generals he nominated first George Izard, a son of the South Carolinian who had served on a peace mission with Franklin and John Adams, who took advantage of his European education to study military engineering in England and Germany and France; and then Jacob Brown, who had rendered such a good account of himself at Sackett's Harbor. Brown was a Quaker schoolteacher with no military training at all, but he showed courage and leadership when they were most needed.

Somehow Madison failed to ward off a series of slights by which Armstrong chivied William Henry Harrison, who, since the recapture of Detroit, had become a hero in the western country, into resigning his commission. At Madison's insistence Andrew Jackson, whom Armstrong was trying to downgrade, replaced him as a full major general. At the same time a number of young colonels were promoted to be brigadiers. Among them were Edmund P. Gaines, who captured Aaron Burr, and that doughty North Briton from Petersburg, Virginia, Winfield Scott. Though often at crosspurposes, Madison and his Secretary of War did manage to establish the solid framework of the army command as it was to continue for the next twenty years.

12. *The Horrors We Have Experienced*

As seen from the hills of Albemarle the prospects for 1814 looked bleak. Jefferson's crops were worse even than in the previous year. Tobacco and flour were unsalable on account of the blockade. The Hessian fly ate up the winter wheat. The depreciation of the paper currency issued by the state banks was assuming alarming proportions. Every traveler from Tidewater brought foreboding rumors of the movements of the British squadrons in and out of the Chesapeake.

July 5 Jefferson wrote John Adams that he had been distressed by a report of Adams' illness.

"Our machines have now been running for 70. or 80. years, and we must expect that, worn as they are, here a pivot, there a wheel, now a pinion, next a spring, will be giving way: and however much we may tinker them up for a while, all will at length surcease motion. our watches with works of brass and steel, wear out within that period. shall you and I last to see the course the seven-fold wonders of the time shall take?"—in spite of himself he had been reading the newspapers; dispatches from Europe were full of Napoleon's fall and the restoration of the Bourbon monarchy in France—"the Attila of the age dethroned," Jefferson declaimed, "the ruthless destroyer of 10. millions of the human race, whose thirst for blood appeared unquenchable, the great oppressor of the rights and liberties of the world, shut up within the circuit of a little island of the Mediterranean"—news had just reached Monticello that Elba had been set as the place of Napoleon's exile and that his first act on taking charge was to double the taxes—"but Bonaparte was a lion in the field only. in civil life a cold-blooded calculating unprincipled Usurper without a virtue, no statesman, knowing nothing of commerce, political economy or civil government and supplying ignorance by bold presumption. . . . to the wonders of his rise and fall may we add that of a Czar of Muscovy dictating, in *Paris*, laws and limits to all the successors of the Caesars, and holding even the balance in which the fortunes of this new world are suspended."

Perhaps Jefferson felt a certain satisfaction over having helped bring this situation about. He wrote that he rejoiced at the deliverance of Europe; but "I see with anxiety the tyrant of the ocean remaining in vigor, and even participating in the merit of crushing his brother tyrant. while the world is thus turned up side down on which side of it are we? all the strong reasons indeed place us on the side of peace; the interests of the continent, their friendly dispositions, and even the interests of England. her passions alone are opposed to it. peace would now seem to be an easy work, the causes of the war being removed. her orders in council will no doubt be taken care of by the allied powers, and war ceasing her impressment of our seamen ceases of course."

Jefferson feared that in a settlement England might try to keep the Americans off the North Atlantic fishing grounds.

"What will Massachusetts say to this? I mean her majority, which must be considered as speaking as the Index of it's will"—in the spring elections the Federalists had carried Massachusetts only by a few hundred votes—"she chose to sacrifice the liberty of our seafaring citizens, in which we were all interested, and with them her obligations to the Co-states, rather than war with England. will she now sacrifice the fisheries to the same partialities? this question is interesting to her alone; for to the middle, Southern and Western States they are of no direct concern; no more than the culture of tobacco, rice and cotton to Massachusetts. I am really at a loss to conjecture what our refractory sister will say on this occasion. I know what as a citizen of the union, I would say to her, 'Take this question ad referendum. it concerns you alone. if you would rather give up the fisheries than war with England, we give them up. if you had rather fight for them, we will defend your interests to the last drop of our blood.'"

"I am bold to say," Adams answered promptly, "neither you nor I will live to see the Course which 'the Wonders of the Times' will take. Many Years, perhaps Centuries must pass, before the current will acquire a settled direction. . . . Government has never been much studied by mankind. But their attention has been drawn to it, in the latter part of the last Century and the beginning of this, more than at any former period and the Vast Variety of experiments that have been made of Constitutions, in America in France, in Holland, in Geneva in Switzerland, and even in Spain and South America, can never be forgotten. They will be studied, and their immediate and remote Effects, and final Catastrophys noted. The result in time will be improvements. And I have no doubt that the horrors We have experienced for the last Forty years will ultimately terminate in the Advancement of civil and religious Liberty, and Ameliorations in the condition of Mankind. . . .

"Our hopes, however, of Sudden tranquility ought not to be too sanguine," he went on, after remarking that the perfectibility of the human mind was a mystical doctrine he never could understand. "Fanaticism and Superstition will still be selfish, subtle, intriguing, and at times furious. Despotism will still struggle for domination; Monarchy will still study to rival nobility in popularity; Aristocracy will continue to envy all above it, and despize and oppress all below it; Democracy will envy all, contend with all, endeavor to pull down all; and when by chance it happens to get the Upper hand for a short time, it will be vengefull, bloody and cruel."

He called Napoleon a "military fanatic" but he doubted whether

Jefferson was fair in calling him "an Usurper." Adams suggested that Napoleon's elevation to the throne was "as authentic a national act" as the coronation of William and Mary in England, or Washington's election "to the Chair of the States."

"Human Nature," he went on in his favorite vein, "in no form of it, ever could bear Prosperity. That particular tribe of Men, called Conquerors, more remarkably than any other, have been swelled with Vanity by any Series of Victories. Napoleon won so many mighty Battles in such quick succession, and for so long a time, that it is no Wonder his brain became completely intoxicated and his enterprises, rash, extravagant and mad. . . . Though France is humbled, Britain is not. . . . John Bull is quite as unfeeling, as unprincipled, more powerful, has shed more blood, than Bona. John by his money his Intrigues and Arms, by exciting Coalition after coalition against him made him what he was, and at last what he is. Now shall the Tyrant of Tyrants be brought low. I still think Bona. great, at least as any of the Conquerors. . . . I wish that France may not still regret him. . . . But I agree with you that the Milk of human kindness in the Bourbons is safer for Mankind than the fierce Ambition of Napoleon."

To Adams, as to Jefferson, the most notable feature of the French Emperor's capitulation was the part played by the Russian Czar: "The Autocrator, appears in an imposing light. Fifty years ago English Writers, held up terrible Consequences from 'Thawing out the monstrous northern Snake.' If Cossacks and Tartars, and Goths and Vandalls, Hunns and Ripuarians, should get a taste of European Sweets, what may happen? Could Wellingtons or Bonapartes resist them? The greatest trait of Sagacity, that Alexander has yet exhibited to the World is his Courtship of the United States."

Adams might well have added that Jefferson's courtship of Alexander showed also a trait of sagacity. That very summer Lafayette, who often acted as Jefferson's alter ego in Europe, was seeking an interview in which he hoped to convince the Czar that he should bring pressure to bear on the British to insure favorable terms for the United States in the peace negotiation about to begin.

Adams ended that part of his letter with one of his flat statements. "The refractory Sister"—meaning his own state of Massachusetts—"will not give up the Fisheries. Not a Man here dares to hint at so base a thought."

13. *Chippewa and Lundy's Lane*

The day Jefferson wrote Adams a battle was fought on the Niagara peninsula which was to have more influence on the behavior of the British government than the solicitations of the Russian Czar. By the time Adams' answering letter reached Monticello accounts were appearing in the gazettes of the engagements on the Chippewa and at Lundy's Lane where General Jacob Brown proved to friend and foe the truth of Jefferson's contention that the Americans would fight superbly if properly led.

The season had opened inauspiciously on the lakes with a descent by the British naval commander on an American depot at Oswego. In spite of continual preparations chunky Isaac Chauncey never could seem to quite get his ships ready to challenge the enemy on Lake Ontario. At the same time Brown, a Quaker who believed in fighting, was drilling the regiments he was able to salvage from Wilkinson's command. Under him he had two able brigadiers. Winfield Scott, who had collected a small library of military manuals he took everywhere with him, was putting himself and his troops through a stiff course of training among the rebuilt shanties of Buffalo. His colleague, Eleazer Wheelock Ripley, an inhabitant of Maine who was Speaker of the Massachusetts House of Representatives, set out to demonstrate to the world that there were some New Englanders who weren't skulking out the war or enriching themselves by trading with the enemy. Both men were natural leaders, Scott a dashing hothead and Ripley a thoughtful tactician.

In all, Brown's little army didn't amount to more than three thousand men. Facing them were about as many British regulars, holding the heights above Niagara Falls on the Canadian side.

Though he was never furnished with sufficient boats Brown managed to get his whole army across the Niagara River in the early dawn of July 3 and to invest Fort Erie. The fort capitulated towards the end of the same afternoon.

With Winfield Scott's brigade in the van the Americans marched as fast as they could next day to attack a British force deployed behind a creek in front of the village of Chippewa before reinforcements should arrive. The British commander, Major General Riall, was so contemptuous of American troops that he rashly attacked. Scott's brigade met him on an open plain and outfought him in every way. Superior musketry. Superior artillery fire. Superior discipline.

Riall pulled back and the Americans drove him into Queenston opposite Fort Niagara at the eastern outlet of the Niagara River. Since reinforcements for the British kept coming in, and Brown feared for his communications, he had to drop back to Chippewa village.

A few days later Brown met a superior British force advancing on him at Lundy's Lane. Winfield Scott again led the attack. This time the Americans were outnumbered. In spite of Scott's cutting several British regiments to pieces, the day was only saved by a charge through the underbrush by Ripley's column. Ripley overwhelmed the chief British battery, bayoneted the artillerymen, and captured the guns.

In the night fighting that followed both Scott and Brown were severely wounded. Important officers were killed. Since the American forces were without reserves they had to fall back on their camp at Chippewa. There was no pursuit. The British had taken such punishment that they estimated Brown's army at five thousand men.

With most of their officers dead or wounded, the Americans, first under Ripley and then under Gaines, entrenched themselves so successfully around Fort Erie that in the following month they were able to withstand a fulldress assault by a much reinforced British army.

After Chippewa and Lundy's Lane the British commanders treated the Americans with more respect. The American regulars for the first time felt confidence in their ability to stand up against the best of Wellington's redcoats.

14. *Cogitations on the Platonists*

No news of these events had yet reached Jefferson when he wrote John Adams in early July. He had been completely out of the world for five weeks at his plantation at Poplar Forest. There he had been superintending the planting of tobacco and the finishing of his octagon house and the building of a wing for offices and dependencies, on the *"ferme ornée"* plan he had developed at Monticello. "Having more leisure there than here," he wrote Adams, "I amused myself with reading seriously Plato's republic. . . . it was the heaviest task-work I ever went through. . . . while wading through the whimsies, the puerilities, and unintelligible jargon of this work I laid it down often to ask myself how it could have been that the world should have so long consented to give reputation to such nonsense as this? how the soi-disant Christian world indeed should have done it, is a piece of historical curiosity. but how could the Roman good sense do it? . . . in truth he is of the race of genuine Sophists, who has escaped the oblivion of his brethren, first by the elegance of his diction, but chiefly by the adoption and incorporation of his whimsies into the body of artificial Christianity. his foggy mind is forever presenting the semblances of objects which, half seen thro' a mist, can be defined neither in form or dimension. yet this which should have consigned him to early oblivion really procured him immortality of fame and reverence. . . . the doctrines which flowed from the lips of Jesus himself are within the comprehension of a child; but thousands of volumes have not yet explained the Platonisms engrafted on them: and for the obvious reason that nonsense can never be explained.

"But why am I dosing you with these Ante-diluvian topics?" Jefferson exclaimed as he started a fresh page. "Because I am glad to have some one to whom they are familiar, and who will not receive them as if dropped from the moon"—he had evidently been trying the topic out with little success on some of the young men who came to him for advice and for courses of reading. "our post-revolutionary youth are born under happier stars than you and I were," he told his old crony in ironical vein, "they acquire learning in their mothers' womb, and bring it into the world ready made. the information of books is no longer necessary; and all knolege which is not innate, is in contempt, or neglect at least. every folly must run it's round and so, I suppose, must that of self-learning or self-sufficiency; of rejecting the knowledge acquired in past ages, and starting on the new ground of intuition."

"I am very glad you have seriously read Plato," Adams answered in his next letter, "and still more rejoice to find that your reflections upon him so perfectly harmonize with mine. Some thirty years ago I took upon myself the severe task of going through all his Works. With the help of two Latin Translations, and one English and one French translation and comparing some of the most remarkable passages with the Greek, I labored through the tedious toil. My disappointment was very great, my Astonishment was greater, and my disgust was shocking. Two Things only did I learn from him, 1. that Franklin's ideas of exempting Husbandmen and Mariners, etc. from the depredations of War were borrowed from him. 2. that Sneezing is a cure for the Hickups."

15. One of the Conquerors

While Jefferson, far from the scene of combat at Monticello, was reflecting on the follies of Platonism, and John Adams, a solitary patriot amid the disaffected Federalists in Quincy, was sketching his panorama of history, dire events were brewing for the Chesapeake Bay country.

Vice Admiral Sir Alexander Cochrane arrived at Bermuda to relieve Admiral Warren in the early summer of 1814. He had served under Rodney and Nelson and seen the Royal Navy sweep the seas of its enemies. Adams would have called him "one of the conquerors." His fleet outnumbered the remnants of the American frigates twenty to one, and more. He was determined to teach the Americans a lesson.

He declared a blockade of the entire coast from Maine to the Mississippi. Since the people of Massachusetts and Connecticut were so laggard in throwing off the yoke of the Washington government he would cease coddling the New Englanders.

In retaliation for the burning of Newark and York he issued orders to his captains to burn every American town within reach: "You are hereby required and directed to destroy and lay waste such towns and districts as you find assailable. You will hold strictly in view the conduct of the American army towards his Majesty's unoffending Canadian subjects, and you will spare merely the lives of the unarmed inhabitants of the United States."

Although no particular measures were to be taken to provoke the slaves to rebellion, such Negro volunteers as applied were to be formed into a special corps under His Majesty's protection. The vice admiral further declared that the "intimate and unnatural connection" of the executive government of the United States "with the late government of France has led them to adopt the same system of plunder and devastation," and stated that "it is to their own government the unfortunate sufferers must look for indemnification for their loss of property."

A fleet of transports soon arrived from Bordeaux bringing detachments from Wellington's crack troops left idle by the capitulation of Bayonne. Their commander was Major General Robert Ross, who had made a name for himself under Sir John Moore in the retreat to Coruña. Further reinforcements from the Garonne disembarked at Quebec. The government at Washington was to be crushed by simultaneous onslaughts from the St. Lawrence and from Chesapeake Bay.

Towards the end of July the gazettes of Richmond and Baltimore and Washington began to publish reports of squadrons of twenty and thirty enemy sail seen cruising in the bay. This threatening news was offset by a triumphant letter describing how Captain David Porter had retired to the far Marquesas to refit the *Essex* after a successful cruise in which he had taken some British whalers and a mass of other rich prizes. Porter raised the Stars and Stripes over those palmfringed isles.

By an odd quirk of communications almost simultaneously there appeared advices from Valparaiso that the *Essex* had been cornered by two British ships in an inlet on the Chilean coast and forced after a bloody engagement to strike her flag. Not long after Captain Porter himself appeared, cured of his wounds and paroled by his captors, to report to the Secretary of the Navy. To his amazement he was hailed as a hero.

July 22 enemy shipping was reported in the mouth of the Patuxent River. British barges were landing at Leonardtown. From Maine came reports of the occupation of Eastport by British troops. Castine fell and everything east of the Penobscot. July 26 a story from Fredericksburg told of the burning of Westmoreland Court House. The British were carrying off slaves, tobacco, and cattle from plantations along the Potomac and the Patuxent. Dwellings were burned, storehouses pillaged.

August 2 the enemy was in the Yeocomico. Chaptico was taken and all the tobacco in it. August 12 British barges were repulsed at Kinsale by the militia under Captain Parker. The same newspaper described a landing at faraway Stonington near the mouth of Long Island Sound in Connecticut. August 16 more fighting was reported at Kinsale. The militia had retired. The town was attacked by twentyseven barges. Every house at Mundy's Point and twenty or thirty houses in Kinsale were burned and everything movable carried away. Admiral Cochrane was described as superintending the pillage in person.

Meanwhile General Ross, assisted by Rear Admiral Cockburn in command of the shipping, established his camp at Benedict on the Patuxent. Thirty sail of reinforcements were seen off Point Lookout. From Baltimore came the report of a meeting of militia officers called by General Samuel Smith to concert the defense of the city.

On August 19 Commodore Barney, who had been placed in command of the American gunboats in the Chesapeake as the result of his exploits on the privateer *Rossie* the year before, reported to Washington that he had retreated as far as he could up the Patuxent. He itemized the British ships beating their way up the river in pursuit: one 80-gun line-of-battle ship, four 74s, six frigates, ten smaller vessels averaging 34 guns each, a large schooner, a small schooner, and thirteen bay bugeyes.

In Washington a strange paralysis had seized hold of the administration. Secretary of War Armstrong was sulky as a result of a calling down by the President, who pointed out to him in a querulous note on August 13 that in important matters "the acts of the Department ought to be either prescribed by him"—the President—"or preceded by his sanction." Monroe's complaints to Madison about Armstrong's appointments were taking effect.

Monroe and Armstrong were openly at loggerheads. Secretary Jones of the Navy, who considered Armstrong to be "without one useful and valuable quality, either social, civil or military," sided with Monroe. Richard Rush, the new Attorney General, had all along been in favor of making Monroe Commander in Chief.

In meeting after meeting of the heads of departments called by Madison to consider the danger of an attack on the capital Armstrong expressed the opinion that the British would never risk it. Baltimore was in greater danger. Secretary of the Treasury Campbell agreed with him. He remarked furthermore that the news of measures being taken to fortify the city might frighten off investors from a loan he was trying to float.

Indecision ruled. Since the President had put through the appointment of a Baltimore lawyer, William Henry Winder, a cousin of Governor Winder of Maryland, to command the 10th District, which included all the great neck of land between the Potomac River and Chesapeake Bay, Armstrong took the attitude that he had no further responsibility in that direction. Winder had just been exchanged as a prisoner of war. His chief military exploit so far had been to get himself captured in his tent during one of the unsuccessful forays into

Canada. In the few days since he had assumed command he had been out riding back and forth across southern Mayland in order to raise the levies of militia that Congress called for. The drafted men came in slowly and reluctantly.

Before the militia could be properly mustered, before sufficient arms and rations could be furnished, before the men knew who their officers were, or the officers who their generals were, news arrived that the redcoats were on the march from Benedict. Monroe, out of patience with Armstrong's management of affairs, went on a scouting trip of his own.

With a squad of dragoons he rode over to the Patuxent and looked down on the British camp. The country was deserted. He found no one to inform him and returned to Washington no wiser than he left it; but he did instruct John Graham to have the records of the State Department packed in canvas bags and transported across the Potomac.

Meanwhile General Winder was wearing out his horses and himself riding around the country on a personal reconnaissance. When regimental commanders tried to get orders from his headquarters no one could find out where he was.

To keep them from falling into Admiral Cockburn's hands Joshua Barney landed his cannon, blew up his gunboats, and led his four hundred sailors and marines in good order to the Washington Navy Yard. At the same time the officer in charge of Fort Washington, which was supposed to keep the enemy fleet from entering the upper reaches of the Potomac, was sending plaintive messages to the War Department. He had guns but no block and tackle to hoist them on their carriages with. He even had some columbiads—a new invention of Robert Fulton's supposed to shoot missiles under water to pierce enemy ships below the water line—but no way of mounting them. Getting no answer to his pleas, he blew up the fort and retired to Virginia at the sight of the first British frigate.

General Ross had about four thousand men. Admiral Cockburn went along with a marine detachment to see the sport. The weather was intensely hot and sultry. They advanced unopposed up the shore of the Patuxent to Nottingham. In Nottingham they found well-stocked barns but no sign of an inhabitant. Without exchanging a shot with the Americans they proceeded next day through pleasant woodland roads to Marlborough. They had no cavalry, only a few small cannon, and a batch of Congreve rockets.

In Washington little President Madison was riding around with his heads of departments reviewing the troops. Everybody was still trying to guess whether the British would make for Annapolis or Baltimore.

The citizens of the District, led by the mayor of Washington City, desperate that nothing was being done for their defense, offered to dig entrenchments round Bladensburg at their own expense. General Wilkinson, who was in Washington waiting for his courtmartial, in a final gasconnade, offered his services to Secretary Monroe; if the charges against him were dismissed and he were placed in command he promised to defend Washington or perish in the attempt. When his letter was ignored he prudently retired with his family to Fontaine Springs in the Maryland hills.

Winder kept giving orders and countermanding them. He couldn't make up his mind whether or not to blow up the bridges over the Eastern Branch. His second in command wouldn't obey his orders, anyway. Armstrong was no help; he had taken the position that Winder was responsible for the defense of the capital.

Monroe started disposing of troops on his own. It was Monroe who, on the night of August 23, first notified the President that the British were surely on the march to Washington, that Winder would fall back until he could collect his troops, and that the government departments must evacuate their records.

Next morning Winder's forces were still in confusion. A lastminute decision was made to defend the hills back of Bladensburg. When the President and several of the heads of departments rode out to see what was going on, they got ahead of their own troops and were very nearly caught by a British column advancing towards the Bladensburg bridge.

Ross's redcoats were welltrained experienced soldiers. Winder's men barely knew closeorder drill. He never managed to set up a chain of command. He had worn his men out by continual night marches. As soon as Ross's grenadiers started shooting their astonishing rockets, the militia broke. Weary as they were, they ran. A few regular units fell back in good order towards Capitol Hill.

The only real stand was made by Joshua Barney and his sailors. After bullying Secretary Jones into giving him orders to advance from the navy yard, Barney set up his guns on a hill overlooking the Bladensburg road. His gunners were first rate. He inflicted heavy punishment on the enemy, until, surrounded and outflanked, and himself severely wounded, he had to order his surviving men to take to their heels. Barney was given every care by the British, who expressed themselves as full of admiration for his gallantry.

After silencing Barney's guns Ross rested his troops on the battlefield for a couple of hours. He had lost something like five hundred men killed and wounded while the American casualties amounted to less than a hundred. Right away the Federalists started calling the affray the Bladensburg races.

In the evening the British march was resumed. The army made camp in the dark behind Capitol Hill. Immediately Cockburn and Ross, eager to carry out Admiral Cochrane's instructions, set out with a detachment carrying incendiary materials to burn the capital buildings.

A shot supposed to be from the house where Gallatin had lived killed the general's horse, so that house was burned too, though Ross had made up his mind to spare noncombatants. The British marched fast through the darkness along Pennsylvania Avenue to the President's house. Ross told the story of finding the table set for forty covers and dinner laid out. He and his officers ate the meal and toasted "poor Jemmy" in his own claret before setting fire to the mansion.

The French minister's messenger, asking for a guard for the Octagon House, which was then the French Legation, found Ross and Cockburn personally superintending the breaking up of the drawing-room furniture before putting the torch to it. Ross carried off the President's hat as a souvenir.

Meanwhile Secretary Jones ordered the navy yard burned.

Three great fires lit the sky—"I never saw a scene more terrible or more magnificent," wrote Serurier, the French minister. A thunderstorm with torrential rains put the fires out, so that next morning fresh troops with torches had to be sent into the sopping ruins to finish the work.

The government offices were destroyed and Admiral Cockburn saw to it that the presses and types of the *National Intelligencer* should be broken up. He was particularly eager for his men to get rid of the C's "so that the rascals can no longer abuse my name."

Dr. Thornton, the Capitol's first architect, then in charge of the Patent Office, argued a British officer out of setting fire to the Post Office Building where the models were kept, by explaining that they would destroy valuable scientific material which would benefit mankind as a whole.

A second thunderstorm, accompanied by what was described as a tornado, interrupted the work of destruction. The same night, leaving campfires burning to deceive any lurking Americans, and abandoning their wounded who lay in the Bladensburg hospital, Ross and Cockburn broke camp and marched hastily back to their ships.

They left Georgetown undamaged. In the columns of the *Federal Republican* Hanson exulted in the loss suffered by his rival editor, Republican Joseph Gale of the *National Intelligencer*. Hanson claimed Gale had come off easy. The mob's wrecking his press in Baltimore had cost him far more.

During the fighting at Bladensburg Dolley Madison loaded the presidential plate and what valuables she could collect on a wagon. She would not leave the President's house until she had seen to it that the large portrait of Washington was carried off to safekeeping.

It was about that time that Serurier, looking out from the Octagon House, observed the little President, displaying "a coolness and constancy worthy of better success," trying to stem the flight of the militia. While his wife took refuge with the Carrols in Georgetown the President, finding that his appeals were unavailing, crossed on the ferry to Virginia.

The rains and the thunderstorms, and the panicstricken militia that trod every road into muck, caused the fleeing Madisons more inconvenience than the enemy. It wasn't until two days later that, after all sorts of wanderings, the President had a proper dinner at the house of a Quaker in Brookville, up in the hills of Montgomery County.

On the way back to Washington after the British had left, Mrs. Madison retrieved her pet macaw, which had been left with a friend for safekeeping. The Madisons were finally reunited at the house of Mrs. Madison's sister Mrs. Cutts in Washington City.

All military authority had broken down. In spite of General Winder's orders to fall back on the heights behind Georgetown most of his troops went off to Baltimore. The general had no choice but to follow them. The Secretary of War and the Secretary of the Treasury were said to be in Frederick Town, while Secretaries Jones and Monroe and Attorney General Rush were doing their best to stand by the President. When John Armstrong reappeared in Washington, at the President's urgent request, he was annoyed to find that the Secretary of State had taken over his duties at the War Office.

After a heated exchange of words, President Madison remarked that the militia were refusing to serve under Armstrong and that perhaps he'd better retire. Armstrong offered to resign then and there, but Madison said no, he meant retire temporarily from the scene. The more Armstrong thought of this conversation the less he liked it. He immediately left the city and sent in his resignation to the President from Baltimore by mail.

Meanwhile refugees from Alexandria brought news that the mayor and council had capitulated to the captain of His Majesty's frigate *Sea Horse*. To save the city from destruction they were giving up all the merchandise in it. Details of British tars were busy plundering the warehouses and loading their ships with tobacco and flour. It was only Monroe's firmness that headed off an attempt by the citizens of Washington and Georgetown to send a flag of truce to the *Sea Horse* offering to surrender on similar terms.

As news of the burning of Washington and the capitulation of Alexandria spread through the country panic gripped the exchanges. Banks refused specie payments. The value of paper money plummeted. Only in New England the banks stood solid. Their vaults were stacked with gold. Many countinghouses closed their doors. To

Pickering and the Essex Junto Federalists drumming up support in town meeting after town meeting for a convention to be called at Hartford to discuss secession, it seemed as if the prayed-for moment had come to break off their unholy alliance with the Jacobins and slaveholders of Virginia.

16. Some Countervailing Events

The militia was in deep disgrace. Everything connected with the War Office was in confusion. It was the sailors ashore who saved the day.

Only Barney's gunners had come out of Bladensburg with credit. Now three more navy men turned up to take charge of defense. Captains John Rodgers, Oliver Perry, and David Porter got together boats and batteries to harass the British in the Potomac. They rigged fire ships to drift into the enemy's anchorages. They set up masked batteries to fire at their barges towing the big ships around the sandspits and shoals. Without being able to inflict much permanent damage they so pestered the *Sea Horse* that her captain abandoned hundreds of barrels of flour and fifteen hundred pounds of fresh beef on the Alexandria docks and dropped down the river.

Once they were assured that the British fleet was leaving the Potomac and the Patuxent the three captains hurried to Baltimore where they found the survivors of Barney's command hard at work preparing new batteries. Each of their names was worth a regiment.

Senator Samuel Smith, who was a major general in the Maryland militia, took charge of the defense of the city. At sixtytwo Smith was a man accustomed to having his own way. Much of his fortune was invested in the city. He had no intention of letting it be plundered by the British.

When Winder tried to outrank him Samuel Smith shouted him down. In spite of appeals to the President and to his cousin the governor, Winder finally submitted to becoming a sort of fifth wheel on General Smith's staff.

In Baltimore there was no skulking by the Federalists. The Federalist officers were as determined to resist as the rank and file of the militia, who were mostly Republicans. Entrenchments were thrown up with wellplanned redoubts on the landward side. Under orders from the three famous captains sailors gleefully manned the shore batteries. Lieutenant Colonel Armistead of the U.S. artillery headed about a thousand regulars and volunteers in Fort McHenry to defend the harbor entrance. Sunken hulks blocked the Patapsco.

When the British arrived Baltimore was ready for them. On September 11 General Ross landed his veterans at North Point at the river's mouth and at daybreak next morning started a quick march towards the city. He had about five thousand men.

Smith sent out Brigadier General Stricker with thirtytwo hundred militia, some of them recruits who had barely got their wind since the flight from Bladensburg. Stricker's men were outnumbered. They were forced to fall back but in the first volley of musketry General Ross, walking with Admiral Cockburn at the head of the advance column, was shot through the breast and died instantly.

The Baltimoreans inflicted such heavy casualties on the British that the redcoats encamped on the field without pursuing the retreating militia. Next morning it rained. The Americans contested every step of the British advance. When the new commander came in sight of the entrenchments on the hills around Baltimore he halted.

A message had arrived from Admiral Cochrane that he wasn't making any headway either. After pounding Fort McHenry and Fort Covington with shells, bombs, and rockets night and day for twenty-four hours he had made no impression on the defenders. The redcoats turned tail. The warships anchored out of range. September 15 the troops were loaded back aboard. The great fleet took advantage of the first favorable wind to set sail and disappeared down the bay.

When Jefferson got news of the disaster that had befallen Washington City his first thought was for the feelings of his friends Madison and Monroe. He wrote them each a consoling letter.

"For altho' every reasonable man," he wrote Madison, "must be sensible that all you can do is to order, that execution must depend on others & failure be attributed to them alone, yet I know that when such failures happen they afflict even those who have done everything they could to prevent them. had Gl. Washington himself been at the head of our affairs the same event would probably have happened."

At the same time he congratulated them both on a "countervailing event" which must surely dispel the gloom of the session of Congress now opening among the ruins.

The countervailing event was an unexpected victory over the British at Plattsburg. Coming on the heels of Jacob Brown's successful defense of Fort Erie, it meant that the British invasion from the St. Lawrence was petering out as fruitlessly as their assault from the Chesapeake.

The defense of Fort Erie was coupled with Isaac Chauncey's recovery of the offensive on Lake Ontario, but the British defeat at Plattsburg was more impressive. Lake Champlain was essential to the British strategy. With the American fleet in control of both Lake Erie and Lake Ontario, Lake Champlain was the only invasion route left to a British army. Furthermore the New York and Vermont shores were the main source for the British army's supply of beef.

In spite of orders from Secretary Armstrong to fortify a point on the La Colle River which turned out to be already in the hands of the enemy, General George Izard used his knowledge of military engineering to dig trenches and throw up redoubts round Plattsburg at the mouth of the Saranac. He was protected on his lake front by a recently built American flotilla under a thirty year old navy lieutenant. Thomas Macdonough was the son of a Delaware physician. He had learned seamanship as a midshipman on the *Constellation* and the unlucky *Philadelphia* in the war against Tripoli.

General Izard wanted to use Plattsburg as a fortified base from which to threaten British communications on the St. Lawrence, but Armstrong, who was suspicious of him as an adherent of Monroe's, thought otherwise and ordered him to march his four thousand regulars west to Sackett's Harbor. The British were quick to take advantage of this opening in the American defenses and immediately sent their fleet down the lake. At the same time they marched against Plattsburg the most powerful army ever assembled on the American continent, amounting to eleven thousand men outside of the reserves, under two lieutenant generals and a flock of major generals, with Sir George Prevost in overall command. Armstrong had left Alexander McComb, the ranking brigadier, a bare fifteen hundred effectives to man the works.

On September 11, the same day that the assault began on Baltimore, Sir George Prevost mounted a simultaneous attack by his fleet against Macdonough and by his troops against the American strongpoints. Since there was almost no wind the naval engagement was fought at anchor. Though the British had more firepower Macdonough had the advantage of having chosen his anchorage in advance.

The British commander was killed early in the action. After two and a half hours of pointblank cannonading, Macdonough, by skillfully winding his *Saratoga* around with the windlass, was able to present his undamaged broadside to the British flagship. As his fresh guns found their targets the *Confiance* struck her colors. Three smaller vessels followed suit and the gunboats took off up the lake. Meanwhile Prevost's troops were making little impression on the American defenses. Appalled by the loss of his fleet and by the marksmanship of the American gunners, Prevost turned round and marched his great army back into Canada again.

17. *"The Star-Spangled Banner"*

Though Madison and Monroe appreciated the value of these "countervailing events" they knew but too well that, with the enormous forces available to the British, the American administration could only play for time.

The Treasury was empty. Secretary Campbell, held in scorn by the Federalists since his duel with their champion Barent Gardinier in the days of Jefferson's first embargo, was proving ineffectual as a promoter of loans. The currency was in confusion. Banks all over the United States had suspended payment in specie. The paper money issued by the multiplicity of state banks was subject to discounts and often worthless—"as oakleaves," so Jefferson put it—outside of the state it was issued in. Inflation and the blockade had paralyzed commerce. The secessionist movement seemed to be sweeping the New England states. The prospects were desperate for raising the men or the money needed for next summer's campaigns.

It was no longer a question of winning the war; it was a question of maintaining the Union.

The houses of Congress met at first in the common room of what was known as the Great Hotel. Rooms at the Post Office were cleared out for committee work. Congressmen grumbled over the discomfort of their situation. The New Englanders talked in threatening terms of the coming convention at Hartford where they would demand satisfaction of their grievances. Motions were introduced to abandon Washington altogether and to move the capital to a more convenient location. The Federalist press was calling on President Madison to resign. Even the most ardent Republicans were disheartened.

William Wirt, who was in the city during this distracted session of the Thirteenth Congress, described the ruins of the President's house as "a mournful monument of American imbecility and improvidence and of British atrocity." He was amused by the way the members of Congress kept their spirits up by crowding with unusual enthusiasm out to the October races. When Wirt visited President Madison he found him "miserably and shattered and woebegone. In short he looks heartbroken. His mind is full of the New England sedition." October 12 Monroe wrote Jefferson a discouraged letter: peace negotiations had been suspended at Ghent.

Though the Washington debacle and the victories at Baltimore and on Lake Champlain failed to unite the nation as the Republicans hoped they might, there was, particularly among younger people, a stirring of patriotic feeling. A prominent Georgetown attorney, a convinced Federalist named Francis Scott Key who saw the bombardment of Fort McHenry from a sloop in the bay, celebrated the event by dashing off a poem. "The Star-Spangled Banner" was set to a tune which had been preempted by the Federalists for a song called "Adams and Liberty." It was printed in the Baltimore American on September 21 and from that day on was sung in heartfelt choruses by Republicans and Federalists alike.

Washington Irving, that very superior young man, who had been brought up among Federalists and New York Burrites, and had described President Madison as "a poor little withered apple-John" almost picked a fight on the Hudson River steamboat with a man who made a sneering remark about the burning of Washington. Irving was so filled with patriotic fervor that he got himself appointed a military aide to Governor Tompkins. When he arrived on some sort of inspection trip aboard Chauncey's flagship at Sackett's Harbor the dumpy commodore growled out: "You here! I'd as soon have expected to see my wife."

18. *A New Library for Congress*

Jefferson failed to share in the general gloom. He kept writing his friends that he could not believe in the secession of the New England states. He pointed out the closeness of the vote in recent elections in Massachusetts. Though the Federalists were temporarily in the ascendant he believed the masses of the people there were sound Republicans. Even if it had been politically feasible secession was economically impossible. The New Englanders were dependent on the middle states and on the South and West for their flour and foodstuffs and for the cotton for their mills. Now that they were a manufacturing as well as a seafaring people they would never cut themselves off from their best customers.

He was not completely discouraged about the course of the war. In late November he wrote William Short, who had lingered on in France after the breakdown of his diplomatic career: "All men know that War is a losing game to both parties. but they know also that if they do not resist encroachment at some point all will be taken from them and that more would be lost even in Dollars and cents, by submission than by resistance. . . . I consider the war then as entirely justifiable on our part altho' I am still sensible it is a deplorable misfortune to us. it has arrested the course of the most remarkable prosperity any nation ever experienced, and has closed such prospects of future improvements as were never before in the view of any nation. farewell all hope of extinguishing the public debt. farewell all visions of applying the surplus of revenue to the improvements of peace rather than to the ravages of war."

Short was very close to his heart. Jefferson loved him as a son. He wrote him frankly of the desperate financial situation he personally faced: "to me this state of things brings a sacrifice of all tranquility & comfort through the residue of life . . . by the total annihilation of the value of the produce which was to give me subsistence and independence. . . . we can make indeed enough to eat and drink & clothe ourselves; but nothing for our salt, iron, groceries & taxes which must be paid in money. for what can we raise for market? Wheat? We can only give it to our horses as we have been doing ever since harvest.

Tobacco? it is not worth the pipe it is smoked in. some say whiskey; but all mankind must become drunkards to consume it."

The direct tax had to be paid. Sums borrowed on the prospects of future crops would now have to be repaid in cash. Interest charges were accumulating on outstanding notes. Jefferson faced bankruptcy.

As soon as he heard of the burning of the Capitol and with it the very considerable library which had been accumulated there, largely on his recommendation, he thought of a remedy. He could perform a public service and at the same time avert his family's ruin.

Jefferson offered to sell his entire library to the United States Government at a valuation to be arrived at by whatever means Congress saw fit. He confided his offer to Samuel Harrison Smith, who after selling his share of the *National Intelligencer* to the younger Joseph Gales had remained in Washington as commissioner of revenue.

Senator Samuel Smith, who, though in bad odor with the Federalists who ran the Maryland legislature, was at the height of popular fame since his defense of Baltimore, immediately wrote Jefferson that he approved of the proposition. The debate was on stark party lines. Rufus King led the opposition in the Senate. In the House Timothy Pickering opposed the acquisition by the government of the works of French infidels. A young congressman from New Hampshire named Daniel Webster, whose style of oratory was already attracting attention, agreed with him. For once Smith's invisibles worked with the Republicans from the South and West. Congress voted to accept Jefferson's offer and set the value of the library at twentythree thousand dollars.

According to Dr. Thornton, fifty thousand dollars would have been cheap. A correspondent of the *National Intelligencer* wrote that "the library is such as to render all valuation absurd and impossible." Its value was inestimable. Joseph Milligan the Georgetown bookseller, who had helped in the appraisal, declared that Jefferson's acceptance of such a low figure was "truly magnanimous."

Jefferson had a good head for figures about government finance, but he was quite feckless in regard to money matters that affected him personally. He accepted the offer with relief. The news that Congress was preparing to pay him twentythree thousand dollars would at least instill patience into his creditors.

19. *The Hartford Convention*

News of the impending transfer of Jefferson's library aroused interest in a group of bookish young Harvard men in Cambridge and Boston. Perhaps it was a pretext to lay eyes on the infidel monster their elders so excoriated. Edward Everett, the learned and fashionable minister of the Brattle Street Church, applied to John Adams for a letter of introduction to Mr. Jefferson. When Everett's "calls at home forced him back from Washington," Adams wrote out introductions for two more of "the most exalted of our young Genius's" who had "an Ambition to see Monticello, its Library and its Sage."

These were Francis Calley Gray, the son of the richest shipowner in Massachusetts, a young man who had recently visited John Quincy Adams in St. Petersburg in the course of his grand tour of Europe; and George Ticknor.

Both Ticknor's father and mother were fervent educators. His mother conducted a young ladies' seminary and his father devoted most of his life to the improvement of the Boston grammar schools. Though he trained for the law, the reading of Madame de Staël's book on Germany gave Ticknor the notion that he wanted to study languages at the German universities. Before proceeding to Europe he wanted to see some of the notabilities of his own country.

George Ticknor was twentythree, slight of build, with eyes so dark they looked black, and wavy black hair. He was a dutiful young man thoroughly saturated with every prejudice of the Boston Federalists. A couple of years before he broke off some pleasant walks on the Common with Samuel Dexter when that gentleman delivered himself of a speech in town meeting in which he supported the war and opposed a convention of the New England states.

In his journal Ticknor described his visit to John Adams whom he asked for letters to Jefferson and Madison: "When I visited him in Quincy to receive these letters I had a remarkable interview with him which at the time disturbed me not a little." To Harvard right thinkers John Adams' notions were considered almost as mistaken as Thomas Jefferson's. "The Hartford Convention, about which I had known a good deal from Mr. William Sullivan and Mr. Harrison G. Otis was then in session. Mr. Adams was bitterly opposed to it. Mr. George Cabot, who was my acquaintance, and in some degree my friend, was its President.

"Soon after I was seated in Mr. Adams' parlor—where was no one but himself and Mrs. Adams who was knitting—he began to talk of the condition of the country, with great earnestness. I said not a word; Mrs. Adams was equally silent"—Ticknor evidently felt Mrs. Adams was on his side—"but Mr. Adams who was a man of strong and prompt passions, went on more and more vehemently. He was dressed in a single-breasted dark green coat, buttoned tightly with very large white metal buttons over his somewhat rotund person. As he grew more and more excited in his discourse he impatiently endeavored to thrust his hand into the breast of his coat. The buttons did not yield readily. At last he forced his hand in, saying as he did so in a very loud voice and most excited manner 'Thank God, thank God, George

Cabot's close buttoned ambition has broke out at last: he wants to be President of New England, Sir.'

"I felt so uncomfortably, that I made my acknowledgements for his kindness in giving me the letters and escaped as soon as I could."

Ticknor had been brought up in veneration of wealthy whitehaired George Cabot. Possibly he was enough in his confidence to know that Cabot had consented to preside over the twentysix delegates from the New England states, whom Gouverneur Morris, still a frantic anti-Republican, dubbed the "Wise Men of the East," to try to restrain them from precipitate action.

The calling of the Hartford Convention to meet on December 15, 1814, was the climax of years of agitation by a few men of the Essex Junto shade of opinion, which began with Pickering's and Hillhouse's project for the secession of New England that Aaron Burr found so intriguing in 1804. Madison's embargo opened the old wounds left by President Jefferson's attempt to coerce the commercial and shipping interests of New England. Elbridge Gerry's defeat for the governorship of Massachusetts, just before his election to the vice presidency in 1812, was brought about by an upsurge of Yankee protest, against his famous gerrymander in particular, and against government by Virginia Republicans in general.

Pickering himself took no direct part in the Hartford Convention, because he was already in Washington for the session of Congress.

Spurred on by the petitions of a host of town meetings, the Massachusetts General Court elected delegates, John Lowell, writing in the Boston *Advertizer*, laid down a program. His plan was to declare New England neutral for the remainder of the war and to declare the Constitution suspended until the Union could be thoroughly reorganized.

Lowell shared in Timothy Pickering's expectations that the expedition under Sir Edward Pakenham, the great Wellington's brotherinlaw, known to be approaching the mouths of the Mississippi, would surely reduce New Orleans and shut off the western states from their outlet to the sea. In the settlement expected to follow, the thirteen original states, under the leadership of New England, which was the only part of the country not bankrupted by the war, would form a new compact, leaving the states and territories to the south and west to go their own way. Since news had reached them of Vice President Gerry's death in Washington, even moderate Federalists wrote of the expediency of forcing Madison to resign and placing Rufus King in the presidency.

George Ticknor set out on his travels on December 22 in the company of Samuel Perkins, a Boston merchant whose wife was the daughter of Stephen Higginson, one of the Charter conservatives of

Essex County. Their first objective was Hartford where they were put up by their mutual friend Harrison Gray Otis, who was living with the gentlemen of the Massachusetts delegation in a rented house. Ticknor was introduced to a number of delegates who came on Christmas Day to pay their respects to Mr. Cabot.

The delegates were closemouthed. "I of course, learnt nothing of the proceedings of the convention, which sat with closed doors," noted Ticknor in his journal, "but it was impossible to pass two days with such men, and hear their free conversation on public affairs, without feeling an entire confidence in their integrity and faithfulness to duty."

The administration in Washington was better informed than young Ticknor. According to Charles Jared Ingersoll, then a Republican congressman from Pennsylvania, Monroe sent Lieutenant Colonel Jesup, one of the heroes of Lundy's Lane, to open a recruiting center in Hartford. Monroe instructed him to concert with Governor Tompkins on the way for the dispatch of New York militia if they should be needed. Meanwhile he was to report to the War Office any treasonable or seditious proceedings.

Colonel Jesup, who seems to have been a gentleman of discretion and tact, struck up an acquaintance with Chauncey Goodrich, then mayor of Hartford, who was a delegate from Connecticut. He found Mr. Goodrich more amenable than he had expected. He reported to Monroe that even Hillhouse had mellowed with the years. Without actually betraying the confidence of his associates Mayor Goodrich managed to keep Jesup informed of the general trend of the convention's doings. Jesup reported the information in daily letters to Washington.

At Monroe's suggestion Jesup tried to distract the New England leaders from their flirtation with treason by interesting them in Monroe's plans for next summer's campaign against Halifax. If the maritime provinces could be added as new states to the north and east, the New Englanders would no longer feel outnumbered by the slave states to the south. Mr. Goodrich seemed particularly pleased by this prospect. In fact Jesup got on so well with the Hartford Federalists that when the city council tried to pass an ordinance against federal recruiting the mayor helped him talk them out of it. He wrote Monroe that all "the young and fighting" men of Connecticut were on the side of the government.

20. *Two Harvard Men Journey to Virginia*

After spending Christmas with the mysteriarch of Hartford, as Ingersoll called George Cabot, Ticknor proceeded to New Haven. There he attended one of Professor Silliman's lectures on chemistry, and visited the arms factory where Eli Whitney produced muskets with interchangeable parts on the assemblyline system. Ticknor was in New York, the largest city he had ever seen, in time for the Dutch-style observance of New Year's Day.

One of the sights of New York was Robert Fulton's floating battery. "The mighty leviathan I saw this morning," he wrote his father, "is the Fulton No. 1. It is in fact two frigates joined together by steam-enginery, which is placed directly in the center and operates on the water which flows between them. It has two keels and two bows and will be rigged so as to navigate either end first. Its sides are five feet thick, and its bulwarks will be in proportion; so that it is claimed that it will be impervious to cannon shot. It will carry forty 32-pounders and is intended chiefly for harbor defence."

In Philadelphia he joined his friend Frank Gray in whose company he would make the arduous winter journey into Virginia. Both Bostonians were impressed by the high style of the Philadelphia magnates. Ticknor described to his father in awestruck terms the solid silver service for twenty he saw at the table of David Parish the banker. The dinner—"in the French style, really so," wrote Gray—was passed around by servants in full livery with epaulets.

At Mr. Parish's table they met John Randolph, a house guest, very much at loose ends since his defeat for Congress by Jefferson's son-in-law, Jack Eppes. Randolph of Roanoke made a disagreeable impression on Ticknor, until he began to speak with gratitude of "the hospitality he had found in Philadelphia, and the prospect of returning to a comfortless home, with a feeling that brought me nearer to him for the moment; and of the illness of nephew Tudor, and of the hopes it had blasted, with a tenderness and melancholy that made me think better of his heart than I had before. At table he talked little, but ate and smoked a great deal."

As Ticknor's stage drew near to Washington City, Ticknor wrote his father that he climbed up with the driver "that I might see all that was strange or new. . . . In the midst of a desolate-looking plain over which teams were passing in whatever direction they chose I enquired of a driver where we were. 'In Maryland Avenue, sir.' . . . The hill of the Capitol rose before us. I knew it was a ruin, but I had formed no conception of that what I was to see—the desolate and foresaken greatness in which it stood, without a building near it, except a pile of bricks on its left more gloomy than itself."

The letters from John Adams opened every door in the capital. When Ticknor dined with the President he found an atmosphere of tension and constraint: "The company amounted to about twenty. There were two or three officers of the army with double epaulets and somewhat awkward manners, but the rest were members of congress, who seemed little acquainted with each other.

"The President too, appeared not to know all his guests, even by name. For some time there was silence or very few words. . . . After a few moments a servant came in and whispered to Mr. Madison, who went out, followed by his secretary. It was mentioned about the room that the Southern mail had arrived, and a rather unseemly anxiety was expressed about the fate of New Orleans, of whose imminent danger we heard last night. The President soon returned, and with added gravity, said there was no news! Silence ensued. No man seemed to know what to say in such a crisis, and, I suppose from the fear of saying what might not be acceptable, said nothing at all.

"Just at dark dinner was announced. Mr. Madison took in Miss Coles. General Winder followed with Mrs. Madison. The Secretary"—Edward Coles—"invited me to go next; but I avoided it, and entered with him, the last."

To his considerable embarrassment, the President insisted on seating George Ticknor at the head of the table between himself and Mrs. Madison; "this was unquestionably the result of Mr. Adams' introduction," explained Ticknor. "I looked very much like a fool and behaved awkwardly. As in the drawing room before dinner, no one was bold enough to venture conversation. The President did not apparently know the guest on his right, nor the one opposite to him."

The President did most of the talking. "I found the President more free and open than I expected . . . making remarks that sometimes savored of humor and levity. He sometimes laughed and I was glad to hear it, but his face was always grave. . . . He spoke to me of my visit to Monticello and when the party was separating told me that if I would go with him to the drawing room and take coffee, his Secretary would give me the directions I desired. So I had another tête à tête with Mr. and Mrs. Madison in the course of which Mr. M. gave amusing stories of early religious persecutions in Virginia, and Mrs. M. entered into a defence and panegyric of the Quakers of whose sect, as you know, she once belonged."

Ticknor and Gray found it rough going when they left Crawford's Hotel in Georgetown on the Richmond stage. "Rain and warm weather," noted Gray, "had softened the rich soil of Maryland to the consistence of hasty pudding and filled the gullies and hollows with water."

There had been frost and then a heavy snow on top of that. The horses kept breaking through. The carriage was occasionally mired up to the hubs. Soaked, frozen, and almost starved, they reached Port Tobacco, where they remarked in their journals on the excellence of the inn. Gray described Charles County as "one of the most fertile and federal in Maryland. Of 2000 voters," he noted with satisfaction, "there are about 90 Democrats."

At Ludlow's ferry they had to help the ferryman chop the boat out of the ice. On the Virginia side they found the roads much improved, but frozen rivers and the breaking down of stagecoaches kept delaying them. A week out of Georgetown, riding the stage horses and having left their baggage to follow in a cart, they arrived in Richmond and repaired to a boardinghouse kept by a Mrs. Randolph.

After two days in Richmond, during which they paid their respects to the luminaries of the Virginia bar: Judge Marshall, whom Ticknor described to his father as "the first lawyer, if not indeed the first man in the country," Mr. Wickham—"far too well bred to let me learn anything more of him in the course of a visit of twenty minutes than that he was an uncommonly courteous elegant gentleman"; and William Wirt—"If I had not known better, I might have set him down for one of those who were 'pretty fellows in their day.'"

Ticknor and Gray rode the stage to Charlottesville and hired a hack at the inn to take them up to Monticello.

Ticknor described to his father "the ascent of this steep savage hill. . . . We were obliged to wind two thirds round its sides before we reached the artificial lawn on which the house stands. . . . The fine growth of ancient forest trees conceals its sides and shades part of its summit. The prospect is admirable."

Not finding any bell or knocker, they walked into the hall unannounced. They were astonished by the elk and buffalo horns and the "curiosities which Lewis and Clarke found in their wild and perilous expedition" which hung on the wall. Opposite was a mastodon's head, and Indian paintings on leather. Finally they found Colonel Randolph, who took their letters to Mr. Jefferson.

Ticknor had been surprised to find Mr. Madison so short. Now he was surprised to find Mr. Jefferson so tall. Gray described their host, at seventytwo, as "standing six feet, one or two, face streaked and speckled with red, light gray eyes, white hair, dressed in shoes of very thin soft leather with pointed toes and heels ascending in a peak behind, with very short quarters, gray worsted stockings, corduroy small clothes, blue waistcoat and coat made of stiff thick cloth made of the wool of his own merinos and badly manufactured, the buttons of his coat and small clothes of horn, and an under waistcoat of flannel bound with red velvet. His figure bony, long and with broad shoulders, a true Virginian."

Mr. Jefferson insisted that they spend the night and sent down to Charlottesville to have their things brought up from the inn. While waiting for dinner they sat in the large drawing room.

"Here," Ticknor wrote his father, "are the best pictures of the collection. Over the fireplace is the Laughing and Weeping Philosophers dividing the world between them: on its right the earliest navigators to America,—Columbus, Americus Vespucius etc, copied,

Mr. Jefferson said, from originals in the Florence gallery. Further round, Mr. Madison in the plain Quaker-like dress of his youth, Lafayette in his revolutionary uniform, and Franklin in the dress in which we always see him." There were other pictures and a copy of Raphael's *Transfiguration*.

"On looking round the room," Gray reported, "the first thing which attracted our attention was the state of the chairs. They had leather bottoms stuffed with hair but the bottoms were completely worn through and the hair was sticking out in all directions." A servant was at work substituting a wooden panel for one of the large glass panes which had been broken out of the glass doors that led out on the lawn.

It had come on to rain. Gray noted that they spent the whole afternoon in conversation with Mr. Jefferson and Mr. Randolph. At four toddy was brought but, as neither of the New Englanders drank it, it was not presented again.

At the dinner table they were introduced to Mrs. Randolph, Mr. Jefferson's only daughter, to his sister, Mrs. Marks, and to the younger Randolphs.

"The drinking cups were of silver," noted Gray, "marked G.W. to T.J., the table liquors were beer and cider and after dinner, wine." "I assure you," Ticknor wrote his father, "I have seldom met a pleasanter party."

He described Jefferson's discursive manner and love of paradox and his appearance "of cool reason and sobriety." He showed enthusiasm for American antiquities, particularly for those of his native state. In everything he said he exhibited a love for "old books and young society."

They took tea in the same room and retired at ten. In the morning a servant lit a fire in their room before they climbed out of their recessed beds. "At fifteen after eight we heard the first breakfast bell and at nine assembled in the breakfast room." After breakfast Mr. Jefferson produced a catalogue of his books and led them into the library.

Gray was particularly struck with the completeness of his sets of the classics, "though very careless as to the editions." He admired a blackletter Chaucer and a first edition of *Paradise Lost*. The collection of works "valuable to a biblical critic" was very complete. He was impressed by the variety of books on law including the complete laws of the state of Virginia in manuscript. English history was covered all the way back to King Alfred and the Anglo-Saxon chronicles. In Gray's opinion Jefferson had probably the world's greatest collection of books on the history of North and South America. Gray particularly remembered an edition by the Archbishop of Toledo of

Cortés' *Cartas de Relación*. The three men talked books till their ears rang.

Jefferson was taken with Ticknor. He discussed the young scholar's plans for a tour of Europe and, though he explained that many of his friends were dead, promised to furnish him letters to the survivors. Ticknor offered to be on the lookout for a few books to replace the library Jefferson was selling. Jefferson was genuinely disappointed when the young men announced they must start back to Richmond. He had hoped they would spend the week with him.

"Two little incidents," Ticknor noted in his journal, "which occurred while we were at Monticello should not be passed by. . . . One morning, when he came back from his ride, he told Mr. Randolph very quietly, that the dam had been carried away the night before. From his manner I supposed it an affair of small consequence, but at Charlottesville on my way to Richmond I found the country ringing with it. Mr. Jefferson's great dam was gone and it would cost $30,000 to rebuild it."

The second "little incident" was the arrival of the news that Jackson had won the Battle of New Orleans.

21. *General Jackson's Breastwork*

One of John Armstrong's more fortunate appointments was that of Andrew Jackson to the 7th Military District, which included New Orleans and Mobile. Jackson was a naturalborn militia leader. During the two years he fought the Creeks he learned the practice of war. After forcing a capitulation on the Creeks by which the Indians, whether they had been loyal or disloyal, lost most of their lands to the whites, the new major general made his way to his headquarters at Mobile. He saw in this command his chance to carry out his project of conquering all Florida. The pretext was the appearance of a small British force at Pensacola to rally the remnants of those Creeks, Choctaws, and Chickasaws who refused to submit, and fled into the swamps and pine barrens. During the fall of 1814 Jackson's mind was on Pensacola. The defense of New Orleans he left to Governor Claiborne.

Monroe wrote him forbidding an attack on Pensacola which Monroe feared would embroil the United States with Spain. He kept warning Jackson to look after New Orleans. Jackson, never much on obeying orders, answered that he would do that as soon as he'd taken care of Pensacola. In November, with the help of a fresh force of Tennessee militia under his old retainer John Coffee, Jackson duly occupied the little settlement. The British blew up their fort and moved east along the coast.

In spite of warnings from the War Office on the extent of the British army on its way to the Mississippi, Jackson wouldn't be hurried. He was worn out with the dysentery he'd contracted up in the Alabama country. He could keep nothing on his stomach but a few spoonfuls of rice and a little coffee. His scrawny frame was skin and bones. All he seemed capable of was the leisurely reconnoitering of the swamps and bayous in the direction of New Orleans. He seemed General Winder all over again until the enemy were almost upon him. There the resemblance ceased.

December 10 Jackson was informed that the British fleet lay off the entrance to Lake Borgne. Four days later the sloops and barges of their landing parties captured the six American gunboats which were the city's only defense to the eastward.

Jackson sent off expresses to gather his scattered troops. He proclaimed martial law in New Orleans and governed the city Wilkinson-fashion.

He struck up a partnership with Edward Livingston, who headed the municipal Committee of Safety, whom he'd known and liked as a sprightly waggish fellow when they served in the House of Representatives together. Livingston became his French-speaking aide, wrote his proclamations, and translated his speeches. Between them they quelled the incipient panic and galvanized Creoles, Americans, Germans, and free mulattoes into a common effort. It was through Livingston's influence that the Lafitte brothers who led the smugglers and pirates of Barataria were induced to turn down tempting offers from the British and to devote themselves to the American cause.

Before Jackson had time to throw up defenses news came that a British force was seven miles from the city. Colonel Thornton, a veteran of Bladensburg, had pushed his barges up the bayou from Lake Borgne, surprised a company of Louisiana militia, and taken over Villeré plantation for British headquarters.

Jackson immdediately marched his troops out to attack the redcoats before they could settle into their camp. Though he was driven off by constantly arriving reinforcements from the fleet, he scored a point. Before risking an assault the British officers decided to wait for their heavy artillery and for the arrival of Sir Edward Pakenham, who had been appointed Commander in Chief when news reached England of General Ross's death.

Sir Edward Pakenham was a popular young general. He covered himself with glory at Salamanca. Lord Wellington was married to his sister. His ship was held up by adverse winds and it wasn't until Christmas Day that he assumed command at Villeré plantation.

The delay gave Jackson two weeks to build breastworks about five miles below the city behind an abandoned canal that cut across the plain from the Mississippi to a cypress swamp. He protected his batteries with bales of cotton plundered from the merchants' warehouses.

The British allowed him another six days while they built emplacements for their artillery. They used bags of sugar which proved even less protection than the baled cotton. At the same time they were digging a canal through the levee through which to push boatloads of troops to perform a flanking operation on the west bank of the river.

January 1 the preliminary artillery duel began. By the end of four hours superior American gunnery had silenced the British batteries. While he landed fresh guns from the fleet General Pakenham, full of confidence in his overwhelming forces, allowed Jackson another week of grace. Jackson's breastworks were well manned now from the river to the swamp, but the militia on the west bank still lacked muskets and ammunition.

At dawn on January 8 the redcoats were seen advancing through the white morning fog. Serried ranks firing by platoon advanced across the slimy flats. At the same time twentyseven boatloads of British troops were crossing the Mississippi.

Regiments lost their way in the fog. Men slipped in the gumbo and fell. Shell and cannister from the American batteries plowed through the ranks. As the British emerged from the mist in front of the breastworks American marksmanship shot them down man by man. General Pakenham was killed by a burst of grapeshot early in the day. His second in command was killed. A third major general was wounded. Scores of officers fell. By the time they retired to the camp the British had lost seven hundred killed and fourteen hundred wounded.

The American casualties were seven killed and six wounded. "This disproportion," wrote Jackson in his report, "must I know excite astonishment and may not be everywhere fully credited."

On the west bank of the Mississippi the British made such headway that Jackson did not dare pursue the broken battalions in front of his breastwork back to their camp. He kept his men in their entrenchments until the British flanking party, dismayed by the loss of their generals, took to their boats. Meanwhile expresses were galloping north with the news that New Orleans was saved.

It took nearly a month for the news to reach Monticello. Jefferson's grandson, Thomas Jefferson Randolph, rode up the mountain with it in great excitement. "The night before we left young Randolph came up late from Charlottesville and brought the astounding news that the British had been defeated before New Orleans by General Jackson," wrote George Ticknor on February 7. "Mr. Jefferson had made up his mind that the city would fall. . . . He had gone to bed like the rest of us but of course his grandson went to his chamber with the paper containing the news. But the old philosopher refused to open his door, saying he could wait till morning." This struck Ticknor as very odd indeed. "There is a breathing of notional philosophy in Mr. Jefferson, —in his dress, his house, his conversation," Ticknor reflected. At breakfast, before Ticknor and Gray left for Charlottesville next morning, they were amazed to discover that Mr. Jefferson had not yet read the newspaper.

CHAPTER VIII

The Easy Work of Peace

1. A Sort of Family Quarrel

More astonishing than the success of American arms at New Orleans were the results of the peace negotiations at Ghent. Four months of diplomatic skirmishing amid the canals and the mossy spires and gray gothic portals of the dank little Flemish city left the British team of negotiators outreasoned and outmaneuvered by the Americans. So far as the original American aims were concerned the War of 1812 was a lost war; the peace of Ghent turned it into a kind of a victory.

No negotiation ever began under less auspicious circumstances.

Back in July 1813 Gallatin and Bayard reached St. Petersburg after a stormy Atlantic crossing, followed by a tedious month beating against head winds into the Gulf of Finland. They were immediately greeted at their lodgings as warmly as his nature allowed by the third member of the peace commission.

John Quincy Adams and his wife and small Charles were thawing out after their third ferocious Russian winter. Adams had made himself respected at the Russian court by never trying to appear different than he was. He lived the life of a frugal New Englander, making no effort to compete with the ostentation of the representatives of the great powers. During his tour of duty in St. Petersburg he actually managed to save enough money out of his allowances to form the foundation of what Ingersoll described as "a modest competence." Finding himself with very little to do, during the Czar's absence on the fighting fronts, he spent the long dark winters reading the classics and composing letters on religion and ethics for the edification of his older sons, whom he had left at school in Massachusetts.

Gallatin and Adams got along. Gallatin was six years Adams' senior. Under the slightly ironic selfeffacement of his demeanor, he displayed a quick prehensile mind that immediately won the New Englander's respect. Adams had been raised to diplomacy almost from the cradle. He was up on all the tricks and subterfuges of the European scene. Bayard, whom they nicknamed the Chevalier, proved to be a not too energetic gentleman of affable manners. He was well read in international law. The three men found it easy and agreeable to work together.

Adams immediately explained that their prospects were poor. The Czar Alexander was at allied headquarters in Bohemia, having a hard time, in spite of vast British subsidies, holding his army together against the counterattacks of Napoleon's fresh levies. St. Petersburg at the moment was a diplomatic vacuum. Count Roumanzoff, the imperial chancellor, favored President Madison's theories of the rights of neutral shipping but his star was on the wane. The anglophile policy of Count Nesselrode, the Foreign Minister, was in the ascendant. Adams suspected that Castlereagh would resent Russian intervention. At a moment when the Russian government was dependent on the English for funds Alexander might find the appearance of American negotiators at his capital somewhat embarrassing.

While the American commissioners were still drafting their aide mémoire for the information of the chancellor, Gallatin received a letter from London that clinched the matter. Alexander Baring, who since his father's death headed the banking house of Baring Brothers, was an old friend. Gallatin knew him in Philadelphia when as a young man Baring was attending to the family interests there and courting the daughter of the William Binghams who were the arbiters among the wealthy and fashionable of what was then the American capital. The Barings were influential in every department of the British administration. Gallatin was taking advantage of old acquaintances, and of the prestige his conduct of the Treasury had won him in financial circles, to open a private avenue of communication with the Tory cabinet. Baring told Gallatin that the British definitely would not accept Russian mediation. Castlereagh felt that outsiders had no business in what was "a sort of family quarrel." Baring explained that in the present state of European affairs it was feared that efforts might be made "to make a tool of America" in ways that he was sure the American government would not approve.

The problem for Gallatin and Bayard was now how to retire politely from St. Petersburg without injuring Count Roumanzoff's diplomatic sensibilities. Bayard felt that the Neva water was damaging his already poor health. Gallatin's personal position was rendered delicate when the news reached him in October that the Senate had rejected his appointment.

There was some argument among the commissioners about what course he should take. Roumanzoff was reluctant to allow either

Gallatin or Bayard to leave until they received a formal letter of recall. Bayard's chief thought was to get out of Russia before the climate killed him. Gallatin wanted to see what he could do through the Barings in England. Adams had doubts about the plan. He reported huffily in his diary that Gallatin's argument was "that he was no longer a member of the commission: he was a private gentleman and might go home by way of England or any other way he pleased. That, as to the approbation of the government he should not trouble himself about it. He would not disobey their orders but if he was right he should not too much regard it whether they liked it or not."

President Madison's tepid support of Gallatin's efforts in the Treasury, the failure of the bank bill, Duane's appointment, the slights and humiliations he had been allowed to endure; these things still rankled.

Paying their respects at court on the occasion of Prince Michael's name day, the American envoys found themselves confronted by a new British ambassador, Lord Walpole. He declared bluntly that the last thing Castlereagh told him before he left England was that he would never accept Russian mediation. When Adams tried tactfully to discover something further the Britisher, perhaps feeling he had already said too much, would only talk of roast goose. That was how they celebrated Michaelmas in England. It was the day when members of Parliament were dined by their constituents, very good dinners, "And we do not get drunk," added his lordship jovially, "but something devilish near it."

2. The Salons Take up the American Cause

Both Gallatin and Adams were in communication with Lafayette. Jefferson had seen to it that his administration supported the policy of friendly assistance to the marquis in his chapter of misfortunes, and induced Congress to make him a huge grant of land in Louisiana. Jefferson hoped that Lafayette would take advantage of his American citizenship to accept the government of New Orleans which he offered him soon after the purchase. Now Lafayette, whom Napoleon had tolerated so long as he remained at La Grange and kept quiet, was in financial difficulties and wanted Gallatin to procure him the patents for some of this land so that he could effect a sale. To Adams Lafayette was writing on a more pressing and personal matter. His son George had married the daughter of Destutt de Tracy, the liberal "idealogue," the commentator on Montesquieu, and Jefferson's faithful correspondent. Her brother, Victor de Tracy, was a prisoner in some village in the far interior of Russia and reported to be ill. Could Mr. Adams effect his exchange?

Adams went to work with his usual persistence and managed in a couple of months to get the young man paroled to St. Petersburg.

Meanwhile, frustrated in every effort to initiate negotiations, the American envoys faced the prospect of being frozen in for the winter. They had visited all the palaces and pleasure gardens, they had heard the marvelous singing in the famous cathedrals. After the first snows there came a spell of sparkling clear weather. Adams reported in his diary on the brilliance of the stars seen out of his chamber window. For the first time in his life he distinguished the constellation Orion. In a characteristic mood of selfdepreciation he noted: "That I should have lived nearly fifty years without knowing him shows too clearly what kind of an observer I am."

In January 1814 with their carriages mounted on sleds, Gallatin and Bayard broke away from the tangle of protocol and made a dash for the west. Along the Baltic coast they were beset with snow and sleet. The inns were so filthy they slept in their carriages. In Berlin they found the bankers uncivil, a sure sign that American credit was low, but they did receive a letter from the American consul in Amsterdam telling them that Great Britain had proposed direct negotiations at Gothenburg and that President Madison had accepted the offer. Russian pressure had forced Castlereagh's hand.

At last, after thirtyeight days on the road, they reached Amsterdam more dead than alive. While they rested in a comfortable Dutch hostelry, Gallatin read his mail. Good news from Hannah: she and the children were well. A frustrating letter from Monroe. Thinking that Gallatin wanted to resume the Treasury, the President had failed to appoint him to the new peace commission.

Gallatin had had enough of Madison's administration. He had lost the hope of accomplishing the Jeffersonian aim of a perfect republic that had buoyed him up through twelve years of drudgery. He no longer felt he cared to face the backbiting and slander of Washington politics. In Europe as "a private gentleman" he was courted and admired for his achievements. His native language was French, the language of scholarship and diplomacy. As plain Albert Gallatin he was a power in the world. He immediately wrote that he preferred the diplomatic appointment.

While Gallatin and Bayard waited for Baring to procure them a permit to cross over to England they saw the sights of Amsterdam, they read the gazettes, visited the theatres, were entertained by the Dutch bankers and by the Prince of Orange himself. Everywhere they could see the results of Napoleon's defeat at Leipzig. The Low Countries were free from French troops. The Grande Armée had been driven across the Rhine and was falling back on Paris. There was an exhilaration of peace in the air.

Peace everywhere except in America. Two days after Gallatin and Bayard and their young secretaries reached London and settled into lodgings on Albemarle Street, Napoleon abdicated unconditionally at Fontainebleau.

The English were dizzy with victory. The London newspapers made painful reading for an American. The British public was convinced that the secession of New England was imminent. "As we urged a principle, no peace with Bonaparte," wrote an editorial writer in *The Times*, "so we must maintain the doctrine of no peace with James Madison." Another inveighed: "He must fall a victim to the just vengeance of the Federalists." The Louisiana Purchase was to be called into question: "Mr. Madison's dirty swindling manoeuvres in respect to Louisiana and the Floridas remain to be punished."

"That such opinions should be almost universally entertained here by the great body of the people is not at all astonishing," Gallatin wrote William Crawford, still in Paris as American minister. "To produce such an effect and render an American war popular, the Ministerial papers having nothing more to do than to transcribe American Federal speeches and newspapers. If Pickering, Quincy, Strong, Hanson &c have not brought a majority of the American people to their side, they have at least fully succeeded here, and had no difficulty in convincing all that part of the English community which derives its information from political journals that we had no cause of complaint and acted only as allies of Bonaparte."

In the same letter he suggested to Crawford that he should try to seek an interview with the Czar Alexander, who was now in Paris with the King of Prussia and a flock of princelings of the Grand Alliance for the installation of Louis XVIII. He should point out to him that a year had gone by since the United States had consented to negotiate and beg him to use his friendly offices in any way he could to speed up the peace.

Gallatin also wrote Lafayette, enclosing the titles to the marquis' land and explaining that this was the first time he had found a safe conveyance for them. He had left Lafayette's friend Victor de Tracy in good health in St. Petersburg.

"I believe I am not mistaken in offering you my congratulations on the late events in France," continued Gallatin. "It would certainly have been more desirable that the changes should have been produced by the spontaneous will of the French people rather than to appear to have been forced by a foreign army."

Gallatin added that he thought it fortunate that Alexander was one of the prime movers. He hoped that the foundation would be laid for institutions "as free and liberal as you are susceptible of."

He warned Lafayette that "the United States . . . are placed in a more critical situation than ever they were since the first years of their revolution." Gallatin was desperate for peace before Great Britain could bring her full military might to bear on the American war. He expressed his confidence that Lafayette would do everything he could to bring it about.

Gallatin well understood that Lafayette was a great man again. Already, wearing his uniform of a general in the National Guard and with a white cockade in his hat, the American marquis had paid his respects to Louis XVIII at the Tuileries Palace.

In Paris, from the moment Bonaparte was bustled off under British escort to Elba, it was as if time had rolled back a quarter of a century. Again there was a fat Bourbon king in the Tuileries. Again the salons hummed with talk of a constitutional monarchy in the English style. Talleyrand was Prime Minister. Such of the enlightened nobility as had survived the Terror and Napoleon's wars were coming out of their holes. The Jeffersonian liberals of the Institut de France were looking forward to a return of freedom of publication.

Crawford was an able Georgia lawyer and had made a name for himself in the Senate, but he was out of his depth in the quicksands and crosscurrents of treatymaking in Paris. He failed to obtain an audience with the Czar Alexander. Count Nesselrode was *désolé* but he was much too busy to see Mr. Crawford. There was no response when he left cards on the King of Prussia and his Foreign Minister, who was Wilhelm von Humboldt, the geographer's equally learned brother. He couldn't even get admitted to the court of Louis XVIII on the day set for the reception of foreign envoys. Nobody had any time for the American minister.

Lafayette went to work for Crawford as years before he had guided Jefferson through the bureaucratic maze of Versailles. Discovering that real efforts were being made to keep people suspected of attachment to the United States from seeing anyone in authority, he threw himself at the feet of Madame de Staël.

Madame de Staël was in her glory. Ever since she had reached Paris from exile in England generals, statesmen, dukes, princes, and kings crowded into her drawing room. The daughter of Jacques Necker, the Swiss banker who had tried to stave off the bankruptcy of the old regime, and of a bluestocking mother, she was the true child of the eighteenth century enlightenment. As a tiny tot she sat on a stool in her mother's salon joining in the conversations of the Encyclopedists. A prudent marriage to a selfeffacing Danish diplomat to whom, for all her frenzied social life, she managed to bear three children, gave her a title and cosmopolitan status.

Now she appeared as the heroine of a decade of persecution and harassment by the fallen tyrant. In the heyday of the political salons under the Directory, young Bonaparte had put himself out to win her favor, but she insisted on denouncing him as the destroyer of the liberties of France. Two of his brothers were among her friends. Their vendetta was savage as a Corsican quarrel.

When Bonaparte achieved power as First Consul, he ordered her to stay at a distance of forty leagues from Paris, and Paris was her life. She took refuge in Weimar where she shone amid the luminaries of Goethe's literary court. She published a volume on Germany full of romanticism and of the spirit of liberty. She wrote continuously. The more she wrote the more she irritated Bonaparte, now become the all-powerful Emperor of the French. The presses were closed to her. He had her publications seized. She was harried about Europe by the imperial police.

Her refuge at Coppet, on Lake Geneva, became unsafe; and besides, the astonishing appearance of a fourth child with no visible papa, when she was well into her forties, scandalized the puritanical Swiss. In 1812 she fled to the protection of Alexander's court. Her carriage dashed through Moscow just ahead of the French invaders. From St. Petersburg she moved to Sweden and then to England. She was well received there because all along she had defended the English as the true paladins of individual liberty.

Madame de Staël had for years been an enthusiast for America. She had large sums of money invested in New York State lands, of which she bought heavily on the advice of Gouverneur Morris. That philandering diplomat, when he first met her, confided to his journal that she looked like a chambermaid, but later he admitted that her wit left him speechless. Occasionally she had entertained a project of retiring to America to escape the Napoleonic tyranny. She corresponded with Jefferson.

In London she was charmed by Gallatin when she invited him to call on her for consultation about her investments. Gallatin was taken aback by her dumpiness but noted her charm and her fine eyes. He interested her as one of the most distinguished Americans; they were compatriots in another way, being both of them originally Swiss. When Lafayette appeared to enlist her sympathies in the American cause she declared that perhaps now, as the British had been when they fought to overthrow Napoleon, the Americans were the true sons of freedom.

She arranged things so that General Lafayette should find himself in conversation, in her salon one evening, with the Czar Alexander. In reply to Lafayette's plea that he press the American cause Alexander cried out that he had twice tried to bring about a peace. "Make a third attempt," said Lafayette. "*Ne vous arrêtez pas en si beau chemin.*" As Lafayette described the conversation in a letter to Crawford—with the suggestion that he forward his account to Gallatin—Alexander promised to try again during his forthcoming trip to England.

Madame de Staël tactfully kept America the topic by describing a letter she had received from Thomas Jefferson, listing the outrages which had forced the United States into the war with England, and speaking warmly of his desire for the mediation of "the virtuous Alexander." The Czar joined in a chorus of praise of the philosopher President.

"You see, my dear sir," added Lafayette, "I had fully the opportunity we were wishing for. If it has not been well improved, the fault is mine."

In June, when Alexander crossed to London with the whole train of princes and potentates to continue the discussion of the European settlement, he granted Gallatin an interview. The Czar's report of his efforts with Castlereagh was discouraging. He had made his third attempt and it had failed. It was reported that His Majesty said something in French which amounted to "Keep a stiff upper lip."

It was the very day of the state reception at Guildhall where the Prince Regent, the King of Prussia, and the Russian Czar, sitting on massive gilt chairs placed on an elevated dais, amid the clangor of bands playing national anthems and fanfares of trumpets, dined off turtle soup and a baron of beef furnished by the City of London. The day was described as the sunniest in the gayest London season in years. The streets were filled with gorgeous equipages. All the finest horses in England were out in glittering harness. The lackeys all wore fresh liveries. Tapestries hung from the windows. Handsomely dressed women leaned out over them waving white handkerchiefs. The cobbles where the royal progress would pass were strewn with flower petals.

Gallatin, and Levitt Harris, the American consul in St. Petersburg who had introduced him, drove away from the imperial residence in a hackney cab. According to a story Ingersoll repeated in his history, they left amid the hoots of a beery crowd jeering at the woebegone aspect of the American diplomats. In another street Gallatin was taken for the Prussian General Blücher and roundly cheered. Alexander von Humboldt was in the city and was reported to be applying his prestige as the foremost natural scientist in Europe to help the American cause. It was some consolation to have the great geographer declare, when he appeared at Gallatin's lodgings with a packet of mail from Paris, that he was bored to death with the ceremonies. Since his brother the etymologist led the Prussian diplomatic service, he'd been forced to attend in King Frederick Wilhelm's suite. *"Que je suis ennuyé des* Magnanimous Sovereigns *et de la croisade des héros!"*

3. *A Mansion on the Rue des Champs*

By July 5 the American plenipotentiaries had assembled at Ghent which had been agreed on as more convenient than northerly Gothenburg. Gallatin and Bayard came from London, and Henry Clay and

Jonathan Russell from Gothenburg, bringing along Gallatin's credentials. John Quincy Adams, accompanied only by a Finnish servant, traveled alone the long rough road from St. Petersburg. They all put up at the Hôtel des Pays Bas, reputed to be the town's most substantial hostelry.

Gallatin had gone to some pains, when the original documents were drafted in Washington, to see that they were so worded as not to wound the touchy susceptibilities of the American minister to Russia. He now found himself last on the list in the new credentials. In spite of protocol he could not help assuming the position of chairman.

His first business was to keep the peace between Adams and Henry Clay. The men were complete opposites. The son of an impoverished Baptist minister in Hanover County, Virginia, Clay had risen, by oratory and brains and a masculine charm that swept not only women but men off their feet, from clerking in a Richmond store to being Speaker of the House of Representatives and the most commanding politician in Kentucky. A great drinker and roisterer, a desperate all-night gambler, a gay dog with the ladies, he had soared so fast to opulence and power there was no limit to his ambition. "The cock of Kentucky" was John Randolph's nickname for him.

Adams, who in spite of the selfdoubt of his private meditations, had rather a high opinion of himself, smoldered inwardly under the challenge of Clay's overbearing high spirits. Russell immediately became Clay's vassal. Bayard, the man of the world, maintained a gentlemanly aloofness. It became Gallatin's business to keep these disparate characters working together.

The American envoys had plenty of time to debate their strategy. It was a full month before the British appeared. The Americans were heartened meanwhile by the hospitable attitude of the people of Ghent. The mayor came wearing his sash and full regalia to invite them to a public ball. The intendant of the Department of the Scheldt was lavish with invitations. When they visited the court of assizes the judge interrupted his trial to deliver an address of welcome. Owners of art galleries were eager to show their collections. At a municipal celebration they were asked to give out the prizes for contests in drawing and painting and architecture. The burghers of Ghent did everything to show that they held their American visitors in high esteem.

The plenipotentiaries found themselves a mansion with a pleasant garden that had large rooms suitable for conferences. While it was being prepared for them they met in the inn at noon every day to work up their documentation. After two or three hours of discussion they dined.

Adams complained in his diary it was a waste of time to sit so long after meals while his colleagues drank bad wine and smoked cigars.

In the evening Clay and his group played cards and billiards. Adams, occasionally accompanied by Gallatin, took long walks through the narrow stone streets. Often he would walk out one city gate and return by another, taking a tour in the country, which he described as "a continual garden." Fields of barley, rye, and wheat were turning to gold as harvest approached. The flax was in bloom. Elms, lindens, and poplars lined the roads. Sundays there was music in little booths under the trees. Townspeople and peasants ate and danced and drank beer under the arbors.

July 8 Adams reported "the weather has changed suddenly from the heel of winter to heart of summer." During the next month he suffered so from the heat and the mosquitoes he had to spread his mattress and featherbed on the floor of his room to get any sleep. On one of their long twilight walks Gallatin showed him a place where he could bathe in the river Lys. After that Adams took to rising at five for a morning swim. He was back in his room by seven to write letters and to work on the position papers. At eight he breakfasted and then wrote again till twelve. For a while he tried to save time by taking his dinner at the table d'hôte but Clay raised such a clamor that he went back to dining and wining with his colleagues. Adams was a great theatregoer. At least once a week he attended a drama or farce or an *opéra comique*.

4. *The Sine Qua Non*

On August 6, a week after the Americans had settled into their mansion on the Rue des Champs, the Britishers put in an appearance at the Hôtel du Lion d'Or. Immediately the delegations started skirmishing for position. The Britishers sent a secretary to invite the Americans to wait on them at their hotel. Absolutely not. The Americans made the suggestion that they had a conference room all ready at their Hôtel d'Alcantara. The Britishers wouldn't look at it. They settled on the Hôtel des Pays Bas as neutral ground.

At one in the afternoon on August 7 they met to exchange credentials. The British team was led by Baron Gambier, a whitehaired retired naval officer who had commanded part of the fleet during the bombardment of Copenhagen. The working members proved to be a pert young civil servant named Goulburn and Dr. William Adams, an obscure admiralty lawyer. It was immediately obvious that these men were mere mouthpieces; they were to make no commitment without instructions from Castlereagh or Lord Bathurst, the Secretary of State for War and the Colonies.

Gallatin's conversations with Baring in London had led him to expect a tough stand. Since the end of the war rendered the question of impressments and neutral rights less urgent he was prepared to play down the original *casus belli*, but he was as shocked as his colleagues at British demands which Goulburn brashly developed at a series of meetings. The Canadian boundary was to be "rectified" in favor of Canada by the accession of territory in Maine. Sackett's Harbor and Fort Niagara were to be ceded to Britain. The Americans were to be prohibited from maintaining a fleet on the lakes. The British right to navigate the Mississippi was to be balanced off against the access of the New Englanders to the northern fisheries. Both countries were to pledge themselves to make no further purchases of Indian lands. The entire Northwest Territory was to be returned to the tribes who originally owned it. This last was the *sine qua non*.

What was to become of the hundred thousand American settlers? "They'll have to shift for themselves," replied Dr. Adams.

5. Uti Possidetis

The Americans labored mightily over the reply to be forwarded to Westminster. Adams drafted it. Bayard revised it. Clay, to Adams' great annoyance, deleted Adams' figurative language. To break the stalemate Gallatin had to rewrite it himself. The one thing they agreed on was that negotiations were certainly at an end. Nothing for it but to go home and prepare for a desperate war for national survival. Only Clay kept his spirits up. He was a great hand at a card game known as brag. He said the British were bluffing.

Castlereagh himself brought his commissioners their reply to the American note when he and his brother passed through Ghent in a train of twenty state carriages on their way to the Congress of Vienna. Bathurst, who had been schooled in aggressive statesmanship under Pitt and had long been president of the Board of Trade, from which most of the projects for destroying the commercial competition of the United States had emanated, was to keep the American negotiation dangling while Castlereagh coped with the manifold intrigues of the European coalition.

Meanwhile the Americans were giving out that negotiations were on the verge of rupture. On August 23 the intendant invited both sets of plenipotentiaries to what might have been a farewell dinner. Clay, who sat next to Goulburn, told him that the British propositions were equivalent to asking for the cession of Boston or New York. After dinner Bayard took Goulburn into a corner and tried patiently to explain that such demands would make it impossible for the Federalist party of which he was a member to support a policy of peace with England. "I have dryly stated," Goulburn wrote Bathurst, "what the American plenipotentiaries said to me . . . it has not made the least impression upon me or my colleagues."

While they waited for something more definite from Lord Bathurst, the Americans were much taken up with the social life of the town. They attended a number of churches. Adams visited the public library and collections of medals and antiquities. A fulldress call was made on the Prince of Orange when he passed through.

The Americans responded to Flemish hospitality by inviting all the local authorities to meet the British plenipotentiaries at a grand dinner at their lodgings at the Hôtel d'Alcantara. The garden was illuminated with colored lamps. After dinner the ladies and gentlemen played whist. When the guests left the American plenipotentiaries were still in a sportive mood. Even dour little Adams was drawn into a gambling game with Clay called "all fours." He lost an oil painting he had previously won in a lottery and young Todd lost a bunch of flowers he had won in the same way.

The British responded to this entertainment by asking the Americans to dine a few days later. Already they were forced to admit that the American gentlemen were their social equals. Before long it would become painfully obvious that they were their intellectual superiors.

In his journal Adams kept complaining that late hours and dissipation were interfering with his early rising and with his long walks. He vowed to continue his regular habits of exercise.

Bayard's argument that the British would lose the support of the Federalist party made an impression on Bathurst if it didn't on Goulburn. Though couched in unpleasant terms, the next British note showed signs of giving ground on the *sine qua non*. Castlereagh's plan now was to let negotiations drag on until the British armies in America could report some signal victory and then to dictate a peace on the basis of *uti possidetis:* "each holds on to what he's got."

October 1 news came of the British raid on Washington. Adams noted that he spent a sleepless night. The weather had turned cold. The following evening he tried to distract himself by going to a play. "I was too drowsy, cold and distressed to be amused."

Gallatin meanwhile received a disturbing letter from Madame de Staël. She wrote in a great flurry from Paris to ask him whether she should sell out her American investments. She had more than a million and a half francs invested in banks, public funds, and landholdings. Hadn't she better send her son over to liquidate what he could? She must know Gallatin's opinion. She had earned any benevolent efforts he might make in her behalf, she added insinuatingly; whenever she saw the Duke of Wellington she preached America to him.

If there was a barometer of public opinion in Europe at that moment it was Madame de Staël's salon. Gallatin answered immediately. The negotiations had not broken down. This act of British vandalism, such as one couldn't duplicate in the history of the past twenty years of war in Europe, certainly raised fresh obstacles to peace. In his opinion the burning of Washington would unite the American people as nothing else had. So long as the nation held together American credit would be good. Look how the debt left by the Revolutionary War had been paid off. Now the country had twice the population and constantly increasing resources. Before selling her American holdings at a loss Madame de Staël should at least wait for peace.

Gallatin ended on a personal note. Before he met her, he wrote, he had respected her for being Madame de Staël and her mother's daughter. "I must admit that I was scared of you, such an elegant and beloved woman," he wrote in French, "the first genius of her sex; one couldn't help trembling a little. You had hardly opened your lips before I was reassured, in less than five minutes I felt with you as I would with a friend of twenty years' standing. I would only have admired you from afar, but your goodness proved equal to your talent and that is why you are dear to me."

On the heels of news of the British raid came an ultimatum from the British. The Americans must accept the British proposition as to the Northwest Indians or else they would break off negotiations. Henry Clay took it upon himself to answer this demand. He took the position that the United States was already at peace with these Indians, an amnesty had been declared for those who laid down their arms. Nothing was left to argue about on that score.

At the same time the American plenipotentiaries were letting it be known that they were authorized to drop their demands on impressment and blockade. Since the world was at peace these topics could well be left for later discussion.

By the time Clay's reply reached Westminster Bathurst had lost interest in the *sine qua non*. News had reached him of General Ross's death and of the failure of the assault on Baltimore. He fell back on *uti possidetis*. The Americans confronted the Britishers with a brief note refusing to treat further on that principle. The *status quo ante* must be the basis for negotiation from now on.

While they were waiting for a reply from the Foreign Office the Britishers had the Americans to dinner again at their Carthusian monastery. "A dull dinner," noted Adams. The Britishers were finding Ghent boresome. Lord Gambier asked Adams rather wistfully if the Americans had made any pleasant acquaintances there. "Yes indeed," said the Americans. Lord Gambier admitted he hadn't met a soul.

That same evening the friendly attentions of the people of Ghent were bestowed in such a form as almost to break up the American mission. Messrs. Gallatin, Adams, and Bayard were invited to become members of the Society of Arts and Letters. At the same time Messrs. Clay, Russell, and one of their secretaries were invited to become members of the Society for Agriculture and Botany. Henry Clay was furious. Arts and Letters rated higher than Agriculture and Botany.

Russell was so nettled he refused an invitation to a dinner the intendant was giving to celebrate these honors. Adams noted in his diary that Mr. Clay was daily more peevish and fractious; he warned himself to keep a firm grip on his temper.

6. *Status Quo Ante*

If they had known the state of affairs at the Foreign Office, the American plenipotentiaries would have forgotten their squabbles. The curt American note arrived almost simultaneously with dispatches describing Sir George Prevost's unseemly retreat from Plattsburg and the capture of the British squadron on Lake Champlain. Lord Bathurst consulted Lord Liverpool, the Prime Minister. Liverpool consulted the Chancellor of the Exchequer, who informed him that a continuation of the American war would cost at least ten million pounds. Their lordships were nonplused.

Meanwhile the news from Vienna was of disquieting disagreements. There was a Bonapartist uprising in the Massif Central. At home the government was short of funds, the lower classes were rioting to protest the high price of bread. Merchants and shipowners were suffering from the reprisals of American privateers. The burning of Washington had not gone over well with enlightened opinion either in England or on the Continent. From St. Petersburg Walpole reported a powerful faction at the Russian court urging Alexander to back the American cause.

At a full meeting of the cabinet it was decided to put the whole problem of the American war up to the Duke of Wellington, then serving as British ambassador to the French Bourbon court. November 4 Liverpool wrote him in Paris of "the many inconveniences" resulting from the American war and asked him whether he would consent to take command in America with full powers to "bring it to an honorable conclusion."

The duke may well have become leery of pulling chestnuts out of the fire for the administration. Perhaps he was affected by the preachings of Madame de Staël. He answered that as the war stood at that moment the British had no grounds on which to base the principle of *uti possidetis*. He hoped New Orleans would soon be in British hands. The cession of that province might well form a separate article in a treaty of peace. He tactfully evaded the offer that he assume the American command.

The negotiators of Ghent settled down to a long wrangle which took up most of the month of November as to whether the northern fisheries were equivalent to the navigation of the Mississippi. Adams

and Clay were as much on the outs on that topic as were Great
Britain and the United States.

John Quincy Adams took to reading four or five chapters of the
Bible as soon as he woke every morning. He had arranged for fires
to be made in his room. In his diary he complained of the relaxation
of selfdiscipline, of too much conviviality, too much theatre, too little
exercise. He was growing uncomfortably corpulent.

Gallatin's correspondence with Alexander Baring was giving him
an inkling of the state of opinion in the City. American bills were
being protested as fast as they appeared on the exchange. Baring, who
for years had acted as the American Treasury's European correspondent, showed signs of scruples about advancing funds which might
further the American war effort; but at the same time he expressed
a hope that "some favorable change" might occur before the next
payment of interest on Louisiana stock became due on the first of
January. Gallatin jumped at the conclusion that the British cabinet
was willing to sign an immediate peace.

7. The Treaty of Peace

On December 14, overruling two of his colleagues—Clay, who
was for refusing to give ground on the Mississippi, and Adams, who
wouldn't yield an inch on the fisheries—Gallatin drafted a new suggestion which was sent over to the monastery the same day. The
Americans were willing to sign a treaty which would leave all points
of dispute open without prejudice for further negotiation later.

The Britishers had already been instructed to sign. On December
23 both sets of plenipotentiaries agreed on a text. On Christmas Eve
they all put their names to one of the few treaties in history that
haven't raised more problems than they solved.

"The day of all others in the year most congenial to proclaiming
Peace on Earth, Good Will to Men," wrote Adams effusively to open
his Christmas Day entry in his journal. Gallatin wrote Hannah: "My
dearest wife, We signed yesterday a treaty of peace . . . it is as good
as . . . we had at this moment a right to expect. For not having had
a better peace & six months sooner we are solely indebted to the New
England traitors." He would start home in the spring. "Now no other
obstacle but the Atlantic remains between us."

The burghers of Ghent celebrated the American peace as if it
were their own. The Americans particularly were congratulated on
every side. When they dined the Britishers at their Hôtel d'Alcantara
the local St. Cecilia Society appeared to serenade them. They al-
ternately sang "God Save the King" and "Hail Columbia." John
Quincy Adams offered a toast to "His Britannic Majesty" and Lord

Gambier drank "To the United States of America." From Vienna Castlereagh wrote thankfully to Liverpool, "I wish you joy of being released from the millstone of the American war."

The American plenipotentiaries wasted their last days in Ghent in a complicated squabble as to who should have custody of the peace mission's papers. Clay wanted them sent to the State Department. Adams insisted that since his name was first on the list of envoys they should remain in his hands. When Bayard and Russell showed signs of agreeing with Clay, Adams accused Clay of raising a cabal against him. Clay denied it hotly. All the accumulated tension of the last four months flared up in a shouting match between them.

Gallatin and Bayard calmed them down. Gallatin with his cool humorous manner managed to quiz them out of their tantrums. He thought Adams should have most of the papers; others might go to Washington. Clay and Adams parted on terms of aggrieved civility and they went their several ways to London where they were to start work on a treaty of commerce.

8. Three Birds of Ill Omen

After an unusually speedy crossing on the sloop of war *Favorite* a British diplomatic courier arrived in New York on February 11. Postriders set off to Boston and Charleston to announce the peace. Three days later the text of the treaty reached the Department of State. Monroe carried it himself to the President the same evening. Next day Madison sent it to the Senate where it was ratified without the crossing of a *t* or the dotting of an *i*. The same day a British diplomat reached Washington from Norfolk with the copy bearing the Prince Regent's signature. Ratifications were exchanged immediately. February 17, 1815, President Madison proclaimed hostilities to be at an end.

Commodity prices boomed. Fortunes were made and lost speculating on the great stores of American products awaiting shipment to Europe. In Amsterdam American stock rose fifteen per cent over night. A sudden gust of prosperity swept the seaboard cities. The Virginia farmers found themselves selling their flour and tobacco with bonanza profits. Even the depreciated paper money of the state banks rose in value. The Madison administration, which had been on the verge of disintegration a few days before, was suddenly hailed on every hand. The Federalist papers copied the triumphant slogan of the Republicans: "Not an inch ceded or lost."

Outside of the upstate New Yorkers and the Vermonters who had been growing rich selling supplies to both armies, the chief sufferers from the peace were the three Massachusetts gentlemen who had been deputed by Governor Caleb Strong to lay before Congress the demands of the Hartford Convention.

Dapper and fashionable Harrison Gray Otis was one. Another was his old friend and schoolmate, Thomas H. Perkins, who made a fortune in the Canton trade and was consequently tarred as an opium merchant by the Republicans. The third was William Sullivan, the Federalist son of the deceased Republican governor of Massachusetts. Like his father, he was a man of letters as well as a politician. All three were members of a convivial group of Bostonians known as the Saturday fish club, and had been active as any Essex men in fomenting the convention.

Their immediate aim was to confront the Madison administration, which they expected to find tottering from the fall of New Orleans, with the demand that the New England states be immediately empowered to use the direct tax for the support of their own armies.

The delegates had emerged from their secret sessions on January 5 with a report that had one foot in the Union and one foot in secession. George Cabot had seen to it that a moderate tone should be preserved. "A rupture of the union is the worst evil that could assail us," the report declared, "except a submission to the present order."

The question of secession was left pending while efforts should be made by the New England state legislatures to promote seven amendments to the Constitution. First: slave representation must be abolished. Taxation and representation should be proportioned to the free voting population. Second: no new states should be admitted to the Union without the concurrence of two thirds of both houses of Congress. Third: any future embargo must be limited to sixty days. Fourth: nonintercourse acts directed against any foreign nation must have the concurrence of both houses of Congress. Fifth: two thirds of both houses must concur in a declaration of war. Sixth: no one naturalized after the present year should be eligible for any elective or appointive office. And seventh: no President could be reelected. No state could provide a President twice in succession.

The amendments could wait for due process. The immediate demand was on the subject of the militia. Though most of the New England state governments seemed willing to abide by the outcome of a bill pending in Congress which would obtain the same result in a different way, Governor Strong was spoiling to teach the administration a lesson. Hence the illfated journey of the three Massachusetts ambassadors.

They left Boston on February 3. The blue laws held them up in New Haven over Sunday. They lost two days in New York on account of pack ice in the Hudson. From Philadelphia Otis, who must have already had misgivings as to the success of his mission, wrote his wife: "We have been exceedingly amused by the circumstance of *three* black crows, constantly preceding us from New York to Philadelphia. . . . These are *ill omen'd* birds and in days when augury was in fashion would have been considered as sad precursors of the three Ambassadors."

Otis guessed right. Arriving in Baltimore, they were greeted by the news of Jackson's victory at New Orleans. Otis described the event to his wife as miraculous, and reported that there were "floating rumors of peace." He described himself as "quite willing to take peace when it comes, with all the inconveniences resulting from the benefit which bad men will derive from an event, for which they deserve no credit."

From Georgetown on February 14 he reported the peace of Ghent. "God's holy name be praised." He added that now he could give all his attention to making money for the support of his wife and children.

Immediately the Republican gazettes began to poke fun at the New England ambassadors. A New York paper printed an advertisement in the Lost and Found column:

> Missing: Three well looking responsible men, who appeared to be travelling towards Washington, disappeared suddenly from Gadsby's Hotel in Baltimore on Monday evening last and have not since been heard from. . . . Whoever will give any information to the Hartford Convention of the fate of these unfortunate and tristful gentlemen by letter (post paid) will confer a favor on humanity. The newspapers, particularly the *Federal* newspapers, are requested to publish this advertisement in a conspicuous place and send their bills to the Hartford Convention.

The joke caught on. Soon every newspaper in the country was carrying quizzing notices about the misplaced ambassadors from Hartford. A comic song on the theme of "the three wise men of Gotham who went to sea in a bowl" was distributed from tavern to tavern. The Hartford Convention, which began as a threat to the integrity of the nation, ended in a gale of laughter.

Besides having to endure ridicule Harrison Gray Otis had the ill luck to come down with a fit of gout at his Georgetown hotel. He vented his spleen in a letter to his wife: "I presume I've already told you that we have rec'd no invitation from Madison. What a mean and contemptible little blackguard."

By February 22 Otis had recovered enough to attend two Washington's Birthday balls. The Georgetown ball he found genteel. Of the ball in Washington he complained that Mrs. Madison entered the room "upon a flourish of drums and trumpets," on the arm of Joe Gales, the editor of the *National Intelligencer*.

"What can be more characteristic of the style of the place, of the knowledge of propriety, and of the subservience of dignity and decorum to Party views and services. . . . Uncovered benches, naked walls, fiery muslins, and bloody flags, Clerks and Clerkesses, Members of Congress, Officers of the Army with fresh epaulettes that will never now be tarnished. The old gentleman . . . was not present. He is obliged to wear a muffler round his face. The dry rot which attack'd his jaw had stopped of itself as it sometimes does on a Crab Apple tree, which bears sour fruit for years after an incipient decay. . . ."

He added that Ticknor and Frank Gray, back from their visit to Monticello, spent half their time in his drawing room. "We have all a great deal of conversation and good humor."

By the last day of February Otis was able to write his wife from Baltimore that he was on his way home. He had already remarked on the civility with which he had been received by Monroe and by Alexander Dallas. Gallatin's resourceful and crotchety lawyer friend from Philadelphia had recently consented to take over the Treasury, which Campbell had left in distressing disarray. Otis' mission with these gentlemen had been to take advantage of the good feeling of the time to obtain the quashing of federal suits against several clients, Hampshire County saloonkeepers who had refused to pay their wartime taxes to the federal government.

The President consented that the indictments be dropped. Otis' letter of thanks to the Secretary of the Treasury took a far different tone from his private scribblings to the wife of his bosom. "I have lost no time in taking measures to apprise those persons of the prompt condescension," wrote the Massachusetts lawyer, "manifested by the President in the accordance of this favor, and have no doubt it will produce the impressions which ought to be expected from acts of bounty upon grateful & generous minds. I pray you Sir to tender to the President my respectful thanks for permitting this favor to be granted through my instrumentality."

9. Not an Inch Ceded or Lost

The peace united the country as the war never had. Back home in Boston Harrison Gray Otis was one of the first to let the bitterness seep out of his Federalism. When he was elected senator a couple of years later he wrote William Sullivan that he was accepting the honor because he felt he was best able to explain to the nation Massachusetts' part in the war, "to soften the prejudices and dilute the venom of party feeling to which she was exposed."

The Federalist politicians immediately became strangely forgetful of the parts they had played in the Hartford Convention. When a reverential biographer completed his son Octavius' life of Timothy Pickering he never even mentioned it.

Jefferson never forgave the Essex Junto, any more than he forgave Aaron Burr, for their efforts to break up the Union. He wrote of the mortification of the New England clergy, whom both he and Madison blamed for the Federalist excesses, exulting bitterly in "the disgrace with which they have loaded themselves in their political ravings, and of their mortification at the ridiculous issue of their Hartford convention. no event more than this has shown the placid nature of our constitution. under any other their treasons would have been punished by the halter. we let them live as laughing stocks for the world, and punish them by the torment of eternal contempt."

10. *The Complicated Science of Political Economy*

In the course of the war the Republicans had switched politics with the Federalists. The Federalists were now defending nullification and states' rights as Jefferson and Madison had defended them at the time of the Kentucky Resolutions. The Republicans were now the party of central government, a standing army, and a navy capable of meeting force with force in relations with foreign nations. To that they were about to add a tariff for the protection of manufactures.

To a correspondent who wrote asking Jefferson whether he still believed in his theory laid down in the *Notes on Virginia,* that the United States should remain an agricultural country and depend on Europe for manufactured goods, Jefferson answered that twenty years of worldwide war had changed his views: "in so complicated a science as political economy no one axiom can be laid down as wise and expedient for all times and circumstances." With piratical navies ravaging ocean commerce it would be folly for the United States to remain dependent on European manufactures. In another letter he expressed his new theory more succinctly: "We must now place the manufacturer beside the agriculturalist."

When the news of the Treaty of Ghent reached Monticello Jefferson was getting ready a packet of letters of introduction to friends in Europe for George Ticknor to take along on his tour. He still warmed to the recollection of the eager intelligence of that very civil young man. He added a series of postscripts on the peace.

He wrote William Crawford in Paris how much he regretted no provision had been included on impressment: "It is in fact but an armistice, to be terminated by the first act of impressment committed on an American citizen. it may be thought that useless blood was spilt at New Orleans, after the treaty of peace had been actually signed and ratified. I think it had many valuable uses. it proved the fidelity of the Orleanese to the United States. it proved that New Orleans can be defended both by land and water; that the Western country will fly to its relief (of which ourselves had doubted before); that our militia are heroes when they have heroes to lead them on; and that when unembarrassed by field evolutions, which they do not understand, their skill in the fire arm and deadly aim, give them great advantages over regulars."

In a letter to Lafayette he reiterated his longheld beliefs that the constitutionalist party, which had been Lafayette's, had been right all along in trying to establish a limited monarchy in France. He expressed the hope that the Bourbon regime would "be contented with a certain portion of power, secured by a formal compact with the nation, rather than, grasping at more, hazard all upon uncertainty, and risk meeting the fate of their predecessor, or a renewal of their own exile." He repeated his statement to Crawford that he considered the peace with Great Britain merely a truce. "The first act of impressment she commits upon an American will be answered by reprisal. . . . we have much to do, in fortifying our seaport towns, providing military stores, classing and disciplining our militia, arranging our financial system, and above all, pushing our domestic manufactures, which have taken such root as never again can be shaken."

Madison had sent Jefferson the administration pamphlet: *An Exposition of the Causes and Character of the War*, which the President had laid out and which the indefatigable Dallas, who was ably taking his friend Gallatin's place as the hand and brain of the administration, had finished. Madison was in doubt as to whether he should publish it now that peace was agreed on.

Jefferson urged him to let it be printed and suggested that Gallatin should have it translated into French.

"We need it in Europe. they have totally mistaken our character. . . . it is necessary for the people of England, who have been deceived as to the causes and conduct of the war and do not entertain a doubt that it was entirely wanton and wicked on our part and under the order of Bonaparte. . . . it is necessary for our own people, who, though they have known the details as they went along, yet have been so plied with false facts and false views by the federalists, that some impression has been left that all has not been right. it may be said that it will be thought unfriendly. but truths necessary for our own character, must not be suppressed out of tenderness to it's calumniators. . . . indeed I think that a soothing postscript, addressed to the interests, the prospects, the sober reason of both nations, would make it acceptable to both."

He added that he would like to see at least a few copies printed with an appendix which should contain all the documents referred to, "to be preserved in libraries. and to facilitate to the present and future writers of history, the acquisition of the materials which test the truth it contains."

No sooner had Jefferson's letter reached Washington than a copy of the administration pamphlet was sent to Charles Jared Ingersoll with the suggestion that it be not printed as authorized by the administration. A few days later Madison's justification was appearing serially in the Philadelphia *Aurora*.

Jefferson couldn't get over his pleasure in the visit of the two scholarly young New Englanders. These were the kind of men needed to leaven the prejudice and wrongheadedness of the Essex Junto. When he sent his packet of letters to Ticknor, ardently recommending him to a list of European worthies, he included a word for Frank Gray.

He congratulated him on the peace. "our second and third campaign here, I trust, more than redeemed the disgraces of the first, and proved that although a republican government is slow to move, yet, once in motion, its momentum is irresistible." Experience was just beginning to bring officers "with talents for war" to the top. "under the guidance of these one campaign would have planted our standard on the walls of Quebec, and another on those of Halifax. but peace is better for us all; and if it could be followed by a cordial reconciliation between us and England, it would ensure the happiness and prosperity of both. the bag of wind, however, on which they are now riding, must be suffered to blow out before they will be able soberly to settle on their true bottom. if they adopt a course of friendship to us, the commerce of one hundred millions of people, which some now born will live to see here, will maintain them forever as a great unit of the European family. but if they go on checking, irritating, injuring and hostilizing us, they will force on us the motto *Carthago delenda est* and some Scipio Americanus will leave to posterity the problem of conjecturing where stood once the ancient and splendid city of London."

Jefferson, who described himself at about the same time to Caesar Augustus Rodney as being, at the age of three score and ten, "in habitual good health, great contentedness, enfeebled in body, impaired in memory, but without decay in my friendships," was as permeated as many a younger man with the new spirit of aggressive nationality that was abroad in the land.

11. *Another Corps of Discovery*

George Ticknor sailed for Europe April 16 on the Liverpool packet. Aboard was a group of friends and acquaintances who were taking advantage of the peace to make the crossing. There was the Samuel Perkins with whom Ticknor had traveled to Hartford and his charming wife, and the prodigious Edward Everett, and John Quincy Adams' two sons, George and John, both fresh from Harvard College.

The first news that reached the passengers, when the pilot came aboard in the Mersey, was that Bonaparte had broken out of Elba. Almost as disconcerting to George Ticknor as the fact that Napoleon was on the throne of France and that Europe was at war again were the political attitudes of Englishmen of wealth and scholarship to whom he had been furnished letters.

In Liverpool he dined with William Roscoe, whom he described as a "mild and philosophical man" who was "the Lorenzo of his native city." Roscoe had started life as a market gardener, "shouldering his father's potatoes to market." He had acquired wealth, was a banker, a Whig member of Parliament, a botanist, philanthropist and bibliophile, and renowned as the historian of the Medici. He was the center of a literary coterie which flourished in Liverpool. He shocked Ticknor, who still wore, in spite of his candid and inquiring mind, the blinders of all the Boston prejudices, by delivering himself at table of sentiments distressingly Jeffersonian. He declared that from the first he had been thoroughly opposed to the American war. For less offensive sentiments than this Ticknor had broken off friendly relations with Samuel Dexter.

Mr. Roscoe showed Ticknor his collection of the manuscripts of Robert Burns, love letters and Jacobite poems, and pieces that certainly wouldn't have been handed around in a Boston drawing room. For a man of sixtyfive Ticknor found his vivacity and enthusiasm very remarkable; his political opinions he could only deplore.

Ticknor was even more astonished when he stopped off in Hatton, at Roscoe's suggestion, to visit the famous Dr. Parr. Samuel Parr was a prodigious classical scholar. He had made a reputation as a schoolmaster. He had been a friend of the thoroughly Tory Dr. Johnson. Ticknor was a young man who knew how to please. Dr. Parr insisted that he stay to dinner, and in a conversation "full of declamation and sounding phrases . . . and dictatorial as an emperor's" emitted opinions on American politics which to Ticknor seemed quite incorrect.

Dr. Parr thought "we had ample cause for war, and seemed to have a favorable opinion of our principal men, such as Jefferson and Madison, and our late measures, such as Monroe's conscription plan, and the subject of taking Canada."

Parr was wont to boast of having voted for Wilkes in the Middlesex election. He declared that he turned on his heel in those days when anyone spoke of the Americans as rebels. According to Ticknor, Parr, who was a Church of England clergyman and vicar of Hatton, spoke with a lisp. Ticknor quoted him as declaring, "Thir, I would not think I'd done my duty if I went to bed any night without praying for the thuccess of Napoleon Bonaparte."

Ticknor arrived in London at the height of the season. He found liberal and literary circles in full reaction against the Tory government. Americans were popular just because they were Americans, and Ticknor, an eminently personable young man, was received everywhere with almost affectionate hospitality.

He found the city a little overwhelming. "I felt no uncommon elation," he wrote his father, "at finding myself in the world's metropolis. I only feel I am in the midst of a million of people whom I know not, and that I am driven forward by a crowd in whose objects and occupations and thought I have no care or interest."

He reassured his father as to the safety of traveling on the Continent. He had just called on Mr. Adams, recently appointed by President Madison minister to the court of St. James's. Mr. Adams arrived from Paris the same day Ticknor arrived from Liverpool and assured him he would meet with no hazard or embarrassment. Since the peace of Ghent American prestige was on the ascendant. "Americans are now treated," Adams told him, "with the most distinguished kindness and courtesy wherever they are known to be such."

Englishmen of all sorts and conditions opened their hearts to the attractive young Bostonian. He had breakfast with Sir Humphry Davy. The handsome Cornish scientist who, having started life as a poet and ballad collector, had won the applause of the Royal Society by his experiments with galvanism and chemistry, was still in his thirties but looked much younger. He had recently married an heiress and was at the height of his scientific fame. Ticknor was surprised to find him an enthusiastic angler. If he had to renounce fishing or philosophy Davy declared he hardly knew which he'd choose. He was just back from Italy which he pronounced, next to England, the finest country in the world.

The high point of Ticknor's London stay was his friendship with Lord Byron. He was introduced by William Gifford, the Tory satirist who edited the *Quarterly Review*. Ticknor had expected Byron to be deformed but, except for his feet, found him remarkably handsome. "I found his manners affable and gentle, the tones of his voice low and conciliating, his conversation gay, pleasant, and interesting in an uncommon degree."

Byron was twentyseven. He'd already published *English Bards and Scotch Reviewers* and *Childe Harold* and was the darling of the literary scene and of John Murray, the bookseller, who paid him a thousand guineas for a poem. He was half apologetic about *English Bards*, said he'd written it when he was very young and very angry, and that he'd made up with most of the men he had satirized. He was friends with Tom Moore and greatly admired Sir Walter Scott as a poet, a lawyer, a scholar, and a citizen.

Byron showed Ticknor his collection of Romaic books and rattled on about his travels in Greece and the Near East. He was interested in America, wanted to go there, asked a little quizzically whether Americans considered Joel Barlow to be their Homer, and exclaimed that Lewis and Clark were two of the men he most envied in the world.

Ticknor was a good listener. Byron talked about his early follies "with that simplicity which I have uniformly found to mark his character." Byron talked modestly about his own work and with "justice, generosity and discriminating praise" about the works of his contemporaries.

"After all," wrote Ticknor in his journal, "it is difficult for me to leave him, thinking either of his early follies or present eccentricities; for his manners are so gentle and his whole character so natural and unaffected that I have come from him with nothing but an indistinct though lively impression of the goodness and vivacity of his disposition."

Ticknor was so delighted with the noble poet he wasn't too much shocked by his political opinions. He happened to be calling on Lord Byron when a British political figure dashed into the room and said abruptly, " 'My lord, my lord, a great battle has been fought in the Low Countries, and Bonaparte is entirely defeated.'

" 'But is it true?' said Lord Byron, 'Is it true?'

" 'Yes my lord, it is certainly true. An aide-de-camp arrived in town last night; he has been in Downing Street this morning, and I have just seen him as he was going to Lady Wellington's. He says he thinks Bonaparte is in full retreat towards Paris.'

"After an instant's pause Lord Byron replied 'I am damned sorry for it'; and then after another short pause he added: 'I didn't know but I might live to see Lord Castlereagh's head on a pole.' "

CHAPTER IX

The More General Diffusion of Knowledge

1. Little Madison's Hour of Glory

Madison's last year in the presidency was as placid as Jefferson's last year had been stormy. He even attained an effective cabinet. Alexander Dallas performed miracles at the Treasury. Monroe had the War Office so well in hand that when Crawford came back from Paris to take it over Monroe was able to return to the Department of State. The Navy Department, in the hands of Benjamin W. Crowninshield, of the great shipbuilding and shipdesigning family from Salem and Boston, was securing appropriations to build new 74-gun ships and to keep its entire force cruising on the high seas. Dr. Rush's lawyer son Richard was not only conducting the Attorney General's office with distinction but was editing a notable collection of the laws of the United States from the beginning of the federal government. "Notwithstanding a thousand Faults and blunders, his Administration" —said John Adams summing up Madison's presidency for Jefferson —"has acquired more glory, and established more union, than all his three Predecessors, Washington, Adams and Jefferson, put together."

The peace of Ghent freed the United States from entanglement in European quarrels. When Napoleon's reappearance in Paris for the hundred days that ended in Waterloo and his exile to St. Helena had all Europe marching to the battlefield again, neither Republicans nor Federalists felt it was any of their business. Monroe put the new consensus of national opinion into words when he rose at a public dinner on the occasion of the Fourth of July 1815 with the toast: "American Neutrality; should Europe again be embroiled let our neutrality be founded on justice and maintained with firmness."

Though President Madison had no knack for the management of

men he understood diplomacy. He had stripped his administration of its ablest supporters in Washington to furnish a firstrate mission to negotiate the peace. Now he had John Quincy Adams in London and Albert Gallatin in Paris. He wanted to send James A. Bayard to Russia but the poor Chevalier was carried ashore desperately ill on his return from Ghent and died a few days later.

American prestige was on the rise. As soon as trade was resumed and the pentup flood of American products, cotton, tobacco, grain, lumber, was released into commercial channels, specie began to move out of England into American banks. British manufactured goods, in return, flooded the American market. Though the British insisted on retaining the right of impressment, the officers of the Royal Navy were instructed to treat American ships with courtesy and tact. The Duke of Wellington himself called at the American legation in Paris, before Crawford sailed home, to congratulate him on the peace.

In the fall of 1815 advices from the Mediterranean added new luster to the reputation of American fighting ships. Stephen Decatur, who had the misfortune to be forced to strike his flag on the frigate *President* to a pair of British cruisers about the time the war ended, retrieved his reputation by capturing the finest frigate the Dey of Algiers possessed. The Barbary pirates had been taking advantage of American involvement with England to seize American merchant ships and to hold their crews for ransom. They were now bludgeoned into a treaty under the most favorable terms ever for the United States.

In Europe Americans could indeed hold up their heads. At home writers in the newspapers were already hailing an era of good feelings.

2. *Would You Live Your Life Over Again?*

At Monticello Jefferson was engaged in urgent projects that kept him chained to his desk writing, writing, writing in his plain squarish hand on the polygraph. Amid the epistolary drudgery he so often complained of his correspondence with John Adams was pure pleasure.

They fell into a discussion of European history as they saw it in retrospect. The reasonable eighteenth century order they had both first known had backslid into the tyrannies and massacres of the Terror and of the Napoleonic wars. To Jefferson it seemed a return to the days of the Borgias.

"You must have observed," he wrote of what was beginning to seem a golden age, "as I thought I did, that those who administered the governments, of the greater powers at least, had a respect to faith, and considered the dignity of their government as involved in it's integrity."

"It would seem," replied Adams, "that human Reason and human Conscience, though I believe there are such things, are not a Match for human Passions, human Imaginations and human Enthusiasm. . . . You ask how has it happened that all Europe has acted on the principle 'that power was Right.' I know not what Answer to give you, but this, that Power always sincerely conscientiously de très bon Foi, believes itself Right. Power always thinks it has a great Soul, and vast Views, beyond the comprehension of the Weak; and that it is doing God service, when it is violating all his Laws. . . . Power must never be trusted without a check."

On March 2, 1816, with that bubbling youthful spontaneity he never lost, Adams broke out: "I cannot be serious! I am about to write you the most frivolous letter you ever read. Would you go back to your Cradle and live over again Your 70 years? I believe You would return me a New England Answer, by asking me another question 'Would you live your 80 years over again?' "

"You ask," Jefferson answered, "if I would agree to live my 70 or rather 73 years over again? To which I say, Yea. I think with you it is a good world on the whole, that it has been framed on a principle of benevolence, and more pleasure than pain dealt out to us. . . . my temperament is sanguine, I steer my bark with Hope in the head, leaving Fear astern."

Adams threw his next letter into the form of an imaginary dialogue between himself and his friend. He too answered yes: "I can speak only for one. I have had more comfort than distress, more pleasure than paine, ten to one, no, if you please, a hundred to one." . . . "How valiant you are!" he has Jefferson exclaim. "Aye," answers Adams, ". . . but who can tell what will become of his Bravery when his Flesh and his heart shall fail him?"

3. Unresolved Problems

Behind the thoughts of both men was the knowledge that death was not far off. Before that moment came Jefferson had an appalling amount of unfinished business to dispose of. Two of the great projects of his early life had been the gradual abolition of slavery and the establishment of a system of public education for Virginia.

During the war his conscience had been stirred on the subject of slavery by a correspondence with Madison's private secretary, Edward Coles. The Coles boys of Enniscorthy in Albemarle County had been raised, like so many of the more promising sons of the neighboring planters, to look up to Jefferson as their teacher and friend. They had been students at the unending informal seminar Jefferson conducted at Monticello. Isaac Coles, the elder brother, had served as his presidential secretary after Meriwether Lewis went off to the West.

Edward and John, when they visited John Adams on a trip to New England, had helped Dr. Rush bring about the reconciliation that meant so much to both old men. Now, while Isaac, who was in the militia, was forwarding long accounts to Monticello of the imbecility of Mr. Madison's generals, Edward was writing Jefferson earnest letters urging him to take a stand for abolition. As soon as the fighting stopped, wrote Edward Coles, he was determined to take his own slaves to Ohio, find them public lands, and set them free.

It was hard for Jefferson to find proper words to answer young Coles's challenge. He still believed, as he had written in his *Notes on Virginia*, that the continuation of slavery was unthinkable. Slavery destroyed the moral fiber of both slave and slavedriver. "Indeed," he had written, "I tremble for my country when I reflect that God is just; that His justice cannot sleep forever; that considering numbers, nature and natural means only, a revolution by the wheel of fortune; an exchange of situation is among possible events. . . . the Almighty has no attribute which can take sides with us in such a contest."

Over the years he had tried to promote his program for gradual emancipation by establishing a date after which all children of slaves would be born free. Now he had to admit his ill success. Eli Whitney's cotton gin had made slavery profitable in the vast cotton plantations of the far South. In Virginia, as a result of the deepening agricultural crisis, slaves were becoming the farmers' chief source of income.

By inference young Coles was asking him to lead the way by emancipating his own slaves. There were two reasons why Jefferson could not meet this challenge. First, his creditors would never allow it. His slaves furnished the best part of the security for his enormous debts. Second, he was throwing all the energy of his last years into the struggle to set up a system of public education in Virginia. If he added outraged slaveowners to the already virulent opposition his plans for education would never get through the legislature.

Jefferson answered Coles that he was too old to undertake such a task. It was like "bidding old Priam to buckle on the armor of Hector. . . . No, I have outlived the generation with which mutual labors and perils begat mutual confidence and influence—this enterprise is for the young—for those who can follow it up, and bear it through to it's consummation."

He reiterated his belief in gradual emancipation followed by resettlement of the freed Negroes outside of the confines of the United States. He begged Coles to give up his plan of moving out of Virginia. Young men like him were needed there. He hoped that "on the contrary you will come forward in the public councils, become the missionary of this doctrine, truly Christian, insinuate and inculcate it, softly but steadily, through the medium of writing and conversation, associate others in your labors, and when the phalanx is formed, bring on and press the proposition perseveringly, until it's accomplishment."

Jefferson insisted to Coles that emancipation was inevitable. He found the laws against the slave trade recently put through the British Parliament very encouraging. He showed a flash of the old sanguine spirit. "No good measure was ever proposed which, if duly pursued, failed to prevail in the end."

4. The Pleasures of Albemarle

The summer of 1815 was one of Jefferson's happiest. The war was over. There was a good market for his crops. The twentythree thousand dollars he received from Congress for his library had relieved the pressure from his creditors. His oldest grandson, Thomas Jefferson Randolph, who was as tall as he was and broader of build, was old enough to take over most of the drudgery of overseeing his farms.

He was busy at his drafting board sketching out the first tentative plans for an "academical village." At the same time he completed an elaborate design for a new house his friend Randolph Harrison was building at Ampthill. Furthermore he was unusually active in mechanical inventions. The family dated from that summer his contriving of a convertible leather carriage top and of a machine to crush hemp for the extraction of the fiber.

He found Albemarle County society unusually agreeable. The Madisons, now that the President dared take more time off from his fever-stricken capital, made visits to Monticello. Jefferson's grandchildren always remembered the long day's drive to Montpelier and the stop at noon for a picnic by a cool woodland spring when the family returned these visits by repairing en masse to the Madisons'. Monroe turned up occasionally at nearby Ashlawn. A new friend, a Portuguese botanist who arrived with letters of introduction from Humboldt and Du Pont de Nemours, was a particular delight. Jefferson declared that the Abbé Correa de Serra was the most learned and agreeable man he had ever met.

José Francisco Correa de Serra, a Brazilian born, was the founder of the Portuguese Academy of Sciences. Troubles with the Inquisition had forced him to flee to England where he became an intimate of Sir Joseph Banks and a fellow of the Royal Society. After forming a part of the scientific coterie that revolved around Humboldt in Paris during the Napoleonic era, he had come to America to investigate the New World flora. As well as being one of the foremost botanists in Europe, he was Portugal's leading historian. At sixtyfour he retained the curiosity and enthusiasm of youth. Jefferson found him indeed a kindred spirit.

Jefferson's health was so good that fall he was able to go on a five-day excursion in the mountains, with the abbé and the son of his old friend Dr. Gilmer, to measure the height of the Peaks of Otter. Francis Gilmer was one of those scholarly young men with scientific interests whom Jefferson had the knack of turning into disciples. Jefferson had been practicing with his theodolite all summer, on Monticello and the adjoining hills. Now, with young Gilmer's help, he had the satisfaction of establishing the exact altitude of the two rocky pinnacles back of Roanoke which the local country people had judged much higher than they actually were.

Although President Madison, who had made such an effort in his younger days to put Jefferson's bill "For the More General Diffusion of Knowledge" through the Virginia legislature, kept loyally urging the establishment of a national university in each of his annual messages to Congress, he failed, as Jefferson had, to convince the federal legislators. Now Jefferson, who knew that his years were running out, determined to drop everything else and to devote every spark of influence he had left to setting up a great educational institution for his home state.

His first thought, during his talks and walks with the abbé, was how to attract him to his college. The abbé declined a professorship, but he did sketch out a course in botany and furnish detailed instructions for establishing a botanical garden. In the following year Jefferson was delighted to receive the news that the abbé had been appointed minister to the United States by the royal court of Portugal. At least he would remain in the country.

All his political life Jefferson had been trying to induce learned foreigners to settle in the United States. As Vice President he had stepped into a hornet's nest by espousing the cause of Joseph Priestley and his associate Thomas Cooper, the pioneers in chemistry and physics who were being excoriated by the Federalists as infidels and Jacobins. When he heard a rumor that the professors of the College of Geneva, whose liberties were threatened by the expanding French, were planning to emigrate in a body, he offered them the hospitality of Virginia.

He was convinced that the Republic would fail without universal education in republican principles. Through endless discouragements he bided his time, collecting, from every scholar he came into contact with, additions to his archive of plans for education.

5. A Man to Rely on

During his second term as President he hit upon just the man he needed to help him. Joseph Carrington Cabell called on him in Washington. Cabell was a boyhood friend of Isaac Coles. Then twentyeight, he had just returned from three years of travel and study in Europe where he became an enthusiast for the system of education for small children of Johann Heinrich Pestalozzi, whose school he visited in Switzerland. Joseph C. was one of the very capable descendants of the lively Dr. Cabell who first settled Nelson County. His brother William was governor of Virginia. As soon as he reached home he became a member of the famous grand jury that brought the indictments against Aaron Burr. He was well connected, energetic, tactful, and persistent.

Cabell went to Jefferson with a plan to reform William and Mary. Since his friend Bishop Madison's death, Jefferson had lost interest in William and Mary. For him Williamsburg was lost in Tidewater apathy, in chills and fevers, and in the doctrines of John Randolph's quids. Exercising his extraordinary ability to charm younger men, he convinced Cabell that the place for the university was the healthy Piedmont section, where people had sound republican principles and from which they both hailed. He urged Cabell to seek election to the legislature.

Cabell served two years in the House of Delegates and many more in the state Senate and virtually gave up his life to the Jeffersonian causes of local selfgovernment, free public education, and a great university for Virginia.

As soon as Jefferson shook himself loose from the trammels of the presidency he turned his attention to promoting an academy or grammar school for Albemarle County. By the fall of 1814 this had turned into a more ambitious project named Central College. Funds were pledged, and Peter Carr, Jefferson's favorite nephew, became chairman of the Board of Trustees. Listed as members were the names of Jefferson, Madison, and Monroe, of Jefferson's friend General Cocke, the temperance advocate, whom he helped plan his uniquely elegant dwelling house at Bremo, and of course Joseph C. Cabell.

Jefferson took the occasion to summarize his present theories in a letter to Carr which was published a year or so later, about the time of Carr's untimely death, in the Richmond *Enquirer*. He insisted again that every child should have at least three years of free primary education. After that Jefferson was now willing to see his fellow citizens divided into what he called the learned and the laboring.

On graduating from primary school where he would learn reading, writing, and arithmetic the laboring youth was to go to work on the farm or to be apprenticed in the crafts and trades. The learned were to continue on to secondary school. There Jefferson made another division. He separated those who would have to make a living in the professions from "the wealthy, who possessing independent fortunes, may aspire to conducting the affairs of the nation." In the early part of the course they were to study together the three branches of language, mathematics, and philosophy before being separated into professional schools for law, medicine, and agriculture.

Jefferson made provision for the teaching of the deaf, dumb, and blind. Architecture and landscape gardening were not to be neglected. There were to be free night schools for teaching the practical arts and crafts, which he grouped under the heading "technical philosophy," to young men who had to work for their living during the day.

For a beginning, the trustees of Central College could only see the funds in sight to support four professors. One should teach languages, belles lettres, rhetoric, and history, another mathematics and physics; a third zoology, botany, chemistry, and mineralogy; a fourth philosophy, in which were included ethics, government, and political economy. Jefferson expected his professors to be as manysided as he was.

6. The Years of the Orators

In this last decade of his life Jefferson was fixing all his attention on his projects for Virginia. With the defeat of his soninlaw Jack Eppes, who had been chairman of the House Committee on Ways and Means, by John Randolph for the Fourteenth Congress he had lost whatever direct influence he had ever had on Capitol Hill. For a dozen years Congress, with the exception of occasional revolts of small groups of legislators, had been subordinate to the executive. Now the House of Representatives was taking the center of the Washington stage. The debates on the floor were being listened to for their own sake as were the debates in the British Commons.

The era of oratory was beginning. As the earnestness faded out of party convictions attention focused on the sayings and doings of political leaders. As Speaker of the House, the voluble and magnetic Henry Clay personified the impatient ambitions of the western frontier. Daniel Webster, first from New Hampshire and later from Boston, spoke, out of the sculptural dignity of his massive head and broad brow, for the bankers and manufacturers of New England. John Randolph, more trenchant and truculent than ever, propounded the strict-construction views of agrarian and slaveholding Virginia. John C. Calhoun of South Carolina, still a fervent nationalist and an advocate of internal improvements, charmed the public galleries with the musical and speculative expression of his thoughts.

Among elder members there were the dignified William Pinkney of Maryland, Timothy Pickering of Massachusetts, indestructible at seventy, and Samuel Smith, the opinionated Baltimore merchant.

These were all highly individual and articulate men, driven more by their own ambitions than by political convictions. Visitors crowded the galleries of the temporary Hall of Representatives, more to listen to the ringing cadences of their favorite speaker than from any passion for the matter in hand.

The Republican majority of the Fourteenth Congress went to work with a will to strengthen the national administration in a manner which would have delighted Alexander Hamilton. Appropriations were made for a standing army and to increase the navy. Indiana and Mississippi were admitted to statehood. To protect American manufactures western Republicans joined with New England Federalists in levying a tax of twentyfive per cent and more on imported woolens and other merchandise. With the hope of remedying the confusion of the currency, Calhoun introduced a bill to charter a second Bank of the United States. To the surprise of his colleagues Daniel Webster proved his friendship for the commercial banks by delivering himself of a fulldress oration in opposition to the measure. It passed nevertheless and, at least temporarily, resulted in better order in the national finances. Specie payments were resumed within a year.

So confident were the members of the Fourteenth Congress that they had deserved well of the country that they put through a bill, known as the Compensation Act, setting the salary for members of Congress at fifteen hundred dollars a year. Up to then they were supposed to subsist on an allowance of six dollars a day while in session, to which was added another six dollars' traveling expenses for every twenty miles a man had to traverse between his constituency and Washington.

To their amazement the Compensation Act aroused a storm from one end of the country to the other. It was denounced by New England town meetings and by the Massachusetts legislature. Grand juries in Vermont and Georgia brought in pronouncements against it. Local conventions registered their violent opposition. Many of the men who had voted for it were defeated in the fall elections. Even Henry Clay, the most popular man in Congress, had trouble getting himself reelected in Kentucky.

When the houses reassembled to hear James Madison's last message in December 1816, and to receive the confirmation of James Monroe's election to the presidency in his stead, congressmen fell over each other in the scramble to repeal the hated law. Turning to more constructive endeavors, both houses passed a clearcut Navigation Act which imposed the same restrictions on foreign vessels which their nations should impose on American shipping, and a Neutrality Act which authorized the collectors of the customs to seize any ship "manifestly built for warlike purposes against the commerce of any friendly state." These acts did much to establish a legal code for maritime commerce during the remainder of the century.

Their last efforts were directed towards setting up a fund to be used to implement Gallatin's and Jefferson's plan for a network of roads and canals to tie the states together. Party lines had been so far obliterated that Calhoun and Pickering concurred in its passage. To everybody's astonishment, since several passages in his messages to Congress were interpreted as favoring such a measure, Madison's last official act was to veto the bill for internal improvements.

7. Qualms on Consolidation

Madison's veto reflected a change in the climate of opinion at Montpelier and Monticello. During Jefferson's presidency, under the influence of Gallatin's eminently pragmatic mind, Madison had gone along with the theory that the public good came first. The Constitution might be strained a little in an emergency. At that Jefferson had wanted a constitutional amendment to justify the Louisiana Purchase, and hoped for another to authorize his program of internal improvements. Now both Jefferson and Madison agreed, in their earnest private consultations, that the time had come to put a limit to the accretion of federal powers.

Though Madison, ever since writing his essay on the subject in *The Federalist Papers*, had supported the interpretive powers of the Supreme Court, he could not help but be affected by the shocked dismay which Jefferson shared with the great mass of Virginia Republicans, at that court's decision in the case of Martin vs. Hunter's Lessee.

Jefferson, always ready to believe the worst of his cousin John Marshall, couldn't help but feel that the Marshall family stood to benefit financially by the decision. John Marshall to be sure had disqualified himself and allowed the opinion to be written by Joseph Story, a brilliant young Massachusetts Republican lawyer whom Madison had appointed to the court. Though the words were Story's, the doctrine was Marshall's.

The case arose from the longcontinued efforts of a syndicate of real estate speculators, in which James M. Marshall, one of the Chief Justice's brothers, was heavily interested, to establish their title to a tract acquired from heirs of the Fairfax family, who still claimed ownership by royal grant of great regions in the Northern Neck. This particular tract was in Frederick County, where the Marshall interests won their first round in the local court. When the case was appealed, Judge Spencer Roane of the Virginia Court of Appeals ruled against James Marshall and his associates on the theory that the sovereign state of Virginia had extinguished the Fairfax title by confiscation during the Revolutionary War.

Spencer Roane was the Virginia judge whom Jefferson had hoped to appoint Chief Justice, if his plan of ridding the bench of Federalists had succeeded during his first administration. He was considered the most eminent Republican jurist in the nation.

In an opinion delivered on March 15, 1813, Justice Story overruled Judge Roane. His argument was that the Fairfax title to lands they had not yet sold had been reestablished under the Jay treaty. This decision was greeted with indignant protest by Ritchie's Richmond *Enquirer* and by most of the state's Republican leaders. At the next term of the Court of Appeals, the Virginia judges, with Spencer Roane in the lead, refused to accept the·judgment of the Supreme Court, claiming lack of jurisdiction under the Constitution.

James Marshall returned the case to the Supreme Court on a writ of error. Again John Marshall refrained from sitting. Justice Story in due time delivered an opinion, soon to become famous, in which he expounded the powers of the supreme bench as court of last appeal from the state courts. The Supreme Court was paramount under the Constitution. "It is the opinion of the whole court that the judgement of the Court of Appeals, rendered on the mandate of this cause be reversed." The case was returned to the local court in Winchester where the Marshall interests reestablished their title to the land.

The decision so intensified the revulsion of the Virginia Republicans against the Supreme Court that their representatives in Congress took the lead in cutting a raise in salary for the justices out of the Compensation Act. The writings of John Taylor of Caroline, the theorist of the states' rights wing of the Virginia Republicans, became gospel in many a Virginia household.

John Taylor of Hazelwood near Port Royal was ten years younger than Jefferson. Left an orphan when a tiny child, he had been reared by Edmund Pendleton, the great conservative jurist of the old school who was Jefferson's colleague on the commission to revise the Virginia legal code in 1776. Taylor grew up an ardent and enthusiastic farmer. He corresponded with Jefferson on the rotation of crops and every agricultural topic. He was a great man for green manures. He served in the House of Delegates, and for two terms in the United States Senate, wrote voluminously for the newspapers, and became the dogmatist of the extreme agrarian theory of government. Long after Jefferson had come to admit that manufacturing was as important as agriculture for the prosperity and progress of the nation, Taylor clung to the thesis that a farm economy was the only proper foundation for republican institutions.

Jefferson's national patriotism and his long experience with government ended by convincing him that, in times of stress and danger, the whole nation was more important than its parts, but John Taylor entrenched himself in the localist view. He was for Caroline County against the state and for the state of Virginia against the federal government. In 1814 he published a disquisition which found eager acceptance among Virginians.

Taylor had started his *Enquiry into the Principles and Policies of the Government of the United States* twenty years before in an effort to disprove what he felt were the aristocratic conclusions of John Adams' *Defense of the Constitutions of the United States.* In its final form his treatise became a plea for a balance of powers between the federal government and the states and for a careful division between the legislative, the executive, and the judicial arms. He considered banks and bank paper an abomination. With the establishment of a new national bank he saw the federal government entrenching itself as "an aristocracy of paper and patronage."

Adams read the book first. When he wrote about it to Jefferson he showed himself more pleased than not to have his half forgotten writings brought again into the public view. "The Conclusion of the whole is that an Aristocracy of Bank Paper, is as bad as the Nobility of France or England. I, most assuredly will not contravert this point. . . . I thought my Books as well as myself were forgotten. But behold! I am become a great Man in my expiring moments."

Jefferson had not read it yet. There was no bookstore in Albemarle County and he had not seen any notice of it in the papers. He replied that in John Taylor's previous writings he had found some good things, "but so involved in quaint, in farfetched, affected, mystical conciepts, and flimsy theories, that who can take the trouble of getting at them?"

Returning from a two weeks' trip to Poplar Forest, he found a copy of Taylor's book waiting for him at Monticello. As soon as he had read the thick volume through he wrote John Taylor that he saw in it "much matter for profound reflection." After this there was no more talk of Taylor's "flimsy theories" in Jefferson's correspondence. Taylor's argument caused him to redefine the term "republic" for his own satisfaction. "Purely and simply it means a government by its citizens in mass, acting directly and personally, according to rules established by the majority." He admitted that a pure republic was not practical for a larger area than a New England township.

8. *Selfgovernment Begins at Home*

Talk was beginning among Jefferson's friends and adherents of the need for a new constitution for Virginia. Taylor's book tended to crystallize many of Jefferson's unresolved musings on the subject. As always the fullest selfgovernment was his aim. "The purest republican feature in the government of our own State," he wrote Taylor, "is the House of Representatives. the Senate is equally so the first year, less the second, and so on. the executive still less, because not chosen by the people directly. the Judiciary seriously antirepublican, because for life; and the national arm wielded, as you observe, by military leaders, irresponsible but to themselves. add to this the vicious constitution of our county courts (to whom the justice, the executive administration, the taxation, police, the military appointments of the county and nearly all our daily concerns are confided) self-appointed, self-continued, holding their authorities for life, and with the impossibility of breaking in on the perpetual succession of any faction once possessed of the bench. they are in truth, the executive, the judiciary, and the military of their respective counties, and the sum of the counties makes the State. . . . one half of our brethren who fight and pay taxes, are excluded, like Helots, from the rights of representation, as if society were instituted for the soil, and not for the men inhabiting it."

Taylor replied with a defense of the county courts. Jefferson admitted that they did a great deal for very small pay. "It is their self-appointment I wish to correct," he wrote in a second letter, "to find some means of breaking up a Cabal, when such a one gets possession of the bench. when this takes place it becomes the most afflicting of tyrannies, because it's powers are so various, and exercised on everything most immediately around us. and how many instances have you and I known of these monopolies of county administration: I know a county in which a particular family (a numerous one) got possession of the bench, and for a whole generation, never admitted a man on it who was not of it's clan or connection. I know a county now of 1500. militia of which 60. are federalists. it's court is of 30. members of which 20. are federalists. . . . the remaining 1440, free, fighting, & paying citizens are governed by men neither of their choice nor confidence & without hope of relief. . . . this solecism may be called anything but republican, and ought undoubtedly to be corrected."

The more Jefferson studied the society around him the more he had to admit to himself that the selfgoverning republic to which he had dedicated his life was far from being established even in his own beloved Virginia. The week before he wrote Taylor he had written Samuel Kercheval, who was trying to get his support for the calling of a constitutional convention for the state—after the usual disclaimer of any participation in the politics of the moment—pointing out the unrepublican formation of the county governments as one of the weaknesses that stemmed from the Virginia constitution of 1776. In this letter he again put forward his project to divide the counties into selfgoverning wards, which would have charge of local courts, schools, and police. Thereby every citizen would become "an acting member of the government." Again he described the New England townships as "the wisest invention ever devised by the wit of men for the perfect exercise of self-government.

"The true foundation of republican government is the equal right of every citizen, in his person and property, and in their management." To the framers of a new constitution for Virginia he recommended: "1. General suffrage. 2. Equal representation in the legislature. 3. An executive chosen by the people. 4. Judges elective or amovable. 5. Justices, jurors and sheriffs elective. 6. Ward divisions and 7. Periodical amendments to the constitution."

He ended by begging Kercheval so to use his suggestions "as to preserve me from the gridiron of the public papers."

From the cool reappraisal of disinterested old age Jefferson could see only too clearly that the federated Republic as a whole was no more than Virginia on the path to selfgovernment. He believed fervently that the application of proper principles would bring amendment. For Virginia he hoped that equal representation of all free citizens would restore government to the people. The people must understand how to operate it. Everything depended on the education of a new generation. There was still fight left in him for one more struggle for that education.

9. *The Bank Bubble*

In so far as the state's relation to Washington went, his distaste for John Marshall's arrogation of powers to the Supreme Court was swinging him more and more in the direction of the uncompromising dogmas of John Taylor of Caroline. He agreed with John Taylor, too, on the subject of paper currency. In spite of a growing agricultural depression, the business boom that had set in at the end of the war still continued. The inflation of the currency favored all sorts of paper speculations. Jefferson, like John Taylor, laid the speculative fever to the evil influence of the banks.

Writing Charles Yancey, who represented Buckingham County in the legislature, to ask his patronage for Central College, which Jefferson recommended "as a germ from which a great tree may spread itself," he exploded: "We are under the bank bubble, as England was under the South Sea bubble, France under the Mississippi bubble, and as every nation is liable to be, under whatever bubble, design or delusion may puff up in moments when off their guard. We are now taught to believe that legerdemain tricks upon paper can produce as solid wealth as hard labor in the earth. it is vain for common sense to urge that *nothing* can produce *nothing*; that it is an idle dream to believe in a philosopher's stone which is to turn everything into gold, and to redeem man from the original sentence of his Maker, 'in the sweat of his brow shall he eat his bread.'"

Jefferson viewed inflation with foreboding. "Confidence is already on the totter," he wrote Yancey, "and everyone now handles this paper as if playing at Robin's alive. . . . the bubble may burst from one moment to the other."

10. *The Secrets of an Old Virginia Manor House*

Jefferson's own private anxieties were such as might well distract his mind from his apprehensions for the common weal. The rebuilding of his gristmill and sawmill and the repairs to the long canal that supplied them with water power soon ate up the money he had received for his library. He became involved in a tiresome litigation over the use of the Rivanna River with a company that was trying to establish barge transportation up to Charlottesville. His letterbooks filled up with explanations to various creditors that as the result of a series of disastrous crop years it was impossible for him to pay amortization and interest as they came due.

1816 was "the year without a summer." In explaining why he would have to delay repayment of a sum he owed to his old friend Mazzei's estate, Jefferson described the past three seasons: "few farmers have made enough of other things to pay for their bread; and the present year has been equally afflicting for their crop of wheat by such an inundation of the Hessian fly as was never seen before. a great part of my own crop has not yeilded seed. whole fields do not give an ear for every square foot; & many turned their cattle on the wheat to make something of it as pasture." "We have had the most extraordinary year of cold and drought, ever in the history of America," he told Gallatin in Paris. "The summer too, has been as cold as a moderate winter. in every State north of this there has been frost in every month in the year; in this State we had none in June and July, but those in August killed much corn over the mountains." He feared the farmers would not harvest enough for their own food. "My anxieties on this subject are the greater because I remember the deaths which the drought of 1755 produced from want of food."

Family worries compounded Jefferson's financial anxieties. The clash of personalities disturbed the halcyon peace he had dreamed of for Monticello during his years of public service. Though a man of some intellectual brilliance, who sympathized with most of Jefferson's opinions and interests, Thomas Mann Randolph was impossible to live with. As Edmund Bacon, Jefferson's overseer, used to say, "The Randolphs were all strange people."

Bacon claimed that Thomas Mann was just as eccentric as John Randolph. Though full of inventive ideas about agriculture he was proving incapable of making a living for his family. He continued recklessly to pile up debts. After the war he came home more moody than ever, having resigned his commission in the U. S. Army in a

quarrel with Secretary of War Armstrong. He lost heavily in a speculation on flour. He was coming bitterly to resent his position as a
dependent in the Jefferson household.

Jefferson's daughter Martha and her children were the mainstay of
his life. His other grandchild, Frank Eppes, whom Bacon described
as "a fine little fellow," was often at Monticello. Bacon remembered
Mrs. Randolph as being just like her father. "Few such women ever
lived. I never saw her equal." Bacon reported that he never remembered seeing either one of them out of temper. She was nearly as
tall as her father, had the same clear bright complexion, the same
blue eyes, and the same habit of humming over her work. She had
six daughters and five sons. Thomas Jefferson Randolph, his grandfather's favorite, the eldest boy who was known as Jeff, was taking
Thomas Mann's place in the management of the plantations. Anne,
the eldest daughter, was married to a handsome heartylooking man
named Charles Bankhead who turned out a drunkard.

Bacon vividly remembered Bankhead's violence. "I have seen him
ride his horse into the bar-room at Charlottesville and get a drink of
liquor. I have seen his wife run from him when he was drunk and
hide in a potato-hole to get out of danger." Bacon remembered Anne
as being, like her mother, "a perfectly lovely woman, a Jefferson in
temper."

Bankhead was dangerous when he was drunk. "One night he was
very drunk and made a great disturbance, because Burwell"—the
butler—"who kept the keys would not give him any more brandy.
Mrs. Randolph could not manage him, and she sent for me. She
would never call on Mr. Randolph at such a time. He was so excit-
able. But he heard the noise in the dining-room and rushed in to see
what was the matter. He entered the room just as I did, and Bankhead,
thinking he was Burwell, began to curse him. Seizing an iron poker
that was standing by the fireplace he knocked him down as quick as
I ever saw a bullock fall. The blow peeled the skin off one side of his
forehead and face and he bled terribly."

Thomas Mann Randolph had an ungovernable temper. According
to Bacon, "his mind became shattered and he pretty much lost his
reason before he died." Suspicion of his eldest son became obsessive. "I have seen him cane his son Jeff after he was a grown man,"
Bacon reported. "Jeff made no resistance, but got away from him
as soon as he could."

Such was the awe in which every member of the family held
Thomas Jefferson that they conspired to shield him from the ugly
passions that smoldered under the surface of domestic life at Monticello: but he was early aware that all was not well between Thomas
Mann Randolph and Jeff.

During the last years of Jefferson's life, Jeff Randolph was his right arm. It was Jeff who carried out his instructions on the farms and was his messenger to political friends and adherents. Their affection was mutual.

The granddaughters and the younger children were a continual pleasure. Jefferson delighted in romping with the little ones on the lawn. Cornelia, one of the younger girls, early showed a knack for sketching. She became so proficient with her pencil that he let her do some elevations for his designs for the University of Virginia.

11. *Planning the Academical Village*

Jefferson could never be for a moment idle. In letters to friends he laid his comparative good health and mental vigor to the work he put in on his two hobbyhorses, as he called them, architecture and the university. In the spring of 1817, when he was seventyfour years old, he went to work in earnest to draft designs for the "academical village" he had been planning for so many years.

He had in mind something on the order of Louis XVI's château at Marly, where the main building was flanked by arcades round three sides of a grassy square. The arcades linked a series of smaller detached pavilions into a unified design. Jefferson had reason to remember Marly with pleasure. He first visited it when he was minister to France during his giddy gust of sightseeing with the fascinating Maria Cosway. He already had a rough sketch of buildings round a square.

During the previous winter Joseph Cabell had managed, after a long struggle, to put a charter for Central College through the legislature. The appropriation was insufficient but Jefferson decided to go ahead anyway. The time would never be more propitious. His good friend Wilson Cary Nicholas, whose daughter Jeff Randolph was soon to marry, was governor of Virginia. He had a number of friends besides Cabell in the Assembly.

Early in 1817 he started looking for a suitable piece of land on the outskirts of Charlottesville. When the first full meeting of the Board of Visitors, which included Madison and President Monroe, was held at Monticello on May 5, Jefferson was able to report the purchase of two hundred acres from a man named Perry.

With the help of Bacon and Dinsmore, his Irish cabinetmaker and joiner, Jefferson laid out the enclosure himself. He had Bacon hire ten hands to dig the foundations. Years later Bacon remembered how they rode down to Charlottesville and bought a ball of twine at Davy Isaacs' store and how Dinsmore cut pegs from some old shingles and how Mr. Jefferson stuck in the first peg and measured off the distances with his pocket rule.

The lay of the land forced Jefferson to change the original plan from a square to a long rectangle. He was planning separate pavilions for the professors' residences and lecture halls with rows of monastic cells for the students in between. He wanted the pavilions to represent various classical styles so that they could be used as models of the orders for architectural lectures. In laying out the rectangle he took advantage of a gentle landscape of green hills and valleys which would be seen, framed by the colonnades, through the open southern end.

As was his wont he sought the best advice he could find. Right after the Board of Visitors voted to go ahead at once on one pavilion and ten dormitories on either side of it, Jefferson wrote William Thornton in Washington asking for his suggestions.

Thornton, an ingenious and imaginative amateur, whose practical sense was somewhat erratic, was the author of the first plan for the United States Capitol which had delighted George Washington and which Jefferson had so much trouble in realizing with the help of the accomplished French architect, Stephen Hallet. Jefferson had appointed Thornton to the Patent Office, and during the late war had leased him his Natural Bridge to drop lead shot from in the manufacture of bullets for the army. Thornton wrote back promptly suggesting columns instead of piers for the colonnades, and porticoes over the arches.

Wanting more specific suggestions, Jefferson wrote Thornton's bitter rival, Benjamin Henry Latrobe. During the war Latrobe had been engaged with the Livingston-Fulton concern in a speculation in steamboat building in Pittsburgh, which in the litigation that followed Fulton's death turned out, for Latrobe at least, a financial disaster. Monroe invited him back to Washington to superintend the restoration of the public buildings.

Latrobe at fiftythree was at the height of his powers. He was the only architect in America with a thoroughgoing education in the craft. He was a skillful and original watercolorist, and a man of great classical learning. Though born in England he was educated in Germany and traveled widely in Italy and France in his formative years. His father was a Moravian schoolteacher with a taste for literature and music who moved in Samuel Johnson's and Dr. Burney's circle of scholars and conversationalists. His father intended young Latrobe for the Moravian ministry but instead he studied engineering with John Smeaton, the builder of the Eddystone Light, and took up architectural drafting in the office of Samuel Pepys Cockerell. Cockerell, in reaction against the spindly Pompeian designs of the Adam brothers, found a point of departure for his neoclassic style in the massive forms of the original Greek buildings. Under his influence Latrobe executed the plans for an English country house, Hammerwood Lodge, in which he used porches of primitive Doric columns reminiscent of Paestum.

Latrobe had every prospect for a brilliant career in England when the death in childbirth of his first wife disrupted everything. He was left at twentynine with two small children. His republican sympathies were beginning to raise difficulties in his way in Pitt's England. As his mother was an American, related to the Philadelphia Rittenhouses, he decided to seek his fortune in Virginia.

Arriving in Norfolk in the spring of 1796, he found that Jefferson's Virginia state Capitol had opened the way for his practice of the Hellenic style. He immediately started designing dwelling houses and public buildings. His greatest work in Richmond was the penitentiary, built according to the specifications which Jefferson had outlined for the new penology. Latrobe and Jefferson seem to have first met in Fredericksburg when Jefferson was Vice President, about the time of Latrobe's visit to George Washington at Mount Vernon, which he commemorated with some lighthearted watercolors of the mansion.

As soon as Jefferson was settled in the presidency he called Latrobe, then established in Philadelphia where he'd married the daughter of a New Jersey merchant and furnished the city with its first system of waterworks, to Washington to design the drydocks he projected for the preservation of navy ships when they were not in use. When Congress failed to appropriate the money for the drydock project Jefferson appointed Latrobe Surveyor of the Public Buildings.

Together, amid a great deal of half bitter, half friendly controversy in which Jefferson complained of Latrobe's extravagance and Latrobe complained that Jefferson's ideas were more Roman than Greek, they worked on the Hall of Representatives, which became the handsomest feature of the Capitol before the fire, and on the President's house.

In spite of many a difference of opinion, Jefferson never ceased to consider his Surveyor of Public Buildings the architect of the most originality and genius in America. As an engineer Latrobe had no peer. Already it was possible to view Latrobe, with his pupil Robert Mills, whom Jefferson started off as a nineteenyearold boy drawing elevations at his own drafting board at Monticello, and his second assistant, William Strickland, as the leading practitioners of the classical style, with its Roman- and Greek-inspired variations, which was to furnish what Jefferson considered the proper setting for republican institutions. Jefferson hoped his academical village would become the model for college buildings throughout the newsettled lands of the West. He felt that it was essential to appeal to Latrobe's unflagging inventiveness.

Latrobe went to work with a will and within sixty days forwarded sketches for the pavilions. He urged Jefferson to put sloping roofs instead of flat roofs on his dormitories. Jefferson proved stubborn about flat roofs. He wanted them for a walk between the buildings in fine weather. Latrobe's most useful suggestion was for a domed lecture hall to accent the center of the long colonnade. Jefferson seized on the notion with enthusiasm and produced a halfsize reproduction of his favorite Pantheon. This rotunda he placed at the crest of the long vista, on the low hill that furnished a gentle terraced slope for the lawns.

He destined the rotunda for a library. He figured out three handsomely proportioned oval rooms for the lower floor. The floor above was to be a circular hall with a domed ceiling. For the ceiling he planned to design a planetarium arrangement with the constellations moving along slots worked by a hidden operator for the use of astronomy courses.

That fall there was another meeting of the Board of Visitors. On October 6 the cornerstone was laid for Pavilion VII, West Lawn. Jefferson incorporated some of Thornton's suggestions in the façade. "The old field was covered with carriages and people," Bacon told the Reverend Mr. Pierson. "There was an immense crowd there. Mr. Monroe laid the cornerstone. He was President at that time. He held the instruments and pronounced it square. . . . Mr. Jefferson—poor old man—I can see his white head just as he stood there and looked on."

According to Bacon, Jefferson never missed a day at the construction project after that. Unless the weather was very bad he would ride down from Monticello to oversee the work. "He looked after all the materials and would not allow any poor materials to go in if he could help it. He took as much pains seeing everything was done right as if it had been his own house."

12. An Utopian Dream

That same fall of 1817 Jefferson laboriously wrote out and copied on his copying machine a new bill on public education which Cabell hoped to get through the winter session of the legislature. "I have only this single anxiety in the world," Jefferson told Cabell in his covering letter; "it is a bantling of 40. years birth & nursing, and if I can once see it on its legs, I will sing with sincerity & pleasure my nunc dimittis."

This bill represented his plans for an educational system for Virginia in their finally matured form. Outside of the free primary schools for each ward or district, it called for nine colleges, roughly equivalent to modern high schools, and a state university. Provision was made for scholarships for able students too poor to pay for their higher education. "The object," wrote Jefferson explaining the bill to Correa de Serra, "is to bring into action that mass of talents which lies buried in poverty in every country for want of means of development, and thus give activity to a mass of mind, which in proportion to our population, shall be double or treble of what it is in most countries."

Jefferson believed with his whole soul in the latent possibilities of the American people. Still he had misgivings that he might, in this project as in so many others, be ahead of his time. "Mine may after all be an Utopian dream," he confided to the abbé, "but being innocent I have thought I might indulge in it till I go to the land of dreams and sleep there with the dreamers of all past and future times."

Jefferson's misgivings proved justified. The bill was hopelessly mangled in its passage through the legislature. It was hard to squeeze money for education out of the Virginia politicians. January 5, 1818, Cabell wrote Jefferson in despair. The prospects were "by no means flattering." Jefferson wrote him back not to worry too much about the form of the bill. He had no pride of authorship. He didn't care how they worded the law so long as it furnished free public education.

A few days later Cabell wrote back. The education bill had passed in fragmentary form. Even cutting their number down to four hadn't saved the colleges. The act as signed by the governor established a single University of Virginia. Fortyfive thousand dollars a year was appropriated for the education of the poor and fifteen thousand for the university. The governor was empowered to appoint a commission, one member from each of the senatorial districts, to meet the following August 1 at the tavern up on Rockfish Gap to choose a site for the university.

Immediately new dangers threatened Jefferson's project. Local interests bestirred themselves. The president of William and Mary was lobbying to have his college transferred to Richmond as the nucleus for a state university. Washington College at Lexington, which was well endowed and backed by the powerful Society of the Cincinnati, became a candidate. The graduates of Hampden-Sydney put forth their claims. The citizens of Staunton, who had been working to have the state capital moved west of the Blue Ridge, started vigorously promoting their town as the site for the new university.

Cabell urged Jefferson to use every dollar available out of the subscriptions for Central College, borrowing if he had to, to get the buildings as far advanced as possible by August. In spite of a certain amount of ill health and a couple of twoweek trips to Poplar Forest, Jefferson speeded the work along. His prospectus was ready. With Cornelia's help he put the finishing touches on the floor plans and elevations of the buildings. Everything depended on the decision of the commissioners.

For the past couple of years Jefferson's letters to John Adams had been full of his preoccupation with the university. He early asked Adams for his theories of education. Adams replied with characteristic hyperbole: "Education . . . is a Subject so vast, and the Systems of Writers are so various and contradictory that human Life is too short to examine it; and a Man must die before he can learn to bring up his Children. . . . The Science has so long labored with a Dropsy; it is a wonder that the Patient has not long since expired." He added that "the Universities in Protestant Germany have at present the Vogue and the Ton in their favour."

When Adams read that there had finally been a meeting of the trustees of Central College he wrote rather mischievously: "I wish you, Mr. Madison, and Mr. Monroe Success with your Collegiate institution, and I wish that Superstition in Religion, exciting Superstition in Politicks, and both united in directing military Force, alias glory may never blow up all your benevolent and phylanthropic Lucubrations. But the History of all Ages is Against you." In a second letter he again paraded his doubts. "From such a noble Triumvirate, the World will expect something very great and very new. But if it contains anything quite original, and very excellent, I fear the prejudices are too deeply rooted to suffer it to last long." He added that he would like to see a prospectus.

Jefferson referred him to the Central College prospectus which had already been printed in Niles' Register. The Visitors were already on the lookout for professors, "meaning to accept none but of the very first order." His own first choice was George Ticknor. "A critical classic is scarce to be found in the US."

In the same letter he congratulated John and Abigail on the return to America of their eminent son John Quincy Adams, whom Monroe had appointed Secretary of State. The younger Adams brought his family home to Quincy. "To receive them all in fine health and good Spirits," John Adams replied, "was a greater Blessing, than at my time of Life when they went away, I had any right to hope or reason to expect. If the Secretary of State can give Satisfaction to his fellow Citizens in his new Office it will be a Source of Consolation to me while I live: though it is not probable that I shall be long a Witness to his good Success or ill Success. I shall soon be obliged to say to him and to you and to your Country and mine, God bless you all! Fare Ye Well!"

He added that he highly approved of the fourth Virginia President. "Mr. Monroe has got the universal Character among all our Common People of 'a very smart Man.' And verily I am of the same Mind."

13. Era of Good Feelings

Monroe's administration opened as auspiciously as Madison's had closed. He picked a firstrate cabinet. He induced his chief rival for the Republican nomination, William H. Crawford of Georgia, to become Secretary of the Treasury. The brilliant if unpredictable Calhoun was Secretary of War. Crowninshield was staying on at the Navy. When Rush was sent to England, William Wirt took his place as Attorney General.

Not long after his inauguration Monroe pulled a leaf out of George Washington's book by showing himself to the country in an official tour. Traveling with a dignified retinue through Baltimore, Philadelphia, and New York City, the new President was greeted everywhere by public dinners, toasts, and military bands. He traveled New England from Connecticut to Maine and, swinging west, drove through the rural districts of New Hampshire, Vermont, and upstate New York. He sailed up Lake Erie as far as Detroit and rode back through the forests of Michigan Territory and the prosperous states of Ohio and Pennsylvania. Now in his sixties, and still affecting the old style of dress, Monroe exhibited a somewhat stodgy Republican pomp that just suited the mood of the country.

During Monroe's first administration there hardly existed an opposition on Capitol Hill. When the Fifteenth Congress assembled the Republican majority was overwhelming. In the Senate the only Federalists of stature were Rufus King and Harrison Gray Otis, who were beginning to wear their Federalism with a difference, and Alexander Hanson, Madison's gadfly through his editing of the *Federal Republican*. There was a swarm of able Republican senators: George Campbell of Tennessee; plainspoken Nathaniel Macon of North Carolina, so long the Speaker of the House in Jefferson's day. Louisiana had Jefferson's appointee to the territorial governorship, William C. C. Claiborne, and Virginia had Jack Eppes, Jefferson's soninlaw, and Jefferson's good friend James Barbour, for whom he was preparing a magnificent domed design for the family mansion at Barboursville. In the House John Randolph's sarcasms stirred Daniel Webster to fresh bouts of reverberating oratory which still carried echoes of New England Federalism. Webster's forensic rival, Henry Clay, ruled the roost from the Speaker's chair.

14. *The Florida Controversy*

John Quincy Adams' first business, when he settled in busily rebuilding Washington City, was to renew the long negotiation with Spain for the acquisition of East Florida. As a result of Andrew Jackson's subjugation of the Indians in Mississippi and Alabama Territory desperate bands had fled to the swamps and pine barrens of the peninsula. There they mingled, sometimes peaceably and sometimes in battle, with escaped Negroes from the cotton plantations. According to the American frontiersmen, these outlaws, now known as the Red Sticks, were furnished with arms and encouraged in their belligerence by British traders from the Bahamas who did a flourishing business with them, bartering for furs and naval stores.

It was war without quarter along the illdefined frontier. White settlers, whether men, women, or children, were indiscriminately scalped, tortured, or burned alive when they fell into the hands of the Red Sticks. The Spanish garrisons at St. Marks and Pensacola were helpless to keep order. From Tierra del Fuego to the Rio Perdido the Spanish empire in the Americas was in a state of dissolution.

Several times American detachments had been forced to take over Amelia Island near the mouth of the St. Johns River to drive off buccaneers and pirates. In the spring of 1817 Andrew Jackson decided that as major general in charge of the military district it was his business to put an end to these outrages.

As the United States forces under Edmund Gaines were far from sufficient, Jackson went back to Tennessee and raised a couple of thousand of the mounted militia who had proved so redoubtable under his command at New Orleans, and marched them south along the Flint River. With only the slimmest authorization from Washington, Jackson charged into Florida, occupied St. Marks, and surprised some chiefs of the Red Sticks at an Indian town on the Suwanee River. There two Bahamians, whom he accused of encouraging Indian raids, fell into his hands. He called a courtmartial, saw to it that they were sentenced to death, and marched off through the wilderness to occupy Pensacola.

When news of Jackson's raid reached Washington, most of Monroe's heads of departments were for reprimanding the general. Nobody worried about the executed Indians, though one of them wore a frock coat presented to him by the British government when he was hanged, but the Bahamians, Arbuthnot and Ambrister, were British subjects. Calhoun and Crawford expressed the fear that their execution, on evidence that would hardly have stood up in a court of law, might disrupt the friendly negotiations being carried on in London by Richard Rush, who was ably succeeding the younger Adams at the Court of St. James's, for a settlement of the northern boundaries and of the fisheries question.

In Washington John Quincy Adams stood up vigorously for General Jackson. He held the Bahamians responsible for the burning alive of an American sailor and for the massacre of a boatload of settlers on the Flint River. Senator Barbour's brother Philip used the same arguments defending Jackson in the House of Representatives. When Madison wrote to ask for Jefferson's opinion Jefferson answered that at first he had been shocked by the execution of the two traders but that Barbour's speech had convinced him that Jackson acted under military necessity. It was noted as an indication of the rise in American prestige since the Treaty of Ghent that, when questions were asked in Parliament about Arbuthnot and Ambrister, the answer from the government benches was that the men were freebooters and had forfeited the protection of the Crown. Negotiations at Westminster went on without interruption.

15. *A Vacation at the Warm Springs*

The public prints were full of the Florida controversy when in July of 1818 Jefferson hurried back to Monticello from Poplar Forest to get ready for the meeting at Rockfish Gap. As usual he was out of cash. July 28 he wrote James Leitch, the Charlottesville merchant with whom he traded for supplies, asking for the loan of a hundred dollars, explaining most ingenuously that he had just discovered that he was overdrawn at his banker's in Richmond by three or four hundred. A couple of days later he was writing Barnet, who ran the tavern up in Rockfish Gap, asking the innkeeper to reserve him a room to himself no matter how small. Since the governor had appointed twentyfour commissioners he suspected beds might be scarce up at the tavern, so he was bringing his own mattress and trussles.

At Rockfish Gap Jefferson carried all before him. He was elected presiding officer of the commission. He exhibited his prospectus for the university curriculum, his handsomely executed drawings for the buildings of the "academical village," and a relief map of Virginia, ingeniously molded out of cardboard, on which he drew lines to indicate the density of the white inhabitants as proof of his contention that Charlottesville was the population center of the state. To demonstrate the healthiness of the locality he produced a list of local octogenarians. So convincing were his arguments that the commissioners voted not even to view any other sites and chose Central College by fifteen votes to seven. Jefferson, Madison, Judge Roane, James Breckenridge of Botetourt County, and a couple of others were appointed a select committee to prepare a report for the legislature on the organization of the college. Jefferson had the report all ready in his portfolio.

His successes at Rockfish Gap left Jefferson in such high spirits that he decided on an excursion in the mountains. For the last few years he had suffered from rheumatism. Friends had been telling him of the marvelous properties of the Warm Springs at the other end of Augusta County. In the company of Colonel Breckenridge, with whom he became fast friends in spite of the fact that Breckenridge had voted for Staunton, he spent two weeks at the springs. He became so friendly with the Breckenridge family that he promised to draw them up a design in the Roman style for the new courthouse they were planning for Fincastle.

Another new acquaintance of Jefferson's at the Warm Springs was

Colonel William Alston of North Carolina. Colonel Alston's eldest son, Joseph Alston, who had married Theodosia Burr and been so bamboozled by Burr during the little colonel's operations on the Ohio, had, after serving creditably for two terms as governor of South Carolina, succumbed to a sudden illness. The Alston family seemed to share in the curse of Cain that descended on everyone connected with Aaron Burr.

During the last year of the younger Alston's life Burr, who had never quite given up hope of accomplishing some miraculous political rehabilitation, tried to interest him in a movement to back Andrew Jackson for the presidency in 1816. In the fall of 1812 Burr had slipped back in disguise to New York where he was sheltered by the Swartwout brothers, who still wielded considerable political power in the city. When it became clear that the prosecutions against him had been dropped he ventured to open a law office on Nassau Street under his own name.

Burr's wanderings during his years of exile in Europe were as abracadabrating as his performances on the Western Waters. In England he ingratiated himself with Jeremy Bentham, the political economist whose utilitarian theories Burr claimed to find admirable. Bentham put him up and furnished him with funds while the little colonel tried to interest Castlereagh in the conquest of Mexico. When Lord Liverpool's administration turned his proposition down, and sought to expel him from Great Britain, Burr had the effrontery to claim that, having been born under King George, he was a British subject. He ran up so many bills that he had to take it on the run, nevertheless, to escape imprisonment for debt; and retired to Sweden. There he panhandled his way from nobleman's seat to nobleman's seat, keeping all the while, expressly for the eyes of Theodosia and little Gampillo, as he called his grandson in his letters, one of the most extraordinary journals in the history of the human mind.

Using a curious code compounded of German and English and Swedish and French, he noted for the edification of the only two people he loved in the world, almost hour by hour, every detail of an existence dedicated to a conscienceless depravity without match in confessional literature. Every page betrayed Burr's inner emptiness. He noted every subterfuge he indulged in to cadge a meal or a handout; every time he drank too much; his efforts to ease the vacant spirit with opium; every success with a woman, were she duchess or chambermaid; the price he paid his harlots and whether they were worth it or not. Intermingled were sparkling descriptions of weather and places, shrewd estimates of people, philosophical disquisitions on the meaninglessness of life, but never a word or a phrase that betrayed a moment's escape from the straitjacket of self-worship.

When he wore out his welcome in Sweden and Germany he made his way to Paris. There he presented to the Emperor Napoleon's Foreign Office a scheme even more fanciful than the scheme he had presented at Downing Street. If only the Emperor would furnish him with the funds he would descend on Bermuda with five hundred men and use that island as a base for the reconquest of Louisiana and Canada for France. The response of Burr's old idol was to have him carefully watched by the secret police.

In the end Burr somehow managed to shake down the French Foreign Office for his passage home and to procure an American passport through Jonathan Russell. He had barely settled in New York before a distracted letter reached him from Theodosia. His grandson was dead. He would never see Gampillo again. Desperate with grief, Theodosia could only think of joining her father. Too ill to travel by land, she tried to run the British blockade and was lost at sea on the pilot boat *Patriot*.

Friends remarked how nobly Burr bore his affliction. The stoicism of total disaster fitted into his philosophy of total nothingness. He managed to make a scanty living at the law, surrounded himself with a new family of outcasts, unfortunate women, and foster children some of whom were reputed to be his own bastards, whose education he supervised with pedantic care. With Joseph Alston's death he gave up hope of any comeback in politics. He lived on for years as one of New York's minor notorieties. Men pointed him out on the street to their sons as the wickedest man alive.

When Jefferson parted with Colonel Alston at the springs, he made him promise to visit Monticello the following summer. As soon as he reached home he made up a case of wines to ship to Alston through Charleston. There were bottles of Jefferson's favorite Hermitage, of Roussillon and Montepulciano. In his conversations with the colonel he had been talking up the superior healthiness of light wines over port and madeira and spirituous liquors. He urged him again to come to Monticello. If his health were good enough next summer he would show the colonel the Natural Bridge.

Jefferson got a heartbroken letter in reply from Colonel Alston. His younger son had just been killed in a fall from a horse. Joseph had been the comfort of life; he was gone, and now this young boy who had shown such promise. Colonel Alston would never leave his home again.

16. *Ill Health and Affliction*

The use of the waters proved disastrous to Jefferson's health. Ever since an unfortunate experience in France he had been suspicious of mineral waters. From Monticello he wrote John Adams apologizing for having taken so long to answer his last letter: "Having been subject to troublesome attacks of rheumatism for some winters past, and being called by other business into the neighborhood of our Warmsprings, I thought I would avail myself of them as a preventive of future pain. I was then in good health," he added wryly, "and it ought to have occurred to me that the medicine that makes the sick well may make the well sick. those powerful waters produced imposthume, general eruption, fever, colliquative sweats, and extreme debility, which, aggravated by the torment of a return home over 100. miles of rocks and mountains reduced me to extremity."

Adams immediately answered consolingly that Jefferson's symptoms "often indicate Strength of Constitution and returning vigour. I hope and believe they have given you a new Lease for Years, many Years. Your letter which is written with your usual neatness and firmness confirms my hopes.

"Now Sir, for my Griefs," John Adams added. Abigail, who was going on seventythree, was desperately ill of typhoid fever. "The dear Partner of my Life for Fifty Four Years as a wife and for many Years more as a Lover, now lies in extremis forbidden to speak or be spoken to."

A few days later Jefferson read in the gazettes of Mrs. Adams' death.

"If human Life is a Bubble," wrote John Adams, "no matter how soon it breaks." Even in his grief he could find in himself no will to die. "If it is as I firmly believe an immortal Existence," he declared to his friend, "we ought patiently to wait the Instructions of the great Teacher."

Jefferson hastened to write back: "The same trials have taught me that, for ills so immeasurable, time and silence are the only medicines . . . nor . . . will I say a word more, where words are vain, but that it is of some comfort to us both that the term is not very distant at which we are to deposit, in the same cerement, our sorrows and suffering bodies, and to ascend in essence to an ecstatic meeting with the friends we have loved and lost and whom we shall still love and never lose again. God bless you and support you under your heavy affliction."

Jefferson's health returned with the cold weather. By the following March he was able to reply to a certain Dr. Utley, who had written inquiring how Mr. Jefferson's regime differed from that perscribed by Dr. Rush, that his health was very good indeed: "I have lived temperately, eating little animal food and that not as an aliment, so much as a condiment for the vegetables, which constitute my principal diet. I double, however, the Doctor's glass and a half of wine, and sometimes treble it with a friend; but halve it's effects by drinking the weak wines only. the ardent wines I cannot drink, nor do I use ardent spirits in any form. malt liquors and cider are my table drinks, and my breakfast, like that also of my friend, is of tea and coffee. I have been blest with organs of digestion which accept and concoct, without ever murmuring, whatever the palate choses to consign to them, and I have not yet lost a tooth by age. I was a hard student until I entered on the business of life, the duties of which leave no idle time to those disposed to fill them; and now, retired, and at the age of seventy six I am again a hard student. . . . I never go to bed without an hour, or half hour's previous reading of something moral whereon to ruminate in the intervals of sleep. but whether I retire early or late, I rise with the sun. I use spectacles at night, but not necessarily in the day."

He explained that his stiff wrist made writing slow and painful. His hearing, especially if several people were talking round a table, was not so good as it had been. His sick headaches had disappeared with advancing age. "I enjoy good health; too feeble indeed to walk much but riding without fatigue six or eight miles a day, and sometimes thirty or forty." He ended what he described as "these egotisms" with a quotation from Horace to the effect that, changing the name, his story would fit any other man just as well.

17. The Panic of 1819

The winter of 1818–19 was an anxious time at Monticello. Cabell's first letters from the legislature meeting in Richmond were discouraging. The commissioners' choice of Charlottesville as the site for the university was stimulating the opposition to fresh efforts. There was an ominous stirring among various Protestant ministers, particularly the Presbyterians, who were dismayed by the absense of religious teaching in Jefferson's prospectus. Though the aspect of national politics was still serene Jefferson could see the portents of a coming split in Congress between the apologists for slavery and its opponents. In Virginia the economic situation was desperate. The effects of the postwar depression of trade and commerce in Europe had reached America. Agricultural prices were sinking. Land values, which had been inflated in the speculative boom that followed the profitable years of the first renewal of trade with Great Britain, were on the way down. Financially 1819 was a panic year.

Thomas Hart Benton, a rising politician in Missouri Territory, who'd first gained notoriety by having figured in a famous brawl in a Tennessee tavern in which Andrew Jackson was winged by a pistol shot, opened his *Thirty Years' View* with a description of the grim years during which he initiated his political career. Like Jefferson, he blamed the panic on the mishandling of credit by the United

States Bank: "The whole paper system, of which it was the head and the citadel, after a vast expansion, had suddenly collapsed, spreading desolation over the land and carrying ruin to debtors. The years 1819 and 1820 were a period of gloom and agony. No money, either gold or silver: no paper convertible into specie: no measure or standard of value left remaining. The local banks (all but those in New England) after a brief resumption of specie payments again sank into a state of suspension. The Bank of the United States, created as a remedy for all those evils, now at the head of the evil, prostrate and helpless, with no power left but that of suing its debtors and selling their property and purchasing for itself at its own nominal price. No price for property or produce. No sales but those of the sheriffs and the marshal. No purchasers at execution sales but the creditor, or some hoarder of money. No employment for industry— no demand for labor—no sale for the product of the farm—no sound of the hammer but that of the auctioneer knocking down property."

Jefferson's own fortunes were heavily involved in the general disaster. His financial situation was bad enough before, but in the fall of 1818 he put his name on two notes for ten thousand dollars each at the urgent entreaty of Wilson Cary Nicholas. Nicholas had just retired from the governorship.

Besides being the fatherinlaw of Jefferson's favorite Jeff Randolph, Nicholas was a lifelong friend and political adherent. He was one of four sons of Robert Carter Nicholas, the respected old Treasurer of Virginia during the last years of the colony. It was his brother George who, as a rash young man, rose in the Assembly to move an investigation of the conduct of the executive at the end of Jefferson's unlucky second term as governor; George had promptly repented and become one of Jefferson's most enthusiastic supporters after his move to Kentucky. All four brothers had espoused the Jeffersonian causes. As governor, Wilson Cary Nicholas had seconded Jefferson's plan for education and, as a director of the Richmond branch of the Bank of the United States, he'd been helpful about credit to him personally. Now, having invested extensively in James River lands which were steadily dropping in value, he was caught in the toils of his own bank. Jefferson, who never could get it through his head that he was no longer a wealthy man, put his name on the notes.

An even more worrisome topic cropped up that winter in his correspondence with Nicholas. Bankhead in a drunken fit stabbed Jeff Randolph, who was remonstrating with him over his abuse of Jeff's sister. Bacon, who was present, claimed years later to the Reverend Mr. Pierson that it was only his stepping between them that saved Jeff's life.

"Jefferson's wounds are nearly healed," Jefferson wrote Nicholas in early March, "but I fear he will never recover much use of his arm. with respect for Bankhead there is room for fear but mostly for his wife. I have for some time taken for granted that she would fall by his hand and yet she is so attached to him that no persuasion has ever availed to induce her to separate and come to live with us with her children. he has failed to appear on his recognizance." Jefferson hoped Bankhead would be put safely away in jail, but he feared the leniency of the county courts towards people of family. "The penitentiary is the only thing which can produce safety to others or reformation to himself."

18. *The University of Virginia Elects a Rector*

The news was not all bad at Monticello that spring of 1819. In late January Cabell's exertions in the legislature were crowned by the passage of a bill adopting the recommendation of the commissioners that Central College be chosen for the university. March 29 the new Board of Visitors, almost a duplicate of the old, except that President Monroe declared that his duties in Washington would keep him from serving, met at Monticello. Their first act was to appoint Thomas Jefferson rector of the new university. A proctor was appointed to oversee construction, and Jefferson's nominee, Dr. Thomas Cooper, was chosen as professor of natural philosophy.

For several years Jefferson had been struggling with the problem of securing really firstrate men for the faculty. He tried to lure Nathaniel Bowditch from Salem. He wrote imploring letters to George Ticknor at Göttingen. When Ticknor politely refused an appointment in Virginia, explaining that, aside from the ties that bound him to Harvard, he was an only son and had to settle where he could be a comfort to his parents in their old age, Jefferson exclaimed: "Would to god we could have two or three duplicates of yourself, the original being above our means and hopes."

Ticknor made up for his refusal by a copious and chatty correspondence about his meetings with European men of letters and by the diligence with which he collected editions of the classics for Jefferson's new library. Before leaving Göttingen he sent Jefferson a lively account of the freshness of the new German literature. He was delighted by the freedom of opinion he found in Protestant Germany, by the scholarly textural criticism of Homer and even of the Bible, and by the industry of the German professors. Jefferson responded by sending young Ticknor letters of introduction to speed him on his travels. George's father Elisha wrote Jefferson thanking him fervently for the help he was giving his son to meet the right people.

In August 1818 Ticknor wrote from Madrid giving Jefferson an accounting of his three years in Europe. He was finishing his work on the Spanish language. He had already learned German, Swedish, Danish, French, Provençal, and Italian, including a smattering of the Venetian and Sicilian dialects. "My object in all of this has been to get general philosophical notions of the genius and history of each of these literatures and to send home good collections of books relating to the history of their languages and representing the whole series of their elegant literatures." He had already collected four thousand volumes beside the books he had shipped to Monticello. Only Portuguese was left on his list. After a few weeks in Lisbon he would revisit Paris, London, and Edinburgh and "as soon as the fine season commences, embark for my home."

Like so many other young men, Ticknor asked Jefferson's advice on the shape of his career. He would be starting out in life at twentyseven. He had no thought of political distinction. If the federal government had a department of general instruction he might have been interested. As it was he would probably lecture at Harvard where he had been offered a professorship. In the summer of 1819 Jefferson got a last letter from Ticknor written as his ship approached the New England coast. He recommended a German professor he'd met in London for modern languages at the University of Virginia. Though he had hobnobbed with every literary figure in Europe from Byron and Goethe to Sir Walter Scott, he had learned to appreciate his own country.

In the search for professors Correa de Serra was Jefferson's chief confidant. When not on his annual excursion to Monticello, the abbé spent most of his time in Philadelphia. There he helped unearth several of Meriwether Lewis' notebooks, mislaid after his mysterious death, for the complete publication of the findings of the Corps of Discovery which Jefferson hoped to promote.

Already people were bringing Jefferson tales about Dr. Cooper. The Presbyterians considered him an atheist. It was whispered in the ears of some of the Visitors that he drank. Since the abbé knew him well Jefferson begged him for a confidential appraisal. Correa answered that he'd never seen a sign of intemperance in all the years he'd known Cooper. Cooper was a bitter enemy of hypocrites. "He will always have the cordial hatred, and interested too, of the literary fireflies who shine only in the dark."

The abbé wrote that he wanted to see Virginia the head of the Union in an intellectual way, as France was of Europe, but he dreaded "the contagious mediocrity" he found in American colleges. "God grant you may get over all the snares that will surround your institution of learning."

Already the funds for the university were exhausted. The buildings were begun, forty bricklayers were at work on the pavilions and dormitories, but fresh appropriations were needed to finish them.

Jefferson chose the moment to spend a long period of rest at Poplar Forest. He had to get away from the drudgery of letter writing and from the constant visitors who filled every bed at Monticello. The family told of strangers who crowded into the entrance hall and, knowing Mr. Jefferson to be very punctual, stood waiting watch in hand to stare through the glass doors when the old man walked across the drawing room to the dining room on his way to dinner. In June he wrote the abbé he would not be back at Monticello till the first of October when there would be a meeting of the Board of Visitors. He hoped for a visit from Correa and Dr. Cooper about that time.

At Poplar Forest that summer he completed the decorative plaster-work and saw to the laying of the marble hearths. In Bedford County Jefferson was far from the main traveled roads but not far enough to escape the news that the bank had foreclosed on Nicholas and was about to hold Jefferson liable for the notes he had endorsed. August 11 he wrote Nicholas that he had just suffered the severest bout of rheumatism he had ever experienced.

"A call on me for the amount of my endorsements for you," he complained, "would indeed close my course by a catastrophe I had never contemplated. but the comfort which supports me is the en-tire confidence I repose in your friendship to find some means of warding off this desperate calamity."

There was no warding off the calamity. A few days later Jefferson was writing a Joseph Marx, who represented the Bank of the United States, that as soon as he returned to Monticello he would execute a deed of trust to the bank on his best tobacco lands at Bedford, which he estimated as worth thirty or forty dollars an acre. Jefferson summoned all his philosophy and wrote sympathetically to Nicholas: "Have no uneasiness, dear Sir, for any part I bear in this painful business. I know well how apt we are to be deluded by our calcula-tions and to be innocently led into error by them."

Stripped of everything, a disgraced bankrupt, Nicholas took ref-uge at Tufton with Jeff Randolph and his daughter. There he died the following year. During the remaining years of his life Jefferson faced a similar calamity. The value of the lands he had relied on to cover his indebtedness shrank month by month. "Lands in this state cannot now be sold for a year's rent," he informed John Adams in December.

19. *The Missouri Question*

Desperate as his financial condition was, Jefferson managed a certain lightheartedness about it. It was his fear for the prospects of the Union under the slavery question that gave him sleepless nights. "The banks, bankrupt law, manufactures, Spanish Treaty are nothing," he wrote John Adams during the last days of the year, "there are occurrences which like waves in a storm will pass under the ship. but the Missouri question is a breaker on which we lose the Missouri country by revolt and what more, God only knows. from the Battle of Bunker's hill to the treaty of Paris we never had so ominous a question. it even damps the joy with which I hear of your high health, and welcomes me to the consequences of my want of it. I thank god I shall not live to witness it's issue."

The question exploded suddenly during the last sessions of the Fifteenth Congress when Representative James Tallmadge of New York offered an amendment to a bill admitting Missouri Territory to the Union. A constitutional convention had set up Missouri as a slavery state. The Tallmadge amendment prohibited any further importations of slaves into the state and provided that children thereafter born of slave parents should be free when they reached the age of twentyfive. Immediately Congress split into proslavery southerners and antislavery northerners. James Barbour of Virginia exclaimed in the Senate that the Missouri question was "an ignited spark which, communicated to an immense mass of combustion would produce an explosion which would shake the union to its centre." Walter Lowrie of Pennsylvania answered: "If the alternative be as gentlemen thus broadly intimate, a dissolution of the union, or the extension of slavery over this whole western country, I for one, will choose the former."

John Randolph and Henry Clay by sheer fervor of oratory defeated the Tallmadge amendment in the House but Congress adjourned without voting on the admission of Missouri. When the Sixteenth Congress assembled the debate rose to such fury that Henry Clay presented a compromise solution. Missouri should be admitted as a slavery state. The Massachusetts province of Maine should be admitted as a free state. At the same time slavery should be prohibited throughout Louisiana Territory north of latitude 36°30'. That would leave twelve states on each side of the line.

When the Missouri and Maine bills passed President Monroe collected his heads of departments and asked their opinion in writing on two propositions. Did Congress have a constitutional right to prohibit slavery in a territory? Would the prohibition of slavery apply only to the territories north of the dividing line or to the states which might be formed out of them?

Monroe's cabinet agreed that Congress had a right to prohibit slavery in the territories. On the second question there were various opinions but President Monroe was supported in his intention of putting his signature to the bills. John Quincy Adams noted in his diary that in his opinion the prohibition would be binding on all states and territories north of the dividing line forever.

After the argument Adams and Calhoun walked home together from the President's house. Calhoun told Adams in his disarming way that Adams' principles were just and noble but that he must remember how people felt in the Southern country. Certain sorts of labor were for slaves only. Calhoun told Adams he was the most popular man in his district, but if he should employ a white servant in his house his character would be ruined.

Adams argued that confounding the idea of labor with servitude was one of the evil effects of slavery; but Calhoun said, not at all; it produced a dignified equality among whites. Work on the farm was not considered degrading: he and his father had often put their hands to the plow; nor was manufacturing or mechanical work, but purely manual labor was the proper work of slaves. Adams told Calhoun tartly that he did not see things in the same light, but they parted on friendly terms.

When Adams got back to his desk he noted his estimate of the southerners in his journal. "The discussion of this Missouri question has betrayed the secret of their souls . . . they show at the bottom of their souls pride and vainglory in their condition of masterdom. . . . They look down upon the simplicity of a Yankee's manners, because he has no habits of overbearing like theirs and cannot treat Negroes like dogs."

Adams further noted his private doubts as to the outcome: "I have favored this Missouri Compromise, believing it all that could be effected under the present Constitution, and from extreme unwillingness to put the Union at hazard. But perhaps it would have been a wiser as well as bolder course to have persisted in the restriction upon Missouri, till it should have terminated in a convention of the states to revise and amend the Constitution. This would have produced a new Union of thirteen or fourteen States unpolluted with slavery, with a great and glorious object to effect, namely, that of rallying to their standard the other States by the universal emancipation of their slaves. If the Union must be dissolved, slavery is precisely the question on which it ought to break."

Adams closed his entry on a more optimistic note. "For the present however this contest is laid asleep." Such was the public impression throughout the nation. The press hailed the compromise as "oil upon the troubled waters."

Jefferson, looking out from the vantage point of Monticello, refused to be comforted. "This momentous question," he wrote a rising Democratic Republican politician from Alfred, Maine, named John Holmes, "like a fire bell in the night, awakened and filled me with terror. I considered it at once the knell of the Union. it is hushed indeed for the moment, but this is a reprieve only, not a final sentence. a geographical line, coinciding with a marked principal, moral and political, once conceived and held up to the angry passions of men, will never be obliterated; and every irritation will mark it deeper and deeper."

He tried to explain to Holmes the feelings of the Southern slave-owner. "The cession of that kind of property, for so it is misnamed, is a bagatelle which would not cost me a second thought, if in that way a general emancipation and *expatriation* could be effected; and gradually, and with due sacrifices, I think it might be. but as it is, we have the wolf by the ears, and we can neither hold him, nor safely let him go. justice is on one scale and self-preservation on the other."

He added that he considered that the prohibition of the movement of slaves across this arbitrary line was unconstitutional. He did not think that the diffusion of slavery would hinder emancipation. It might alleviate the condition of the slaves. Congress had no right "to regulate the condition of different conditions of men composing a State. . . . could Congress for example, say that the non-freemen of Connecticut should be freemen or that they shall not emigrate into any other State?"

20. *John Marshall's Court*

Each revolving year found Jefferson more obsessed by the danger to selfgoverning institutions he saw in the arrogation of powers by the central administration in Washington. "The great object of my fear is the federal judiciary," he wrote Spencer Roane; "that body, like gravity, ever acting with noiseless foot, and unalarming advance, gaining ground step by step, and holding what it gains, is engulphing insidiously the special governments into the jaws of that which feeds them."

Ever since John Marshall, on grounds Jefferson considered trivial and tinged with personal prejudice, had upset his prosecution of Aaron Burr for treason, Jefferson had thought of his cousin as a great spider stealthily weaving a web of power round himself and the Supreme Court. In Marshall's solution of the long litigation which grew out of the disputed disposition of the prize money from the brig *Active* the Chief Justice had enforced the subordination of the state of Pennsylvania to the federal government. Martin vs. Hunter's Lessee had done the same thing for Virginia. In Fletcher vs. Peck he had upheld the sanctity of commercial contracts against a law passed by the Georgia legislature to repeal grievous inequities. Now during the February term of the 1819 session of the court Marshall upheld the same principle by declaring a New York bankruptcy law unconstitutional in the case of Sturges vs. Crowninshield.

The second sensation of that term of court was the setting aside of a law passed by the state of New Hampshire to take over the administration of Dartmouth College. The trustees, claiming that Dartmouth

was a private institution, refused to give up their charter when the
state tried to absorb their college into a system of public education.
They hired Daniel Webster to speak for them. When the case came
up before the Supreme Court Joseph Hopkinson, the cultured and
subtleminded dean of the Philadelphia bar who, as a sparetime poet
and musician, was the author of "Hail, Columbia," joined Webster.
They convinced the court. John Marshall cited the constitutional
prohibitions against "any bill of attainder, ex post facto law, or law
impairing the obligation of contrasts" and found that the original
charter of the college as an eleemosynary institution could not be set
aside by any act of government.

In a third case, McCulloch vs. Maryland, the court outlawed an
attempt by the state of Maryland to tax the Baltimore branch of the
Bank of the United States.

In this case Webster joined William Pinkney and William Wirt on
the side of the national bank, while the versatile Joseph Hopkinson
and seventyfive year old Luther Martin, who in spite of fifty years of
excessive drinking could still speak forcefully for three solid days in
court, appeared for the state of Maryland.

The Bank of the United States was a touchy topic. The public outcry against it was enormous. While the argument went on before the
Supreme Court, efforts were being made in Congress to abolish the
bank. Its opponents claimed mismanagement and corruption and
pointed out its failure to stem the tide of financial panic. It was hardly
a popular institution that John Marshall was defending when he declared: "This great principle is that the constitution and the laws
made in pursuance thereof are supreme; that they control the constitution and laws of the respective states, and cannot be controlled by
them." The court pronounced the Maryland statute unconstitutional.

Hezekiah Niles attacked Marshall's decision in three numbers of his
Register as a breeder of financial monopoly and moneyed privilege.
Spencer Roane denounced it under various pseudonyms in the Richmond *Enquirer*. In a long pamphlet which he called *Construction
Construed* John Taylor held up to ridicule Marshall's passion for
sovereignty and denounced his three latest opinions as fostering "a
fanaticism for wealth" and setting up "an aristocracy of money."

Ritchie and Judge Roane combined to convince Jefferson that he
must allow a statement of his approval of Taylor's book to be printed.
Jefferson prepared a special letter declaring his agreement, under a
few reservations, with Taylor's argument. He admitted that Taylor
had corrected "some errors of opinion into which I have slidden without sufficient examination." He summarized Taylor's underlying thesis in his own words: "It is a fatal heresy to suppose that either our
State governments are superior to the federal or the federal to the
States. . . . The people, to whom all authority belongs, have divided

the powers of government into two distinct departments, the leading charters of which are *foreign* and domestic; and they have appointed for each a distinct set of functionaries, these they have made coordinate, checking and balancing each other, like the three cardinal departments in the individual States: each equally supreme as to the powers delegated to itself, and neither authorized ultimately to decide what belongs to itself or to its copartner in government . . . each party should prudently shrink from all approach to the line of demarkation, instead of rashly overleaping it, or throwing grapples ahead to haul to hereafter."

At the same time he explained his sidelines position to Judge Roane: "I should not shrink from the post of duty, had not the decays of nature withdrawn me from the list of combatants. great decline in the energies of the body import naturally a corresponding wane of the mind." It was the business of the next generation to "preserve for their sons the political blessings delivered into their hands by their fathers. . . . the University," he added in conclusion, "will give employment to my remaining years, and quite enough for my senile faculties. it is the last act of usefulness I can render, and could I see it open I would not ask an hour more of life."

21. *A Hopedfor Solution*

In spite of strident opposition the university was coming ahead. When Jefferson's old Quaker friend Isaac Briggs visited him in 1820, Jefferson was able to show the seasoned surveyor of so many grand projects, who was now working for the state of Virginia, some pretty complete buildings. Briggs wrote his wife that the work was "so far advanced as to exhibit, to one acquainted with these things, a very good idea of the design, scope and probable fruits of the institution." He added that he found Mr. Jefferson, in his seventyseventh year, "strong and active and in full possession of a sound mind. . . . He rides a trotting horse and sits him *as straight as a young man*."

When Briggs arrived one late November afternoon at Monticello the family was still at the dinner table. Briggs told his wife an amusing story about finding a stranger sitting in the hall. The stranger admitted he had no sort of introduction but just wanted to catch a glimpse of Mr. Jefferson. When Jefferson came out to ask Briggs in for a glass of wine the stranger tagged along. Jefferson, thinking he was a friend of Briggs's, set him at the head of the table. Only Mrs. Randolph, Mrs. Marks, and the girls were present as Thomas Mann Randolph was in Richmond, where he had recently been elected governor of Virginia. After the stranger had modestly excused himself, saying he was on the road south and that his friends were waiting for him at Charlottesville, Jefferson asked Briggs who the man was and Briggs admitted he didn't have the slightest idea.

After they had laughed over that Jefferson launched into his anxieties over the Missouri situation. If things continued the way they were going he saw civil war as inevitable. Briggs wrote his wife that he would try to put down what "the dear venerable old man" said as exactly as possible in the words he used.

If such a civil war broke out, between slavery and antislavery states, Mr. Jefferson feared it would turn into a war of extermination against the Africans. "Instead of improving the condition of this poor, afflicted, degraded race," Briggs quoted Jefferson as saying, "terminating in ordering of wisdom, in equal liberty and the enjoyment of equal rights (to which public opinion is advancing in rapid strides) the course pursued, by those who make high pretensions of humanity and friendship for them, would involve them as well as us in certain destruction. I believe there are many, very many, who are quite honest in their humane views and feelings towards this people, lending their efforts, with an amiable but misguided zeal, to those leaders—those master spirites who raise the whirlwind and direct the storm—who are *not honest*, who wear humanity as a mask, whose aim is power and who would 'wade through slaughter to a throne, and shut the gates of mercy on mankind.' "

Jefferson, as Briggs wrote his wife, felt that the crisis was of far more than national significance: "I have considered the United States as owing to the world an example . . . an example which by its mild and steady light, would be far more powerful than the sword, in correcting abuses,—in teaching mankind that they can, if they will, govern themselves . . . but if our union be broken, this duty will be sacrificed—the bright example will be lost—it will be worse than lost. The predictions of our enemies will be fulfilled in the estimation of the world, that we are not wise enough for self government and the chains of despotism would be rivetted more firmly than ever."

At eight o'clock Jefferson excused himself. "I feel I am an old man and it is proper for me to retire early to bed." Briggs sat up a couple of hours more chatting with the ladies of the family.

In Richmond, in spite of the bitter ambivalence of his personal feelings towards his fatherinlaw, Governor Randolph was vigorously espousing the Jeffersonian causes. Cabell wrote Jefferson from the legislature that, though the governor's friends regretted his having recommended in his message legislation setting a term to slavery in Virginia, "his triumph over his enemies was compleat." The triumph was purely personal; the legislators would not touch emancipation with a tenfoot pole, but they reelected Thomas Mann Randolph governor for three successive terms.

Notwithstanding the rising power of the cotton planters, whose dollars and cents attitude was rationalized by the plantation intellectuals into an apology for slavery built out of their romantic estimate of the slavelabor economies of the Greek and Roman republics, the Virginia abolitionists were active and persistent. Though their motions for even a debate on emancipation always failed, the Virginia legislature had passed a series of resolutions requesting the federal government to help solve the problem of colonizing the free blacks.

Slaveholders, and antislavery men managed to agree on at least one part of the plan Jefferson suggested in his *Notes on Virginia,* which he made several efforts to put in effect while he was President. The British had already started a colony of free Negroes, some of them descended from slaves lured from American masters during the Revolutionary War, in Sierra Leone. When Rufus King was minister in England, Jefferson instructed him to sound out His Majesty's Government on the possibility of settling American Negroes there in case of an emancipation. The British showed no enthusiasm for the plan. A similar refusal came from the authorities in Brazil. For a while some hope was entertained that an agreement to receive colonists might be concluded with Negro leaders in Santo Domingo but the War of 1812 put the whole business on the shelf.

The resolution of the Virginia Assembly was now echoed by similar resolutions in Maryland, Tennessee, and Georgia. At that point Dr. Robert Finley, a Presbyterian divine raised under the protective wing of Dr. Witherspoon at Nassau College, a fervent opponent of slavery who was headmaster of a respectable boys' school at Basking Ridge in New Jersey, arrived in Washington City and organized the American Colonization Society. In this organization Dr. Finley managed to induce the slaveowners who wanted to get rid of the free blacks and the northerners who wanted emancipation to work together.

The first meeting was signalized by the sponsorship of President Monroe and by addresses by John Randolph and Henry Clay. Bushrod Washington, George Washington's nephew, the heir to Mount Vernon and Associate Justice of the Supreme Court, consented to serve as president. The dandified Robert Goodloe Harper, who had been transformed through the years from a South Carolina Republican into a fashionable Baltimore Federalist, gave his enthusiastic support. Funds were raised and agents were dispatched to the West African coast.

In 1820 Congress passed a rigorous law which provided that every person engaged in the slave trade was guilty of piracy for which the penalty was death. The navy set up a patrol of the West African coast to enforce it. By that time the American Negro settlements around Cape Mesurado had weathered the fevers and attacks by local chieftains, who didn't want to see the slave trade interfered with, but they still numbered barely a hundred souls. A devoted clergyman named Jehudi Ashmun was sent out as U.S. agent. Extensive lands were bought from the occupying tribes by the Colonization Society. An armed U.S. schooner furnished protection. At Harper's suggestion the new American protectorate was named Liberia and the capital, in compliment to the President, Monrovia.

Meanwhile in Albemarle County Jefferson's young friend Edward Coles took the positive steps he had promised some years before. He sold his plantation near the Blue Ridge and moved his slaves out to the Illinois country. Coles, after resigning as President Madison's private secretary, had made a reputation for himself by his skillful completion of an emergency diplomatic mission to the Czar Alexander in St. Petersburg. As soon as he settled in the blacksoil belt at Edwardsville, Monroe appointed him registrar of the Land Office there. He had already, during the trek out, one balmy May day on a flatboat drifting down the Ohio, declared to his slaves that they were free.

Coles's career in Illinois was brilliant and stormy. The new state was torn by conflict between proslavery and antislavery factions. An attempt was made to prosecute him in the courts for bringing in free Negroes. In spite of every kind of opposition, within three years he was elected governor. Though in the end he sacrificed his political career in the struggle, he was generally credited with being one of a handful of men responsible for the establishment of Illinois as a free state.

When Jefferson's overseer, Edmund Bacon, who had saved up three thousand dollars, toured the west, along with Coles's brother John, in search of land for settlement, his party stopped for several days at Edwardsville. Bacon reported when he got back to Monticello that Edward Coles had vast landholdings where his former slaves were working happily for wages. When Coles was finally swept out of Illinois politics by the Andrew Jackson tidal wave, he was able to sell his land at such a profit that, having married a Pennsylvania girl, he spent the rest of his life in opulent retirement in Philadelphia.

Jefferson knew only too well the storm of passions that would be aroused by the slavery question. He was torn between his desire for emancipation and his understanding of the slaveowners' problems. Always foremost in his mind was the question of what to do with the slaves when they were freed. In January 1821 he wrote John Adams: "The real question, as seen in the states afflicted with this unfortunate population, is Are our slaves to be presented with freedom and a dagger? for if Congress has the power to regulate the conditions of the inhabitants of the states, within the states, it will be but another exercise of that power to declare that all shall be free. are we then to see again Athenian and Lacedemonian confederacies? to wage another Peloponnesian war to settle the ascendancy between them? or is this the tocsin merely of a servile war? that remains to be seen: but I hope not by you and me, surely they will parley awhile and give us time to get out of the way. what a Bedlamite is man!"

"Slavery in this Country I have seen hanging over it like a black cloud for half a Century," answered Adams. ". . . I have been so terrified by this Phenomenon, that I constantly said in former times to the Southern Gentlemen, I cannot comprehend this object. . . . I will vote for forcing no measure against your judgements. What we are to see, *God* knows, and I leave it to him, and his agents in posterity. I have none of the genius of Franklin, to invent a rod to draw from the cloud its Thunder and lightning."

Jefferson in replying congratulated Adams on having "health and spirits enough to take part" in the convention that met in Boston to revise the Massachusetts constitution. He liked what he read in the papers of the amendment Adams proposed eliminating state recognition of the three chosen religious sects. "This country, which has given to the world the example of physical liberty, owes to it that of moral emancipation also. for, as yet it is but nominal with us. the inquisition of public opinion overwhelms in practice the freedom asserted by the laws in theory."

"My appearance in the late convention," Adams answered, "was too ludicrous to be talked of. I was a member in the Convention of 1779, and there I was loquacious enough. I have harrangued and scribbled more than my share, but from that time to the convention of 1820 I never opened my lips in a publick debate. After a total desuetude for 40 years I boggled and blundered more than a young fellow just rising to speak at the bar. What I said I know not; I believe the Printers have made better speeches than I made for myself. . . . What would I give for nerves as good as yours? But as Wesley said of himself at my age, 'Old time has shaken me by the hand and parallized it.'"

Both men made a point of avoiding topics which might cause friction between them. They never came to an end of the things they could discuss amicably. Adams didn't tell Jefferson, whom he knew to be in favor of unrestricted manhood suffrage, that his chief effort in the convention was a defense of the property qualification for voting. A small property qualification, he maintained, would encourage enterprise. Without a property qualification the rich would have undue influence over the poor, by buying their votes and thus corrupting the electorate. Neither did Adams admit that the effort, which was unsuccessful, had so worn him out that he'd gone home to Quincy with a fever that kept him several weeks in bed.

22. *Republicanism Abroad*

Adams and Jefferson, at that moment, were profoundly interested in events to the southward. The Spanish empire in America had for years been in the agonies of dissolution. Independent republics were springing up with pronouncements of constitutions based on the Declaration of Independence and French proclamations of the Rights of Man. Jefferson's advice would have been, had he known of any way of getting it listened to, the same that he gave to Lafayette in Revolutionary Paris: go slow. He was horrified by the tales of despotism and bloodshed brought back by American shipowners.

"I feared from the beginning," he wrote Adams, "that these people were not sufficiently enlightened for self-government; and that after wading through blood and slaughter they would end in military tyrannies . . . yet as they wished to try the experiment I wished them success in it. they have now tried it, and will probably find that their safest road will be an accommodation with the mother country, which shall hold them together with the single link of the same chief magistrate, leaving to him power enough to keep them at peace with one another, and to themselves the essential powers of self-government and self-improvement, until they shall be sufficiently trained by education and habits of freedom to walk safely by themselves"—in short a federal system under a Spanish viceroy. "representative government, native functionaries, a qualified negative on their laws, with a previous security by compact for freedom of commerce, freedom of the press, habeas corpus and trial by jury, would make a good beginning. this last would be the school in which the people might begin to learn the exercise of civic duties as well as rights."

He was encouraged in these conclusions by news that the Spanish patriots had managed to extort a liberal constitution from their sulky Bourbon despot. This, with a similar revolt in Naples, gave him fresh hope that Europe was once more on the road to free institutions. With his own peculiar sort of selfdeprecating humor he added, "You see, my dear Sir, how easily we prescribe a cure for their difficulties, while we cannot cure our own."

John Adams in his reply was categorically pessimistic. "I have long been decided in opinion that a free government and the Roman Catholick religion can never exist together in any nation or Country, and consequently that all projects for reconciling them in old Spain or new are Eutopian, Platonick and Chimerical."

Adams, always skeptical of popular outbursts, was looking forward, with considerable foresight, to the black reaction, largely led by priests and monks, which had already arisen to crush the liberal movements of 1820. "I have seen," he declared, "such a prostration and prostitution of Human Nature to the Priesthood in old Spain, as settled my judgement long ago, and I understand that in new Spain it is even worse."

"The Art of Lawgiving," Adams added after ruminating on the subject for a couple of months, "is not so easy as that of Architecture or Painting. . . . I may refine too much, I may be an Enthusiast. But I think a free Government is necessarily a complicated piece of Machinery, the nice and exact Adjustment of whose Springs, Wheels and Weights, are not yet well comprehended by the Artists of the Age and still less by the People."

23. *Florida at Last*

As dispatches accumulated in the gazettes telling of renewed turmoil in Spain and in the Spanish Americas, Jefferson had to agree that free governments were proving hard to come by. Through occasional visits and consultations with Madison and President Monroe he was kept posted on Secretary of State Adams' difficulties in procuring ratification of the treaty with Spain for the cession of Florida. John Q.'s vehement defense of Andrew Jackson's arbitrary measures had produced a sort of shocked acquiescence in the Liverpool cabinet to American annexation, but Fernando VII's court was beset with speculators angling for land grants before the territory changed hands. One happy result of the liberal revolution in Spain was that the Cortes during its short season of power ratified the treaty and annulled the grants to Fernando's favorites.

On February 22, 1821, the younger Adams was able to enter in his journal: "Ratifications of the Florida Treaty exchanged." The same day he sent to Congress a massive report on the history and theory of weights and measures which the Senate had requested three years before in the course of a debate on the feasibility of adopting the metric system. "And thus have terminated, blessed be God, two of the most memorable transactions of my life. This day two years have elapsed since the Florida Treaty was signed. Let my sons, if they ever consult this record of their father's life . . . meditate upon all the vicissitudes that have befallen the treaty. . . . Let them remark the workings of private interests, of perfidious fraud, of sordid intrigues, of royal treachery, of malignant rivalry, and of envy masked by patriotism, playing to and fro across the Atlantic into each other's hands, all combined to destroy this treaty between the signature and the ratification, and let them learn to put their trust in the overruling providence of God."

The moment the Spanish treaty was out of the way the question arose of the recognition of the South American republics. President Monroe, whose blood kindled as Jefferson's did to the republican watchwords, had been waiting for the favorable moment. In the first year of his presidency he sent Caesar Augustus Rodney, Jefferson's old Attorney General, and John Graham, whom Jefferson had sent as his private investigator to the Western Waters during Burr's adventure, down to the river Plate to report on the stability of the government established in Buenos Aires.

The estuary of the Río de la Plata was particularly interesting to American commerce. Great Britain had sent two small armies there without being able to obtain a political foothold, but still managed to retain a near monopoly of the carrying trade. It was a region of rising commercial importance. The reports that came back were mixed. Rodney told Jefferson that personally he had great hopes for the future of what was then known as the United Provinces. All vestige of Spanish authority had been long since wiped out there. The pacification was so complete that the local General San Martín was preparing an army to march across the Andes for the liberation of the Pacific coast.

In the north fighting still continued. Spanish remnants held out in Peru. In Venezuela and Colombia the fortunes of war seesawed back and forth. The leadership of the revolt, first instigated in Venezuela by the indefatigable Miranda, had, since his capture and death in a Spanish dungeon, fallen into the hands of the mercurial and dictatorial Liberator, Simón Bolívar. Mexico had just proclaimed independence. Since the flight of the Braganza court to Rio, the Brazilians were coming to consider themselves the equals of the mother country in the farflung Portuguese empire. In Congress and out Henry Clay was advocating immediate recognition of the new nations.

24. Canning Incites President Monroe to a Doctrine

James Monroe's second inauguration was on March 5, 1821, because the fourth fell on a Sunday that year. "The President," reported John Quincy Adams, "attired in a full suit of black broadcloth of somewhat antiquated fashion, with shoe-and-knee buckles, rode in a plain carriage with four horses and a single colored footman." The heads of departments each followed in a carriage and pair. "There was not a soldier present, nor a constable distinguishable by his badge of office."

The crowd was packed so dense around the Capitol that arriving dignitaries had trouble getting in. The new British minister, the elegant Stratford Canning, a cousin of George Canning's, who arrived betimes decked out in a full court uniform, was unable to make his way in the crush until he managed to squeeze through a door in the backwash of the presidential party.

During this fifth year of Monroe's administration foreign affairs were as relaxed as domestic. Even an occasional clash of temperaments between crusty little Adams and Stratford Canning, who in spite of his rather frozen good looks was absentminded and eccentric in the upperclass English manner, had no ill results on the relations between the United States and Great Britain.

Adams reported in his journal one conversation which became a classic of diplomatic history. Canning called one morning at the State Department and inquired testily if the story he'd read in the *National Intelligencer* were true about American settlements on the Columbia River. Adams bristled and intimated that this sort of question should be made in writing. When they met again next day the argument became blistering. Adams laid down the law. Canning cried out that he was being treated like a schoolboy.

Adams demanded to know whether Great Britain had any claim on the Columbia River. "Why, do you not know," Canning replied, "that we have such a claim?"

"I do not know," said Adams, "what you claim nor what you do not claim. You claim India; you claim Africa. You claim . . ."

Canning interrupted. "Perhaps a piece of the moon?"

Adams pretended to take him seriously. "No," he said, "I have not heard that you claim exclusively any part of the moon; but there is not a spot on this habitable globe that I could affirm you do not claim; and there is none which you may not claim with as much color of right as you can have to Columbia River or its mouth."

"And how far," asked Canning, "would you consider this exclusion of right to extend?"

"To all the shores of the South Sea," said Adams. "We know of no right that you have there."

"Suppose," said Canning, "Great Britain should undertake to make a settlement there, would you object to it?"

"I have no doubt we should," said Adams.

The gentlemen parted in great disaccord. Stratford Canning reported the tiff to Downing Street but was advised to pay it no heed. No more than the execution of Arbuthnot and Ambrister was this little row allowed to strain the improved relations between the two countries.

When Congress passed a Navigation Act levying duties on British shipping entering American ports, the British retaliated but without real animus. A subtle change was coming over the Tory administration. During the depression that followed the Napoleonic wars, Liverpool and Castlereagh, though neither of the noble lords was much versed in economics, had somehow discovered that the United States was Great Britain's greatest overseas market. The cabinet was yielding to influences from the City and the Board of Trade. The British were coming to think of Americans as potential customers instead of as upstarts and rebels.

The development of the South American question, which a few years back would have been the source of bitter rivalry, now drew the two countries together. Lord Liverpool's government was pulling away from continental entanglements. Though George IV and his court tended to sympathize with the fervent reactionaries at Vienna, the commercial interests deprecated the idea of spending any more money on the Hapsburgs and the Bourbons.

Metternich, who had so carefully clamped a lid down on the people of Europe, began to let drop acid comments about Castlereagh's defection. His whole careful repatching of the old regime was threatened by the transatlantic revolutions. He knew too well that revolt was contagious. It was the mutiny of the troops being drilled at Cadiz for fresh repressions against the American colonists that had touched off the liberal uprising that shut Fernando VII up in his palace and forced him to grant a constitution.

The principalities and powers huddled together in the Holy Alliance began to concert measures against the South Americans and the Spaniards. Even the Czar Alexander had lost the youthful liberalism that had entranced Thomas Jefferson. His plan was to march Russian troops across Europe and over the Pyrenees to stamp out the Spanish constitution of 1812.

It was in this context, when news reached Washington of Bolivar's victory at Carabobo, soon followed by his entry into Caracas, that Monroe and his Secretary of State decided that the time had come for a decisive move. On March 8, 1822, the President sent a special message to Congress recommending the recognition of the independence of the United Provinces of the Rio de la Plata, of Colombia, Chile, Peru, and Mexico. He further recommended that the United States should observe "the most perfect neutrality" between all warring factions. Monroe was not a hasty man. Though Congress was prompt in appropriating the necessary funds he let almost a year go by before he appointed ministers to the new nations.

Meanwhile Richard Rush's letters kept him up to date on the continuing transformation of the Tory administration at Westminster. In the summer of 1822 the imperturbable Castlereagh began to crack. Tapping his forehead with his fingers, he confided to his private secretary, as the two men stood beside the river in front of his mansion at North Bray, "I am quite worn out here." At court he made wild statements about being a fugitive from justice. He threw himself on a sofa in the Duke of Wellington's library and accused himself of every crime on the calendar. Hurried home to his country place by his wife, he was put to bed and given sedatives. Though razors and pistols were taken away he managed to hide a little penknife. He cut his throat one August morning and bled to death in the arms of his physician.

Castlereagh's death made way for the return of George Canning to the cabinet. The Canning who returned to power was a different man from the Canning who had thrown up his political career after their duel. He had shown an ability, rare in statesmen and in Tories particularly, to grow with the times. During his retirement he interested himself in the *Quarterly Review*. He became warm friends with Sir Walter Scott. He traveled on the Continent and served for a while as ambassador extraordinary to the court of the Braganzas. An admirer of Edmund Burke, he did not feel that the system of the Holy Alliance was a system the great conciliator would have approved of. Furthermore he was thoroughly aware of the rising power of the businessmen and manufacturers who had their hands on the levers of the industrial revolution.

There was a new spirit in the air, a backdraft from the enthusiasms of the romantic poets. British statesmen of the day whether Whig or Tory could not help being stirred by the Greek revolt against the Ottoman Turks, which exploded in Wallachia and Moldavia just as Metternich's pupils were putting the quietus on the liberals of western Europe. Members of Parliament were brought up on the classics. Many of them read Byron. Sympathy with the latterday Hellenes, struggling to establish their nationality against fearful odds, spread through all literate Britain. When Alexander, whose agents had done so much to encourage the revolt, turned against it at Metternich's insistence, the British Tories felt the whole depth of the chasm that separated their John Bull kind of conservatism with that of the Holy Alliance.

When the Duke of Wellington appeared to represent Great Britain at the congress at Verona, he wrapped himself in a chill formality which filled Metternich with misgivings. When the duke returned home with nothing good to report Canning sent an urgent note to the French Foreign Minister begging him to desist from the plan hatched at Verona for the invasion of Spain.

The French let it be known that if Louis XVIII didn't go to the assistance of his brother Bourbon the Czar Alexander would. Their Foreign Office turned down an offer of Canning's to mediate between France and the Spanish constitutionalists. When in the spring of 1823 a French army crossed the Bidassoa the only opposition was a group of exiled French liberals dressed in Napoleonic uniforms. They waved the tricolor and called on the French soldiers to mutiny. They should march on Paris instead of on Madrid. The liberals were answered by a volley of musketry. The French marched on through Spain, greeted in every village with flowers and wine by adherents of the Bourbons.

Addressing the House of Commons, George Canning expressed the pious hope that the constitutional regime would triumph in the struggle.

In the summer that followed Richard Rush was agreeably surprised by Canning's affability. Canning intimated to him slyly that he was modeling his system of neutrality on that of George Washington when Jefferson was Secretary of State. In August 1823 he began making veiled suggestions to Rush that the United States and Great Britain might go "hand in hand" in checking Bourbon designs on Spanish America. Rush, as an astute diplomat, waited to see how far Canning would go. He made the countersuggestion that perhaps the time had come for Great Britain to recognize the independence of the new nations.

Canning answered with an "unofficial and confidential" note. The recovery of the colonies by Spain was patently hopeless. British recognition was a question "of time and circumstance." Great Britain would throw no impediment in the way of an amicable arrangement between the colonists and the Spanish government. "We aim not at the possession of any part of them ourselves. We could not see any portion of them transferred to any other Power with indifference."

These formulations were not too far from the theories John Quincy Adams had been elaborating in the State Department since his tiff with Canning's cousin in Washington. The policy of the United States must be to oppose any European colonization on the American continent; there must be no interference in the internal affairs of any American nation.

Monroe, too, in his slow careful way, had been ruminating over these problems ever since his message on recognition. The matter was made urgent by a flight of fancy on the part of Czar Alexander. The erstwhile liberal czar had issued a ukase ordering all foreign ships to keep one hundred Italian miles off the coast of "Russian America." Since the British, the Russians, and the Americans had furtrading posts scattered indiscriminately along the northern Pacific shoreline, Adams, as soon as the Russian minister reported the wording of the ukase, immediately started a negotiation to set a southern limit to Russian claims.

The capture of Madrid and the flight to Seville of the Spanish Cortes opened up the possibility of new threats to South America. Monroe immediately sought the advice of Jefferson and Madison. He furnished them both with copies of Rush's letters and asked their opinion.

Jefferson was hoping that all Europe might yet catch fire from the Spanish constitution. In the spring of the year he sent Monroe a copy of what he called "a reverie" he'd fallen into in a letter to their mutual friend William Short, in which he imagined the French troops marching on Paris instead of crossing into Spain and setting off a general insurrection against Metternich's absolute monarchs. This "reverie" must have been based on some inkling of the plans of Lafayette's conspiratorial friends, the French branch of the Italian Carbonari. With Europe in turmoil again, went Jefferson's daydream, "Great Britain and U.S. prepare for milking the cow; and as friend to all parties, furnish all with cabotage, commerce, manufactures and food. . . . she goes hand in hand with us in reaping this harvest and on fair principles of Neutrality, which it will be now to her interest to settle and observe: She joins us too in a guarantee of the independence of Cuba, with the consent of Spain, and removes thus this bone of contention from between us."

He went on to imagine a liberal Spain freeing her colonies voluntarily, and representative governments established all over Europe.

In June he had answered a query of Monroe's as to whether the United States could "take a bolder attitude than formerly in favor of liberty" with an outburst of indignation against "the presumption"— of the Bourbons of France—"of dictating to an independent nation the form of it's government." At the same time he reiterated Washington's advice never to take part in foreign quarrels. He didn't trust the new liberalism of the Tory administration. He considered Canning's remonstrances a farce "to gull her own people."

Rush's communications changed his mind. After reading them over and over he wrote President Monroe a letter.

"Our first and fundamental maxim should be, never to entangle ourselves in the broils of Europe. our second never to suffer Europe to intermeddle with cis-Atlantic affairs. America, North and South, has a set of interests distinct from those of Europe, and peculiarly her own. she should therefore have a system of her own, distinct from that of Europe. while the last is laboring to become the domicil of despotism our endeavor should surely be to make our hemisphere that of freedom."

He was for taking up Canning's proposition.

"Great Britain is the nation that can do us the most harm. . . . with her on our side we need not fear the whole world. . . . not that I would purchase even her amity at the price of taking part in her wars. but the war in which the present proposition might engage us, should that be its consequence, is not her war but ours. . . . I am clearly of Mr. Canning's opinion, that it will prevent instead of promoting war. with Great Britain withdrawn from their scale and shifted into that of our two continents, all Europe combined could not undertake such a war."

He added in parentheses that he had to admit that he would like to see Cuba eventually admitted into the Union.

"The controul which, with Florida Point, this island would give us over the Gulf of Mexico, and the countries and isthmus bordering it, as well as those whose waters flow into it, would fill up the measure of our political wellbeing."

As second best, in order to avoid a war, he would be willing to join with Great Britain in guaranteeing Cuban independence.

He ended the letter by saying, in his usual selfdeprecating way, he had been so long weaned from political subjects he doubted if his opinions were worth much. "But the question now proposed involves consequences so lasting . . . as to rekindle all the interest I have hitherto felt on such occasions . . . and praying you to accept it at only what it is worth, I add the assurance of my constant and affectionate friendship and respect."

Madison wrote the President from Montpelier a few days later. He agreed with Jefferson. The British overtures must be encouraged.

"Our co-operation is due to ourselves & to the the the world; and, whilst it must insure success, in the event of an appeal to force, it doubles the chance of success without that appeal. . . . Will it not be honorable to our Country, & possibly not altogether in vain," he added somewhat wistfully, "to invite the British Govt to extend the avowed disapprobation of the project agst. the Spanish colonies, to the enterprise of France agst. Spain herself, and even to join in some declaratory Act in Behalf of the Greeks."

With Jefferson's and Madison's letters on his desk and Rush's communications spread out before him, Monroe went to work to compose a message for the opening of the forthcoming session of the Seventeenth Congress. His effective cabinet now consisted of John Quincy Adams; John C. Calhoun; Samuel L. Southard of New Jersey, an old friend from the days when Monroe had his law office in Fredericksburg, recently installed as Secretary of the Navy; and William Wirt. Secretary Crawford of the Treasury was desperately ill in Virginia of a sickness from which he never recovered. The five men discussed the situation from every angle at a series of meetings, sitting perched on the ornate French chairs with which the Monroes had furnished the restored presidential mansion.

Two fresh pieces of news, coming in since the government had returned to Washington after the dog days, added new hazards to the prospect. One was a message from the Czar Alexander: he would receive no envoys from the South American states; at the same time he went out of his way to congratulate the United States on their neutral position towards them. He followed this note a few days later with a grandiose statement in which Secretary Adams discerned a threat: the Czar Alexander was willing "to guarantee the tranquility of all the states of which the civilized world is composed."

The second piece of news was even more alarming. Cádiz had fallen to the French. The deputies of the Spanish people were in flight or in prison and Fernando VII was back on his absolute throne.

Cogitating on these developments, Monroe instructed Adams to go to work, in Washington and through Rush in London, on the joint declaration with Great Britain which Jefferson and Madison had approved.

Adams reported that Monroe appeared profoundly depressed. Calhoun, according to Adams, who by this time disliked him heartily, was "perfectly moonstruck at the surrender of Cadiz," and talked wildly of war to defend the liberties of America against the Holy Alliance. Adams quoted himself as remarking scornfully, "They will no more restore Spanish dominion . . . than Chimborazo will sink beneath the ocean."

At this juncture a latest dispatch arrived from Rush. Canning had lost interest in a joint declaration. Monroe and his heads of departments were puzzled and dismayed. It was not till much later that they learned that Canning had used the pressures of the moment to accomplish an agreement with the French ambassador. In a secret document known as the Polignac Memorandum Great Britain declared that the reduction of Spanish America was hopeless, that all restrictive laws against foreign commerce were in abeyance; and that trade was now open; if any nation questioned her right to trade there, she would immediately recognize the independence of the Spanish-American states. "The junction of any foreign power in an enterprize of Spain against the Colonies" would be viewed by His Majesty's Government "as an entirely new question, and one upon which they must take such decision as the interest of Great Britain would require."

France declared, on her part, that she had no designs on Spanish America but that she reserved the right to trade there on the same terms as Great Britain: she abjured, in any case, "any design of acting against the colonies by force of arms."

Canning had won his point from the Bourbons in their moment of triumph. He had no further need for the cooperation of the United States.

President Monroe decided to go it alone. The discussion in the cabinet room from this point on was entirely between the President and his Secretary of State.

Monroe wanted to make a public declaration before Congress. Adams wanted to expound the principles upon which the heads of departments were agreed in his diplomatic correspondence.

The President read a draft of his proposed message to Congress. It was full of republican fire, a fresh outburst of the spirit of '76 he'd imbibed from Jefferson's and Madison's letters. Adams begged him to tone down the paragraphs denouncing the invasion of Spain and Turkish reprisals against the Greeks. "The ground I wish to take," he explained, "is that of earnest remonstrance against the interference of the European powers by force with South America, but to disclaim all interference on our part with Europe; to make an American cause and adhere inflexibly to that."

Monroe was impressed with the wisdom of Adams' remark. The message he sent to Congress on December 2, 1823, like most state papers of lasting import, was a collaboration. Behind it lay a mingling of the libertarian enthusiasms of Jefferson's aggressive republican nationalism with Madison's aspirations for an international rule of reason and law; their ardor was checked and pointed up by John Quincy Adams' matter of fact knowledge of the exigencies of diplomacy. Albert Gallatin, in Washington at the time, added some advice based on his experience with the French. The final draft was suffused by a sort of sturdy rightmindedness, which in his maturity was the characteristic of Monroe's role as a statesman. Even the awkwardness of some of the phrasing expressed the processes of Monroe's slow but accurate thinking.

After describing the amicable negotiation now in course with Russia and Great Britain for a limitation of their claims on the northwest coast, the President solemnly laid down what later became known as the Monroe Doctrine.

The first significant paragraph was Adams': "The occasion has been judged proper, for asserting as a principle in which the rights and interests of the United States are involved, that the American Continents, by the free and independent condition which they have assumed and maintain, are henceforth not to be considered as subjects for future colonization by any European power."

The President then remarked on the regret with which Americans must view the suppression of the "Great effort . . . in Spain and Portugal to improve the condition of the people of those countries" in spite of "the moderation with which it had been conducted. . . . Our policy in regard to Europe, which was adopted at an early stage of the wars which have so long agitated that quarter of the Globe, nevertheless remains the same, which is, not to interfere in the internal concerns of any of its powers; to consider the Government *de facto* as the legitimate for us; to cultivate friendly relations with it, and to preserve those relations by a frank, firm and manly policy, meeting in all instances, the just claims of every power; submitting to injuries from none."

The declaration concerning the Americas was in Monroe's own words: "in regard to those continents, circumstances are eminently and conspicuously different. It is impossible that the allied powers should extend their political systems to any portion of either continent, without endangering our peace and happiness, nor can anyone believe, that our Southern Brethren, if left to themselves would adopt it"— the despotism of the Holy Alliance—"of their own accord. It is equally impossible, therefore, that we should behold such interposition, in any form, with indifference."

It was said that Canning was delighted when he first read President Monroe's message. Though he must have known that there had not been time for the brief summary of that secret document he whispered confidentially in Rush's ear to cross the Atlantic, it seemed an obedient echo of his Polignac Memorandum. On a second reading the paragraph on colonization stuck in his craw. "There was not a man in the British councils whose blood did not tingle at his finger ends on reading that proposition of President Monroe," a Britisher told one American diplomat.

In any case Canning took all the credit to himself. In a vainglorious statement he made in Parliament a few months later the declaimed: "I called the New World into existence to redress the balance of the Old."

25. *The Search for Professors*

Thomas Jefferson's collaboration in the Monroe Doctrine was his last and final encounter with statesmanship on the grand scale. He was eighty. He was feeling his years. Some months before he and John Adams had exchanged views on the miseries of their time of life.

"When our faculties have left, or are leaving us," Jefferson wrote, "one by one, sight, hearing, memory, every avenue of pleasing sensation is closed, and athumy, debility and mal-aise left in their places, when the friends of our youth are all gone, is death an evil? . . . I have ever dreaded a doting old age and my health has been generally so good, and is now so good . . . I dread it still. the rapid decline of my strength during the last winter has made me hope sometimes that I see land. during summer I enjoy it's temperature but I shudder at the approach of winter, and wish I could sleep through it with the Doormouse."

"I answer your question, Is Death an evil," John Adams answered from Quincy. For some years now he had amused himself with the whimsy of calling his establishment there, in his letters to Monticello, Montezillo. "It is not an evil. It is a blessing to the individual and to the world. Yet we ought not to wish for it till life becomes insupportable; we must wait the pleasure and convenience of this great teacher. Winter is as terrible to me, as to you, I am almost reduced in it to the life of a Bear or torpid swallow."

Time was short. Jefferson's every effort must again be concentrated on the university. The legislature that met in the winter of 1822–23 was favorably inclined. As early as January Cabell could write from Richmond: "I am happy to inform you that our prospects are now very favorable. . . . Everything is understood . . . everything is arranged."

The pavilions were nearly completed. Sixty thousand dollars was now appropriated for the rotunda. The prospects for opening in 1824 were excellent if only the Visitors could find the firstrate men Jefferson insisted on to do the teaching. While Cabell wrestled with the Assembly, Jefferson wrestled with the difficulty of finding professors.

The hue and cry among the Presbyterians and the Methodists and the Baptists rose to such a pitch against Dr. Cooper that Jefferson had to allow himself to be overruled on his appointment by the other Visitors. Dr. Cooper regretfully accepted a compensation for the canceling of his contract and went to the University of South Carolina.

Jefferson had canvassed every other competent man in the United States. When he found he could attract none of them to Charlottesville he decided that somebody must be sent abroad to engage teachers, preferably in England. George Ticknor had already recommended Dr. Blaettermann, a cultivated German who had studied all over Europe and who had recently been teaching in London, for the chair of modern languages. Someone must be sent to interview him. The university's emissary must be a man in whom the Visitors had absolute confidence. When Cabell begged off, for family reasons and because he was needed in the legislature, Jefferson rode over to Montpelier. Jefferson and Madison put their heads together and decided on Francis Walker Gilmer.

One of the younger sons of the beloved Albemarle County physician who was a friend of Jefferson's younger days, Frank Gilmer was left an orphan at an early age. He was partly raised at Monticello. Jefferson advised him in his studies and loaned him books and Martha Randolph helped him with his French. As a youth he fell in love with Jefferson's granddaughter Ellen. Her turning him down combined with mounting ill health to throw his life off balance. When William Wirt married Frank Gilmer's older sister, the warmhearted Wirt was charmed by a sparkle he found in the boy. He coached Frank in the law and treated him as his own son.

With Wirt as a foster father, and Jefferson taking the place of a grandfather, the young man was encouraged to develop every aptitude. He grew up with a scholarly mind, a knack for graceful writing, and a grasp of intricate legal reasoning that delighted his wellwishers. His many friends saw him as one of the coming leaders of Virginia, but nobody could quite guess what channel his talents would take.

At Monticello he met Correa de Serra, whom he described in an enthusiastic letter to one of his brothers as "the most extraordinary man now living or perhaps who ever has lived." Probably under Jefferson's influence he'd already done some botanizing in the Albe-

marle County hills. Now he took up botany in earnest. When Correa
returned to Philadelphia he went along. Jefferson gave him a letter
to Dr. Caspar Wistar, the learned Scottish anatomist whose "Wistar
evenings" were the sociable reflections of the American Philosophical
Society's meetings. With two such sponsors young Gilmer was immediately taken into the circle of scientists and litterateurs which
made Philadelphia at that moment the intellectual center of the United
States.

When the invitation reached Gilmer from the members of the
Board of Visitors to represent them in Europe, he was practicing law
in Richmond. His practice was flourishing, he was highly regarded
at the bar, already he was being spoken of for Congress. Friends
tried to talk him out of taking on the mission, but Gilmer had an
itch for travel and a high sense of public duty. He convinced himself
that he would be doing Virginia a service. At the same time he would
be emulating George Ticknor, with whom he became friends at a
Wistar evening in Philadelphia when the Bostonian was starting on his
European tour, by broadening his mind among the eminent and
learned of Europe. The trip, as he envisioned it, would hardly take
longer than his yearly vacation at the Virginia springs. His clients
would hardly know he'd been away. To Jefferson's delight he accepted.

By this time the projected opening of the university had been
postponed to January 1, 1825. It wasn't until April 5, 1824, that
Gilmer was formally appointed by the Board of Visitors. At the
same meeting Jefferson received his formal investiture as rector of the
university. Carrying a great bundle of letters of introduction from
Jefferson and Madison and from his own contemporaries, Gilmer
sailed in May from New York on the ship *Cortes*.

He had hoped to have John Randolph's company, as that eccentric
gentleman, having finally paid off every cent of indebtedness on his
paternal estates, was about to embark on a longcontemplated European
tour. In spite of having been brought up in the circle of Randolph's
bitterest enemies, and of the seventeen years' difference in their ages,
Randolph and Gilmer had become fast friends. The fastidious Randolph was unstinting in his affection for brilliant young men. He
wrote Gilmer letters as doting as those he wrote to his own nephews.

Landing in Holyhead after a rough crossing, Gilmer's first call,
like Ticknor's a few years before, was at Hatton to seek the advice
of Dr. Parr. Dr. Parr was away from home so Gilmer rode posthaste
to London. There he promptly engaged George Blaettermann, whom
he knew Jefferson would accept on Ticknor's recommendation. He
spent a few hours with John Randolph, whom he found "looking
badly." Poor Randolph had shown every sign of mental illness on the
Alexander coming over. He'd made a scene with the captain and

refused to pay his fare on the steamboat which was to take the passengers ashore.

Gilmer's letters were mostly to members of the liberal opposition. He found the American minister, Richard Rush, too busy to be of much help. The famous lecturer, Sir James Mackintosh, was too absorbed in his lobbying in Parliament for the recognition of the South American republics to do more than furnish letters of introduction. Gilmer found Henry Brougham, another man who never had a moment to spare, definitely interested in Jefferson's project. Brougham was himself planning a new university for London on similar lines, to furnish the scientific and technical training needed in the industrial age.

Brougham and Mackintosh prepared the way so well that Gilmer was warmly received at Cambridge. He was invited to take rooms at Trinity College.

"The tone of feeling in England is undoubtedly favorable to us of the U.S.," he wrote Jefferson. "The lawyers are beginning to read our reports, the courts and even Parliament have in several things followed, and somewhat boastfully, I may say, our example." He added that Brougham had inquired about Mr. Jefferson "with the greatest interest."

At Cambridge he discovered with dismay that the long vacation was on and that most of the professors had disappeared into the country. The same thing at Oxford.

Gilmer enjoyed himself immensely nevertheless. He saw all the sights. Writing Wirt from Stratford, he quoted the inscription on Shakespeare's tomb. He found the countryside lovely, but he preferred Virginia: "I like the elbow room we have, where the wild deer cross the untrodden grass. . . . There is nothing in England so beautiful as Albemarle or the view from the window"—in ex-Governor Cabell's house at Montevideo—"from which you used to gaze on the deep blue depth of those silent and boundless mountains."

When Gilmer finally caught up with Dr. Parr the venerable scholar proved a disappointment. Parr was in his late seventies. He knew every pedagogue in Britain but he couldn't remember their names or addresses. He did help prepare a list of books for the university library.

Gilmer made for Edinburgh as fast as the coaches would carry him up the Great North Road. His letters home were rhapsodic about the beauty of the city of squarecut blue stone set in "flinty hills, veiled in eternal mist."

He put himself out to charm the dour Scots and, like Ticknor before him, won all hearts. Everywhere he was regaled with good dinners and sage advice, but he started back to London again without having signed up a single professor.

Sir John Leslie, the most renowned of Scottish scientists, did offer to visit the University of Virginia for a few weeks and to give the Visitors his patronage and advice. His fee would be a thousand pounds to cover the expenses of the trip. Jefferson had to write back himself explaining, with his usual tact, that at this stage of the institution's development they needed permanent professors. With Leslie's offer as a feather in his cap Gilmer journeyed back to London.

There he managed to get hold of a Fellow of Trinity College named George Long to teach Latin, Greek, and Hebrew. Dr. Long turned out to be a great find. Another outstanding Cambridge man named Thomas Hewett Key accepted the chair of mathematics. After that his work was easy. By September he was able to write his friend Dabney Carr that he had four professors signed up.

He explained his tardiness in embarking for Virginia: "At this season of the year no man in England is where he ought to be, except perhaps those of Fleet and of Newgate"—the famous London prisons. "Every little country schoolmaster who never saw a town, is gone, as they say, to the country, that is to Scotland to shoot grouse, to Doncaster to see a race, or to Cheltenham to dose himself with that vile water. With all these difficulties, and not only without assistance but with numerous enemies to one's success (as every Yankee in England is)"—Gilmer was convinced the New Englanders had been spreading evil reports and that even Rush, as a Philadelphian, wasn't any too willing to put himself out to help Virginia start her university—"I have done wonders. I have employed four Professors of the most respectable families, of real talent, learning, &c., a fellow of Trinity Col. Camb. and a M.A. of the same University. . . . If learning does not revive its drooping head it shall not be my fault. . . . My intercourse with professional and Literary men here has fired again all my boyish enthusiasm and I pant to be back at work."

Gilmer had taken advantage of some spare hours during the weeks he spent bargaining for books with the London booksellers and for laboratory equipment with the mathematical instrument makers to do a little research on his favorite topics, the life and writings of Captain John Smith.

"Virginia must still be a great nation," he went on to Dabney Carr: "she has genius enough, she only wants methods in her application." He had met most of the eminent Scottish and English lawyers. With the exception of Brougham, whom he thought prodigious, he didn't find them any brighter than their Virginia counterparts. "The University will open in February, and I shall be with you in time to give you a greeting at the court of appeals. . . . Keep me alive in the memory of my friends & do not let them suppose I have deserted the bar." Before he left England he had a fifth professor engaged.

On October 5 Gilmer sailed home from Liverpool on the *Crisis*. Thirtyfive days of adverse winds and wallowing seas. Gilmer became desperately ill on the voyage, probably from complications of the tuberculosis that had been smoldering in him since boyhood. He reached New York too weak to walk.

John Randolph, who landed in a quiet and chastened frame of mind two days after his younger friend, nursed him as best he could. In spite of the optimism of the physicians Randolph recognized the disease as consumption from the first. Though Gilmer was confined to his bed for weeks he managed, while in New York, to engage a sixth professor, John Patton Emmet, the nephew of the Irish patriot Robert Emmet, whom the English had done to death, for the chair of natural history.

Jefferson and Madison had insisted all along that the chairs of law and ethics should be occupied by Americans. In spite of his refusing the post, they still hoped that Gilmer himself would eventually consent to become their professor of law. For ethics they picked Congressman George Tucker, of the brilliant Tucker family of Virginia and Bermuda, whose destinies became involved with the Randolphs when St. George Tucker married John Randolph's widowed mother.

Although some effort had been made to keep Gilmer's mission a secret the newspapers by this time had got wind of the composition of the University of Virginia faculty. The New England press erupted into patriotic protests.

"We wish well to this college, but think it a pity, that an agent should be dispatched to Europe for a suite of Professors. Mr. Gilmer could have fully discharged his mission with half the trouble and expense by a short trip to New England," remarked the Boston *Courier*. The Philadelphia *Gazette* considered that "This sending of a Commission to Europe to engage professors for a new University is, we think, one of the greatest insults the American people have received."

These expostulations, though Ritchie's reprinting of them in the Richmond *Enquirer* was followed by a friendly exposition of Thomas Jefferson's reasons for picking professors in England, found echoes in Virginia. Jefferson had tried to appease the Protestant divines by offering to arrange facilities for schools of theology at Charlottesville, affiliated with but separate from the university; but many of them were still unreconciled. They denounced the university as a school for teaching the infidelities of Voltaire and the devilments of French Jacobinism. Jefferson was reduced to despair by the virulence of the opposition which appeared in the legislature in the winter of 1824–25 just at the moment when victory seemed within his grasp.

"The attempt," he wrote Cabell, "in which I have embarked so earnestly to procure an improvement in the moral condition of my native State, although in other States it may have strengthened good dispositions, it has certainly weakened them in my own. the attempt ran afoul of so many local interests, of so many personal views, of so much ignorance, and I have been considered so particularly its promoter that I see evidently a great change of sentiments towards myself. . . . I feel it deeply and very discouragingly, yet I shall not give way." He spoke of the multitude of fine young men who would benefit from the university. "We will not then be weary of well doing," he exclaimed. In another letter he spoke of himself as "discharging the odious function of a physician pouring medicine down the throat of a patient insensible of needing it."

26. *The Nation's Guest*

Jefferson was cheered that winter by a number of enlivening visitors at Monticello. The first was an old friend and lifetime correspondent. One of the last acts of Monroe's administration was to arrange a state visit for Lafayette.

The Bourbon ministry in Paris seems to have consented to the journey on the theory that a sight of the American marquis would put fresh polish on American friendship for France, admittedly somewhat tarnished by the events at Cádiz. At least it would get him out of France where his drawing room had become a hive of liberal conspiracies. A tour abroad, with all expenses paid, was at that moment even more grateful to Lafayette than his absence was to the Bourbons. Lafayette was out of funds. He had been pouring out money in behalf of the liberal revolution now engulfed by the reactionary wave sweeping across Europe. He had lost his immunity from prosecution with his seat as a deputy. Louis XVIII was on his deathbed. His brother who would succeed him as Charles X made him seem a liberal by comparison.

Furthermore Lafayette was in trouble with the *conseil de famille*. Even more than by his politics his vast family connection among the provincial *noblesse* was scandalized by his liaison with a tall handsome opinionated Scottish girl named Frances Wright. To make amends for having kept a mistress during her lifetime, Lafayette had sworn on his wife's deathbed never to remarry. Now he was introducing Fanny Wright and her sister Camilla everywhere as his adopted daughters. Lafayette, accompanied by his son George Washington Lafayette and a numerous retinue, disembarked in New York in August 1824. It had been thought discreet that the Wright sisters should cross the Atlantic on a separate ship.

Immediately he was treated to such a series of functions—state banquets, triumphal arches, singing schoolchildren—as had never been seen in America before. Everywhere he was hailed as "the nation's guest."

After New York it was Boston. There he dined with John Adams, who had just turned ninety. "What a wonderful Man at his Age to undergo the fatigues of such long journeys and constant feasts," Adams wrote Jefferson.

Jefferson, whose role towards Lafayette had always been paternal, immediately warned his oldtime protégé: "I fear they will kill you with their kindness so fatiguing and exhausting must be the ceremonies they force upon you. be on your guard against this, my dear Sir, and do not lose in the enthusiastic embraces of affection, a life they are meant to cherish."

Lafayette throve on it.

Jefferson went on to regret he was "too much enfeebled by age" to journey to Yorktown, where the marquis was to grace the anniversary ceremonies with his presence on October 19. When Lafayette came to Monticello Jefferson promised him that the only official function would be a public dinner which the citizens of Charlottesville insisted on tendering him.

Lafayette replied from Philadelphia. Age had not abated "the canine vanity" Jefferson had noted in the young man. After his political failures at home he was enjoying every moment of popular adulation in America. "The Extraordinary Circumstances of a Reception So Superior to Any Individual Merit Have However, to my Great Regret Mixed with Much delight, prevented My fulfiling the Most pressing duties of a Correspondence with public Bodies or private friends who have the Goodness to Address me." The marquis was so set up every sentence was a public speech.

In the same letter he tactfully explained that Frances Wright and her sister, "preferring American principles to British aristocracy" were joining his party. Jefferson had spoken well of Frances Wright's book, *A Few Days in Athens.* "She is very Happy in your Approbation; for, you and I are the two Men in the World the Esteem of whom she values the Most." He explained that Miss Wright and her sister had spent three years with his family at La Grange. He considered them his daughters.

Fanny Wright was from Dundee, the daughter of a welloff Scottish radical who brought her up in admiration of Tom Paine. As a girl she worshiped Byron from a distance and won the friendship of the eccentric Jeremy Bentham. She had traveled through America three years before and published a panegyric on American democracy which earned her an encomium from Lafayette. She now admitted to the authorship of the little book on Epicurean materialism which Lafayette had lately sent Jefferson. Their mutual friend Short had declared no woman could have written it. Jefferson promptly invited the Wrights to join Lafayette's party when they came to Monticello.

Lafayette spent ten days at Monticello in November. His arrival was preceded by six hundred pieces of mail. The marquis proved as vain and visionary and lovable as ever. Fanny Wright discussed methods of emancipating Negro slaves with Jefferson and Madison. Lafayette joined in her plea for action; slavery was the only blot on the Republic. He was proud to be an American citizen but, in liberal circles abroad, slavery took some explaining away.

Like Edward Coles, Fanny Wright believed in the force of example. She was planning to buy land in Tennessee and to work it with slaves who should receive a yearly credit against their manumission. Her theory was that a slave should be allowed to purchase his own freedom by five years' work. As fast as hers were freed she was planning to resettle them in Haiti. Jefferson acquainted her with the plans of the American Colonization Society. She always claimed that Jefferson approved of her scheme.

The two old cronies spent hours talking over the course of history from the famous evening when Lafayette brought the liberal patriots to Jefferson's legation in Paris to ask his advice on a constitution for France, through their Revolution's subsequent betrayals by Robespierre, Barras, Bonaparte, and the Bourbons.

Although classes had not begun Lafayette had the honor of being the first visitor to be formally entertained by the University of Virginia. Young Jeff Randolph read the welcoming speech which his grandfather had prepared.

In Washingron Lafayette entrusted his bread and butter letter to George Ticknor and Daniel Webster, who were just starting out with Mrs. Ticknor to pay Jefferson a visit: "The Happy Days I have Past at Monticello Are over; But they Have Left on my Heart an Impression, Never to Be effaced. I Rejoice at the Visit you are going to Receive. . . . You will, No doubt talk with Mr Webster of Your ideas to facilitate the Emigration of Coloured people, and Connected with it their Enfranchisement, of His own wishes, expressed in Congress last year with Respect to the Greeks. . . . I Have Seen with pleasure the insistence of the president's Message on the Maintainance of Republican Confederate Institutions in South America."

Lafayette was even more sanguine than Jefferson about the progress of selfgovernment.

27. George Ticknor's Return

The journey from Washington to Monticello proved much easier than when Ticknor made it ten years before. A steamboat carried the party smoothly from Washington to Potomac Creek. They found the Virginia roads and the Virginia inns no worse than they had expected.

They stopped at Montpelier on the way. Ticknor reported that Mr. Madison at seventyfour looked ten years younger than when he had last seen him as President. "Both Mr. Webster and myself were struck with the degree of good-sense in his conversation," noted Ticknor in his journal, "which we did not anticipate from his politics and course of life." The New Englanders were incorrigibly Brahmin in their outlook.

Mr. Madison had three thousand acres, a hundred and sixty slaves, and one of the bestmanaged farms in Virginia. Mrs. M., whom Washington Irving used to say reminded him of one of the Merry Wives of Windsor, was as bouncing and cordial and ceremonious as ever. Her table was luxurious. Mr. Madison liked his wine, which was excellent. She sent her guests delicious little "lunches" to eat in their rooms.

After a night with the Barbours of Barboursville, they arrived early one winter morning at Monticello. They met Mr. Jefferson on the road.

Like all visitors at Monticello during Jefferson's declining years, Ticknor and Webster, each in his journal, minutely described the state of his health. Jefferson still kept up an appearance of wellbeing. Ticknor found that the years had changed him little. He was "very active, lively, happy, riding from ten to fifteen miles every day, and talking, without the least restraint, very pleasantly on all subjects."

Daniel Webster described him as "exhibiting an extraordinary degree of health, vivacity and spirit." His hair still showed sandy traces among the white. He had an easy swinging walk, and a lounging way of sitting. His dress was "neglected but not slovenly." On horseback he wore a gray straightbodied coat with large pearl buttons and black velvet gaiters over loose gray pantaloons.

His habits were very regular. Mr. Jefferson rose, noted Webster, as soon as he could see the hands of his clock. His breakfast consisted of tea and coffee and "bread fresh from the oven, of which he does not seem afraid." Dinner was half Virginian and half French. His talk at table was mostly of science and letters and of the university.

Webster questioned him about the Continental Congress. As a professional orator Webster noted carefully every word about Patrick Henry. Jefferson described Richard Henry Lee and Samuel Adams. He spoke of John Adams as "our colossus." On contemporary politics Webster eagerly set down in Jefferson's own words his opinion of Andrew Jackson, already much talked up for the presidency.

"I am much alarmed at the prospect of seeing General Jackson President. He is one of the most unfit men I know for such a place. He has little respect for laws and constitutions and is in fact an able military chief. His passions are terrible. When I was President of the Senate he was a Senator; he could never speak on account of the rashness of his feelings. I have seen him attempt it repeatedly and as often choke with rage. His passions are no doubt cooler now; he has been much tried since I knew him, but he is a dangerous man."

Both New Englanders spoke approvingly of the cordial family life at Monticello. One house guest was Dr. George Long, the knowledgeable young Cambridge professor who was to take the chair of classical languages at the university. He had just arrived from New York where he landed in the company of Dr. Blaettermann, the modern languages professor. Three more professors, they were told, were daily expected at Norfolk. They were so long overdue that Jefferson was expressing the fear that their ship might have been lost in a terrible gale that had swept the Atlantic. Another Cambridge man was present, Mr. Harrison, a young lawyer who was the son of Jefferson's friends at Ampthill. Mrs. Randolph and her children and Nicholas N. Trist of Louisiana, her new soninlaw, who was the grandson of an old associate from Jefferson's Philadelphia days, made up the household that winter. Of Thomas Mann Randolph not a word was said.

Jefferson lost no time in showing his guests around the university. Though Ticknor was a man of scholarship and somewhat of a dilettante in painting he had little eye for architecture. He described the rotunda as being modeled on the Parthenon. Still he was impressed. He admitted that the buildings were "more beautiful than anything architectural in New England and more appropriate to an university than can be found, perhaps, in the world." He remarked that the academical village had cost two hundred and fifty thousand dollars. "The thorough finish of every part of it, and the beautiful architecture of the whole, show, I think, that it has not cost too much. . . . Mr. J. is entirely absorbed in it and its success would make a *beau finale* indeed to his life."

The Ticknors' and Webster's departure was delayed by heavy rains. They stayed five days. News of the desperate illness of his son Charles caused Webster to hasten back to Washington. The boy was dead when he got there. He found Capitol Hill in a ferment over the presidential race. Jackson had most votes in the electoral college but not the majority he needed for election. Webster had already determined to cast his vote in the House of Representatives for John Quincy Adams, who was the runnerup. Although he lagged far behind in the popular vote Adams was duly elected sixth President of the United States.

28. *The University in Operation*

At Monticello wintry weeks dragged by without news from the missing professors. Word came from Poplar Forest that the octagon house, which Jefferson had gone to such pains to finish, and which he'd made over to his grandson Francis Eppes, at the time of his marriage to one of the great Randolph clan, had been severely damaged by fire. Imperturbable as ever in face of this sort of calamity, Jefferson wrote careful instructions to Frank as to how best to close the house in against the weather until permanent repairs could be effected.

All Jefferson's anxieties centered on the professors. He was sure that they had drowned until, in mid-February 1825, a letter arrived from Cabell in Richmond announcing, to Jefferson's inexpressible relief, that the *Competitor*, with the professors aboard, was safe in Hampton Roads. Another of Cabell's letters reported that the appropriations for the university and for the library and for laboratory equipment had passed the legislature. He added regretfully that the primary schools were languishing.

The weather raised a final obstacle. Weeks of rain turned the roads into swamps. The stages suspended operation. Jefferson sent Jeff Randolph off on horseback to help the professors find their way up from Richmond where he feared they would be too long delayed by Virginia hospitality. Some forty students managed to straggle in, mud-spattered and travelworn. At last classes opened in the schools of language and mathematics, presided over by Blaettermann, Long, and Key. After fifteen years of determined grueling struggle Jefferson's and Cabell's plan was accomplished. The university was no longer a group of empty buildings that smelled of wet plaster. It was a living institution.

On April 12 Jefferson was able to write Joseph Coolidge, Jr., in Boston: "The arrival of our Professors has at last enabled us to get our University into operation. their failure to arrive by the day we had announced for its commencement lost us for a while many students who supposing, with most of us, from the length of time they had been out that they must have perished, engaged themselves elsewhere. we began on the 7th of March with between thirty and forty. since that they have been coming in, and are still coming in almost daily. they are at this time sixty-five."

Coolidge had just won the hand of Jefferson's most soughtafter granddaughter, Ellen. The young Bostonian was wealthy and congenial and, as a further recommendation, was a good friend of Ticknor's. During his courtship he had ingratiated himself at Monticello by making a present of nearly a hundred books to the university library and was helping Ticknor arrange the purchase of more books through a Boston bookseller.

In the course of the letter Jefferson remarked in his sly way that Coolidge's "kind dispositions towards our university" might well prove a source of further trouble to him. The proctor needed a bell for the rotunda which could be heard two miles, "because that would ensure it's being always heard at Charlottesville." Would Coolidge mind finding out how much a Boston bellmaker would charge for such a bell? Coolidge was eagerly awaited at Monticello. "The object of the welcome visit we expect from you soon is such" that it would make the presence of the elder Coolidges "peculiarly gratifying" if their state of health would permit their making the trip. Jefferson added he would be delighted to put up any other friends Coolidge wanted to bring along.

Joseph Coolidge and Ellen Randolph were married at Monticello on May 29. It was a happy time. Ellen was perhaps the granddaughter Jefferson loved best, and she was marrying a man he heartily approved of. The fact that the university was actually functioning afforded him daily satisfaction.

Joseph C. Cabell expressed both men's feeling of triumph in a letter from Norfolk, where he had gone to take his wife on a visit to her family after the legislature adjourned: "I cannot describe the satisfaction which I feel on reflecting on the present prospects of the university. Our corps of professors is full of youth and talent and energy. . . . Like a fine steamboat on our noble Chesapeake, cutting her way at the rate of ten knots an hour and leaving on the horizon all other vessels on the waters, the university will advance . . . and throw into the rear all the other seminaries in this vast continent."

29. *The Preoccupations of a University Rector*

Jefferson's life was running down nevertheless. This was the first spring for which there are no entries in his garden book of vegetables planted. For some years now he had left the flower gardening to his granddaughters. A chronic dysentery which he blamed on his illfated visit to the Warm Springs wore away the strength of his spare rugged frame. He suffered from prostate trouble. His horse had fallen with him fording a creek and he'd injured his wrist again, with the result that letter writing became ever more laborious and painful.

Fortunately Robley Dunglison, the north countryman Gilmer engaged as professor of anatomy and medicine, was one of the ablest physicians of his time. In later life he was to be the author of a physiology and of a medical dictionary which were to be standard reference works throughout the nineteenth century. He agreed with Jefferson that doctors should try to treat only diseases of which they had real experimental knowledge. He proved not only a help with the ailments of old age but a congenial friend. Their only disagreement was about payment. Jefferson insisted on being billed for Dr. Dunglison's visits, and the doctor, probably well aware of the state of Jefferson's finances, wanted to treat him without charge.

In spite of his ailments Jefferson mingled with the life of the university. He often had the professors up to dinner at Monticello.

Once a week he invited a batch of students to his table; the next week another group, and so on in rotation until he got to know them all. He was depressed by the boys' total lack of preparation for university studies.

Every day when the weather was good and his dysentery permitted he would ride down to Charlottesville on old Eagle, his favorite mount. All his life he'd vaulted into the saddle. Now he had to let himself slide onto the horse's back from the edge of the terrace. At the university he would be seen walking under the colonnades or peeping into the lecture halls. Sometimes he would sit silent in the back of the proctor's office listening to the business being transacted, or would ask for a stool in the upper room of the rotunda and watch the carpenters building presses for the books.

When some students petitioned for a ten day vacation over the Fourth of July he told them the rector could not grant vacations without the advice of the Visitors and tried to convert them to his theory that vacations interrupted the thread of study. When a dancing master named Xaupy asked permission to teach the students fencing, Jefferson refused. "Dancing," he wrote, "is generally, and justly I think, considered among *innocent* accomplishments; while we cannot so consider the art of stabbing and pistolling our friends, or dexterity in the practice of an instrument exclusively used for killing our fellow citizens only, and never against the public enemy."

The spontaneity was dropping out of his correspondence with John Adams. Adams congratulated him somewhat charily on the opening of the university. He agreed with the Boston newspapers that it was a mistake to send to Europe for professors. "I do believe there are sufficient scholars in America to fill your Professorships and Tutorships with more active ingenuity, and independent minds, than you can bring from Europe." When Jefferson wrote Adams to congratulate him on the election of his son to the presidency he wrote with constraint.

He feared the victory of the younger Adams was a victory for centralized government over the strict construction of the Constitution he had come to favor most passionately. Then too—though John Adams in one letter recalled the old days in Paris, when Jefferson lived in the Cul de Sac Têtebout and the boy prodigy "appeared to me as much your boy as mine"—Jefferson had never quite forgiven John Quincy's bitter lampooning of his sponsorship of Tom Paine. Evil tongues, furthermore, must surely have whispered in Jefferson's ear of a satirical poem on the subject of Dusky Sall, much giggled over by Federalist politicians, supposed to be from John Quincy's pen.

When the younger Adams' election was an accomplished fact,

Jefferson had to summon all his diplomacy. "I sincerely congratulate you," he wrote John Adams, "it must excite ineffable feelings in the breast of a father to have lived to see a son to whose educ'n and happiness his life has been devoted so eminently distinguished by the voice of his country." Hinting that the younger Adams might encounter difficulties as a minority President, he added consolingly, "so deeply are the principles of order, and of obedience to law impressed on the minds of our citizens generally that I am persuaded there will be as immediate an acquiescence in the will of the majority as if Mr. Adams had been the choice of every man."

To Crawford Jefferson wrote the same day in a different vein: "The disappointment will be deeply felt by our State generally. I confess that what we have seen in the course of this election has very much dampened the confidence I had hitherto reposed in the discretion of my fellow citizens." He was referring to the lastminute coalition between the supporters of Henry Clay and Adams, which embittered not only the partisans of Crawford but the far more numerous partisans of General Jackson.

He was discouraged by the roster of the new Congress. "A decided majority seem to measure their powers only by what they may think or pretend to think for the general welfare of the States. all limitations therefore are prostrated and consolidation, the general welfare in name but not in effect, is now the principle of every department of the government."

John Adams took Jefferson's felicitations at their face value: "Your kind congratulations are a solid comfort to my heart. The good-natured and good-humored acquiescence of the friends of all the candidates gives me a comfortable hope . . . that the ensuing administration will not be as difficult as . . . I had apprehended. . . . I look back with rapture on the golden days when Virginia and Massachusetts lived and acted together like a band of brothers and I hope it will not be long before they may say 'redeunt saturnia regna,' when I hope the world will hear no more of Hartford Convention or Virginia Armories."

He was referring to a virulent speech of John Randolph's in the House some years before in which he claimed without the faintest historical justification that the Richmond Armory was built at the time of the Alien and Sedition Acts "to resist by force the encroachments of the then Administration upon her indisputable rights."

John Adams concluded his letter on a wry note: "I wish your health may continue to the last much better than mine. The little strength of mind and the considerable strength of body that I once possessed appear to be all gone, but while I breathe I shall be your friend. We shall meet again, so wishes and so believes your friend, but if we are disappointed we shall never know it."

It was ten months before Jefferson answered John Adams' letter. The magnificent dialogue which had buoyed both men up through the pains and struggles of the decline of life had run its course.

30. *The Hero of Two Worlds*

In August General Lafayette reappeared for his farewell visit to Monticello. He found Jefferson lying on a couch suffering from a bladder ailment. He spent six days at Monticello telling of his American journey. Since he last saw his old friend it had been a ceaseless round of travel, speeches, parades, military escorts, fireworks, civil receptions, welcoming banquets, a balloon ascension from Castle Garden. He had hardly slept two nights in the same bed.

In Washington he received ovations from both houses of Congress. John Randolph's and Henry Clay's fair words were given substance by an appropriation of two hundred thousand dollars and twentyfour thousand acres of western land as a final reward for his services during the Revolutionary War. From Washington he traveled by steamer to Norfolk. From banquet to banquet he proceeded south through the Carolinas and Georgia until he reached the banks of the Chattahoochee River where the Creek Indians turned out with whoops and war dances to do him honor.

At Mobile the steamboat *Natchez* was placed at his disposal to carry him to New Orleans. The Creoles thronged the Place d'Armes to hail a fellow Frenchman. French plays, *cuisine française*, torrents of oratory in both languages. The real estate interests saw to it that he was present at the inauguration of a new garden suburb to be named the Faubourg Lafayette.

In New Orleans the Wright sisters joined the party on the *Natchez* and accompanied Lafayette on his romantic voyage up the Mississippi. Fanny had come downriver from Robert Owen's communist settlement of New Harmony on the Ohio. She was determined to found a settlement of her own where Negro slaves could earn their freedom. The governor of Tennessee was helping her buy land. The tradition lingered on in Memphis that the elderly general and the tall young woman with the imperious blue eyes clambered together up the red gullies of Chickasaw Bluffs and stood arm in arm, looking out over the green bottomlands, to pick a site for Nashoba.

At St. Louis the general was greeted by Governor William Clark, the surviving leader of the Corps of Discovery that had first trodden the trails to the South Sea. After another procession, a banquet, and a ball he boarded the *Natchez* again and was conveyed downstream to the mouth of the Ohio. It was deemed discreet that the Wright sisters should proceed to Nashville on a different boat.

In the Cumberland the general transferred to the small steamboat

Mechanic which was to take him to Nashville. General Andrew Jackson was waiting in full uniform to receive him. He reviewed the militia, visited an academy and a college, was present at a ball, and partook of a collation spread out by Andrew and Rachel at The Hermitage. There General Jackson presented General Lafayette with a brace of pistols which had belonged to General Washington. Governor Edward Coles of Illinois, who had led the way by emancipating his own slaves, joined Lafayette for the return trip down the Cumberland.

Steaming up the Ohio, somewhere above Shawneetown where Governor Coles had left the party, Lafayette suffered a mishap. The *Mechanic* struck a shoal in the middle of the night and sank. The general was put ashore in a skiff and spent the hours till dawn beside a fire on the riverbank. In the morning most of his baggage was salvaged. The captain of a steamboat proceeding downriver obligingly turned round and conveyed the illustrious shipwrecked passenger to Portland, three miles below Louisville. The ovations recommenced.

Partly by boat and partly by road Lafayette traveled amid the inevitable mounted escorts and cheering throngs from town to town on the Ohio. At Wheeling he left the river and rode up into the Pennsylvania mountains. At New Geneva he dined with Albert Gallatin, now retired from the diplomatic post in Paris and engaged in an effort to bring order into his various investments in real estate and manufacturing. Gallatin had brought a choice collection of wines home from France. Lafayette reported a gay evening.

By early June the general had made his way, under countless triumphal arches, through throngs of pretty girls strewing flower petals in his path, past ranks of hussars in dress uniforms, to Niagara Falls. On the packet *Governor Clinton* he was conveyed to Albany through the Erie Canal. He reached Boston in time for the fiftieth anniversary of Bunker Hill. There he listened to a long address by Daniel Webster. In Portland, Maine, it was Henry Wadsworth Longfellow who greeted him with measured adulation. The governor of Maine refused to escort him out of town on a Sunday.

Everywhere he visited Revolutionary battlefields, presided over the baptism of infants who were named after him, patted schoolchildren on their little heads, reviewed troops, replied to toasts. At Brandywine and Chadd's Ford he revisited the scene of youthful exploits.

In Washington he was present with President Adams at the launching of the new frigate *Brandywine* so named in his honor.

Lafayette planned his last visit to Jefferson as the dramatic climax of this yearlong series of ovations. Ex-President Monroe, who in his fine house in Loudoun County was struggling with a financial situation as desperate as Jefferson's, rode over to Charlottesville to preside at a farewell dinner tendered the general by the Jefferson

Society of the university. The tables were laid in the rotunda, now finished except for the capitals of the columns of the portico, which still lay on a Boston wharf, where they had arrived from Italy, awaiting a decision of the Treasury Department as to whether they were dutiable or not.

Next day Lafayette embraced his old friend and mentor for the last time. "I found him very ailing," he wrote Fanny Wright. "Our mutual adieus very very melancholy as you may believe."

Back in Washington Lafayette was entertained like a visiting monarch at the White House by President Adams. Banquets and receptions continued ceaselessly till the very end. A couple of accidents marred the splendid ceremony of the hero's departure. The *Brandywine* had dropped down the Potomac and was anchored in the bay. The steamboat *Mount Vernon,* with the Lafayettes, father and son, and the leavetaking dignitaries aboard, grounded on an oysterbank and had to wait for the rising tide to lift her off. The sea turned out rough on the bay. Just at the moment when General Lafayette was to be piped aboard the frigate with the whole crew manning the yards, "the nation's guest" was taken with a fit of seasickness and forced to disappear abruptly below.

The last letter Jefferson received from him from Paris still tingled with the glow of the American journey. Lafayette told of the success of the Nashoba project of "our philanthropic young friends now at Memphis, West Tennessee." He ended his letter with an earnest plea. "Indeed my dear Jefferson, the more I see, I Hear, I think and I feel on the subject the greater Appears to me, for the white still more if possible than for the Colored population of the Southern States, the importance and urgency of Measures pointing towards the Gradual Emancipation of Slavery."

31. *A Dark Winter*

Jefferson's health took a turn for the worse after Lafayette's departure. Matthew Maury, the son of one of Jefferson's school friends who visited him about that time, got the impression that he was dying of diabetes. An outburst at the university roused him from his sickroom.

One day in early October a bunch of students disguised themselves in masks, drank themselves silly, and raised a riot on the lawns at the university. When Professors Key and Long sallied forth from their pavilions to quell them, they were assailed with brickbats and foul words. Summoned to an assembly in the rotunda next morning, the students refused in a body to give the names of the guilty parties. Professors Long and Key threatened to resign and sent word up to Monticello. Jefferson summoned what members of the Board of Visitors were available, hoisted himself painfully on old Eagle's back, and trotted down to Charlottesville.

Confronted in a second assembly by the aggrieved faces of two venerable ex-Presidents, the rioters stepped forward of their own accord. Three were expelled and the rest suspended or admonished. Efforts were made to close up the drinkshops that had furnished their liquor. Writing on October 18, Jefferson was able to reassure Madison. The university was quiet and indeed the authority of the professors seemed to have been strengthened. "Everything is going smoothly, the professors are all lecturing, the two Cantabs, however, somewhat in the pouts as yet."

He went on to tell Madison of another painful incident that had weakened him a great deal, a true backlash of fame. A sculptor named Browere was going around taking life masks preliminary to molding busts of the survivors among the Revolutionary great. He had done Lafayette (and Fanny Wright) in Philadelphia. When he appeared at Monticello Jefferson let him go to work.

"I was taken in by Browere," Jefferson complained to Madison. "He said his operation would be of about 20 minutes and less unpleasant than Houdon's method. I submitted therefore without enquiry but it was a bold experiment, on his part, on the health of an octogenary, worn down by sickness as well as by age. successive coats of this grout plastered on the naked head, and kept there for an hour, would have been a severe trial for a young and hale person. he suffered the plaister to get so dry that separation became difficult & even dangerous. he was obliged to use freely the mallet & chisel to break it into pieces and get off a piece at a time. these thumps of the mallet would have been sensible even to a loggerhead. the family became alarmed and he confused, till I was quite exhausted and there became real danger that the ears would separate from the head sooner than the plaister. I now bid adieu forever to busts & even portraits."

Later the same month the news came that all of Ellen Coolidge's personal possessions had been lost in the wreck of the coasting vessel which was conveying them to Boston. Jefferson, who had suffered a similar disaster as a young man when the Shadwell house burned, commiserated with Ellen, in a long affectionate letter, on the loss of her "letters, correspondencies, notes, books &c &c, all gone and your life cut in two, as it were, and a new one to begin without any records of the former."

Among the losses most lamented was a beautiful writing desk made specially for Ellen by John Hemings, the Monticello cabinetmaker. It was Hemings who first heard the news. "Vergil could not have been more afflicted had his Aeneid fallen a prey to the flames!" Hemings declared his eyesight had failed so he could never make her a duplicate, so Jefferson was going to send, as a gift to her husband, a little writing box he had designed himself, and which Ben Randall, the cabinetmaker in whose house he'd lodged in Philadelphia in the spring of 1776, had made for him. It was "plain, neat, convenient"; in fact it was the writing box on which he wrote the Declaration of Independence.

He went on to charge the Coolidges with some commissions in Boston. The university was out of funds for the moment because the Visitors had spent seven thousand dollars on muchneeded additional land, and the federal government was charging them twentyseven hundred dollars' duty on the marble capitals and bases for the columns of the rotunda. Would the Coolidges please inform the clockmaker that it would be February before they could put in a firm order for the university clock?

On his own account Jefferson asked them to send him a kental of salt cod—known as dumbfish in Albemarle—and twenty or thirty pounds of sounds and tongues, which he found particularly tasty. "We should be better perhaps for your recipe for dressing both articles." He charged her husband with procuring him a thirtygallon cask, "doublecased against spoilage," of Marseilles brandy, "if tolerably good at a dollar or thereabouts" a gallon. "The family is well. My own health changes little. I ride two or three miles in a carriage every day."

In spite of Jefferson's protestations about loss of memory and senile decay his mind was keen as ever. He punctiliously performed his duties as rector of the university. His bodily weakness was a constant irritation. He took to writing sharp replies to the importunities of unsolicited correspondents. To a man who complained that Mr. Jefferson hadn't answered a letter asking for help in getting a Washington job he wrote explaining that he had no credit with the new administration. He would answer no more letters on the subject. "The fact was that I had worn out the knees of my pantaloons in the humiliating posture of eternal suppliant at the feet of the gov't. begging favors for others. I became tired of it and thought at length I ought to pay some respect to my own character and to rise from the ground."

To a gentleman who wrote requesting that he not only read a long metaphysical work he was forwarding him but review it for a Philadelphia magazine Jefferson replied testily that he had no use for metaphysical reading. ". . . these dreams of the day, like those of the night, vanish in vapour, leaving not a wreck behind. the business of life is with matter. that gives tangible results. handling that we arrive at knolege of the axe, the plough, the steam boat, everything useful in life. but from metaphysical speculations I have never seen a useful result."

The year 1826 opened darkly. Jefferson's granddaughter Anne Bankhead, after an unhappy life with a drunken husband, had come home desperately ill, bringing her four children with her. Young Gilmer, for whom Jefferson felt great affection, and whom he had finally induced to accept the chair of law at the university, was dying of consumption at Farmington, George Divers' house which Jefferson had in happier days taken such pleasure in redesigning. From the window of an upstairs room Gilmer looked his last on "the red hills, the brown shade, the blue sky of Albemarle" he wrote of with such affection.

Cabell's news from Richmond was all bad; the legislature was dead set against appropriating another cent for the university.

Jefferson was much afflicted by his daughter Martha's unhappiness. After Thomas Mann Randolph's affairs were liquidated he made every effort to induce his soninlaw to rejoin the family circle. Randolph would not forgive Jefferson for not stepping in to save him from bankruptcy. He lurked in the neighborhood but refused to let himself be seen.

A little penciled note in Randolph's handwriting was found on one of Jefferson's conciliatory letters: "I never slept a night from Monticello while my wife was there. But I left it early & returned after dark. After my misfortune I wished to avoid the supercilious looks of Mr. Jefferson's various guests. I still had the house in which I had so long kept my books & papers. Thither I went at an early hour every day & constantly returned when I could cross the river or the rains were not too heavy to brave."

Jefferson tried to make Randolph understand that the only hope he had of leaving the family provided for was to find some way of satisfying his creditors without a forced sale. Land in Virginia which had been rated at a hundred dollars an acre was hard to sell at five or six. If he took on Randolph's obligations it would be hopeless.

If he had wounded Randolph's feelings it had been unintentionally. He explained with a certain pathos that if he had seemed inattentive to Randolph's remarks at table it was on account of his deafness. "Let me beseech you, dear Sir, to return and become again a member of the family . . . rather than continue in solitude, brooding over your misfortunes, & encouraging their ravages on your mind. . . . neither your family, nor yourself can be without any comforts while I have anything, and all I ask is that you be assured of this as well as of my affectionate friendship & respect."

Randolph would not be reconciled.

How to assure these "comforts" to his daughter and her children and grandchildren after his death was Jefferson's constant preoccupation. He hit on the expedient of selling land through a lottery. He figured he could realize enough to save Monticello and the adjoining farm. Authorization would have to be obtained through the legislature. The faithful Cabell went to work to put through the necessary bill. Jeff Randolph was sent off to Richmond to attend to the details. Lottery tickets were printed but there were no takers.

Cabell and his friends in Richmond next threw themselves into an effort to raise a fund by public subscription. The Virginians proved callous to every plea. John Tyler, then governor, did his best. "We had public meetings," he wrote, "and the expenditure of a vast deal of breath, but that was all. The money did not come."

In the darkest days of February Anne Bankhead died. Jefferson took her death very hard. For a while he lost control of himself completely. All his alarming symptoms returned. In one letter he spoke of paroxysms of pain. The news from Farmington was depressing. In spite of tender nursing by his brothers, Francis Gilmer's life was ebbing away.

A week after his granddaughter's death Jefferson was well enough to write Madison a long carefully considered letter which he felt would be among his last. Now that there was no hope of Gilmer's recovery the right man must be found to fill the chair of law. William Wirt had refused it even though the Visitors offered to add the emoluments of another office, that of president, invented for his benefit. In reminding Madison of the qualities he insisted on in a professor of law, Jefferson was stating in final succinct form his philosophy of education. The aim of the university must be to train men devoted to the progress of selfgoverning institutions.

"In selecting a Law-Professor we must be vigorously attentive to his political principles. you will recall that before the revolution Coke-Littleton was the universal elementary book of Law Students; and a sounder whig never wrote, nor of profounder learning in the orthodox doctrines of the British constitution, or in what were called British liberties. you remember also that our lawyers were then all whigs. but when his blackletter text and uncouth but cunning learning got out of fashion, and the honied Mansfieldisms of Blackstone became the student's Hornbook, from that moment, that profession (the nursery of our Congress) began to slide into toryism, and nearly all our young brood of lawyers are now of that hue. they suppose themselves to be whigs because they no longer know what whiggism or republicanism means. it is in our seminary that the Vestal flame is to be kept alive. and thence it is to spread anew over our own and the sister states."

Jefferson felt himself weakening from day to day. His rheumatism was torture. The dysentery continued unabated. He was planning his will. He concluded his letter with a personal goodbye to his old friend.

"The friendship which has subsisted between us, now half a century, and the harmony of our political principles and pursuits have been sources of constant happiness to me."

He had explained that in case of a forced sale he would have to move to Bedford "where I have not even a log hut to put my head into . . . and if I remove beyond the reach of attention to the university, or beyond the bourne of life itself, as I soon must, it is a comfort to leave that institution under your care. . . . to myself you have been a pillar of support through life." Jefferson was bitterly aware that his reputation had sunk to nothing in Virginia. "Take care of me when I am dead," he added, "and be assured I shall leave with you my last affections."

March 8 he wrote Monroe, with whom he'd been carrying on a melancholy correspondence; from one ruined landowner to another: "To keep a Virginia estate together requires in the owner both skill and attention: skill I never had and attention I never could have, and really, when I reflect on all the circumstances my wonder is that I should have been as long as 60 years in reaching the result to which I am now reduced."

He hoped Monroe would have better luck, that his affairs would "wind up to your wishes." He had long since turned over all business to his grandson.

Dr. Dunglison was up at Monticello two or three times a week, but there was little he could do but prescribe palliatives. In March Jefferson's resilient spirit reasserted itself. Letters had come from North Carolina telling of a public subscription. The mayor of New York had raised eightyfive hundred dollars. Five thousand was promised from Philadelphia. Jefferson was delighted. "Not a cent of this," he wrote, "is wrung from the taxpayer—it is the pure unsolicited offering of love." He looked forward to closing "with a cloudless sun a long and serene day of life."

32. *One Last Spring*

At the end of March he sent Jeff Randolph north up the coast to try to get his hands on some of these promised funds. Since Jeff was going as far as Boston, his grandfather gave him a letter to John Adams: "Like other young people he wishes to be able, in the winter nights of old age, to recount to those around him what he had heard and learnt of the Heroic age preceding his birth, and which of the Argonauts particularly he was in time to have seen . . . gratify his ambition then by receiving his best bow, and my solicitude for your health by enabling him to bring me a favorable account of it. mine is but indifferent, but not so my friendship and respect for you."

An afterglow of the old friendship suffused Jefferson's relations with the Adamses during that last spring. John Adams and Jefferson had been induced to bury the political hatchet years before by the friendly interposition of Dr. Rush and the Coles brothers. Now the common enmity of Timothy Pickering caused a certain cordiality to arise between Jefferson and President John Quincy Adams.

Pickering, having proved his physical vigor by winning a plowing contest at seventyfive, was proving his mental acuity by penning a series of vituperative attacks against public men whose policies he had disapproved of in the past. In the course of this vendetta he tried to entice John Adams, whom he never forgave his dismissal from the State Department, into an argument with Jefferson about which of them was most responsible for the Declaration of Independence. Both men showed better sense than to fall into that trap. His feud with the Adamses culminated in a bitter exchange of letters with John Quincy Adams that covered the whole history of New England Federalism and for months brought eager readers to the Massachusetts newspapers.

Finding a mutual enemy in Pickering made President Adams feel more cordially towards Thomas Jefferson. He was aware of how large a part Jefferson's correspondence played in his adored father's happiness during his old age.

While he was still Secretary of State he had politely sent Jefferson a couple of engraved facsimiles of the Declaration of Independence of which he promoted the publication as a Fourth of July observance. As President he forwarded to Monticello a copy of his first message to Congress; and asked Jefferson's advice, on behalf of the South American emissaries in Washington, as to how they could best go about seeking the recognition of their independence by the great powers.

It was gratifying to Jefferson to feel he had not been entirely forgotten. He replied in a cordial letter that the simplest method would be for them to negotiate commercial treaties with the powers, as he had tried to do on his first diplomatic mission. These would amount to recognition without more ado.

Life at Monticello was further enlivened that spring by the arrival of a pianoforte shipped from Boston by the Coolidges. Mrs. Randolph and musical friends gave little concerts.

Jefferson took advantage of his improved health and spirits to write his will. He weighed every word with unusual care so as to leave no loophole by which Thomas Mann Randolph's creditors could get their hands on the farms he now hoped would be saved by the public subscription to support his daughter and her children and their teeming broods.

"Considering the insolvent state of the affairs of my friend and son-in-law Thomas Mann Randolph and that what will remain of my property will be the only recourse against the Want in which his family would otherwise be left," Jefferson left what property would remain to him in trust for Martha Randolph for the duration of the life of Thomas Mann Randolph. The trustees were Thomas Jefferson Randolph, Nicholas N. Trist, and Alexander Garrett. He appointed Jeff Randolph sole executor. In a codicil he entrusted the care of his sister Anna Scott to Martha Randolph and explained that the only reason he made no provision for the comfortable maintenance of Thomas Mann Randolph was the fear that his creditors would thereby be able to deprive his family of their sustenance.

He left his "gold-mounted walking stick of animal horn" to James Madison, and his library to the University of Virginia, except for duplicates of books they already had. These duplicates were to be divided between his grandsonsinlaw Nicholas Trist and Joseph Coolidge. He left his silver watch to Jeff Randolph rather than his gold one because it kept better time. His literary and business papers were to go to Jeff Randolph.

To his body servant Burwell he gave his freedom and three hundred dollars to set himself up in trade as a glazier. One year after his death he desired to free John Hemings and Joe Fosset, deeding them the tools from their workshops and directing that a comfortable log house be built for each of them on his land, in a spot convenient to Charlottesville and the university. He further gave John Hemings, of the mulatto Hemings family which was the subject of so many surmises, the services of his two apprentices, Madison and Eston Hemings, until they reached their majority, when they were to have their freedom. "And I humbly and earnestly request of the legislature of Virginia a confirmation of the bequest of freedom to these servants, with permission to remain in this State, where their families and connections are."

He completed the winding up of his affairs by tracing out a design for his tomb, an obelisk of the rough stone which he had used for the columns at the university. For three achievements only he wanted to be remembered: the American Declaration of Independence, the Virginia Statute for Religious Freedom, and the University of Virginia.

In April he was well enough to be driven down to the university to superintend the installation of the capitals on the columns of the rotunda. At the last moment the administration in Washington had remitted the duty, so Jefferson had the satisfaction of sending to Boston for the clock and ordering more books and equipment for Dr. Dunglison's classes in anatomy.

At the same time he took up with the natural history professor John Emmet the question of opening a school of botany. Jefferson had long had in his files his departed friend Correa de Serra's specifications for a botanical garden. Now he suggested that six acres be laid off adjacent to the Lawns and enclosed by one of the serpentine brick walls that were his particular hobby. A stream would run through the midst of it. The terrain was to be laid out in terraces and planted with seeds of exotic trees and plants he promised to procure through a correspondent of his who headed the Jardin des Plantes in Paris.

Jefferson loved trees. Just writing their names down was a pleasure. He listed for Dr. Emmet's benefit varieties of larch, cedar of Lebanon, the French marronnier, the Spanish cork oak, teak, mahogany, and the "Indian rubber tree of Nepul" which might be adapted to the Albemarle climate. He could furnish larch seed from his own tree at Monticello.

Already he was too feeble to walk so far as his own flower garden. The jouncing of his gig on the roundabout road was agony. Some mornings he was still strong enough to let himself down from the edge of the terrace on old Eagle's back and to ride slowly around the lawn behind the house.

Rheumatism crippled his hands. He had to have his meals brought to his room, but he still carried on all the paperwork of the rector of the university.

He kept the minutes of the meetings of the Visitors, wrote Dr. Emmet thoughtfully about how to get the most out of the fifteen thousand a year grant which was all the legislature would dole out, and corresponded with Dr. Dunglison about setting standards for graduation from the different schools and about the arrangement of medical works in the library. Problems of discipline still worried the faculty. Jefferson had never imagined the young men would prove so unruly.

When he wrote for advice to his old friend Cooper at the University of South Carolina, the reply was discouraging. Cooper's students were worse than Jefferson's. They kept taking horses out of their stables without the owners' permission and stealing saddles and bridles.

33. *The Fiftieth Anniversary*

On June 24 Jefferson refused an invitation from Mayor Weightman and the citizens of Washington City to take part in their celebration of the fiftieth anniversary of American independence. "It adds sensibly to the sufferings of sickness to be deprived by it of a personal participation in the rejoicings of that day." He remembered as he wrote that it was his action as President that substituted July Fourth for the President's Birthday as the national holiday. For a last time he restated the old war cry: "All eyes are opened, or opening, to the rights of man. the general spread of the light of science has already laid open to every view the palpable truth that the mass of mankind has not been born, with saddles on their backs, nor a favored few booted and spurred ready to ride them legitimately by the grace of God."

The same day he sent a note down to Dr. Dunglison begging him for a visit as he was "not so well."

One late June morning a stranger appeared at Monticello. Mrs. Randolph told the man, who came in compliance with an appointment arranged during May, that Mr. Jefferson was too ill to see him, but when Jefferson heard who it was he insisted on the visitor being admitted to his bedroom. The importunate caller was Henry Lee.

Henry Lee was the son of the General Lee usually known as "Light Horse Harry," who was Jefferson's bitterest enemy throughout his life. It was General Lee who poisoned Washington's mind against Jefferson after Washington returned to Mount Vernon by bringing him tales of Jefferson's political machinations. It was General Lee who stirred up Jefferson's boyhood friend Jack Walker to bring forward the charge of adultery which humiliated him during his campaign for the presidency. While in prison for debt General Lee had tried to make a little money by writing his *Memoirs of the War in the Southern Department*. There he revived all the charges Jefferson's enemies made during his harassed second term as governor of Virginia.

Now General Lee was dead. Bankruptcies and foreclosures had dissipated the great Lee estate. Henry Lee, Light Horse Harry's son, though a Federalist, was picking up a precarious living from such odd jobs as he could cadge off the Republican administrations and political hack writing for Calhoun.

To his father's veneration for Washington Henry Lee added a passionate admiration for Napoleon Bonaparte. For some years he had been engaged in a project of rehabilitating his father's name and assuring his own sustenance by rewriting the history of the campaign of 1781 in the Carolinas. He sent Jefferson an early edition of this work accompanied by a fulsome letter of praise for the "efficient and patriotic labors" to which Mr. Jefferson had devoted his life. Jefferson replied civilly as was his wont.

Henry Lee wrote back from Fredericksburg enclosing a copy of a newspaper he was editing. In an answering letter Jefferson remarked somewhat pointedly on the respect and affection he had felt "for the grandfathers of the present generation of yr Family" and sent him five dollars for a subscription.

Lee took advantage of Jefferson's halfcordial tone by asking whether he might consult Jefferson's notes and records for data for the biographies and historical works he was planning. When Jefferson held him off, Lee ingratiated himself by promising to send three youths, whose parents had engaged him to oversee their studies, to the University of Virginia.

In May 1826 Lee announced that he was preparing a new edition of his father's memoirs and hoped to include Jefferson's reply to his father's strictures. He spoke disarmingly of the natural divergence of opinion between military and civilian leaders in wartime.

Jefferson replied that Jared Sparks had recently uncovered Jefferson's own correspondence as governor in the council chamber at the Richmond State House. Warning him against possible lapses in memory, Jefferson sent Lee a careful account of his recollection of events in Virginia at the time of Tarleton's raid. When Lee insisted on a personal interview Jefferson finally consented.

It was near the close of June before Lee reached Charlottesville. Immediately after the interview he wrote down his impressions for the press. He found Mr. Jefferson "extended prostrate in the alcove where he slept." He noticed that Jefferson would not let his body servant brush the flies off his face but insisted on brushing them off himself.

"The fine and clear expression of his countenance not all obscured by illness," Lee noted. "The energy of his grasp and the spirit of his conversation were such as to make me hope he would yet rally."

Jefferson "spoke of the freshet in the James . . . said he had never known a more destructive one." The dam that supplied the Shadwell mills had washed out again. Jefferson expressed no anxiety on that score. He even managed a short laugh. He insisted that Lee take dinner with the family though he regretted he could not be of the party.

Though his subsequent writings leave little doubt that Henry Lee came to Monticello as an enemy, in the hope of picking up what damaging admissions he could, he couldn't help a surge of admiration for the man's fortitude. "He alluded to the probability of his death," Lee wrote, "as a man would to the prospect of being caught in a shower."

July 1 Dr. Dunglison wrote Madison that he would have to put off a projected visit to Montpelier because Mr. Jefferson was very low. July 2 Jefferson fell into a coma. At around seven in the evening of July 3 he roused himself enough to ask Dr. Dunglison if it were the Fourth of July yet. The doctor said no, but it soon would be. The doctor reported that his patient's pulse by that time had become almost indistinguishable.

Next day, while a cannon boomed down in the valley to call the citizens of Charlottesville to the reading of Jefferson's Declaration of Independence from the courthouse steps in celebration of the jubilee, somewhere around noon, Dr. Dunglison pronounced Thomas Jefferson dead.

Later the same afternoon John Adams' life slipped quietly away in the old family mansion at Quincy. He too was quoted as saying something about the Fourth: "It is a great day. It is a good day." The doctor in attendance told President John Quincy Adams, who was notified too late to arrive in time from Washington, that his father's last words were something about Thomas Jefferson. "Thomas Jefferson still" . . . the last word was indistinct. Perhaps it was "survives."

One of Jefferson's nephews and Alexander Garrett, whom he had appointed as trustee for Martha Randolph's property in his will, fixed the shroud over the long body as best they could. Next day the students met in the rotunda. The courthouse bell was tolling. Matthew Maury wrote he had never seen young men so affected. They voted to procure mourning bands and to attend the funeral in a body.

Jefferson was buried on July 6 in the family burying ground he had laid out, where so many men and women he loved had gone before him. It came on to drizzle. The burial service was read by Mr. Hatch, the minister of the Episcopal Church in Charlottesville which Jefferson had designed. Thomas Mann Randolph stood at the head of the grave and Thomas Jefferson Randolph at the foot. Of Martha Randolph, who had her father's build and her father's selfcontrol, a relative reported, "She has yet to shed a tear." The students from the university, toiling up the hill in the rain, arrived too late for the ceremony.

On the day of his grandfather's death Jeff Randolph listed the family indebtedness. Thomas Jefferson died owing $107,273.63. Jeff Randolph had himself assumed indebtedness amounting to around sixty thousand dollars, which included some sixtythree hundred he still owed to Thomas Mann Randolph's creditors as the result of having bid in some of his father's land in the forced sale. For the support of his mother, Thomas Jefferson's daughter, and of her children and grandchildren, there was nothing except what could be raised by subscription and by possible grants from state legislatures.

Four days after his grandfather's burial Jeff Randolph wrote his cousin Dabney Carr, begging him to find a tailor to make him two pairs of black pantaloons and also a suit of mourning for Nicholas Trist. Since Jeff had neither cash nor credit would Carr please stand security for him. Jeff's mother would be dependent on the public bounty. "My father who has shown a spirit more ferocious than a wolf & more fell than a hyena, hating him in life, neglecting him in death, and insulting his remains when dead: is already in motion to get hold of these sums by fraud or force if possible."

It was not long before Monticello and everything in it fell to a forced sale. Jeff Randolph, who turned out to be a young man of some financial skill, was able to establish his mother and the younger children at Edgehill. Though not a man of letters, he immediately went to work to preserve and edit his grandfather's papers.

CHAPTER X

Of Democracy in America

1. *Messieurs de Tocqueville and de Beaumont Embark on an Expedition*

On the morning of April 2, 1831, two young Frenchmen boarded the New York packet at the port of Le Havre. Alexis de Tocqueville was a small, darkhaired, darkeyed, intense young man of twentyfive who was never in the best of health. Gustave de Beaumont was three years older, taller, more athletic and easygoing, with a good deal of the bigboned Norman in his makeup.

Both came of families of the provincial noblesse who were intensely loyal to the Bourbon cause. Tocqueville was the greatgrandson of Malesherbes, who had been the first to encourage philosophical ideas at the Bourbon court and the last man to stand up in defense of Louis XVI and Marie Antoinette when they were on trial for their lives. Beaumont was a relative of Lafayette's. Family connections had launched both on careers in the royal judiciary which were suddenly called into question by the Revolution of 1830. They were drawn together early in their lives by their divergence from the political ideas traditional in both their families, by their ardent love of country, and by an allabsorbing passion for research and adventure.

Tocqueville particularly saw in the insurrection that ousted Charles X omens of the triumph of something he called *la démocratie*. To him it meant social leveling and participation in the government by the lower orders. As a member of the old noblesse he could hardly be expected to approve of it, but as a young man of eager intelligence with an analytic bent, whose curiosity was whetted by Guizot's exhilarating lectures on political evolution at the Collège de France, he was interested in every manifestation of this onrushing political wave.

During the July days Tocqueville enlisted in the National Guard at

Versailles. Tears came to his eyes when in the early dawn of a late summer morning he saw the long train of carriages, carrying Charles X and his family from abdication into exile, drive slowly past him along the boulevard. As a guardsman Tocqueville's Commander in Chief was General Lafayette. All his life Lafayette had represented *les américains* among French republicans. He had come back with his political personality much refurbished by the triumphs of his American tour. The July Revolution constituted the ultimate triumph and the ultimate failure of his political career. For an hour amid cheering crowds at the Hôtel de Ville he was on the verge of being proclaimed provisional President of a French republic.

The story went around that the American minister arrived at the moment of decision to congratulate him on the success of his insurrection. This was William Cabell Rives, one of the Albemarle County youths on whose education for statesmanship Jefferson had lavished particular pains. Lafayette asked him what the Americans would say when they heard the French had proclaimed a republic. "They will say," answered Rives, "that forty years' experience has been lost on you."

While Tocqueville was standing guard at Versailles, Beaumont was dodging bullets between barricades, running back and forth across Paris to try to find out what was going on. The July days culminated in a dramatic scene. Lafayette, having refused the presidency, and seeking to quell cries of "No more Bourbons" that could be heard from the crowd, led plump Louis Philippe out on the balcony of the Hôtel de Ville and, beneath the folds of an enormous tricolor, introduced him to the Parisians as constitutional King of the French.

Neither Tocqueville nor Beaumont approved of the Commander in Chief of the National Guard. Between themselves they referred to him sarcastically as *le héros des deux mondes*. They feared that his revolution was laying France open to the ravages of republicanism. As a moderate liberal Tocqueville had been planning a trip to England to discover at first hand what lessons the French could learn from the revolution of 1688 which established a constitutional monarchy there, but now both he and Beaumont decided that the United States was the place to study *la démocratie*. To combat it they had to find out how it worked.

After much soulsearching both of them signed the oath of allegiance to Louis Philippe. Their families and friends were shocked. Tocqueville's father, who had been a member of the House of Peers and had served as prefect under Charles X, retired haughtily to his château. Louis Philippe was abhorred by the men of the Bourbon restoration as the son of that Judas Iscariot, Philippe Egalité of Orléans.

These young men overflowed with filial piety. To avoid arguments in the family their first thought was to get out of France. They needed time for reflection to decide what the attitude of a liberal public servant should be towards the new government. They managed somehow to have themselves appointed by the Ministry of the Interior, now pledged to humanitarian reforms, as commissioners to inspect the penal institutions of the United States. The American penitentiary system was then considered the most enlightened in the world. The Ministry of Justice granted them leave of absence, but both ministries drew the line at paying expenses. Their families furnished them funds.

They packed fashionable regalia for city life along with equipment for a journey through the wilderness into two leather trunks, procured the best fowling pieces money could buy and a great mass of blank paper and notebooks; Beaumont took along his watercolors, some sketchpads, and his flute, and they were off on the stage to Le Havre.

Tocqueville had made up his mind to write a book on American democracy. Beaumont began to plan to do the same. "It is of the most extreme importance for us to have English at the tips of our fingers, to understand its idioms, to be aware of all its fine distinctions; and to appreciate all its shades of expression: otherwise we shall not be certain to understand what we are told," Beaumont wrote home during the crossing.

They considered it their good fortune that most of the passengers on the packet were American. They had hardly gotten their sea legs before they threw themselves into the study of English. They found the passengers very kind and helpful, particularly a young lady named Miss Edwards who treated them "like a sister."

They were full of unabashed curiosity, they were tirelessly cheerful and accommodating, their manners had something of the candor and generosity of the old regime. Within a week they were the most popular young men on the ship. Everybody helped them with their English. People filled their ears with curious details of American politics.

They exclaimed with rapture over every manifestation of the New World. Beaumont wrote his father of a charming little blue bird, the size of a sparrow, that lit on the deck in a squall. Tocqueville climbed out on the bowsprit one stormy night when the ocean was phosphorescent. "From there at some distance I could see the prow, which seemed to rush upon me with the sparkling wave it spurned before it. The spectacle was more admirable and sublime than I can paint it."

"We are meditating great projects," Beaumont confided in his father. "First of all we shall accomplish to the best of our ability the mission given us. . . . But while working on the penitentiary system we shall see America . . . we shall come to know the mechanism of its republican government. Would not that be a fine book which would give an exact conception of the American people, would paint its character in bold strokes, would analyze its social conditions and would rectify so many opinions which are erroneous?"

Their high spirits were contagious. One delicious spring evening in mid-Atlantic Beaumont got the passengers dancing on deck to the sound of his flute. They were exhilarated by the gales that buffeted them on the Grand Banks. Thirtysix days out the lookout at the masthead shouted, "Land." They were beginning to rhapsodize over the sight of grass and green trees on the Long Island shore when the wind switched into the northwest and the captain, who was afraid of running short of food and water, put his ship about and ran into Newport with a quartering breeze.

A fishing dory landed them after dark at the Newport wharf. When they felt the firm ground underfoot they jumped for joy. The earth still seemed to heave from the motion of the ship. Next morning they were entranced by the neatness of the whitepainted clapboard houses, "small as chicken coops." The customs officers greeted them civilly and, after they'd sworn on the Bible they had nothing dutiable, let them pass with hardly a glance into their trunks. They were surprised that the inhabitants didn't look too different from the French.

Beaumont found the women ugly but admired the town. "It has 17,000 inhabitants, a magnificent harbor, newly fortified, tiny houses modeled one would say on the kitchen at Beaumont-la-Chartre"—the provincial hamlet where he'd been brought up—"but so clean they resemble opera scenery." One of the passengers had been impressing on them the fact that the Americans were essentially a commercial people. This dictum was confirmed by the discovery that even a small city like Newport supported five banks. While they waited for the New York steamboat Beaumont sat down and did a sketch of the Wrenstyle steeple of one of the churches, which he found *remarquable*.

The trip through Long Island Sound on the steamboat *President* was a revelation. The swiftness of this "immense machine" which covered eighty leagues against the wind and a contrary sea in eighteen hours; the saloon, the dining hall, the tiers of bunks which could accommodate eight hundred people; it was all "magical." They uttered "cries of admiration" at their first sight of the environs of New York. The rocky shoreline variegated with bays and inlets, the slopes covered with lawns and blossoming trees right down to the water, the multitude of country houses, "small as candy boxes but showing careful workmanship." They found neatness and prettiness and an air of convenience about every dwelling. Tocqueville promised to send home a sketch plan of a couple of those he liked best. Beaumont wrote: "We have things as beautiful in France, but we haven't anything of the same kind." They couldn't get over "the animation given this majestic tableau by the immense number of vessels, brigs, gondolas and boats of all sizes" crisscrossing in every direction. It was surprising how fast they sailed closehauled to the wind.

The *President* docked at the foot of Courtland Street. A friendly passenger introduced them to a boardinghouse. It was four in the afternoon but they were "so tired, so tossed about, so bruised" that they rolled into bed. At eight o'clock the next morning they were still between the sheets.

2. *Usages Américains*

If they were surprised by the beauty of the landscape, they were overwhelmed by the reception they received in New York. They had been planning to wait for the help of the French legation and of the consulates before presenting the seventytwo letters of introduction they brought along, but they had hardly staggered to their feet the May morning after they landed when they were shown an enthusiastic description in the newspaper of the arrival of two commissioners to report to the new French government on the American prison system. Tocqueville and Beaumont had to pinch themselves: it was they—two little bureaucrats of the lower rank—who were to be received as emissaries from the great French nation. The liberal revolution had aroused enthusiasm in America. The idea of a European government seeking guidance in the United States was gratifying to the national pride. The two Frenchmen had barely time to take a quick investigative stroll over the treelined cobbles of Broadway before callers appeared, welcoming messages, invitations.

They had not been twentyfour hours in New York before they found themselves, to their amazement, being introduced to the mayor and aldermen, to several judges. Tocqueville's eyes almost popped out of his head when he found himself shaking hands with the governor of New York State, "who was staying at a boardinghouse, and who received us in the parlor without any ceremony whatever."

Under *Usages Américains*, Tocqueville immediately entered in his notebook: "The greatest equality seems to reign, even among those who occupy very different positions in society. The authorities seem extraordinarily approachable."

Tocqueville and Beaumont found the authorities a great deal more than approachable in New York. Their hospitality ran the young commissioners ragged. They wanted to see the prisons? Well, the mayor invited them on a ceremonial visit. Early one morning they were invited to City Hall. They found all the dignitaries of the city collected to greet them. They left City Hall at 10 A.M. in a train of carriages.

First they visited a house of refuge where efforts were being made to reform youthful offenders before they hardened into professional criminals. From there they drove through country lanes to Blooming-dale, the hospital for the insane. They noted that alcoholism and re-ligious enthusiasm were the chief causes of madness among the Amer-icans.

Tocqueville remarked on the magnificent view of the North River with the Palisades in the distance and the white sails of the shipping in the foreground which they were shown from the belvedere. Next it was an establishment for the deaf and dumb and then the poorhouse.

At the poorhouse they sat down to a public dinner. "Picture to yourself," Tocqueville wrote his old family tutor, "a long table like a refectory table at the high end of which the mayor flanked by your two servants was seated. Next came the guests—*tous grands personn-ages à faire pleuer*—because they laugh very little on this side of the Atlantic. As for the dinner itself it represented the infancy of the art: the vegetables and fish before the meat, oysters for dessert. In a word, complete barbarism. . . . Unfortunately as soon as the soup was removed they brought wine." It was a heavy fortified wine, not the table wine they were accustomed to. "The mayor drank to our health in the English manner, which consists of filling a small glass, in raising it while looking at you, and in drinking it, the whole performed with great solemnity. The person to whom this civility is addressed has to respond to it by doing exactly the same thing. We each then drank our glass, always with befitting dignity. Up to that point everything was going well. But we began to tremble on perceiving that each of our table companions was getting ready to do us the same honor. We had the appearance of hares with a pack of dogs on their trail; and the fact is, they would soon have had us in distress if we had allowed them to. But at the third glass I took the step of only swallowing a mouthful, and I thus happily gained what we in France call the end of the dinner, but which here is only the end of the first act."

The plates were removed. Cigars were brought in, and candles to light them with. "The society enveloping itself in a cloud of smoke, muscles relax the least little bit and they give themselves over to the heaviest gaiety in the world."

The moment had come for the formal toasts. The Frenchmen were not only unhappy at the idea of drinking more wine. They dreaded being forced to reply to a toast to Beaumont's cousin, Lafayette. The "hero of two worlds" had fallen into general disrepute since the July days. The republicans were down on him for not having been republican enough and the royalists were down on him because they feared his republicanism might any day break out in more barricades. A toast to Lafayette would be interpreted in France as a political act. During their whole American trip whenever they attended a public function Tocqueville and Beaumont were on the *qui vive* to avoid having to drink to Lafayette.

This time they were saved by the party's breaking up before the toasts had properly begun. Barges were waiting to take them to Blackwell's Island where they were treated to the edifying sight of three or four hundred convicts cheerfully building their own prison. After some "charming promenades" on the East River they were escorted back through the gloaming to their lodgings in New York by five carriageloads of what Tocqueville described as "honorable gentlemens." It had been a long day.

"You no doubt want to know," Tocqueville wrote his mother during his first days in New York, "what is our present manner of life. . . . We get up at five or six and we work till eight. At eight o'clock the bell announces breakfast. Everyone goes in promptly." They were astounded the first day to see women appear at breakfast "carefully dressed for the whole day." After that they visited jails and made calls on "certain men who are interesting to listen to." They returned to dine at three. After dinner they put their notes in order. Then at seven they went out into society to take tea. Often the evening ended with a dance. They consoled each other on the waste of time with the reflection that everything they did, no matter how frivolous, helped them understand the life around them. They were absorbing America through their pores.

At first they missed light wines with their meals. The food was good but the cookery bad. "We still can't understand the multitude of things that they succeed in introducing into their stomachs here," Tocqueville wrote his mother. "In addition to breakfast, dinner and tea, with which the Americans eat ham, they also eat a very copious supper and often a *goûter*. That up to now is the only indisputable superiority that I grant them over us. But they see in themselves many others. These people seem to me stinking with national conceit: it pierces through all their courtesy."

3. *A Pair of Examining Machines*

Tocqueville and Beaumont were incredibly industrious. They got up at dawn to write in their notebooks. They read all the reviews and gazettes. They saw all the sights. They accepted every invitation. They never tired of asking questions. They listened with careful courtesy to what everybody had to say. After a couple of hours' acquaintance they found the Americans treating them as old family friends.

At the same time, with grim conscientiousness, they visited every penal institution from attic to cellar. They collected a library of pamphlets and newspaper articles dealing with the new penology. They found prison reform the subject of great enthusiasm. Every kind of reform was the rage. The wave of Jeffersonian idealism which had established the Republican party in the government thirty years before was washing back on itself in a thousand new movements for moral improvement. Temperance societies, societies for universal peace, for the establishment of communist communities, for Negro emancipation and resettlement, associations for every type of uplift were proliferating in every town and hamlet. This was the year William Lloyd Garrison published the first number of his *Liberator*.

Tocqueville's first impressions of the Americans were that they were puffed up with patriotic pride; that, in spite of the multiplicity of sects, they were extremely religious; and that "the sole interest which absorbs the attention of every mind is trade."

The purity of morals, the sanctity of the marriage vow he laid to these three causes. Beaumont wrote home that the men were so busy making money they didn't have time to seduce other men's wives. He found "something tempting" in "the happiness which seems to reign in their families." Neither of them could imagine marrying a foreigner but he and Tocqueville had already decided that if some political overturn should exile them from France it would be in America they would take refuge. After he'd been in the country two weeks Tocqueville wrote home: "We have already largely lost our national prejudices in regard to this people."

They were enjoying themselves as they had never enjoyed themselves in their lives. Even the excursion to Sing Sing prison had its picturesque aspects. They boarded with a family at a place called Mount Pleasant overlooking the Hudson and the blue mountains beyond. They remarked on the play of sunlight through yellow haze which became the specialty of the Hudson River school of painters.

Whenever they were free from the prison they spent their time out of doors. It was a relief to escape from the social scamper of the city. Perched in the crotches of an enormous sycamore, Beaumont sketched while Tocqueville filled his notebook with the statistics of what was already the largest prison in America. They had to listen to a lot of bad piano playing in the parlor evenings after tea. They never could get over how badly American ladies played the piano. The singing was atrocious, but they were touched by the naïve friendliness of their fellow boarders.

"We are now examining machines," Tocqueville wrote his father. "We squeeze whoever falls into our hands." He had been in America only a month but he had so far overcome his prejudices as to proclaim: "This people is one of the happiest in the world." His researches led him to believe that the Americans owed their prosperity less to "their truly superior form of government" than to "the peculiar circumstances" in which they found themselves.

"Nature here offers a sustenance so immense to human industry that the class of theoretical speculators is almost unknown. Everybody works and the mine is so rich that all those who work quickly succeed in acquiring that which makes existence happy. The most active spirits, like the quietest, find enough to fill their life without troubling the state." He found society organized on exactly the opposite basis from that in France. "With us the government concerns itself with everything. Here there is, or appears to be, no government."

Back in the city, the "examining machines" found themselves very much the vogue. "The company with whom we eat," wrote Beaumont jauntily, "is always composed of attractive people. Evenings we make calls; and each day we make new acquaintances." Soon Tocqueville would have to revise his notation on the lack of "theoretical speculators."

Among their new acquaintances was the genial Chancellor Kent, who was busy turning his legal practice into legal theory in the first edition of his *Commentaries on American Law*. Jefferson had considered James Kent to be a flagrant example of that unconscious toryism of the American lawyer which he wrote Madison about in his last letter; but Chancellor Kent was generally esteemed, along with John Marshall and Spencer Roane, as among the great legal minds of the century. Now in his early sixties, having been forcibly retired from the Court of Chancery by unsympathetic Republicans, he was lecturing at Columbia. His good friend Edward Livingston was encouraging him to take up the study of Greek. He was so delighted with the young Frenchmen that he immediately had delivered to their lodgings the three volumes of his commentaries, fresh from the press.

They dined with Robert Emmet, another bright lawyer, whose brother was professor of natural history at the University of Virginia. They spent a morning with Albert Gallatin. Gallatin, after an unsuccessful bid for the vice presidential nomination with Crawford, and a term as minister to the Court of St. James's, which he'd found boring after the gaiety of Paris, had given up the public service for good and was devoting his life to the theory and practice of banking and to the development of Indian ethnology. It was a relief for Tocqueville and Beaumont to be able to speak French for a while. Gallatin explained a theory he was developing on the usefulness of lawyers in American political life. In response to a question about the sanctity of the marriage vow which the Frenchmen still found such a surprising feature of American life, he described the premarital sexual habits of the American Indians and of the people of the frontier. Gallatin, more than any man in America, had the anthropological point of view towards human affairs which Tocqueville was in the course of developing.

4. *A Steamboat Race on the Hudson*

No matter how fascinating they found conversations in New York Tocqueville and Beaumont were in a fever to see the impenetrable forests and the proud savages of the interior. They had been brought up on the resounding rhetoric of Tocqueville's cousin, Chateaubriand, the statesman of the Restoration, whose romantic descriptions of his exile in America had infected their whole generation with a passion for the primitive and the primeval. They had devoured the romances of James Fenimore Cooper as fast as they came out. The last day of June they made up their minds they must push on into the interior. Since there was no steamboat that day they took passage for Yonkers on a sloop.

In Yonkers they hoped to renew their acquaintance with the family of Edward Livingston, who was then Secretary of State under President Jackson, but finding that the agreeable and Frenchspeaking Livingstons were away from home, they explored the countryside, shot a number of beautifully colored birds, and swam in the river while they waited for the next steamboat.

Tocqueville somehow found time to write a long letter to a boyhood friend, in which he came back to this mysterious phenomenon he had discovered. It had never occurred to him it could be possible. Here was a country that seemed to get along very well without any government at all.

In spite of "a perpetual instability in the men and in the laws, an outward equality pushed to the highest point, a kind of manners and a turn of thought uniformly shared by all . . . this country on the whole presents an admirable spectacle." Two things he admired: "the extreme respect for law" and "the ease with which they do without government." "Each man here regards himself as interested in the public security and in the functioning of the laws. Instead of counting on the police, he counts only on himself. It results that, on the whole, the public force is everywhere without ever showing itself. It is really an incredible thing, I assure you, to see how this people keeps itself in order through the single conviction that its only safeguard against itself lies in itself."

The weather was hot. The only accommodations they could find in Yonkers were two bad beds in a suffocatingly hot attic. A steamboat appeared in the early morning that carried them to a small village on the western shore. They spent the day climbing Bear Mountain.

That night they were rowed out to the steamboat *North America*, bound, they supposed, for West Point where they wanted to inspect the military academy. The captain only slackened speed enough to throw a towline to the skiff and to haul the passengers and baggage unceremoniously up over the rail. Once aboard they learned that the captain had no intention of stopping at West Point that trip. He was racing the *Constellation* and many bets had been staked that he could beat her to Albany. Opposite Newburgh the Frenchmen were thoroughly alarmed when the *North America* started spouting rockets and bengal lights that lit up the whole river. They had been told tales of how often steamboats blew up. Answering rockets and mortars came from the shore where they could see people crowding the water's edge to watch the steamboat race. The *North America* was well ahead. At five in the morning willynilly they found themselves in Albany.

5. *The Government of the State of New York*

Beaumont wrote home that Albany, besides being the capital of New York State, was, as the junction point between the Erie Canal which brought down all the produce of the lakes and the Hudson River, a considerable seaport. Its importance would soon be enhanced by the completion of a railroad from Schenectady.

The Frenchmen were still amazed at being received like foreign potentates. Archives were thrown open to them. The Secretary of State's office collected documents for them. Officials dropped everything to show them the sights.

On the Fourth of July they found themselves, flanked by the chancellor of the state and by Lieutenant Governor Livingston, in the first ranks of the parade. They were amazed by the unconventional aspect of the militia, by the number of craft associations, newspapermen, mechanics, carpenters, painters, apprentices, who marched behind their banners, and by the ingenuity of the floats, horsedrawn carts decorated with symbolic tableaux. The tricolor flag was much in evidence in their honor.

The procession ended at the Methodist Church, where after a prayer the attorney general read the Declaration of Independence. Both men were profoundly moved. "It was really a fine spectacle," Tocqueville wrote home. "A profound silence reigned in the meeting . . . it seemed that an electric current made all hearts vibrate. . . . There was in the reading of these promises of independence so well kept, in this return of an entire people toward the memories of its birth, in this union of the present generation with that which is no longer, sharing for a moment all its generous passions, there was in all that something deeply felt and truly great."

Both Tocqueville and Beaumont were depressed by the oration that followed. Some bigmouthed lawyer poured out the sort of nationalistic platitudes they were accustomed to at civic funerals back home. "I came out cursing the orator," wrote Tocqueville. He had "succeeded in destroying part of the profound impression that the rest of the spectacle made on me."

Beaumont's musical sensibilities were jarred by the crowd's offkey singing of a hymn to liberty to the tune of the "Marseillaise," to the accompaniment of a single flute, but he admitted that the ceremony affected him more than any of the great state shows he'd seen in Paris. "There is more brilliance in our ceremonies; in those of the United States there is more truth."

They spent several days in Albany trying to pin down the government of the great state of New York, and finally gave up the search and started for Buffalo on the bonebreaking public stages. They caught up with Governor Throop, whom they had met their first day in New York City, at his own little farm on one of the Finger Lakes.

"He is a man of simple manners," Beaumont wrote his sister. "He has little money; the state gives him only twenty thousand francs as a salary. . . . This country place is but a farm which he cultivates. The house he lives in with his wife hardly appears sufficient to lodge them, so tiny it is. It stands however on a charming site. Owasco Lake touches its garden, and on the other side it is surrounded by great high trees. He took us for a walk in the woods. While admiring the beauty of the trees we caught sight of a squirrel. At that the governor began to run as fast as his legs could carry him to get his gun at the house. He soon came out, all out of breath, with his murderous weapon. The little animal had the patience to wait for him, but the big man was clumsy enough to miss him four times in succession."

The governor was a fine fellow, but completely without distinction, Beaumont told his sister. When he asked a noted penologist they interviewed at Syracuse why the people of New York chose such a man for governor, he replied that men of great talent would not accept such employ. "They prefer trade and business where one makes more money. There in two words you have the American character."

6. A Fortnight in the Wilderness

On the road to Buffalo they met their first Indians. They were begging along the road. After a stroll through the town Tocqueville noted his disenchantment. Chateaubriand and Cooper had prepared him for something different. "A multitude of savages in the streets (day of a payment), new ideas that they suggest. Their ugliness, their strange air, their bronzed and oily hide, their long hair black and stiff, their European clothes they wear like savages. . . . Brutalized by our wines and our liquors. More horrible than the equally brutalized peoples of Europe. Something of the wild beast besides. . . . Not one Indian woman passable."

They had been planning to visit Niagara Falls but, finding that the steamboat *Ohio* was about to leave for Detroit, they hurried aboard. They were bound they'd see some wild country. Steamboats, they explained in their letters home, were faster, cheaper, and infinitely more comfortable than any other method of transportation. They had suddenly come to understand that the way to penetrate "to the last limits of civilization" was through the Great Lakes.

They had bad luck with the weather. It took them three days of pounding through rain and head winds to reach the Detroit River. They discovered that freshwater lakes could produce seas as threatening as the Atlantic. Now their blood tingled as they neared a lost outpost of their own France. The houses of Fort Malden, on the Canadian side, had a French look. The steeple surmounted by a weathercock was undoubtedly Catholic. The hamlet reminded them of a Norman village.

Tocqueville noted one of the contrasts that gave him such pleasure. "At our right on the bank stood a Highlander mounting guard in full uniform. It was the uniform made famous by the field of Waterloo . . . his arms sparkled in the sun. To our left, as if intentionally furnishing a contrast, two stark naked Indians, their bodies streaked with paint, their noses pierced by rings, put off at the same moment from the opposite bank. They were in a small bark canoe with a blanket for a sail. Letting their frail boat run with the wind and the current, they shot like an arrow towards our vessel and rounded it in an instant: then they started quietly to fish near the English soldier who seemed placed there as a symbol of Europe's brilliant military civilization."

They hired horses in Detroit. They decided to take their lives in their hands and to ride through the forest to the settlement of Saginaw which an innkeeper told them was *la borne où s'arrête la civilization*. When they went to a drygoods store to buy mosquito netting they were amazed to see on the wall a new French fashion print: *Les Modes de Longchamps: 1831.*

This, combined with the civilized aspect of the little frontier towns with their white churches, their Greek Revival buildings, their stores stocked with French and British and New England merchandise, caused Tocqueville to jot down the discovery of a fresh paradox.

In America there was only one society. He had expected the back country to be primitive as out of the way French villages were primitive. Not a bit of it. "The man you left behind in the streets of New York, you will find again in the midst of almost impenetrable solitude. . . . If night overtaking you does not force you to take shelter under a tree, you have a good chance of reaching a village where you will find everything down to French fashions and poor copies of boulevards. . . . When you leave the main roads you force your way down barely trodden paths. Finally you see a field cleared, a cabin made from half-squared treetrunks admitting the light through one narrow window, you believe yourself to have come to the home of an American peasant. *Erreur.* You make your way into this cabin which seems the abiding place of every misery, but the owner wears the same clothes as you, he speaks the language of the cities. On his rough table are books and newspapers; he wants to know exactly what is happening in old Europe. . . . He will solemnly tell you what still needs to be done to make France prosperous. One might think one was meeting a rich landowner who had come to spend a few nights in a hunting lodge. And in fact the log cabin is only a temporary shelter for the American. . . . When the fields that surround him are in full production . . . a more spacious dwelling and one better adapted to his needs will replace the log cabin and make a home for those numerous children who will also go out one day to make themselves a dwelling in the wilds."

The ride to Saginaw, through primeval forest interspersed with settlements and Indian camps, fulfilled their wildest hopes. They saw an Indian tribe feasting off freshly killed deer after a hunt. At one cabin the settler had a tame bear named Trink to guard his door. They almost got lost. They slept in huts in the forest. They crossed the Saginaw River in an Indian canoe paddled by halfbreed Canadians who spoke French—"the French of a hundred years ago"—and sang an old French ballad: *"Entre Paris et Saint Denis."* They saw masses of game, deer, beautiful hawks, partridges, woodcocks, pigeons they shot for the pot. Though the Indians had ferocious eyes their faces had a special charm when they smiled. Nobody harmed them. They began to see beauty in the halfbreed girls. The only harassment they suffered was from the mosquitoes.

Back in Detroit they had a piece of luck. The steamboat *Superior* was about to leave on a special excursion to the western lakes. Tocqueville celebrated his twentysixth birthday on Lake St. Clair. They entered Lake Huron one cloudy evening with heat lightning flashing on the horizon. The passengers were dancing on deck to a violin and an English horn. For a finale, as a compliment to Tocqueville and Beaumont, the musicians played the "Marseillaise." Beaumont remembered that exactly a year had passed since he had heard the revolutionary hymn for the first time. It was sung by the crowd in the Place Vendôme. It sent a chill up his back "like an echo of the cannon of July still reverberating through the world."

On Lake Huron they marveled at the crystal clearness of the water. The forested shores though not mountainous exhibited a great diversity of foliage. Beaumont sketched and sketched while Tocqueville noted the conversation of his fellow passengers. Michilimackinac, with its blockhouse and its great arch scooped by wind and water out of the natural rock, seemed the most picturesque place they had ever seen. At Green Bay they spent some hours with a group of Indians they felt were unspoiled by contact with the whites. They found them congenial. Beaumont delighted the little band by painting the face of one of the younger boys. He traced a bluebird on one cheek, a galloping horse on the other, and a cat on his chin. An Indian girl bartered a string of wampum for a woodpecker he'd painted on his pad. Beaumont declared he'd learned more about the Indians that half day than reading a hundred books.

7. *The Uncommon Bostonians*

Back in Buffalo they did Niagara Falls. Their meditations on the awful splendor of the scene were somewhat disturbed by the importunities of a halfcracked English spinster who insisted on attaching herself to their party and whom they nicknamed *la folle du Niagara*. Another steamboat took them on a side trip into French Canada. They came back from Quebec and Montreal stirred by ten days spent in a lost enclave of their native land, but pondering one question: why, after expending such energy in the exploration of the continent, had the French stagnated in the St. Lawrence Valley? In Canada as in the United States they found the Anglo-Saxons dominating every avenue of progress.

As soon as they reached Albany again, with hardly a pause for rest, they were off on the stage through the Berkshires and across Massachusetts. During their excursion into the wild they had been neglecting their penitentiaries. The New York penologists had told them that, though the first penitentiary was built under Jefferson's influence in Virginia, Boston and Philadelphia were now the centers of prison reform. Spurred by guilty consciences, they hurried to Boston.

Their first days in Boston were a little forlorn. This was the only city where nobody came to offer his services. They had neglected to bring introductions to any Bostonian. At the post office Tocqueville found bad news from home. The beloved old abbé who had tutored him as a child was dead. With the change of ministry the danger loomed that the liberals might start reprisals against men like his father who had been officials under Charles X. The Asiatic cholera, which had caused hundreds of thousands of deaths in eastern Europe, was spreading into France.

Tocqueville and Beaumont never got over laughing about how

they finally broke into high Brahmin circles. It was at a public meeting on behalf of the revolutionary Poles. Certain Bostonians had already begun to realize that their French visitors were not only noblemen of high degree but interested in prison reform. "In the United States," wrote Tocqueville, "the execution of a fine prison seems as important as the pyramid of Cheops." An invitation was issued them to attend this meeting.

In the parade with which the proceedings began, they found themselves being introduced to Josiah Quincy, who was one of the orators of the day, and to Harrison Gray Otis. Their winning manners did the rest. They were placed in seats of honor in Faneuil Hall, which was decorated with banners lettered with the names of Polish patriots who had served in the Continental Army, and with those of Washington and Lafayette. They had to sit with a look of edification on their faces while a preacher, who was none other than Lyman Beecher, excoriated those who opposed the forces of liberalism in Europe. After an oration by the mayor, a letter was read entrusting General Lafayette, whose name was cheered to the rafters, with two standards he was to forward to the Polish patriots in revolt against the Holy Alliance. The young French nobles, who were at that moment desperately anxious for fear that Lafayette's followers were about to jail the most esteemed members of their families, couldn't help seeing the funny side of their situation. Beaumont in a letter home called the business "patriotic folderol," and pointed out that the poor Poles would be much better served by a little hard cash.

It turned out that among the more cosmopolitan Bostonians there were some who heartily agreed with them. Harrison Gray Otis, who prided himself on making his house a center of political and literary society, invited the Frenchmen home. In his drawing room they met George Ticknor and Francis Colley Gray, Ticknor's companion on his first visit to Monticello, who was now Inspector of Prisons. The Frenchmen were immediately in their element. They wrote home that Boston was more like France than anywhere they'd been in America. They were among people rich enough to think about art and literature and topics of general interest instead of talking money all the time. The ladies all spoke French. Even Beaumont admitted, though he still insisted the Americans were not a musical people, that they showed some slight skill at the piano.

Ticknor, with the knack he had for picking firstrate friends, immediately embarked on a friendship with Tocqueville which was to last through both their lives. One of Ticknor's good friends was Joseph Coolidge, Jefferson's grandsoninlaw, who was now a merchant in the China trade. He had recently moved his family to Cambridge. Sponsored by the Coolidges and the Ticknors, invitations poured in on every side. Their days were even fuller of dinners, teas, and balls than they had been in New York, only in Boston and Cambridge they really felt at home. They found the food good; their only complaint was that the Bostonians drank too much and spent too many hours at the table. Their new friends insisted that the French commissioners should move to the Tremont House, which was the hotel in Boston where everybody who was anybody stayed.

Coolidge and Ticknor were enchanted with their French visitors. Coolidge wrote his brotherinlaw Nicholas Trist, who was then an upper clerk in the State Department and on good terms with President Jackson, that they were "extremely intelligent and interesting men, greatly curious to inform themselves of the true state of things here and very sensible of any attentions they receive." Trist must take good care of them when they reached Washington. Coolidge, who was a practical fellow, immediately went to work to help them collect documents and information. As an earnest of more help to come he took them to see Jared Sparks.

Sparks was at that moment virtually the unique American historian. Starting life as a poor farm boy, he became a journeyman carpenter and, so the story went, was taught Latin while he was shingling a Connecticut clergyman's barn. He showed such aptitude for letters that he worked his way by tutoring through Exeter and Harvard, served as minister of the First Independent Church in Baltimore, as chaplain of the House of Representatives, and as editor and successful owner of the *North American Review*.

He was encouraged by the success of his *Life of John Ledyard* to embark on a life of George Washington and a series of biographies of the Founding Fathers. He had recently arrived in Cambridge to lecture at Harvard after a tour of Virginia, bringing with him several trunkloads of George Washington's letters and records turned over to him for publication, under a special profitsharing arrangement, by John Marshall and Bushrod Washington.

Tocqueville felt a little of the awe he'd felt in the thunder of Niagara in the presence of the great Washington's handwriting. There were account books and business letters in connection with army administration. He was astonished that a man "whose ideas were so broad could bend himself to such details. . . . The whole is kept with a care, a neatness, accuracy and detail which would do credit to a clerk. The handwriting is beautiful, calm and perfectly uniform throughout all the pages. . . . Each signature looks like a facsimile."

Sparks's treasure trove seemed endless. There were letters of members of the Continental Congress, from ministers abroad, from Madame de Staël, from Louis Philippe himself during his exile. Tocqueville even turned up a letter of Lafayette's, written from prison at Olmütz. Beaumont's cousin was protesting the "horrible assassination" of Louis XVI by the Convention. "Poor Lafayette," Tocqueville noted scornfully.

Sparks, a man of infinite selfconfidence and consuming industry, felt he had the history of the Republic well in hand. Like Coolidge, he caught fire at Tocqueville's plan of describing the United States as they were in the year 1831. He promised to help him.

Tocqueville's ability to elicit facts and ideas from each new acquaintance was little short of miraculous. Without knowing it Coolidge and Sparks found themselves collaborating with Tocqueville in the treatise on selfgovernment which he was amassing as he traveled round the country—in his head even more than in his notebooks.

Tocqueville snatched up a phrase Josiah Quincy used to describe the relation of the towns to the state of Massachusetts: "a union of small republics." The president of Harvard College agreed with him that the happiest side of the American system was the absence of government. "Each man learns to think, to act for himself. . . . Man, thus accustomed to seeking his wellbeing only from his own efforts, rises in his own opinion, as in the estimation of others, his spirit expands and grows strong at the same time."

The idea of the state being a union of small republics delighted Tocqueville. He brought it up with everyone he met. He set Francis Gray and Joseph Coolidge to collecting documents on the jury system. Wasn't the jury, outside of its function of administering the law, an organ of selfgovernment? He began to see the New England town as the key to American democracy. The next time he saw Jared Sparks he asked if somebody hadn't written a book describing the administration of what he called *la commune*. Sparks said there was no such book, but he promised that he would himself get up a thorough documentation on the subject.

Tocqueville and Beaumont's New England friends kept referring to the "Godlike" Webster as the greatest orator of the day. He proved hard of access. When the Frenchmen finally obtained an interview it was a disappointment. They felt the great man didn't see anything for Daniel Webster in their project. Hoping that as a lawyer he might have some contribution to make on the topic of the reform of criminals, Tocqueville asked him his usual questions. Webster replied dryly it was no use to try to reform criminals. Tocqueville was disgusted. He told a German acquaintance, right after the interview, that Webster had "the common lawyer's viewpoint." Like thousands of statesmen, he cared only for power.

His impression of another great American was quite different. He and Beaumont felt truly awed when they were invited by the learned Senator Edward Everett's brother Alexander to dinner to meet John Quincy Adams. They looked forward with trepidation to meeting this "sort of deposed king," but when he arrived at the Everetts' "he was received with great politeness as an honored guest but that was all." Another example of the leveling effect of *la démocratie*. Tocqueville was seated beside him. He spoke excellent French, was full of *esprit*, and his conversation was delightful.

John Quincy Adams had retired, bruised and battered, from the presidency two years before. Admittedly he had reached that high office through an unspoken agreement with Henry Clay which his enemies denounced as a corrupt deal. He was not aware of any wrongdoing but his conscience pricked him nevertheless. He had engaged in a public row with his Vice President John C. Calhoun. John Randolph had expended all the dying fires of his invective in lashing his administration.

Adams' first message to Congress, although it was an echo of the great plans Jefferson and Gallatin themselves had drafted during the heady moment when they felt they could pay off the national debt and spend the whole federal revenue on "internal improvements," was ill received by the Democrats in Congress. He advocated a national university, the financing of scientific expeditions, the establishment of astronomical observatories, the setting up of a uniform standard of weights and measures, and added to that Henry Clay's "American system" of turnpikes and canals.

At every turn he was frustrated by Congress and by the political infighting of southern, New York, and western factions until his entire wellintentioned administration was swept away by the rising flood of Jacksonian Democracy. Tocqueville was surprised to learn that the ex-President had consented to election to the House of Representatives. There for the seventeen years of life that remained to him the thorny old public servant was to fight the good fight as he saw it.

Tocqueville didn't get much response to his first remark about how well the Americans did without government, but when he brought up the sudden multiplicity of public conventions: for a protective tariff, against a protective tariff, for temperance, for African colonization of the blacks, for workingmen's rights, Mr. Adams showed interest. He disliked this tendency. He feared these informal associations might tend to take government out of the hands of the elected representatives of the people.

Tocqueville enticed him into evaluating the American character. Adams discerned two main influences, one good and one bad. There was the personal independence and sense of individual responsibility which developed out of the religious basis of the early settlements in the North; there was the debasing influence of slavery in the South. He admitted, hopefully, that slavery was diminishing in every state except where cotton and sugar were cultivated, but it remained a threat to the Union.

Tocqueville, himself a convinced Catholic, was interested in the exuberant Unitarianism he noted in his Boston friends. He asked Adams whether as the Protestant sects proliferated they were not wearing away the basic faith without which Christianity could not subsist? Adams pointed out that the skepticism of Hume and Voltaire, which had been in the ascendant forty years before, had long been on the wane. He did not think the Christian religion was decaying in the United States.

When Tocqueville asked him about nullification in South Carolina, the latest form of the states' rights movement, which seemed to be gaining headway in the slavery states, "Mr. Adams did not answer at all, but it was easy to see that in this matter he felt no more confidence than I did in the future."

8. *Democracy a Style of Living*

Tocqueville noted under *General Remarks* in his diary: "All believe that to be republican a people must be poised, religious and very enlightened. Many admit that, besides these conditions, it is necessary that there be a condition of material wellbeing such that there be hardly ever any interior unrest resulting from unsatisfied needs."

After leaving Boston they traveled from prison to prison through Connecticut. The leaves were turning, the maples were aflame. They made note of the magnificence of the American autumn. In the Connecticut towns Tocqueville was struck more than ever by the intelligence of the common people. In Europe he had been taught that it was specialization that brought out the best in people. Here the opposite was true. Every man was a jack of all trades. "He does each thing less well than the European who does nothing else, but his general capacity is a hundred times greater." This Tocqueville saw as "the chief cause of superiority in the usual affairs of life and in the government of society."

He was coming to the opinion that freedom in education was another factor. "Anyone is free to found a public school and direct it as he pleases. It is an industry like other industries, the consumers being the judges and the state taking no hand," he wrote a friend in Paris. "You ask me if this unlimited liberty produces bad results. I believe it produces only good."

When they reached Philadelphia what struck them most was the geometrical regularity of the squares and numbered streets. "All the edifices are neat," wrote Beaumont, "kept up with extreme care, and have all the freshness of new buildings." He found the city's cleanliness delightful, though the place was "monotonous in its beauty." Tocqueville found the numbering of the streets convenient, but the results of "a frozen imagination." "These people here know only arithmetic. . . . But we must not speak ill of them," he added on second thought, "for they continue to treat us admirably. Philadelphia beyond all others is infatuated with the penitentiary system, and as the penitentiary business is our racket, they vie with each other in pampering us."

Beaumont reported that the Philadelphia humanitarians had really gone too far. "The prison is truly a palace. Each prisoner enjoys all the comforts of life." He tried to figure what each cell would cost in francs. "The building of such a prison must cost *un prix fou.*"

They were entertained by Jefferson's old friend William Short, now retired after his romantic adventures in Europe to a bachelor life which was occupied mostly with attending to his investments in Genesee Valley lands. Short, like Coolidge and Gray, threw himself into collecting documents for the French commissioners.

Though Tocqueville would hardly admit it to himself he was thoroughly bored by this time with prisons and prison reform. The interviews he had with the convicts in the solitary cells which Beaumont found so luxurious were heartbreaking, but they led nowhere.

He wanted to see the American scene as a whole. Already he was sorting out chapters in his mind for his book. He wrote his father that in studying a foreign country one must be careful to separate the features of the social organization which could be imitated from those which would be unworkable in another country. He was coming to the conclusion that the shape of a society depended far more on the customs and habits of the people than on laws and constitutions written in the statute books.

His mind worked in paradoxes. He had to a high degree that clarity of generalization which has often been remarked on as a feature of the French intelligence at its best. In Philadelphia he wrote in his pocket notebook a statement which was to be the core of his final analysis of American democracy:

"When the detractors of popular government claim that, in the many points of internal administration, the government of one man is better than the government of all, they are in my view incontestably right. . . . A republic is less well administered than an elightened monarchy. . . . The wonderful effect of republican governments (where they can subsist) is not in presenting a picture of *regularity* and *methodical order* in a people's administration, but in the *style of living.* Liberty . . . does not always and in all circumstances give the peoples a more skillful and faultless government; but it infuses throughout society an activity, a force and an energy, which cannot exist without it, and which throughout all time has made the greatest nations."

The same day he added an ironic afterthought: " 'The people is always right,' that is the dogma of the republic, just as 'the king can do no wrong' is the religion of monarchic states. It is a great question to decide whether one is more false than the other: But what is certain is that neither one nor the other is true."

9. *Freedom of Association*

Ever since his talk with ex-President Adams he had been obsessed with the problem of freedom of association. Was it a good thing or a bad thing? He was convinced it would never do in France. Industriously collecting statistics, he was appalled to discover that there were in the United States more than two thousand associations dedicated to the cause of temperance alone.

In Philadelphia he brought associations up in the course of a long conversation with Charles Jared Ingersoll. Ingersoll was the kind of man Tocqueville found congenial. He was knowledgeable and witty. He knew his way around in Pennsylvania politics. He'd served in Congress and written a play and a sprightly political history of the War of 1812.

"The power of association," Tocqueville had just noted, "has reached its uttermost development in America. They associate in the interests of commerce, for objects political, literary and religious. It is never by an appeal to a superior authority that success is sought, but by an appeal to individual resources, organized to act in harmony."

Wasn't this, he asked Ingersoll, a dangerous and impracticable consequence of the sovereignty of the people?

Ingersoll thought not. It was like freedom of the press. "When people can speak in liberty you can bet they won't act." Associations were a useful way of ventilating minority opinions. Public meetings produced not laws but speeches. They gave men a chance to put forth opinions which might be unpopular at the time but which eventually might influence the ideas of the majority. They formed the people's protection against the tyranny of the majority.

Tocqueville declared himself unconvinced, but when the time came to set down his considered opinion in his chapter on associations, he found he agreed with Ingersoll. "*En Amérique il y a des factieux mais pas des conspirateurs.*"

It was already late October. Time was getting short. In spite of all their reading, their study of maps and travelers' tales it had never occurred to Tocqueville and Beaumont that the United States covered such an immense territory.

From Philadelphia they hurried to Baltimore. The Baltimoreans received them royally. They hardly had time to wash off the dust of the road before they were driven to a grand subscription ball where they were introduced to the wit and fashion of the city. The girls were lovely, and very flirtatious. One young lady caught Beaumont's eye. She was "roguish as a demon, giddy as a Junebug." He added wistfully that she "might be guilty of some follies when she has chosen someone as ready as she to commit them." The implication was that she had not chosen him.

Next morning they were introduced to another association. This one was dedicated to the racing of horses. Beautiful Arabians. They saw a trotting race for the first time. The costumes of the jockeys they considered ridiculous. Beaumont wrote home that Baltimore was a whirl. "The week we spent in that city was a real carnival; we went steadily from feast to banquet; not a single day did we dine at our inn."

10. L'Esclavage aux Etats-Unis

Maryland was their first slavery state. They had hardly arrived at the race track when they saw a Negro beaten with a cane for entering the paddock with some whites. "One of them gave him a volley of blows with his cane without this deed appearing to surprise either the crowd or the Negro himself."

For Beaumont this was the turning point. The more he saw of slavery the more it sickened him. Before that his profoundest impressions came from his two weeks in the wilderness and his hours with the Indians at Green Bay. Let Tocqueville write about democracy. His book would be about the Indians driven into the wastelands and the miseries of Negro slavery. Even in Boston he had discovered that Negro children were not admitted to the schools. At the Baltimore theatre he saw beautiful welldressed women, who looked white to him, forced to sit in the mulatto part of the gallery because they were suspected of a taint of Negro blood. The plot of his novel would hinge on the plight of a halfbreed. As eagerly as Tocqueville projected his *Démocratie en Amérique,* Beaumont started to sketch out *Marie, ou l'Esclavage aux Etats-Unis.* He wrote home that he was planning a great work which would render him immortal.

The memorable moment of their stay in Baltimore was being taken to call on the last surviving signer of the Declaration of Independence. Charles Carroll of Carrollton was ninetyfour. His mind was clear. He had the manners of the old regime. He owned thirty thousand acres and three hundred slaves. Tocqueville and Beaumont looked upon him with particular veneration because he was a Catholic. It pleased them to learn that it was the Catholic country gentlemen of Maryland who had first established religious toleration in America. Charles Carroll's political opinions had remained those of a British Whig of the past century. "A mere democracy is but a mob," he told them.

"This strain," wrote Tocqueville, "is disappearing today, after having furnished America her greatest men. With them is being lost the tradition of the better born. The masses are growing more enlightened. Knowledge is spreading, a middling capacity is becoming common. The outstanding talents, the great characters are more rare."

11. *Winter on the Western Waters*

In their mail came distressing news. The Ministry of Justice was cutting short their leave. The cholera had appeared in France.

Some physician had told them that cajeput oil from the Moluccas was a sovereign remedy. It was obtainable in Philadelphia. They hurried back to Philadelphia to purchase two bottles—one for the Beaumonts and one for the Tocquevilles; only a few drops were said to be needed—which they expressed to New York where their heavy baggage was awaiting them. They had engaged passage on the French packet for early February.

They couldn't leave America without seeing the Mississippi. Their ears still resounded with the surge of Chateaubriand's description in *Atala* of the mighty tropical river, its banks thronged with blue herons, pink flamingos, gay parrots, and even an occasional monkey.

Their travels became a race with time. From Philadelphia they set out for Pittsburgh. It was already November. They had made no allowance for the American climate. Crossing the Alleghenies on the stage, they met the first blizzard of what was to be the coldest winter since 1776.

They were in Pittsburgh just long enough to notice that the sky was "constantly obscured by the multitude of steam engines that run the shops."

They settled comfortably on the steamboat *Fourth of July* for Cincinnati. They loved the steamboat trips. It was an opportunity to write letters and to make entries in their notebooks.

Just above Wheeling their quiet navigation was rudely interrupted. The *Fourth of July* struck a shoal and, like Lafayette before them, they nearly drowned in the Ohio.

It happened at night. Tocqueville described the accident to a friend: "Our vessel, driven by the current and all the force of steam, smashed itself like a nutshell on a rock in the middle of the Ohio. The cry of 'We sink' resounded immediately; the vessel, the gear and the passengers started in company for eternity. . . . I have never heard a more villainous sound than the water made rushing into the ship."

The river, he observed, was wide and swift and full of cakes of ice.

Beaumont and Tocqueville both remarked on the admirable coolness of the American women in the moment of danger. There was no panic. The *Fourth of July* grounded firmly on the rocks and sank no further. When the day dawned Beaumont found time to make some sketches. Another steamboat came along and carried the passengers to Wheeling.

They pushed on downriver.

They saw enough of the river towns to remark on the vast difference between the states of Ohio and Kentucky. In free Ohio everything was bustle and progress. Cincinnati already had thirty thousand inhabitants and exhibited the same curious contrast between civilization and the frontier they had noticed on the Great Lakes. Kentucky, the slave state, seemed stagnant in comparison. They noted that slavery brutalized the black population and debilitated the white.

At Cincinnati they took passage on another fine steamboat for Louisville. The meals were good, the passengers interesting. The steamboat didn't vibrate as much as the others so that they could write at their ease. Everything was fine except the weather.

About twentyfive miles above Louisville they were put ashore because the river was frozen solid below them. They had to pile their baggage on a cart and walk through kneedeep snow into Louisville.

At Louisville every steamboat was frozen up solid. Nothing to it but to take the stage to Memphis.

The frozen roads were horrible. Most of the way the passengers had to walk through the snow, pushing and shoving when they could.

The stage broke a wheel.

Tocqueville was taken ill.

They found themselves hunched up for several days in a log hut on the side of the trail at a place called Sandy Spring in Tennessee. Although the fireplace roared icy winds seeped through the chinks between the logs.

Their hosts were cordial but utterly shiftless. If wood had to be cut they waited for the Negroes to do it. All the white men did was hunt and talk politics. Tocqueville and Beaumont had plenty of time to observe this race of backwoodsmen who had just come to political prominence in America with Jackson's victory at the polls. At last Tocqueville's fever subsided and he was well enough to stand the jolting of the stage again.

Memphis with such a mighty name, so long looked forward to, turned out to be a miserable little hamlet at the base of some clay cliffs. They could see great ice floes upriver.

The Memphis district, Tocqueville noted, was represented in Congress by one David Crockett, "who had no education, could hardly read, had no property and no fixed residence, but passed his life hunting."

Finding nothing better to do, they took to hunting themselves. Some Chickasaw Indians guided them in search of game. The Indians were not too pleased when the Frenchmen blazed away into a flock of green, yellow, and red Carolina parrots. When they shot one the gay gregarious little birds fluttered around the dead body so it was easy to shoot more.

On Christmas Day a steamboat appeared. She was the *Louisville*, handsome and new, bound upriver. Tocqueville and Beaumont convinced the captain that since he couldn't reach St. Louis on account of the ice he might as well turn around and take them down to New Orleans.

Another inducement was the appearance of a tribe of dispossessed Choctaws, begging to be transferred to the west bank of the Mississippi, where they had been allotted new land. Men, women, and children, with their chattels and possessions, and their aged and infirm, and their dogs and their horses, were loaded aboard the *Louisville*. The government agent paid their passage.

The travelers settled down to shipboard life. The paddle wheels churned the puttycolored water and the steamboat was off into the smooth swift current.

One lovely moonlight night they grounded on a sandbar. Finding that complaints to the captain and the pilot were unavailing, Beaumont got out his sketch pad and Tocqueville philosophically improved his time reading the *Federalist* and Kent's *Commentaries*.

Thaws upriver caused the waters to rise. After two days of hard work by the crew the *Louisville* was pushed off the sandbank.

They stopped again at the mouth of the White River to disembark the Choctaws. There a tall man in a deerskin hunting shirt came riding down to the river shore shepherding another group of Indians. He rode a superb stallion. Everybody knew who he was. It was whispered about that this was Sam Houston, who some years before had walked out on a promising political career in Tennessee. He abandoned his wife on their wedding night, resigned as governor of the state, and went to live with the Indians in the wilderness. He had taken a chief's daughter for a concubine and become a leader among the Cherokees.

He came aboard the *Louisville*. While they steamed downriver Tocqueville, intrigued by the strange and disreputable tales that hung about his name, sought him out. Beaumont, with his projected masterpiece in mind, was all ears. Houston proved to be a man of some cultivation. He was said to be fortyfive but he looked younger. Tocqueville remarked on his athletic build and his look of "physical and moral energy."

Houston talked willingly about Indian customs and religions. He was interested in the mound builders. They had certainly not been of the same race as the present Indians. He connected them with the Aztecs of the Valley of Mexico. Beaumont questioned him sharply about the possibility of survival for the tribes that were being driven out into the Arkansas River region. Houston said that if the United States Government were willing to take the trouble to help the Cherokees, who were already an agricultural people, they could civilize themselves in twentyfive years. Other tribes would take longer. He believed the Indians were as intelligent as anybody.

"The Indian is born free," Tocqueville quoted Houston as saying. "He is left to look after himself as soon as he can act; even a father's power is an imperceptible bond for him. Surrounded by dangers, hounded by needs, able to count on nobody, his mind has to be constantly on the alert. . . . This necessity imposed on the Indian gives his intelligence a degree of development and ingenuity which are often wonderful."

Houston was of the opinion the same thing might have been true of the Negro if he hadn't been born a slave.

They parted at New Orleans. Rumor had it that Sam Houston was coming out of exile. He was said to be on his way to Washington to present President Jackson with a petition on behalf of the Cherokees; he was planning to reconstruct his life. The career of the future victor of San Jacinto was on the march again. Tocqueville and Beaumont had met the great Texan at the turning point of his life.

Having lost so much time, they had to go through the Creole capital they had so looked forward to on a dead run. "The first of January, 1832," Tocqueville wrote home, "the sun rising in a brilliant tropical sky revealed to us New Orleans across the masts of a thousand ships. . . . There was no time to lose: to make the acquaintance of all those to whom he had letters of introduction, to enjoy the pleasures, so celebrated, of New Orleans; to study the laws; to get a notion of how the people behaved; to collect the statistics and learn the history of the country, only twentyfour hours remained to us. . . ."

They hurriedly found quarters in a hotel. "We tried to introduce into our dress as much as possible a happy mixture of the Philosopher and the man of the world. . . . We put on a black tie for the members of the legislature, a white vest for the ladies, we took in our hands a little swagger stick to raise us into the intimacy with the fashionable world, and well pleased with ourselves we walked down the stairs."

They found the French consul in his dressing gown in the middle of a family party. Stepping over the children and the halfunwrapped toys, they bombarded him with questions.

Scribbling desperately fast, they filled their notebooks with observations on the position of the mulattoes, the unique situation of the cultivated octoroons, the state of the Catholic religion, the horrible filth of the jail. . . . The French population was merging with the American. There were marriages between them every day. The overriding characteristic of life in New Orleans was an immense and growing prosperity. As far back as 1828 a thousand sailing vessels and seven hundred and seventy steamboats had entered the port of New Orleans. The number increased from year to year.

Tocqueville tried to relate this hurried jumble to the basic generalizations he was laying away for future use. "The greatest merit of American government is to be *powerless* and *passive*. . . . America needs, in order to prosper, neither skillful leadership nor profound plans . . . but liberty and still more liberty."

12. *A Traveling South Carolinian*

At the end of three days they were on the stage bound north through Mobile and Montgomery and Milledgeville into South Carolina. There was so little time left them they had to bypass Charleston.

At an inn in the Piedmont country they ran into an acquaintance from Philadelphia. Joel Poinsett was on his way back to Washington from a private mission for President Jackson. Alarmed by the secessionist talk in South Carolina, Jackson had sent him down to his home state to argue the militia in the back counties into taking the Unionist side if the planter politicians should try to break up the Union.

Though he kept his mouth shut on these matters Poinsett was a great find. He was the most seasoned traveler in the country. He was a genial man who knew his way around. He took the Frenchmen in charge. They would go to Washington together.

Poinsett was the son of a wellheeled Charleston physician. After some schooling by Timothy Dwight in Connecticut he was sent to Edinburgh to study medicine. Tiring of the Scottish professors, he wandered all over Europe and part of Asia. When he came home he studied law instead of medicine as his father wanted. He had the traveler's itch. He told Beaumont he'd made the Atlantic crossing twentytwo times. He was no stranger to secret missions. President Madison sent him to Chile and the Argentine to report confidentially on the chances for republican government in those countries. In 1822 Monroe sent him on a similar mission to Mexico.

When Poinsett reached Mexico City who should receive him with a magnificent spread but that old intriguer General James Wilkinson. Though well along in his sixties and suffering from a complication of diseases, Wilkinson had almost managed, with the outbreak of independence, to accomplish his lifelong dream of making his fortune at the court of Montezuma.

When he got himself to Mexico he found the imperial crown Aaron Burr had so coveted on the head of a military adventurer named Agustín de Iturbide. Wilkinson always had a way with the dons. He counseled the Emperor on fine points of the United

States Constitution, and somehow acquired a claim on two hundred thousand acres of Texas land.

Poinsett steered his way so successfully through a crowd of connivers motivated mostly by a desire for Texas land that when he reported back to Washington he was appointed by President Adams American minister to Mexico. He had somehow earned Wilkinson's enmity. When he arrived at Vera Cruz the valiant American general was quoted in the newspapers as asking dramatically: "What have the Mexican people done to deserve such a calamity as the appointment of Poinsett?"

Poinsett was a Freemason. His Masonic connections had been useful in dealing on friendly terms with the Mexican politicos. He found the government a republic again, but in the scuffle for the presidency a group of Freemasons who bitterly opposed Poinsett's kind of Freemason came to power.

Meanwhile General Wilkinson succumbed to his chronic diseases. As there wasn't a penny in the house to bury him, the American minister had to handle the obsequies of his distinguished compatriot and to attend to his burial in the Church of San Miguel.

The clamors of the anti-Poinsett faction in the Mexican Foreign Office reached such a point that Andrew Jackson reluctantly consented to his recall. He came away with little to show for his efforts beyond the introduction into the United States of the gaudy pot plant that bears his name.

President Jackson was no man to be impressed by the vituperations of the dons. It was largely as an expression of personal confidence that he sent Poinsett to South Carolina.

Traveling with Poinsett was a pleasure. He was able to conjure up the best of food and drink in the most unlikely places. He had endless anecdotes about the South American peoples. He was skeptical of the success of republics in those countries. He told Tocqueville that, though the Mexicans were trying to adopt North American political constitutions, they were "still in the sixteenth century." Poinsett said he always knew what the Mexicans were going to do if he asked himself "what a sixteenth-century man would do in such a situation." The Mexicans were in the sixteenth century, he added pointedly, but without the savage virtues of that time.

13. Cogitations on the Chesapeake Steamboat

Poinsett saw to it that the moment they arrived in Norfolk they should take passage on the steamboat leaving the same evening for Washington. Steaming up the Chesapeake, Tocqueville had leisure to go over his notes. He was comparing what he'd seen in the

United States with what Poinsett told him of the failure of republican institutions among the Spanishspeaking Americans.

He laid the difference to the "practical political education" of the North American people. Again Tocqueville wrote in his little book that it was habits and customs, not laws, that counted. "Political liberty is a food that is hard to digest. Only the most robust constitutions can support it."

He began to note down his misgivings on the subject of *la démocratie*. The great days of American politics, when men like Jefferson and Madison headed the Republicans and Hamilton and John Adams the Federalists, were over. All he could see now was picayune factions.

"I cannot conceive a sorrier spectacle in the world than that of the different coteries (they do not deserve the name of parties) which today divide the union. You see operating in broad daylight in their bosoms all the small and shameful passions which are usually hidden with great care at the bottom of the human heart.

"As for the interest of the country no one thinks of it: and if they do talk about it it's only for the form. The parties place it at the head of their platforms as our fathers once printed the King's licence on the first page of their books.

"It is pitiful to see what coarse insults, what small vilifications and what impudent calumnies fill the journals which serve them as party organs, and with what shameless scorn for all the social decencies they daily arraign before the bar of public opinion the honor of families and the secrets of the domestic hearth."

Tocqueville was convinced that the American institutions which so filled him with enthusiasm would never do for France; in the long run would they do for America?

Though he had not yet carried his misgivings to their logical conclusion he was already turning over in his mind the doubts he later formulated in his final chapters on the future development of *la démocratie*. Wasn't it a law of history that democracy bred despotism? He discarded the parallel of the Roman Empire. Yet in the coming centuries he saw the independence of the individual and local liberties becoming more and more "an artificial product." Centralization would be the natural government. What he called the "Social-democratic order" which he had observed in America seemed to offer "singular facilities" for the establishment of despotism.

"The sort of oppression," he wrote, "which threatens the democratic peoples will resemble nothing that has happened in the world before; our contemporaries will find no inkling of it in their memories . . . the old words, despotism and tyranny, do not fit. It is a new thing. I must try to define it since I cannot name it.

". . . I see an innumerable crowd of men, alike and equal, endlessly turning in on themselves to procure small and vulgar pleasures. . . .

Each one is alone in his own corner, a stranger to the destiny of all the others; his children and his particular friends represent for him the entire human race; as to his fellow citizens, he is among them but doesn't see them; he touches them but he doesn't feel them; he only exists in himself and for himself, and even if he still has a family one can well say of him that he has no country.

"Above all these there hovers an immense tutelary power, charged with assuring their pleasures and looking out for their fate. It is absolute, detailed, regular, foreseeing and mild. It would resemble the paternal authority if its object were to prepare men for mature manhood; but on the contrary its aim is to keep men children. . . . This power works for the good of the citizenry; but it must be the only agent and the only arbiter; it works for their security, anticipates and assures the satisfaction of their needs, facilitates their pleasures, conducts their business, directs their industry, arranges their line of descent, bequeaths their inheritance; until it has relieved them of the trouble of thinking and the labor of living. . . .

"After having taken each individual in its powerful hands and molded him to its taste, the sovereign power stretches its arms over the whole of society. It imbues the surface of society with a mesh of small rules, complicated, minute and uniform. The more original spirits and the vigorous minds will never be able to break through these rules enough to raise their heads above the crowd. This power does not crush men's wills, but it softens them, bends them and directs them. It does not force people to act but it keeps them from acting. It does not destroy but it inhibits invention. It does not tyrannize but it obstructs, it enervates, it stifles . . . until in the end it reduces the nation to a flock of timid and industrious animals, of which the government is the shepherd.

"I have always thought that this sort of servitude . . . could be combined more easily than we think with some of the external trappings of liberty, and that it is not impossible that it might become established in the shadow of the sovereignty of the people."

14. The Capital of Democracy

Tocqueville and Beaumont had only three weeks left when they reached Washington. "This town, whose population is inconsiderable, is yet immense in area," Beaumont wrote. "Distances are almost as great as in Paris. . . . The houses are scattered here and there without connection between them, without order and without symmetry. Outside of the fact that it makes a very ugly panorama, it is very inconvenient for those who have visits to make."

They found Monsieur Serurier, the French minister, to be an old Washington hand who had known the city under three different administrations. Returning after an absence of twenty years, he said he missed the great political talents of former times. Men had grown smaller.

Their friend Poinsett took them to Capitol Hill. Beaumont found the "aspect of the debates grave and imposing." He remarked on the advantages of establishing the capital in a small town out of the way of the great cities. Tocqueville described the building as "a magnificent monument."

The usual invitations poured in. They found the social life gay, the company good. They were particularly delighted with Edward Livingston, the Secretary of State. Beaumont described him as the "most celebrated writer in America," which was hardly true, and as having been born in Louisiana, which was equally incorrect, though Livingston, to be sure, had lived years in New Orleans. At sixty, at the height of his career, Beau Ned was a sprightly talker, and in spite of his passion for puns an excellent raconteur. He spoke French fluently. Beaumont enthusiastically described a *soirée dansante* at the Secretary of State's house, where, between waltzes and square dances, he discussed the penitentiary system with Mr. Livingston: ". . . All the members of the diplomatic corps gathered in Washington set the tone; French is the common language, and you would believe yourself in a Parisian salon."

When Tocqueville published *De la démocratie en Amérique* some years later Edward Livingston was the only American he thanked for his help. Livingston was American minister to France at the time he was finishing the book and may well have gone over the manuscript with him. Tocqueville may have felt that the lists of his American assistants was too long to name; or, more likely, that they would not care to have their names associated with what he feared would be a very unpopular work. In Washington the man who did most for the inquiring Frenchman was a subordinate of Livingston's in the State Department, Jefferson's grandsoninlaw, Nicholas Trist.

Coolidge had again written from Boston reminding him to be on the lookout for Tocqueville and Beaumont. They were "fine fellows" and would need his help in collecting documents for their studies. While they were in Washington Trist gave up much of his time to searching out materials for them.

Trist came of a family which had been on terms of friendship with Jefferson since before Trist was born. Since his marriage to Jefferson's granddaughter Virginia he had lived for years at Monticello. He was an executor of Jefferson's estate. Only recently he had helped Jeff Randolph edit the *Memoirs, Correspondence, and Miscellanies from the Papers of Thomas Jefferson* which the family published in Charlottesville in 1829. As one of Jefferson's young men he could not fail to be passionately interested in the research Tocqueville was undertaking into the realities of the American democracy of which Thomas Jefferson was the founder.

15. *Les Dieux s'en Vont*

It is notable that in spite of the fact that Trist, Coolidge, and Short, three younger men who looked up to Jefferson with filial reverence and affection, who had virtually been members of his family, were among Tocqueville's and Beaumont's chief informants during their American tour, there is hardly a mention of the founder of democratic republicanism in their notebooks. Later Tocqueville did list the French translation of Jeff Randolph's edition of Jefferson's papers, brought out by Conseil in Paris in 1833 under the title of *Mélanges politiques et philosophiques,* along with *The Federalist Papers* and Kent's *Commentaries,* as the most important literary sources of his studies of American democracy.

Jefferson had been dead only five years but in the American mind of 1831 there was hardly a trace left of the living man.

Jefferson's letters still circulated in the press. His name and a hundred phrases torn from their context were used as slogans by the coteries Tocqueville saw as making such a sorry spectacle of American politics. It was as if the great phrasemaker had been defeated by the success of his own phrases. Expressions of his national patriotism and his clearsighted admission that America had to become an industrial nation became part of the banner of the consolidationists. His doctrine of states' rights became the war cry of slavery advocates struggling to protect their peculiar institution.

While Tocqueville and Beaumont were traveling from New Orleans to Washington, Jeff Randolph, stirred to action in the Virginia Assembly by the hideous bloodshed of a slave rebellion in Southampton County, was making a last unsuccessful effort to put through his grandfather's program for gradual emancipation. The Virginia constitutional convention of the year before had already disregarded the Jeffersonian plea for local selfgovernment by manhood suffrage in the Virginia counties. All that was left of Jefferson's project for free public education was the University of Virginia. His published papers had indeed stirred up a controversy in the American press, but it was a controversy in which partisan prejudices and partisan tactics superseded the sort of rigorous thinking that interested Tocqueville.

As one of the Founding Fathers Jefferson's name was lettered on the patriotic bunting every Fourth of July but its use had already become liturgical. The captious Frances Trollope, who spiced up her bestselling *Domestic Manners of the Americans* with the tale of the infidel lecher amid his brownskinned concubines at Monticello, was not far from echoing the public mind generally when she labeled the Jefferson papers as "a mighty mass of mischief."

When Tocqueville told Trist how much he regretted not having had time to visit Mr. Madison at Montpelier, Trist, his mind still full of the failure of the Jeffersonian cause at the convention and in the Assembly, replied sadly that "Virginia was now only a shadow of her former self . . . the great men, even the noteworthy men had disappeared . . . one no longer saw men of that kind rising up to take their place."

In his notebook Tocqueville jotted down a phrase which he underlined: *"Les dieux s'en vont."*

The French minister took the inquiring Frenchmen to call on President Jackson. Their literary friends had given them a poor opinion of the frontier general as a brawler, a duelist, and a backwoods demagogue whose only credit was having won the Battle of New Orleans. Beaumont wrote home that the President occupied a palace which in France would be considered "a fine private residence. Its interior is decorated with taste but simply. The salon in which he receives is infinitely less brilliant than those of our ministers. He has no guards watching at the door."

They found President Jackson alone though it was a public receiving day. They found him a wellpreserved old man of sixtysix who "appeared to have retained all the vigor of body and spirit."

Andrew Jackson was alone indeed. He had won the presidency at a terrible price. He believed that it was the "coarse insults" and "impudent calumnies" of the campaign that had caused his beloved Rachel's death. The opposition press had dragged out the story that she lived in sin with him for two years before they were legally married. Dumpy, pious, innocently warmhearted, the guardian angel of many a forsaken family in the Tennessee mountains, with a taste for a few quiet puffs on her pipe in the chimney corner in the evening, Rachel Jackson had dreaded going to Washington. In her last illness she said: "I would rather be a doorkeeper in the house of God than live in that palace in Washington."

"In the presence of this dear saint," the heartbroken old campaigner declared at her funeral, "I can and do forgive all my enemies, but those vile wretches who have slandered her must look to God for mercy."

In Washington the bereaved President was tasting to the full the frustrations of the office. He stood at bay against the nullificationists in the South and the northern advocates of a national bank. He had a bad press. Half of Congress was yapping at his heels. He was on the outs with Calhoun, who had been reelected Vice President. In the hope of somehow finding some politicians he could trust he had just performed the unprecedented feat of asking for the resignations of his entire cabinet.

It was a bitter fervent selfopinionated vigorous old man the inquiring Frenchmen found sitting alone in the White House. "Not a man of genius," they noted. Andrew Jackson was no man you could subject to questioning. They found little to say to him and he had nothing to say to them. He courteously invited them to drink a glass of madeira with him. When they left they said, "*Merci, monsieur*," as they would to anybody.

In New York they had to wait a few days because the packet's sailing was postponed. Tocqueville found waiting for him Jared Sparks's "Essay on Town Government," on which he based many chapters of his book. Materials arrived from Joseph Coolidge, a letter from Short, masses of statistics from the records of New York and New Jersey, and an essay on democratic government from the mayor of Philadelphia. They carried so much documentation aboard the *Havre* that neither Tocqueville nor Beaumont ever found time to look at a great deal of it.

Tocqueville already had in his head the salient chapters of the book which was to summarize for all time the achievement and the failure, the satisfactions, the forebodings and portents of the Jeffersonian era in the United States.

They sailed on February 20. In ten months in America Tocqueville had learned more than he was to learn in all the years that remained to him.

AUTHOR'S NOTE: The three principal sources for the Tocqueville material are 1) *Tocqueville and Beaumont in America* by George W. Pierson (Oxford University Press, New York, 1938); 2) Tocqueville and Beaumont manuscripts in Yale University Library; 3) *Alexis de Tocqueville's Journey to America* edited by J. P. Mayer (Yale University Press, New York, 1961).

APPENDIX

Reading on the Jeffersonian Era

With the multiplicity of newspapers, and the ample record left behind in letters and journals by every man of importance, the period 1800–30 is embarrassingly well documented.

A literature of political comment and apologetics had grown up even before the turn of the century. As an example of the genre Humphrey Marshall's *History of Kentucky* is highly partisan but written with a wit and malice that make it thoroughly readable. The same can be said of Charles Jared Ingersoll's *Political History of the War of 1812*, which comes from the Republican end of the spectrum. The easiest access to the journalistic polemics of the time is through the bound volumes of Hezekiah Niles' *Register*, published in Baltimore, which carried reports of the debates in Congress and printed all important documents and statistics. Niles indexed his volumes and was objective enough as an editor to win the approval of gentlemen of such divergent political opinions as Thomas Jefferson and Josiah Quincy.

The best overall account of the first half of the period is to be found in Henry Adams' *History of the United States during the Administrations of Jefferson and Madison*. This is one of the really firstrate historical works written by an American about his own country. Its very excellence was tended to perpetuate, among later historians, Henry Adams' slighting view of Jefferson's acts and pronouncements. You have to keep in mind that it was written by an Adams, and that Henry Adams based much of his narrative on John Quincy Adams' personal observations. John Quincy Adams' *Memoirs* are a gold mine, but the reader has to remember on every page how brilliantly that extraordinary gentleman managed to combine acute personal prejudice with seeming accuracy of detail. Henry Adams was the first man to understand the historical importance of Albert Gallatin. His *Life of Gallatin* serves as an introduction to the whole period.

The *Life of Thomas Jefferson* published in 1837 by Professor George Tucker of the University of Virginia is essential because Tucker knew Jefferson personally and had the advantage of advice and recollections furnished by James Madison and Nicholas N. Trist, and by many other men who were Jefferson's familiars during the last decade of his life. In a sense it is an apologetic work. Tucker was writing in an effort to quiet the chorus of denunciation by political enemies that followed Jeff Randolph's publication in 1829 of his selection of his grandfather's papers under the title of *Memoirs, Correspondence and Miscellanies from the Papers of Thomas Jefferson*.

Henry S. Randall's threevolume life also had the advantage of personal reminiscences. Published in 1847, it set off a reaction against the almost total eclipse of Jefferson's reputation that followed his death. Though somewhat worshipful, Randall's life is stuffed with information that can't be found anywhere else.

To this day Jefferson's reputation as a statesman is subject to periodic eclipse and apotheosis. As Tucker wrote in his preface, "It was the fate of Thomas Jefferson to be at once more loved and praised by his friends, and more hated and reviled by his adversaries than any of his compatriots."

Since the Princeton edition of Jefferson's papers has only reached November 1790 we still have to depend on the Library of Congress, the Massachusetts Historical Society, and the Alderman Library at the University of Virginia for Jefferson's writings during the period 1807–26. A great number of letters were printed in the wretched Memorial Edition and in Paul Leicester Ford's carefully chosen selections; but even Ford, who was a real scholar, occasionally left out passages which for some reason he thought too rank for the public eye. Gilbert Chinard's collections of Jefferson's correspondence with the French are very useful, as is his edition of the Commonplace Book. Edwin Morris Betts's editions of the Farm and Garden Books are invaluable. The Jefferson writings constitute a world in themselves. Lester J. Cappon's edition of the Adams-Jefferson letters has for the first time made that correspondence conveniently available.

The bulk of Madison's and Monroe's papers are in the Manuscript Division of the Library of Congress. Also to be found there are William Plumer's memorandum and autobiography, which are basic for the period, and the Samuel Harrison Smith papers which contain so much gossipy description of the daily life of the national capital by both Mr. and Mrs. Smith. There, too, are to be found a complete microfilm of John Quincy Adams' journal, Henry Adams' famous transcripts from the British, French, and Spanish archives which proved Burr's treason, and John Henry's revelations for which Monroe paid such an exorbitant price.

There are shelves and shelves of descriptions of Monticello by visitors foreign and domestic. Best among the original sources for knowledge of Jefferson's private life are Edmund Bacon's recollections as related by Hamilton W. Pierson, the president of Cumberland College in Kentucky. Bacon was overseer of the Monticello plantations for about twenty years. Then there is the story Old Isaac, who was the Monticello blacksmith, told a man named Campbell, which is among the manuscripts at the Alderman Library. In the last few years a most interesting letter from Randall to James Parton, describing a confidential conversation with Jefferson's grandson Jeff Randolph, has turned up in the Parton papers at the Harvard University Library. Professor Flowers printed it as an appendix to his monograph on Parton. To these must now be added, for the understanding of the history of the Hemings family and of their connection with Jefferson, an account of Madison Hemings' life, under the title of *Life Among the Lowly*, printed in March 13, 1873, in the *Pike County Republican*, a newspaper published at Waverly, Ohio.

I found Bernard Mayo's little volume *Thomas Jefferson and His Unknown Brother Randolph* and the Collection of Dr. Robley Dunglison's correspondence with Jefferson in the last weeks of his life peculiarly revealing. Henry Lee's letter describing his interview with the dying man was printed in Niles's *Register* soon after Jefferson's death.

John Randolph's documents are mostly at the Virginia State Library in Richmond. Timothy Pickering's complete papers are at the Massachusetts Historical Society. The chief source for information on Albert Gallatin is the mass of letters and documents at the New-York Historical Society. There too is a mass of material on Aaron Burr, particularly on his later life. A volume of the complete Bixby edition of Burr's European journal is easily available at the New York Public Library. The most important of General Wilkinson's papers, including the cypher letter which has been the subject of so much controversy, are at the Newberry Library in Chicago. The three obese volumes of the general's *Memoirs of My Own Time* are worth looking into.

Both Washington Irving's and George Ticknor's memoirs and journals help illuminate the period.

James Parton's *Life of Andrew Jackson*, which seems to me the best of his biographies, is very good reading indeed. Among recent works I found Nathan Schachner's biographies of Jefferson and Burr, and Irving Brant's volumes on Madison, thoroughly useful. A good modern analysis of Burr's career can be found in Holmes Alexander's *The Proud Pretender*. For Monroe's and John Quincy Adams' adminstrations nothing approaches George Dangerfield's *The Era of Good Feelings*.

The Yale University Library has an important collection of the letters and papers of Alexis de Tocqueville. Professor George Wilson Pierson based his *Tocqueville and Beaumont in America* on these papers and on his researches in France among the archives of the Beaumont and Tocqueville descendants. This excellent book furnishes an inimitable panorama of the America Jefferson did so much to create. It furthermore constitutes the best introduction I know to a reading of *De la démocratie en Amérique*.

If ever a book grew with the years it is Tocqueville's masterpiece. It should, if possible, be read in French because translation slows the pace and makes the style seem heavy when it is actually effervescent.

Index

BRITISH POSSESSIONS

L. WIN...

THE OREGON COUNTRY

Astoria

COLUMBIA R.

Portland

OCCUPIED JOINTLY
BY
UNITED STATES
AND
GREAT BRITAIN

OREGON TRAIL

SNAKE R.

BOUNDARY LINE OF 1819

MISSOURI TERRITORY

GREAT
SALT
LAKE

N. PLATTE R.

(THE INDIAN COUNTRY)

GREEN R.

S. PLATTE R.

PLATTE R.

OREGON

San Francisco

Monterey

CALIFORNIA

COLORADO R.

ARKANSAS R.

Santa Barbara

Los Angeles

Santa Fe

Albuquerque

San Diego

COLORADO R.

GILA R.

RED R.

AR...

BRAZOS R.

El Paso

RIO GRANDE

PECOS R.

TEXAS

PACIFIC

San Antonio

OCEAN

MEXICO

NUECES R.

RIO GRANDE

0   Miles   300

palacios